DIVORCE AND REMARRIAGE

DIVORCE AND REMARRIAGE

RECOVERING THE BIBLICAL VIEW

WILLIAM F. LUCK

1817

Harper & Row, Publishers, San Francisco

Cambridge, Hagerstown, New York, Philadelphia, Washington
London, Mexico City, São Paulo, Singapore, Sydney

DIVORCE AND REMARRIAGE. Copyright © 1987 by William F. Luck. All rights reserved. Printed in the United States of America. No part of this book may be used or reproduced in any manner whatsoever without written permission except in the case of brief quotations embodied in critical articles and reviews. For information address Harper & Row, Publishers, Inc., 10 East 53rd Street, New York, N.Y. 10022. Published simultaneously in Canada by Fitzhenry & Whiteside Limited, Toronto.

FIRST EDITION

Library of Congress Cataloging-in-Publication Data

Luck, William F.
    Divorce and remarriage.

    1. Divorce—Biblical teaching.   2. Remarriage—
Biblical teaching.   3. Marriage—Biblical teaching.
I. Title.
BS680.D62L83   1987   241'.63   86-45021
ISBN 0-06-065311-6

87 88 89 90 91 RRD 10 9 8 7 6 5 4 3 2 1

To Roger and Carol Thorne, who funded the project, to William Jack, who orchestrated the systems, to the Christian Research Associates of Denver, under whose auspices the writing was accomplished, and to my covenant companion, Joan, who kept the process going, I dedicate this book.

Contents

Preface

This study began over ten years ago with the writing of a book review for a national family monthly. I was a seminarian with some background in Bible and ethics wanting to get into print, and I took with me to the books I reviewed the posture of my upbringing: marriage is a permanent, mystical union of two souls; divorce is always wrong, but sometimes, in the case of adultery, a necessary evil; desertion is an unfortunate reality in a fallen world, but never justifies divorce, only separation; wife abuse is a hateful sin, but the Bible is silent on the matter, and the only action that can be justified is separation produced by the police removing the offending husband; remarriage is never morally permissible, and people who do it are guilty of adultery; the sins of divorce and remarriage are forgivable, but persons tarnished by these sins must forever give up the thought of publicly serving the Church.

As a result of my review, I received a letter from a woman who was living through divorce. She asked the "expert" about her situation, and I tried to answer her according to my understanding. I found writing that letter a thoroughly frustrating experience. In reading the scholars I found all of them quick to say that marriage was permanent but that a person could be released from it on the grounds of adultery, or perhaps desertion. In dealing directly with the biblical material I began to feel uneasy about labeling a woman whose husband had divorced her on other than these grounds an "adulteress" simply because she took advantage of the Mosaic permission to remarry. And what about that Old Testament concession? Would a holy and compassionate God give in to "hard-hearted" men who wanted to divorce their wives? Why did he condemn most sexual sins so severely, but wink at polygamy, which was, in my view, no more than legal adultery? And why, in all those laws, did God pass over the severe physical abuse of wives without so much as a "mumblin' word"?

Other things bothered me too: Why did God divorce Israel and condone the divorcing of the pagan wives in Ezra's time if he hated divorce? How could God change the moral rules of marriage in the New Testament? And why would God use a self-confessed murderer like Paul as an apostle and then inspire that apostle to proscribe those who had been divorced on improper grounds from taking up the collection in the morning worship service?

Of course, behind my confusion stood two convictions that, in effect, created the contradictions: I believed that God was immutable in his righteousness and fairness, and that the Bible was his inspired word, so superintended in its production that its initial text was without error in matters of practice. Because of these convictions, I was led to suspect that many of the problems I had with the morality of divorce arose from misunderstanding of the text. Maybe I had been ill informed by the fallible understanding of my tradition. So I decided to start over.

This is not to say that I disregarded previous attempts at the project. Initially I was helped greatly by the writings of John Murray, the great Presbyterian theologian. His book *Divorce* seemed to be the best thing available. Subsequently, I came across the commentaries of R. C. H. Lenski, a Lutheran and Greek scholar, whose work is of timeless value. He probably stirred my thinking the most and helped me on my way to settling a number of thorny exegetical problems. But neither scholar completely and satisfactorily answered my questions, especially regarding the Old Testament.

From my youth I had been brought up to think of the Old Testament as largely unprofitable (practically speaking), since the Scofield Reference Bible notes relegated it to the dispensational bone pile. What was concealed in the Old was revealed in the New, anyway, and too much concentration on the Old might confuse one into becoming a Seventh-day Adventist or something. But my seminary training had taught me to see the Old Testament as the context for understanding the meaning of the New. So I started at the beginning in Genesis and worked through the biblical materials in the order that they were written to see if there is a harmonious theology of divorce and remarriage.

Along the way, the bits and pieces of a harmonious and comprehensive theology of divorce and remarriage in the Bible seemed to come into place. But although the pieces fit the puzzle of the Bible, they weren't cut the way they should be to fit my tradition. I agonized over many of the conclusions I found myself compelled to accept. I searched for any reasonable alternative to the bizarre ideas that made the most biblical sense. After all, I constantly warn my students never to leave their traditions without good biblical warrant. But I felt that I had good biblical warrant. So I grudgingly altered my preconceptions and adopted new positions. And I began to teach what I had come to accept.

My new views met the same reception in the ears of others that they had initially met in my own. Many hearers turned away in dismay at my "liberalism," while others voiced distress at how my views would "destroy marriage in America." But their epithets were stronger than their arguments. Some even resorted to denying the inspiration of Deuteronomy 24:1–4 or the genuineness of the Matthean "exception clauses." I could not agree with their conclusions, but I never doubted their motives toward the Church or me. Some uttered solemn warnings concerning my spiritual and economic future. I gave them thanks, but reminded them that we must all follow our convictions.

There were those brave souls, however, who saw value in my work and encouraged me along the way: a friend who thought the project worthy enough to purchase a word processor, without which the book would never have been produced; a wife who did not put me away for having an "affair" with my word processor, who kept the kids out of the basement, and who put up with the inquisitive stares of friends who wondered who could be married to a man who would teach such radical views on "this" subject; children who grew to understand the importance of their father's spending so much playtime "down there"; students who said the position made the most sense of all the materials with which we had to work; counselors who felt comfortable applying the position because it seemed to have the weight of truth. For the encouragement of these comforters I offer this work.

Almost by a fluke, the work came to the attention of Roy M. Carlisle at Harper & Row, San Francisco. I was brazen enough to suggest that the work might replace Murray, and, after some convincing, Roy thought the work worthy enough to present it to the press. His and their help has been of great value to a young and unproven writer.

As I say in my ethics classes, there is something in this teaching to offend everyone—not intentionally, but in all likelihood. I have not tried to be controversial, but in dealing with a subject as meaningful and personal as marriage/divorce/remarriage, controversy and impassioned involvement cannot be avoided. Let me say it as clearly as possible: my aim in writing this book has been to find the biblical position or positions. I have been astonished to go back to the book review that started me on my quest and find how my mind has changed over the past decade. Some of what I then condemned I now hold. The changes have come in attempting to deal honestly with the biblical materials.

Though at times the book may ring with polemic, it is "the thrill of the hunt" and the "sweetness of discovery" that pump it with life. If sometimes I seem to vigorously defend the divorced and at others to rattle the rostrum against adultery, it is because I find some of the same fervor on the pages of the Bible. God's laws are not burdensome, but they are righteous. It is my conviction that finding, understanding, and teaching his ways will bring healing to souls caught in the tragedy of marriage covenants going bad or being broken. His way, and mine, is to create guilt when it ought to exist as a prelude to true reconciliation and peace and to remove guilt where it exists only because of the errant teachings of well-meaning human beings.

I anticipate that my critics will fall into widely different schools. Some will be convinced that the book missed the real monolithic biblical position. I encourage them to write their reviews and their books and make good their case. For my part, I am open to correction by sound biblical argument. Others will suggest that the book is more wrong-headed than wrong on any given passage. They may suggest that I have been far too "clever" in the production of a unified theology of divorce and remarriage. They will suggest to me that there are really any number of different theologies of divorce and remarriage, depending upon the given writer or redactor. To them I respond that whenever writers claim to be faithful to their tradition, as the biblical writers do, at least initially the benefit of the doubt should go to them. If Jesus claims that he is correcting contemporary misunderstandings of tradition in favor of the older tradition, and if Paul claims to be teaching in a way that agrees with Jesus, then we should look at their writings with an eye to harmonization. If that harmonization simply cannot make its way, then the multiple theology theory must be admitted.

But at present, I am convinced that the later writers have been faithful to the earlier, and I plan to share my conclusions in this regard with others, whom I encourage to apply what they come to accept. I regret that the length of this work has forced me to omit examples of how the theory presented may be applied. However, to meet that need I intend to write another book along the lines of a "case study." Those who are more than academically inclined may look forward to it.

Finally, I realize that writers always face the risk of being misunderstood or of having their work misused. This fear is heightened when the writing is about Christian ethics. One hates to think of people justifying or condemning themselves out of a misunderstanding of one's writing. And one hates to think of how others might criticize what they do not really understand. Nonetheless, the attempt to get at the truth is worth the risk.

Cohesiveness in the Marriage Union

(Genesis 2:24)

INTRODUCTION

A study of divorce and remarriage should begin with a significant study of marriage. Since the morality of divorce and remarriage is affected by the nature of marriage, we can only appreciate that morality when we know what marriage itself entails. Scripture itself supports the reasonableness of this simple conclusion. When Jesus was questioned about divorce, he responded by directing the Pharisees' attention to the earliest scriptural teaching on marriage, Genesis 2:24 (Matt. 19, Mark 10). In this first chapter, we will concentrate our effort on that verse, looking at each of its important words or phrases as they relate to the context. We will feel free to bring to bear upon this "key verse" other biblical passages and word studies that form the broader context of the verse. In this way, we should come to see the union in marriage as an intimate and complementing companionship wherein two individuals become a unit in order to do the work of God and to experience his blessings. In the second chapter, we will consider marriage as a public commitment that is designed to care for each partner in a manner befitting the nature of each sex. First, let us catch the prior context.

THE CAUSE OF MARRIAGE

For this cause . . .

(Genesis 2:24a)

Genesis 2:24 is masterfully placed in the text of the Bible's first book. It appears as an editorial comment made as the redactor reflected upon the account of the creation of Eve.[1] But the verse is no mere footnote; in a sense, it is the apex of the story of the creation of human beings. As a footnote, it should not be expected to be an exhaustive treatment of the subject of marriage, but, as the apex of the story, it should tell us some essential things about that institution. As we seek to learn these great truths, let us follow the direction of the verse itself and ask why its Author thought it necessary to the text of the story.[2]* What is the "cause" of the marriage comment?

The prior context of the verse reaches back into the first chapter of Genesis. There, in the general account of the creation of the world, we read that God culminated his creative work in the making of Adam, the first human being. Like the animals, human beings are given the divine blessing to "be fruitful and multiply, and fill the earth" (1:28). But we were made unlike the animals in at least two respects. First, human beings are specially said to be created in the "image of God" and "according to his likeness" (vv. 26 f.). The apparent reason for this difference is so that we might be able to accomplish the second difference: the rule of the newly created world (vv. 26, 28). The ability to rule arises from the created similarity of human beings to our Creator. (Of course, the ability of creatures to be "fruitful and multiply" arises from this as well—though in a different way.) Human beings alone are given the task of rule, and the difference between us and the animals is our special creation in the image and likeness of God. We alone are in the image of God, and we alone have a task to do.

It is significant to our study that only human beings are said to be created "male and female." Of course, most of the kinds of animals created were made in this way. Had they not been, it would have been impossible for them to "be fruitful and multiply," which is a blessing given to them as well as to us (v. 22). My point is that only of human beings is it *said* that they are created male and female. I understand this to mean that it is important to know that humans are "di-sexual." And it would seem most reasonable to assume that the importance of knowing this relates to what is peculiar to humans in the text, namely, that we are "in the image" and have been given the responsibility to rule the earth. I concur with Karl Barth[3] when he says that di-sexuality is somehow intrinsically related to God's personality. Scripture is telling us that God has distributed the Image into the genders. "Male" (Heb.: zakar) and "female" (Heb.: negeba) are both "human beings" (Heb.: 'Adam), but they differ from each other in a complementary way. The Hebrew terms are physically descriptive. Neither, alone, exhibits the complete divine Image. And, if it takes the complete Image to form the authority that delegates rule of the earth, then it also requires in-

*Editor's Note: Notes indicated by a number in boldface type (e.g. **12**) contain further discussion; those notes set in regular roman type (e.g. 13) are bibliographic citations.

tegration of the divided Image to accept and implement this delegated rule. This is to say that both sides of the Image must be present and working in harmony.[4]

What is said here about distinguishable personality traits of the sexes is not likely to strike a friendly note among many in the sophisticated Western world today. It is fashionable these days to deny natural distinctions and affirm the similarities of the sexes. I do not follow the fashion, nor does everyone in the secular world. It is true that any given member of one sex possesses those personality traits distinctive of the opposite sex, but this fact does not overturn another fact, namely, that certain traits are dominant among members of each of the sexes.

Obviously, these separate sexes cannot experience the blessing of "being fruitful" and multiplying unless they physically unite. But it is equally true that the blessings of personal happiness and human fulfillment cannot be experienced without social communion between the sexes. For God himself is the happiest of beings, and this cannot but be related to the integrity of his personality. Since each of the sexes alone incompletely exhibits the divine personality, it is necessary for them to share in each other to achieve psychological wholeness. The blessings of personal fulfillment—a necessity for doing the work of God in the world—are dependent on the communion of the sexes.

Now, I am not saying that the sexes have to experience sexual contact to be happy. God is happy, and the physical is not an ingredient in that happiness—God is a Spirit (John 4:24a). I am referring to social relations and the integration of the distinctive personality traits distributed between the sexes. Neither am I saying that the form of social relations need be marriage. Were we to conclude that marriage and essential community are one and the same, we would find ourselves in disagreement with both Jesus and Paul. For Jesus held up to the world the model of the "eunuch," the unmarried kingdom worker (Matt. 19:12)—and his own life on earth was an example of this condition. Paul exhorted the Corinthian believers to consider the economics of Christian service: single persons *theoretically* can spend more time pleasing the Lord (1 Cor. 7:32 f.). Neither Jesus nor Paul, however, isolated himself from the fellowship of women. Jesus' supporters (Luke 8:1–3) and his disciples (Luke 10:39) included women. And Paul reports that his fellow workers included women as well (e.g., Rom. 16:1 ff.).

Sadly, human beings have twisted the biblical teaching on sexual community. We have done so from the beginning. Sometimes the misuse of sexuality has brought rejection of the opposite sex. Monastic isolation and writings against women, sex, and marriage run through history. A less radical, but more perverse, reaction is homosexuality. This unnatural choice (Rom. 1:26 f.) is at root a rejection of God's revealed method of arriving at personal, physical wholeness. It rebukes God, by saying that one sex can find in quantitative addition a solution to a qualitative problem. Though homosexual men may not personally or geographically separate themselves from women, their sexual preference is a denial of God's way: physical union is to be only with the other aspect of the divine Image—the opposite sex. Homsexuality is an attempt to "join together" them that God did not choose to join.

It is natural for two of the opposite sex to seek to become one flesh, for they were once sundered from each other by the hand of a creating God. Their union is a blessed reuniting of the divorced Image.[5] But homosexuality is never proper, because it claims completion when in reality there are either two "heads" or leaders (male homosexuality) or no "head" (lesbianism). According to the descriptive language of the Scriptures, there must be a head and a body—anything else is a monster!

On the other hand, sexual pleasure between men and women—valid candidates for sexual union—which was intended only as the final and optional aspect of social union, has often been the only focus of male-female relations. The man has too often sought sex at the expense of the woman, desiring her not as a person, but as a means to the end of self-gratification. She is "objectified," seen neither as a part of the Image nor as a person for whom Christ died.

That such denigration of personhood is despicable to the Creator is best seen in the section of the Deuteronomical Law that deals with the eighth commandment (contra theft). From Deuteronomy 23:15–24:7, we read a series of legal stipulations, most of which are designed to teach the listener that people are not objects or pieces of property. Chattel slavery is degrading. So is prostitution. And a wife is not a piece of property to be passed back and forth between husbands (24:1–4).

Even when marriage has been understood to involve the union of two persons, the woman has often not been seen as a full partner, but only a second-class human being. The textbook case is found in the Talmud (bMen. 43b): "A man is bound to say the following . . . blessing . . . daily: '[Bless Thou] who hast not made me a woman.'" Men seem bent on continuing to use women as a scapegoat for their failures, instead of properly relating to her to perform God's work in the world. When it comes to reuniting the Image, men and women must treat each other as equal partners—as *persons* rather than objects. There is a pattern to being human and to acting like a human being. By implication, there are also some forms of behavior that are not permitted.

Yet in an age of "victimless crimes" when "freedom of choice" is touted, this is hard to accept. It is presumed that to be human is to be able to make a choice for or against anything. Existential humanism has long seduced us into thinking that we make our essence by the choices we make during our existence. To deny a person the right to choose his or her own experience of sexual union is said to be wrong. To unite at will is paraded as a basic human right.

But the Scripture of God did not understand this to be so. Sex might be the natural direction of the reuniting Image, but uncovenanted sex, in the view of God's word, was either rape (Deut. 22:28 f.), seduction (Exod. 22:16 f.), or harlotry (Deut. 22:20 f.), all crimes. The victim (aside from the two themselves!) of rape or seduction was the father of the woman (Deut. 22:21, 29; Exod. 22:17; and especially Lev. 21:9); to profane any human being is an assault upon the Father, God. In sex, as in other human relations, everything must be done "decently and in order."

On the other end of the continuum is the school of thought that made marriage an expectation of maturity, at least among those not committed to monastic vows. It was so in Jesus' day (cf. Matt. 19:9 ff.); it is so today.

Summing up what we have been saying: God made sexual community essential to produce human wholeness, and physical union the natural culmination of the intimacy of the sexes (since they were once physically united). Given these facts, it is only reasonable for God to protect male-female relations (especially the sexual aspect of them) with a pronouncement about the moral context of such a union.

THE COHESIVENESS OF MARRIAGE

"A man . . ."

Adam, of course, knew nothing of the institution of marriage when God brought the woman to him. He had to be told later what had happened to him when God formed the woman out of his side. He doubtless did not know anything about sexual intercourse. Given all this, it is most unlikely that Adam himself uttered the words of Genesis 2:24. Although it is possible that God uttered them directly, it is far more probable that they are editorial. As Genesis is part of a legal code, it is to be expected that the writer should have added such a moral note to this important event.

The crucial part of this note begins: "a man." The Hebrew term used here (*'ish*) is not the same as those used before to signify humankind (e.g., Gen. 1:26). Neither is it the term used to convey the maleness of "man" (as in Gen. 1:17). Instead it is a word that connotes an *individual male*. The emphasis is on a given male as a distinct person.[6] By using this word, the Scripture is trying to tell us that marriage is a personal decision, by contrast to a corporate or sexual one. Though many societies have practiced arranged marriage, most have consulted the prospective bridegroom. Woman have often had less say about whom they will marry, but there is ample evidence that they often at least had veto power.[7] On the other hand, getting married is not a matter of mere physical connection. It is not simply the male in his sexuality, or "plumbing," that enters into the marriage, but the whole individual person. Men who get married simply to experience genital union are but a little higher in virtue than those who go to a prostitute. Their life-style is barely moral, sadly deficient. It is the job of parents to teach their children that marriage is essentially for interpersonal communication and fulfillment of two people, not a selfish coupling for pleasure.[8]

Note, lastly, that the term for "man" is the same as that commonly used for "husband," and that its counterpart ('*Ishsha*) is used to denote both "woman" and "wife." Only by using the context can one determine whether the *individual* or the *positional* meaning is intended. This is also true of the Greek counterparts: *Anthropos* can mean either "man" (as in Matt. 7:9) or "husband" (as in Matt. 19:3). *Gune* means either "woman" (cf. Matt. 14:21) or "wife" (the probable meaning in Matt. 5:31). Even when they do imply position, these words always stress the individual personhood of the one referred to.

There are, of course, terms that highlight the social position "husband" or "wife" more than the ones just mentioned. For example, in Hebrew a husband is sometimes called "master" (*baali*). In Greek the word used would be "lord" (*kurios*). In these words, one tastes a flavor that is less romantic and personal than it is hierarchical. The role relationship is being stressed by these words. For instance, Peter refers to Sarah calling Abraham "lord" (*kurios*) to show her submission to his authority (1 Pet. 3:6). And in Hosea 2:16, we have the striking statement " 'And it will come about that in that day,' declares the Lord, 'that you will call Me Ishi [personal/romantic] and will no longer call Me Baali [hierarchical].' " Commentators sometimes add that, in addition to the obvious need to change the title of husband from what was the name of a heathen deity (Baal), the future covenant between God and Israel will be of the sort wherein a term of endearment is more appropriate.[9] *Ishi* conveys more affection than *Baali*.

"shall leave his father and mother . . ."

It is this individual person, half the Image of God, so to speak, who the text says "leaves" his "father and his mother." The key word "leave" (*aw-zab'*) means to forsake, leave destitute, refuse. It is used of loosening bands, as of a beast from its bonds. The Arabic equivalent means "single" or "unmarried." The idea here is that the man forsakes his parents. He cuts himself off from them. He breaks the "union" with them almost in the sense of divorcing himself and becoming "subsequently single." It is as if he has been bound to them in a marriage state but, in an act of the will, departs from them regarding responsibility and dependence (if such exists) and becomes alone to unite with the chosen woman.

The bridegroom cannot sustain two primary social relationships at the same time, at least in the sense of being under his parents as the head of a familial social unit and at the same time the head of his own family unit. Even in a world infused with the concept of extended families, priorities must be kept straight.

I note here that the text speaks specifically of the man in this matter. It is he who must be his own head of the household. If in family relations he is dependent upon his father, then to whom do his dependents look for authority? It would create for his wife an unworkable hierarchical arrangement: she would have two heads (i.e., her husband and his father), and that, according to Jesus (Matt. 6:24), is not right. The problem is not so much his as it is hers. He might still be able to relate to his father in honor as master of the extended family, but it is improper for his wife to have to deal with two potentially competing authorities. In such an arrangement the father's authority would probably supersede her husband's, yet, according to the Scripture, his is to be her final authority in family matters (Eph. 5:22 f.).

We can see, then, that the dynamic here does not require an explicit reversal of the clause to tell us that the woman leaves her father and mother. The reason the man must be free of encumbering relationship to his parents is so that his wife may be unencumbered by inappropriate authority. It would be folly to suggest that she may in some manner remain encumbered by a relationship to her own father. The text implies the later custom of "giving the bride away," insofar as God, the Father of Eve, "brought her to the man" (Gen. 2:22).

It is important in this discussion to understand that God does not require the pair physically to leave either parent-pair. For those who can keep their priorities and lines of authority straight, the extended family idea is presented as a desirable option. Remember that Christ intends to take his bride the Church to live "in his Father's house." On the other hand, it is often difficult, if not dangerous, to live in the home of a parent when the line cannot be kept straight. Jacob offers us an example of this in his wranglings with Laban.

It would also be inaccurate to suggest that a man is necessarily a dependent until he gets married.[10] Jacob was independent of his father before he married; he was away from home and entirely on his own. The text is simply trying to say that *if* the "cord has not been previously cut" by the time the marriage is contracted, it must be cut at that time. Childhood, remember, ends when the society (by and large made up of parents) determines that one has reached the age when one must stand on one's own before the community. The issue is not left up to any individual parent, and it is well that it is not.[11]

Lastly, and most important, the term *leave* is a term of strong intention. The man is making a decision to end, once and for all, an intimate relationship of dependence. He is choosing to break off, *with the inten-*

tion never to resume, that aspect of the relationship to his parents. And when the woman is given by her father to the bridegroom, the intention is the same. When it is not, we see the sorrow that results. David was given Michal, but Saul, her father, later took her back. By agreeing to marry another man, she became a party to the return (1 Sam. 25:44). Leaving must be with the intention never to return to the authority of the parent again.

"shall cleave to his wife."

Although most will find agreeable much, if not all, of what I have said so far, the discussion of the next phrase will bring, for many, a parting of the ways. For "and shall cleave to his wife" is at the heart of the divorce issue. See how two recent writers describe the word *cleave:*

> The word means "to cling to, to stick (or glue) to, to hold fast to someone *in a permanent bond.*" . . . Certainly the idea of cleaving is a whole-hearted commitment to another *in an inseparable union.* . . . A man who cleaves to his wife . . . will "glue" himself to her in a *permanent bond.* When two people are married, God provides the glue and seals them in a union which is never to be broken. (Emphasis added.)[12]

> The Hebrew word for "cleave" suggests the idea of being glued together. . . . In marriage, the husband and wife are "glued" together—*bound inseparably* into one solitary unit.
>
> An interesting characteristic of glue is its *permanence.* . . . The same is true of persons "glued" together in marriage. It is a *permanent relationship until death.* There is no allowance made in Genesis 2:24 for divorce and remarriage. (Emphasis added.)[13]

The importance of this matter must not be overlooked. If such writers are correct in their analysis, then the question of divorce is already answered: Marriage is permanent. Divorce is always improper, because it does not legally reflect this couple's real status in the eyes of God. Remarriage is a form of adultery (in at least half the cases), because remarriage brings together partners who have no right in the eyes of God to be joined together. It continues to astonish me that people attempt to hold both to the permanence of marriage and to the moral propriety of divorce. Either one or the other must go. For my part, I choose to deny the former. Moreover, as this book argues, I believe that I have the tacit support of the biblical text. Insofar as the debate continues, I suggest that the authors just quoted have been overzealous in their exegesis. Let us look at the Hebrew and Greek lexicons and uses of this word *cleave* in the biblical text.

CLEAVE IN THE HEBREW

In Hebrew, the word for "cleave" is *dābag* "to adhere, be glued firmly, keep, be joined, follow close, abide fast; to impinge, cling; to repair breaches." This sampling clearly shows that the term implies a tight connection of the cleaving parts. Nothing here implies, however, that permanence is an *essential* or *inherent* ingredient of the "glue" of marriage. I believe it is fair to say that such synonyms give no convincing support to the idea that the word *cleave* (*dābag*) implies permanence. Consideration of the uses of that word in the Old Testament affords little more help, yet the advocates of permanence seek to make their case by appealing to use. Consider the following examples:

The Hebrew word for "cleave" suggests the idea of being glued together. It is used in Job 38:38 of dirt clods which stick together after the rain. It is used by Joshua of a military alliance (Josh. 23:28). The word is also used of the leprosy that would cling forever to dishonest and greedy Gehazi (2 Kings 5:7). In marriage, the husband and the wife are "glued" together—bound inseparably into one solitary unit.[14]

Cleaving is an essential element in the covenant language of the Old Testament. . . . Israel is commanded to cleave to the Lord with intensity, to have a love that will not let go. . . . Certainly the idea of cleaving is a wholehearted commitment to another in an inseparable union.[15]

Close inspection of the verses cited, however, presents a much different picture of the function of this word: As for dirt clods, who is to say that they cannot be separated? If they are still clods, perhaps they can. It is not the point of the story of Job to make a comment on the permanence of the dirt bond. The reader, who should doubtless be concerned with other matters in this story anyway, may rightly feel free to draw different conclusions.

The "military alliance" citation actually proves that cleaving is *not* necessarily permanent. The alliance in question is the forbidden relation between Israel and the heathen nations of Canaan. Anyone who is familiar with the history of Israel in the Promised Land will recall that on many occasions this prohibition was not heeded and such alliances were established. In light of this, the question arises, Did God see these alliances as permanent? The answer is surely no. Time and again, the prophets call the people of Israel to *break off* such cleavings and to return to the God of Israel and be loyal to him (cf. Jer. 3 ff.). Here is a case in which cleaving is improper and leaving is the order of the day.[16]

Of course, the term is used of Israel's cleaving to God, and surely that was supposed to be a permanent commitment. But Israel's continued adultery with the nations reveals that cleaving, as *their* act, was not permanent. If the relationship of God to Israel is permanent, it is not because Israel cleaved to God, but because God cleaved to them. From this we learn that cleaving *may* or *may not* involve an endless bond; that is, permanence is not inherent in the term *cleave*. Whether or not permanence is a part of a particular cleaving must be decided on other grounds than the dictionary. Since this is so, interpreters ought to be less zealous in pounding their pulpits on the matter. Marriage may well prove to be one of those instances wherein the cleaving *ought to be* but, sadly, *may not be* permanent.

Here is an appropriate place to make an important criticism of much writing on divorce. Most writers who propound the permanence of marriage consistently avoid distinguishing between permanence of *intention* and of *fact*. They seem to think that quoting passages that stress that marriage *ought* to be permanent (a moral matter) proves that marriage *is* permanent (an ontological or metaphysical matter). Though we will return to it at a later time, at this point we need to remember that Jesus did not deny the ability of a couple to sunder their marriage but only the morality of doing so.[17]

Returning to the examples cited, note, lastly, that Gehazi's leprosy (2 Kings 5:7) is known to be "forever," not by the word *cleave*, but by the accompanying adjectives. And so it goes through the other uses of *cleave* in the Old Testament; many times the idea of permanence is clearly *not* implicit in the word *cleave*. The rest of the time, the lack of any implication of permanence turns up on closer inspection.

At this point one might be prompted to consider the last synonym offered by the lexicon: "to repair breaches." Perhaps the immediate context will give us a better understanding of the use of *cleave*. In that vein, we should recall from the context that God created a breach in Adam's flesh and out of that created Eve. The union in marriage is an attempt to physically repair the breach in the unity of Adam's flesh by reuniting the two parts of the Image.

At first this might seem promising to those who propound some mystical element in marriage. It might be argued that the marriage partners are so closely united that they are as Adam was before the creation of Eve, that is, one person. Indeed, this might be close to what many people think of marriage. The two individuals lose their individuality and become some third entity. This mystical union is understood as being so ontologically unifying that the resulting "oneness" cannot be broken. "You cannot divide one," we are told.

Of course, it might be mentioned that it was a unity (Adam) that was originally sundered, but doubtless the retort would be that only God could do such separation and that, as far as marriage goes, he would never desire to do such a thing. But this is all vain kibitzing. However organically a married couple may be related, they do not become one person. At best they are like Siamese twins.

Often such discussions come up on consideration of Jesus' statement that "the two shall become one." It is perfectly proper to take that New Testament passage into account, but one must be careful that such a maneuver does not simply beg the question. It is not transparent that the "one" is one "person." It may simply mean that the two independent persons have become one team or unit. Though talk is often heard of "personal" unity in marriage, I have yet to hear a psychological or philosophical or biblical explanation for what this new person is and how the two individual persons have ceased to be. In all marriages with which I am familiar, including happy and intimate ones, I still observe two distinguishable individuals functioning in a harmony—and, if distinguishable, then perhaps separable. In any case, one simply cannot glibly quote the text of Scripture to prove one's point on this matter. Nor should one too hastily agree with A. Isaksson, who tells us that "it is clear from the context of Mt. 19:3 ff. that Jesus was referring primarily to what is written in Gen. 2:24 as proof that marriage is indissoluble."[18] I, for one, would contend not that Jesus sees marriage as "indissoluble" but rather that he thinks it morally improper to dissolve it.[19]

William A. Heth and Gordon J. Wenham seem to be moving in more dependable directions by considering, with Isaksson, the use of *cleave* in *covenantal* contexts (Deut. 10:20; 11:22; 13:4; 30:20), but careful reflection on their work suggests that they ignore the covenantal elements in favor of a reaffirmation of the elusive ontological bond. After noting that parallel terms in these passages are *attitudinal,* they quickly return to consideration of the more metaphysical "bone and flesh."[20]

By way of conclusion, then, I would regard *cleave,* in the Old Testament, as implying a bonding of two individuals that emphasizes intended, but not ontological, permanency. Stressing intention, the term is really closer to the idea of *covenant* than it is to a bonding of being. But what of the New Testament? We must remember that Genesis 2:24 is quoted more than once by the New Testament writers. We must consider how they translated the term from the Hebrew and the uses of that word as well.

CLEAVE IN THE GREEK

proskallao

The Greek word that is used in quoting Genesis 2:24 in the New Testament is *proskallao*. It is a strengthened form of *kallao*, another word used in the marriage discussion. We will look at the strengthened form first, since it is the translators' choice. That word is used three or four times only. Its first occurrence is in the Matthew 19 divorce passage and in some manuscripts of the Mark 10 parallel. Since the manuscript support for its inclusion in Mark is not strong, we will limit our consideration to Matthew 19:5. In this passage, the term is embedded in a quote of the whole Genesis 2:24 verse. Jesus quoted Genesis in response to the Pharisees' inquiry about the propriety of ending marriage. They wished to know if there was any legal way out of marriage. Doubtless, they wished to know Jesus' opinion of the legal grounds for dissolution, but Jesus perceived what was in their hearts. They were focusing on the wrong question. He knew that they were only too ready to be hard-hearted toward their wives. They were interested in how to end marriage. Jesus wished them to look at marriage from another direction—the main reason for marrying in the first place, to be together—so he cited the words of the Law that recall the basics of marriage. *Leaving* was what they did to get into marriage. *Joining* was what they were doing by getting married. When they first made their vows, separation from the spouse was the furthest thing from their minds. Now, it seemed, separation was the focus of marital analysis. How things had changed!

Jesus placed the quote before the words "Consequently they are no longer two, but one, flesh" (v. 6). We will discuss this more later when we analyze "one flesh," but for now, understand that Jesus meant to remind them that the time for deciding to walk away from a marriage is before the vows, not after. By joining as "husband" and "wife" they ended their right to make a unilateral decision. The couple are dependent on each other, not independent. The time to isolate two blocks of wood is before, not after, gluing them together.

But to say all this is not to say that there is *no* cause for divorce insofar as the two have glued themselves together. Rather, it is cause for arguing that there is no cause for separating or sundering the couple. In effect Jesus has not yet answered their question. They asked about divorce, Jesus answered regarding separation. These are not the same. It is not that Jesus confused the two, or that there is no answer to their question. It is because he wished to stress the bond rather than the legal dissolution. It is the Pharisees who were confused. They fancied that marriage was simply a matter of choosing to be or not to be. Jesus wished to bring reality into the fancy.

But they persisted, asking why Moses commanded divorce in Deuteronomy 24. We will reserve detailed analysis of this point for later chapters. Here note that Jesus pinpointed the hardness of heart that both he and Moses recognized in some married men. As an aside to the discussion he did mention an exception to the general rule that divorce should not come between marriage partners. But the stress of the passage is that in cleaving men have "made their bed." They have committed themselves to being glued to their wives.

The second instance of *proskallao* is Acts 5:36. There, Gamaliel is commenting upon earlier messianic groups who had come to nothing. One Theudas had made messianic claims and had gathered about him some four hundred followers. These followers had *joined up* with him. They had apparently remained with him until their band was dispersed at the death of their leader. It would not be appropriate to suggest that these men had become mystically or sexually bonded to Theudas. They certainly did not become one existence with him. But theirs was a bond of intentions and ideas, which determined their subsequent actions. There is no reason to suggest that Gamaliel's word choice could not accommodate a personal betrayal of Theudas by a person such as Judas. In short, the word implies strong social bonding, but not "mystic sweet communion."

The last usage of the term is in Ephesians 5:31—again, a quote of Genesis 2:24. The writer of Ephesians uses the quote in a discussion of marital relations. He places it in a section discussing the need for a husband to provide for his wife as he does himself. More precisely, it follows an analogical reference to Christ's relation to the Church—his Body. Does Paul intend the reader to see in the quote a further expansion of the point about care of the wife? If so, then perhaps the quote is intended to remind the husband that he has committed himself to care for this woman. On the other hand, the quote might intend to broach a new subject: the union of the husband to the wife.[21] Paul may be suggesting that as a husband leaves his parents to join to his wife, the Lord chose to leave his Father to cleave to the Church—a union that is immediately mentioned. The former interpretation is probably preferable, insofar as verse 33 informs us that love and care and respect are the issue still. In either case, what is clear about the use of *proskallao* is that the intention and incumbent obligation to care for the wife are at issue. Nothing inclines us to go beyond these matters to some ontological relationship. To go in that direction is to go well beyond the text.[22]

kallao

Kallao is the Greek word that is the root of *proskallao*. Vine reports that it means "to join fast together, to glue, cement." He reports that it is used in the New Testament only in the passive voice, with reflexive force. Others might choose to say that the voice is "middle (emphatic)." In either case, the emphasis is upon one attaching oneself closely to another.[23]

Although the word is never used explicitly of joining in marriage, it is used of the "one-flesh" relation of a man to a prostitute in 1 Corinthians 6:16. Since this passage involves a quote of the Genesis 2:24 "one-flesh" wording, it is worthy of our consideration. In these verses, Paul is admonishing his readers to put away immoral practices, specifically, the visiting of temple prostitutes as a vent for sexual desire. Says he, "Do you not know that the one who *joins* himself to a prostitute is one body with her? . . . But the one who *joins* himself to the Lord is one spirit with him." Paul is making it clear that even a one-time sexual experience involves reuniting the physical breach between Adam and Eve. (This also shows that the term *cleave* has acquired specific sexual connotations by New Testament times.[24]) Not only that, but (according to Paul) in the fornication the believer becomes part of the body of the prostitute. She is the "head," in control of the relation.

Paul contrasts joining with a prostitute to joining to the Lord. The believer, Paul points out, has already established a living relationship with God; therefore, it is improper for the believer to be joined to this second master at the same time. God and harlots are incompatible. Since the believer has been bought with a price (v. 20) and is the temple of the Holy Spirit (v. 19), the believer must not only break off existing relations with prostitutes, but must never establish any with them again. In other words, there must be a complete divorce between the man and the harlot. He must "flee" or forsake (v. 18).

For our purposes, the point is clear. *Kallao* ("one-flesh") relationships may be as strong as one's relationship with God or as casual as a union with a prostitute, but the word in itself does not imply permanence. The admonition to break off the *kallao* relationship with the prostitute clearly reveals this to be so. The fact that our *kallao* relationship to the Lord is permanent should not mislead us into thinking that our relationship to the prostitute is also permanent. By the same token, the lack of permanence of the relation to the prostitute should not be taken to imply a lack of permanence in the relationship to Christ. *Duration* is not determined by the word *kallao* alone. *Kallao* relationships may be temporary or permanent. We cannot settle questions of duration simply by an appeal to the word used. Neither is it proper to take one type of *kallao* relationship (e.g., union with the Lord), known to be permanent, and glibly suppose that some other relationship (e.g., husband and wife) is therefore permanent. Each type must be understood in its own context. Nonetheless, it is correct to say that the word *kallao* in itself implies no permanent bond. The relationship may in fact be permanent, but that permanence must be proven from something other than the word used for it.

sunzugos

Another word for "joined"—as in the joining of a man to his wife—is the word *su[n]zeugnumi*. It is made up of two words: "with" and "yoked." It means "yoked together," and its root (*zugos*) is the same word used in the Mark 10:9 parallel. In English, we would speak of a "yoke of oxen," that is, two oxen yoked together, and so is it used in the New Testament (Luke 14:19). The picture is of marriage as the creation of a team of persons who are closely related to each other. Like oxen yoked together to do a task, each partner in the married couple has been yoked with the other for the completion of his or her mate so that the two, as a team, can do the work that God has set before each. For Adam, this involved tending the garden as a fulfilled individual male. The resulting translation accurately encompasses the meaning in the Greek: "Consequently they are no longer two *indepen-*

dent individuals [i.e., each able to make a decision to leave the other—unilaterally] but are a unit. What therefore God has made *a team,* let no man separate." Again, there is nothing either mystical or spiritual about being a team.[25]

In 2 Corinthians 6:14 there is another interesting instance of the word *yoked.* Paul tells his followers not to be "unequally yoked" (*heterozugos*) together with unbelievers. The reason for this has already been noted in our treatment of 1 Corinthians 6:16. The believer and the unbeliever are spiritually incompatible. Perhaps Paul felt a need to reaffirm this Old Testament principle (cf. Deut. 7:3) insofar as some of the Corinthians might misunderstand his prohibition of sundering marital relations with unbelieving spouses in 1 Corinthians 7. Lest they think that it was all right to be yoked to an unbeliever as long as it was not a casual liaison, Paul points out that formal unions are unacceptable as well. The harmonization of 1 Corinthians 7 with 2 Corinthians 6 rests in a crucial difference of compatibility *at the time of the yoking.* The former passage speaks of persons spiritually compatible at the time of the yoking; both were unbelievers, and only later was one of them "called" or converted. The latter passage speaks of the marrying of a believer and an unbeliever; that is, they were unequally yoked in the first place.

Paul's admonition to those who have joined themselves together with "Belial" is found in his quote (6:17) of Isaiah 52:11: "Come out from their midst and be separate, says the Lord. And do not touch that which is unclean; and I will welcome you." In substance this is the same admonition Ezra gave to those in the same condition in post-exilic times (cf. Ezra 9 and 10): separate. Paul means to exclude not only new relationships but existing ones as well ("stop being joined," v. 14). It seems hard to conclude that Paul is teaching the permanency of *zugos* by this.

deo and douloō

Two other words that speak of the marriage relation in the New Testament are akin to *sunzugos.* They too speak of joining the two partners together, side by side. The first, *deo,* the common word for binding something, is used to describe both Paul's relation to Christ in Acts 20:22 and the possessed woman's relation to Satan in Luke 13:16. As we have observed before in similar instances, the word itself does convey a strong attachment, but no permanent union—the woman was freed in Luke 13:13. Accordingly, when Paul uses *deo* of the marriage relation in 1 Corinthians 7, we should expect no concept of permanence in the word itself.

Nonetheless, what of the context of the word in those passages? Does it imply that the bonds of marriage are permanent? First Corinthians 7:39 is often quoted as saying it is.[26] First Corinthians 7:27 is quoted as proving it is not! We shall consider this matter in greater detail in a later chapter; let it suffice here simply to say that the word itself cannot settle the matter.

The second term, *douloō*, exhibits a usage similar to *deo*. The strength of the attachment is not to be denied; *douloō* is a common word for enslavement. It is used, for example, of addiction to wine in Titus 2:3 and of being a bondslave to righteousness in Romans 6:18. But it is also used in Galatians 4:3 of the believers' *former* bondage to the "elemental things." And where it is used in the marriage context, a woman whose husband has separated himself from her is specifically said not to be under such bondage any more (1 Cor. 7:15). The effect in this last-mentioned use is that the separated person is no longer under a condition of slavery or contract to the master or head. Clearly, *douloō* does not imply a permanent union.

So, then, our study of the concept of joining in the New Testament confirms our previous work in the Old. The strength of the union in marriage as implied in *cleave* or similar words is profound, but not necessarily permanent. The union seems far more social than ontological. The two individuals lose their independence, but not their individuality. They become a team, tightly tied to each other but not necessarily permanently bound.

"They shall become one flesh."

Genesis 2:24 ends with the clause "and they shall become one flesh." The crucial words are *one flesh*. Here again, one finds a term that has become almost a slogan, a word the mere invoking of which some feel ends the discussion. We turn again to the writers quoted earlier, first Paul E. Steele and Charles C. Ryrie:

God said, "They shall become one flesh" (Genesis 2:24). One cannot be divided and maintain wholeness. . . . Allen Ross says, "To become one flesh means becoming a spiritual, moral, intellectual, and physical unity." . . . Abel Isaksson points out that the term "one flesh" actually refers to a kinship that is so permanent that even if the husband or wife dies, the other is not free to marry those of the partner's family without committing incest.[27]

Then J. Carl Laney:

Becoming one flesh symbolizes the identification of two people with one community of interests and pursuits. . . . Although they remain two persons, the married couple becomes *one* in a mystical, spiritual unity. . . . The concept of "one flesh" is beautifully illustrated in the children God may give a married couple. In their offspring, husband and wife are indissolubly united into one person.[28]

Casting aside Laney's ill-chosen illustration (in which a new and unique *person* arises from biological parents—marriage having nothing to do with the matter), we must ask if the text of Scripture sustains these opinions or whether we must look for another.

OLD TESTAMENT USE

The words *one flesh* are found, in the Old Testament, only in Genesis 2:24, although this passage is quoted several times in the New (Matt. 19:5; Mark 10:8; 1 Cor. 6:16; Eph. 5:31). As we noted with regard to *cleave,* the interpreter should be careful of quick opinions regarding such seldom used words. Nonetheless, the context of the one time it is used in the Old Testament is instructive, insofar as the term *flesh* is used several times in that passage. The idea behind that word is simple. Adam, feeling lonely, is brought animals to name. In the process, he feels his uniqueness even more poignantly. There are no other creatures like him. But when later God presents him with a woman to be his companion, he immediately recognizes an essential relation. He sees that she is one of his kind, with flesh like his and bones like his.[29] He doesn't so much cleave to his wife so that he may become one flesh again as he cleaves because they are the same flesh. Nonetheless, having cleaved, they become "one flesh." I take that to mean that the sexual intimacy, a relation to be entertained only by those who have "cleaved" to each other, reunites the once-sundered flesh *as closely as it ever will be reunited.*

A. Isaksson considers *flesh* or the expression *bone and flesh* to denote here and elsewhere (Gen. 29:12–14; 37:27; Judg. 9:2; 2 Sam. 19:13) kinship or blood relation. These words "speak about a person in his total relation to another."[30] Isaksson would use the words *kin* or *family* to express the meaning of *flesh.*[31] To Isaksson and company, this means that the relationship established by becoming married goes far beyond simple sexual coupling.

Isaksson's understanding of "one flesh" as a *family* relationship deserves further comment, insofar as some modern authors lean heavily upon his Old Testament work to support their case that marriage forms a union that cannot be dissolved.[32] In the first place, though it may be the case that such terms are often found in the context of kinship, one must be careful in applying general use to the text of Genesis 2:24. Trying to apply Isaksson's idea to that text brings a mixed interpretative blessing. On the one hand, the simple terms *flesh* and *bone* in Genesis 2 do indeed seem to bear the sense of family or *species.* As we have already mentioned, Adam takes note of Eve because she is his kind of creature. We might say that she is akin to him or "of his family," as opposed to the animals he has been observing. On the other hand, it does not seem so easy to suggest the translation "shall cleave to his wife; and they shall become one family [or kin]" or *social unit.* It would seem more likely that the "one-flesh" idea means to convey a physical reuniting of those who are of the same "kind" or species.

Thus we do not feel comfortable to argue as harshly as Isaksson does that "one flesh" does not have any specific sexual significance.[33] "One flesh" does seem to speak of physical *reunion,* and under the circumstances it seems strained to avoid the mechanism of sexual intercourse as important to the text of Genesis 2:24. It would seem that Isaksson and Heth and Wenham wish to distinguish "one flesh" from sexuality so as to preclude the inference that sexual misconduct dissolves the "one-flesh" relationship. At least, such is the use to which Heth and Wenham put Isaksson.[34]

There is really a semantic knot here that needs to be untied. Heth and Wenham contend that *one flesh* is synonymous with *marriage* or *marriage bond.* There is a close relationship between the terms, but they are not synonyms. A "one-flesh" relationship seems to be primarily an organic one, which, in the case of human beings, would be sexual.[35] Marriage, however, is not primarily sexual. It is not the "one flesh" but the "cleaving" that constitutes the marriage. The organic union ("one flesh") is the first and consummative right of those who have cleaved. As to whether or not sexual misconduct dissolves the marriage, that has to be proven, and may be, if sexual fidelity is understood as an essential element of covenant. The fact that there exists a "one-flesh" or organic relationship in marriage does not *ipso facto* mean that multiple organic relationships dissolve the covenant. The argument that infidelity does end the marriage bears the burden of proof. Heth and Wenham do not need to argue as harshly as they do.[36]

One other aspect of Isaksson needs to be dealt with rather harshly. According to his understanding, *one flesh* primarily means "relation," the sort of relation spoken of in Leviticus 18. The subject of this passage is kinship as it relates to incest. Isaksson's point is that the marriage union forms a bond of kinship so strong that even if one partner dies, the remaining spouse is still so closely related to the dead partner's close kin that to marry one of them is the same as committing incest.[37]

On this view, the husband and wife become close kin, like brothers and sisters. This kinship then is used to explain why it is an abomination for a woman to return to her former husband after becoming married to someone else subsequent to a divorce (Deut. 24:4). Hear Gordon Wenham:

A spouse's relationship with the family is not terminated by death of the partner who belonged to it by birth nor is it ended by divorce. As far as her husband's family is concerned, the divorced wife still belongs to them and thus may not marry anyone closely related to her husband . . . the horizontal relationships are as enduring as the vertical ones. It thus seems to imply that to seek a divorce is to try and break a relationship with one's wife that cannot really be broken.[38]

Isaksson himself goes further by suggesting that the nature of this relationship is such that for her to return to her "brother" (first husband) after becoming defiled by a subsequent husband is incestuous.

I shall have more to say about this when we consider Deuteronomy 24:1–4, but for now, note that, although the death of a spouse (or divorce from him or her, for that matter) does not erase all aspects of the social relationships the first marriage established, it goes far afield to suggest that kinship relations are ontologically, morally, and legally indissoluble in the sense that divorce and remarriage are impossible or immoral per se.[39]

Heth and Wenham, Isaksson, and company have overread the significance of continuing social ramifications of a marriage. At the point where they infer that such continuing relations inhibit marriage to the non–blood relatives of a former spouse, they leave exegesis and begin speculation.[40] And when Isaksson argues that to return to the former spouse is to commit a form of incest, he presents us with a view that is truly bizarre. For if the act of becoming "one flesh" establishes that kind of kinship or blood relation, then the very act of consummation in any marriage would be incestuous, and all marriages would be incestuous by nature. That seems a bit far-reaching!

It seems better simply to conclude that *one flesh,* in the Old Testament, implies a bond of kinship that speaks of the physical reunification of parts of the Image of God that are of the same kind. The bond established is such a strong one that, even when it is severed (by death or divorce), ongoing social ramifications exist. But it goes too far to suggest that "one flesh" entails a permanent relation such that marriage partners cannot be divorced or remarried to others.

NEW TESTAMENT USE

A careful look at the New Testament quotes of Genesis 2:24 will help fill out our understanding of this word-set. Consideration of *one flesh* in the Gospel passages does not change our conclusion. In Matthew 19, after quoting Genesis 2:24, Jesus says, "Consequently they are no longer two, but one flesh. What therefore God has joined together, let no man separate" (v. 6). Although this may be interpreted as no longer two *distinct* entities but one mystical *unity,* this is not a good alternative. The next verse makes that clear. The two are said to be no longer isolated individuals, but a social unit. They are like two oxen that are joined together. When unyoked they might walk away from each other, but now that they are yoked they form a team. It is not that that team cannot later be broken up as the yoke is removed or broken; they do not become one ox. One must neither understate nor overstate the strength of the bond.[41]

The next usage of the word-set comes in 1 Corinthians 6. There we see that a man who has joined himself to a prostitute has established a "one-body" relationship to her. *One body* appears to be synonymous with *one flesh.* Paul uses *one body* of the liaison with the prostitute to create a linguistic parallel with the relation between the Holy Spirit and the believer, whose body he indwells. Paul uses *one flesh* to remind the Corinthians that sex implies commitment or union,[42] thereby showing that that idea is not implicitly negative in his vocabulary. Nor will it do, for the same reason, to suggest that *one body* is a term that denotes only physical union with no spiritual implications. In the end, it seems that Paul sees the phrases as being nearly synonymous. The *body* theme is his preferred term (he uses it extensively in later chapters of the letter), but he wishes to quote Genesis to show that physical union is God's long-standing concern. Physical union was originally meant to be in the context of leaving and cleaving—actions obviously absent in the temple practices. To be united with a harlot implies a commitment to her. In fact, Paul cleverly insinuates that the harlot is the head, the one in charge: "make [your body to be] members of a harlot" (v. 16). But all this is incompatible with a Christian's previous relation to another master, Christ. We cannot serve both Christ and a prostitute.

In saying this we can see that there are spiritual ramifications of union to a heathen prostitute, and that our relation to her is spiritually unacceptable. That, of course, is the point of the passage. Since such fornication is incompatible with the kingdom (6:9), a willful joining with the forces of Satan's kingdom in this way is treason. It is not as some Platonists or proto-Gnostics were apparently saying, "Food for the stomach and the stomach for food," that is, sexual relations are purely physical. No, there is spiritual alignment with the Devil in willful intercourse with a harlot. But this is not the same thing as saying that the one-flesh relationship is in itself a spiritual relationship, one way or the other. Chapter 7 of 1 Corinthians makes it clear that a one-flesh relationship with an unbeliever is, in itself, not an alignment with the Devil. Were it so, Paul would have told the married believer to flee from her *spouse* just as he tells the believer to flee *immorality*. As we shall see later (in chap. 8), it is probably that very question ("Is being married to an unbeliever in itself acceptable, or should we divorce?) that brought about the admonition about desertion so much argued over today. Thus we conclude that the one-flesh relationship is not a spiritual union, though any given relationship may have spiritual ramifications. It all depends upon whether the relationship is licit or licitly entered into.[43]

The Ephesians passage cites the Genesis text but does so only regarding the believer's relation to God. Paul is identifying the nature of the Christ-Church union. It is a living union and, according to many traditions, a union that is permanent—nothing will ever separate the believer from the Lord. Paul simply wishes to note that the union of men and women is similar at the point of being living union. The *duration* of union is not a point of discussion, however; it is wrong to make it so.

The point here discussed needs clear and careful statement. Paul is presenting an analogy. In interpreting an analogy, we must be careful not to go beyond what is intended. To do so is dangerous; we may infer points never in the mind of the author. Those who suggest points of analogy not specifically mentioned in an analogy have the burden of proving that the similarities are not merely in their own mind. In the case at hand, insofar as permanence is never broached by the apostle, those who would suggest permanence as a feature of marriage on the basis of this text bear the burden of proof. Nor will it do to point out that Christ's relation to the Church is permanent. That need not be denied. The question is not whether Christ is permanently bound to his Church, but whether husbands are permanently bound to their wives.

The fact that Paul himself mentions two or three points that are not parallel between the analogically related pairs should itself give pause to those who wish to force permanence into the analogy. Some things said of Christ and Church may be said of husband and wife. Some things said of Christ and Church may *not* be said of husband and wife. To which category does permanence belong? One cannot tell from Ephesians 5; therefore, Ephesians 5 cannot be the proper basis for a permanence argument.

By stripping *one flesh* of the concept of ontological permanence, we do not mean to take away from the strength of the word *implicit* in both Testaments. The term definitely does imply a strong bond, a bond stronger than one established by a person having "casual sex" might think the act involves. But it does an injustice to Scripture to add strength that the word does not contain, and I fear this is being done. God does not need any help in verbal inspiration. It is enough that the divinely chosen word, like its negative counterpart, *leave*, speaks of a strong action. Marriage is a *commitment* to be joined to the spouse until death sunders the relationship, but it is not necessarily a commitment to a *permanent* relationship. The permanence is one of *intention and commitment*, not of *fact*. Marriage *ought* to be permanent, but, sadly, it may not be. If any given marriage remains "until death" parts the couple, it is by the grace of God, not by the indissoluble nature of the relationship.

It is worth saying at this point that, although by New Testament times the word *cleave* and the words *one flesh* had come to have physical or sexual overtones, it is improper to speak of marriage as essentially a physical bond. Although 1 Corinthians 6 does speak of nonmarital intercourse as such a cleaving, and quotes the Genesis 2:24 terminology, an easy reading of the Old and New Testaments reveals that marriage is not the sexual act (as we have already noted). Premarital intercourse led to a legally forced marriage (cf. Exod. 22:16; Deut. 22:28 f.; etc.), so if we wish to use the term *one flesh* as synonymous with sexual unity, we need to distinguish between becoming "one flesh" and being "married."

What, then, does it mean to become "one flesh," and is this union permanent? The words themselves speak of organic union. Organic relationships are *fundamental* ones involving constitutional union. It is the relationship of one's hand to one's head. But although the head and hand may "team up," their relation is far greater than that of two oxen simply bound together by a wooden yoke. The union appreciated by husbands and wives is spoken of in the language of *inherent* union as well as *extrinsic* grouping. First Corinthians 6:16 emphasizes "organic union," using the analogy of the parts of a body in their relation to each other, and also loosely relating this whole discussion to our personal relationship to Christ. Ephesians 5:31 picks up on the analogical illustrations and expands them to a corporate analogy: the union of husband and wife is like that between Christ and the Church. Again, the two are intimately related, the way an arm is to a shoulder. (Paul explicitly speaks of the wife being to the husband like a part of his own body, Eph. 5:28 f.)

The question arises, however, whether the Scripture intends us to take this talk of "organic union" literally. In other words, is the union itself organic, or only *like* an organic union? Is there really a living organism that the two sexual partners become? What exactly is that "third entity"? Or is it that the Scriptures use the language of organic union to evoke in our minds the profundity of the marriage relation? After all, the more precise use of the organic, "one-flesh" language by Jesus is simply to emphasize that the two are a team, the members of which cannot function as independent individuals.

My own choice is the latter. I admit that marriage is a profound relationship that is best understood by hearing the language of organic union. Scripture, I believe, does not intend for us to speculate on the mystical nature of some "body" that the married couple become but rather to concentrate upon the profound nature of marriage and the tragedy of sundering such a relationship.

Nonetheless, for those who may differ with me here, I shall broach the question of whether the Scripture understands such "organic unions" to be permanent. First, note that, lexically, nothing demands that this be so. Second, be careful about drawing conclusions from the illustrations and analogies that the New Testament uses in connection with our terms. Nothing is stated explicitly in such passages that would imply permanence, and it is risky to presume relations in an analogy that go beyond stated correspondence. Yet this is often exactly what is done. Well-meaning persons go beyond stated similarity in Ephesians 5 to argue for permanence because Christ's relationship to the Church is permanent.[44]

Think of it this way: if God can sunder the unified flesh of Adam, then someone could sunder the "one flesh" of a husband-wife relationship (Gen. 2). Summarizing: in Matthew 19 and Mark 10, people are warned against sundering the "one-flesh" relationship, implying they physically *can* but *shouldn't.* Whatever "one-flesh" relationship may exist between the man and the prostitute, they are specifically told to "flee immorality," that is, break the relationship. It is far beyond the text to suppose that, this admonition notwithstanding, some ongoing bond remains between them. The need for purity of the spiritual bond with the Holy Spirit denies that. And, finally, although the apostle, for effect, says that "no one ever yet hated his own body" (Eph. 5:30), we have already been told by him that *immorality* (*porneia*) is a sin "against [one's] own body" in 1 Corinthians 6:18. Or, if I may be forgiven the crassness, one can separate an arm from a shoulder. One could even cut off one's head. That would be traumatic, but possible. Even if we were to take the language of "organic union" literally, such a union would still be dissolvable.

From the New Testament, then, we discover that the term *one flesh* emphasizes an organic kind of union that is suggested by the same term in its Old Testament use. However, this may be simply a figurative way of expressing the profound nature of the bonding that takes place in the sexual union in marriage. In all, however, we are reminded that a "one-flesh" union may take place outside marriage. Thus, the union is a union *in* marriage and not *of* it per se.

Insofar as the only valid sexual union occurs in marriage, however, these terms came to be near synonyms for marriage itself. They underscore the truth that marriage is undertaken to bring two persons together in intimate and profound relation.

THE CONTEXT OF MARRIAGE

[They] were both naked and were not ashamed.

(Genesis 2:25)

The context of the Genesis verse reminds us that marriage has just been discussed in the context of a sinless world. Although it is true that the Mosaic "footnote" about marriage has elements that existed only after the Fall (e.g., "father and mother"), the discussion has set forth marriage in an Edenic way. Since there was then no sin, there was no need to discuss either immoral marriages or the breakup of marriage. Adam and Eve were acceptable partners. They were not of different religious convictions, one believing and the other pagan; there were no heathens. Nor was there any reason to proscribe homosexual marriages (though that proscription may rightly be exegeted from the text), as there were only one each of the two sexes. There was no need to tell Adam and Eve not to marry in lust like the Gentiles, for there was no lust. There was no reason to caution parents about the marriage of their children as Paul does in 1 Corinthians 7, because there were no parents. That parents are mentioned at all is unusual—it was done only to show how strong the desire for reunion between the two halves of the Image would be.

On the other hand, it is true that the text does not discuss the end of marriage. This has been made much of by those who wish to deny divorce and remarriage. They wish us to remember that marriage *originally* was to be till death parted the couple. But of course this is simply to misunderstand the placement of the Genesis 2:24 text. Before the Fall, there was no discussion of marriage lasting until death, for there was no death, since death comes by the sin of Adam. It is only subsequent to the Fall that the issue of the end of marriage becomes relevant. Had there been no sin, then we may presume that Adam and Eve's marital relation would have lasted as long as God thought it helpful for the fulfilling of their task of caring for the world. But at the point when sin entered the world, and death by sin, and further sin from that sin, shameful behavior by and against marriage partners became relevant. From then on, death might end marriage by natural means, or by execution of one or both of the partners for some crime. Or marriage might end by some serious offense against the covenant, perhaps by divorce. In short, one has no right to deny the right to divorce and remarry just because such activities are not mentioned in Genesis 2:24. Genesis 2:24 never promised us that it would contain everything that could be said about marriage or its ending.

CONCLUSIONS

From our study of Genesis 2:24, we have learned more about what marriage is not than what it is. This has been because we have concentrated upon the themes and terms of union (e.g., *one flesh*) more than on the covenantal themes implicit in the word *cleaving*. Specific major conclusions are restated in appendix A.[45] At this point our findings are summarized in a more general way.

The text of Holy Scripture, from its earliest passages, presents marriage as a profound union of individual persons. From early in its first book, the Bible speaks of marriage in the language of *organic union*. The effect of this talk is to stress the intimacy and the bonding nature of the act that consummates the social-legal contract. This intimacy is presented as the goal of marriage as well as a marriage right. Yet only the legalities sanction such intimacy. This latter fact should increase appreciation for the legalities and encourage their continuation. *Divorce*, on the other hand, is a sidetrack. It remains one of the saddest ironies of human relations that the state of marriage, which was originally designed as the moral context of the drive for "togetherness," has been so abused that discussions of it often center on the "right" to end it. It is a sad commentary on the failure of human beings to live according to the wise counsel of their Creator. The union in marriage was meant to be enjoyed "till death" parted the couple, and the legalities themselves were designed to help ensure continuation. Thus, it is wrong to *under*state the strength of intimate union in marriage.

On the other hand, it is equally improper to *over*state the strength of that union. The cohesiveness in the marriage union does not entail a permanent ontological bond (i.e., a bond of being). None of the crucial terms used in the Bible denote permanency. Though the strength of those terms implies an intention to make the relationship a permanent one, and though there is every indication that God expects the marriage union to go on until the death of the partners, this does not imply ontological finality, in the sense of creating a permanent third entity or being. The couple vows to keep their union inviolate until death, and if violation of the vows occurs, the union is broken thereby. As it was begun by intentional action, it is broken by intentional action. But, of course, marriage need not end in violence. Marriage ought to remain inviolate until death, and, by the grace of God, it might do so! We can see that God intended for marriage to last, but we cannot legitimately argue from the text of Genesis that marriages will be unending in a world of sin.[46]

Our conclusion, then, is that marriage is the moral context of a profound union accomplished by the physical union of two persons. The close relation between the physical union in marriage and marriage itself gives rise to the metaphorical description of marriage as an organic union wherein the partners have so entwined their lives as to render themselves a unity. But their relationship is not for that reason permanent *in fact*, though their marriage *ought* to remain intact until death parts them. The marriage relation is not best typified by mere sexuality, by terms of mystery or an ontological union of spirits. It is a bond based upon intention. It is the establishment of a kinship relationship between two people that, in spite of death or divorce, has ongoing ramifications for them and/or their near kin.

CHAPTER 2

A Covenant of Companionship

(Exodus 20 and 21)

Your companion . . . by covenant

(Malachi 2:14)

INTRODUCTION

The cohesiveness of the bond in marriage is strong, and the interfacing of the marriage partners holds potential for intimate companionship; but marriage itself is more properly a *covenantal* relationship. In Malachi 2:14, God reprimands certain Israelite men for dealing treacherously with the wives of their youth, with whom they had a covenant.[1] These husbands had divorced their wives to marry women of the land. What exactly is a covenant, and what specifically does a marriage covenant involve?[2] A covenant is, simply put, an agreement between two parties. The agreement might be either public (e.g., Gen. 23) or private (1 Sam. 18:3). Generally, a covenant was made to establish some legal position. In fact, the Akkadian word *burru*, which means precisely that, is thought by many scholars to be the basis of our Hebrew word *berit*.[3] Covenantal agreement in biblical times had four elements: parties, conditions, results, security.[4]

THE PARTIES OF THE COVENANT: EQUAL OR UNEQUAL?

The parties in a covenant might be individuals (1 Sam. 18:3) or larger groups (Gen. 23), and the relation these parties bore to each other might be one of parity or disparity. In marriage, were the partners equals, or was one the servant of the other?

"A Helper 'Suitable' "

Given the Old Testament emphasis on the husband paying a price for the bride (e.g., Exod. 22:17) and the New Testament emphasis on the "headship" of the husband (e.g., Eph. 5:22 ff.), one might suppose that the Bible understands the marriage agreement as being between unequals. That is incorrect. In the first place, Genesis 1:26 ff. identifies men and women as equal representatives of the divine Image (see chap. 1). When this is coupled to the second chapter of Genesis, in which God creates the woman as a "helper suitable" for Adam, and when it is understood that these latter words, in the Hebrew, imply not inequality but rather the supportive help of equals, one begins to get a better picture of the nature of their covenant relation. Adam recognized an aspect of their equality when he spoke of their common human bond (v. 23).

Not a Slave

An even clearer picture of their status relation is revealed by a close analysis of the concubinage laws. Leviticus 19:20 states a law governing the infidelity of a concubine to her master. It reads,

Now if a man lies carnally with a woman who is a slave acquired for another man, but who has in no way been redeemed, nor given her freedom, there shall be punishment; they shall not, however, be put to death, *because she was not free.* (Emphasis added.)

What this is saying is that in concubinage the woman is judged differently than in a "full marriage." This reminds us of our previous comments about the terms employed of the partners. *Baali* implied "master," whereas *ishi* implied status equality. Status equality, in turn, reminds us of the intimate companionship of a covenantal relationship. The partners are seen as "companions," that is, two individuals bound together as equals.

None of this should be construed as denying the biblical teaching that, within the marriage relationship, the husband is endowed with the qualities necessary for and has the responsibility to be the leader of the team. Even in teams of horses, one is commonly the lead horse. The fact that the man is the leader of the unit, the "head" as compared to "the body," does not make him higher in personhood. Nor does it mean that his wife is less than an equal in terms of partnership. This is admittedly difficult to grasp. They are equally persons, equal partners, different in role responsibilities (with the husband being the final authority in familial decisions).[5]

Worthy of a "Bride Price"

Modern people, when reading "bride price" passages in the Law, often jump to the conclusion that to pay for the bride amounts to her having been *sold,* and this reduces her to the level of a slave.[6] It is my conviction, however, that the God who is neither male nor female but who is the Judge of all the world would not do wrong. It is he who has inspired these passages. When we fathom his intentions, we come to see the justice and realism such passages express. Recognizing the potential for irresponsibility in husbands, these laws provide one of the best means for the woman's family to discern the sincerity of a potential husband. Only a sincere suitor will place a value on his bride equal to nearly a year's wages.[7] Her father, in turn, was expected to keep— perhaps to invest—the money for the woman's future possible needs (cf. Gen. 31:15). The man who disregarded commitment and had un-covenanted relations with an unmarried woman[8] was required to "pay money equal to the bride price for virgins" to the girl's father (Exod. 22:17). A man who raped a virgin was charged fifty months' wages (Deut. 22:29), and a man who publicly defamed his wife had to pay her father a hundred months' wages (Deut. 22:19). In each case, the money was to ensure proper, future provision for the woman.

It may be that the money functioned as a sort of prepaid alimony, to cover the woman's needs against the possibility of unjust treatment or release by her husband. This is based upon Exodus 21:11, where a mistreated concubine, by contrast, was to be released "without payment of money." Although this passage deals with concubines, it would seem to be in harmony with Genesis 31:15, which deals with full wives that had been "sold" like concubines (as Laban sold Rachel and Leah). There will be further discussion about the use of concubine passages in a later section.

A Willing Partner

If marriage is an agreement between equals, what part, if any, did the woman play in consenting to the marriage? Weren't marriages arranged by the men? Genesis 24 would seem to present us with a more realistic picture. There, in the story of the procuring of a wife for Isaac, the servant of Abraham asks him what he is to do if "the woman will not be willing to follow me to this land." The striking thing about this is that the servant did not know who the woman would be; his question seems to imply that women *generally* exercised the right to determine their marital partner. And though there may have been exceptions, I believe that it is safe to conclude that this was the rule in biblical times, at least among the ancestors of the Israelites.[9]

THE CONDITIONS OF THE COVENANT

If the partners are considered equals in their covenant, we would speak of the covenant as "bi-lateral." And realizing that the marriage covenant is a bilateral agreement is a significant point to which the inquirer into the biblical view of divorce can come. For, as is pointed out about such covenants, they are "entirely conditional upon the acceptance and fulfillment" of the obligations to which the parties have agreed. Indeed, the authors of the article "Covenants" in *Wycliffe Bible Dictionary* state that "all human covenants are bilateral and conditional."[10]

Conditional or Unconditional Commitment?

The astute reader will foresee the implications regarding the breakup of marriage that arise from such a view of covenant, namely, if the marriage vows are broken, the covenant is off, and a divorce writ is only *a public statement of the facts.* Those who are opposed to these implications may respond by opting for the obvious alternative, namely, that marriage is unconditional. Their major source of biblical support comes often from verses that analogically relate human marriages (*a*) to God's unconditional relation to his chosen "bride," the Church (Eph. 5:22–33) and (*b*) to the Abrahamic covenant (Gen. 15). From these passages the argument is drawn that, since God is faithful even though we are not, we should do the same with our spouses, since we should love them the way Christ loves the Church (Eph. 5:25). The husband should present his wife to the Father, just as Christ will present his bride the Church to the Father (5:26–27).

This sort of reasoning has several mortal deficiencies. First, as I have already had occasion to point out, there are dissimilarities as well as similarities in analogical arguments. Just as permanence is not specifically mentioned as a similarity, so too, an "unconditional" aspect of human covenants is likewise not stated. The fact that God makes unconditional covenants and that God draws analogies between his relationships and human relationships does not mean that human relationships are ever unconditional. The burden of the proof rests upon anyone who affirms such a correspondence. It will not do in interpreting analogies to bring in unexpressed elements and compare them simply because they exist in one of the relationships. We must remember that this sort of "smuggling" works in both directions. For example, human husbands do not always know what is best for their wives and families, but this fact does not lead me to suggest that Christ is sometimes unaware of the needs of the Church. By the same token, the fact that Christ may commit himself unconditionally to the Church should not lead us to infer that human marriages are unconditional. The very fact that conditions are not expressly discussed in the passage is prima facie evidence that God does not intend the reader of the Ephesian letter to draw implications about such conditions from it.

Some might suggest that verses 26 and 27 offer support for the existence of an unconditional aspect to human marriages. These verses mention that Christ will present his bride the Church to himself in all her glory. Does this not refer to the eschaton? And does this not imply a permanent and unconditional relationship? And, if these are implied, does this not mean that unconditional elements *are* germane to the analogy to human marriages? Not really. As we noted in chapter 1, there are several aspects of the Christ-Church relationship in Ephesians 5:22–33 that clearly go beyond the analogy to human marriages. The Christ-Church relationship is *mysterious,* according to verse 32, but that verse also mentions that marriage is not. Verse 23 notes that Christ is the *Savior* of the "body," but verse 24 begins with "but": *but* this is not true of the husband's relationship to the wife or of her relationship to her husband; the husband is not the *savior* of the wife. The husband is the "head," but not the savior. So too, husbands should be self-sacrificing for their wives, just as Christ is for the Church (v. 25). But the husband is not the "sanctifier" of the wife (v. 26). In other words, the presence of contrasting elements in the analogy requires us to use caution in drawing correspondences between points that are stated, much less those that are known only from other biblical passages.

Furthermore, it can honestly be questioned whether the covenants of God himself with *individual* human beings are always and in every respect unconditional. The blessings of even the Abrahamic covenant are conditional (Gen. 17:14), even though the covenant itself is not. For although God's promises regarding seed, land, posterity, and so on will be fulfilled to the descendants of Abraham *corporately* considered, the experiencing of any of these blessings by *individual* descendants of Abraham is conditioned upon their being circumcised of heart—an Israelite indeed (Rom. 3). Additionally, the marriage-divorce "metaphor" in the Old Testament is most often tied to the Mosaic covenant rather than to the Abrahamic. With regard to the conditional nature of that covenant, consider Deuteronomy 27–30. If the people then, or in future generations, disregard the unequal treaty of Sinai, cursings will come upon them. Jeremiah records the historical facts of the visitation of these curses, and notes:

"Behold, days are coming," declares the Lord, "when I will make a new covenant with the house of Israel and with the house of Judah, not like the covenant which I made with their father in the day I took them by the hand to bring them out of the land of Egypt, My covenant which they broke, although I was a husband to them," declares the Lord. (31:32 f.)

Sinai was a "bilateral," or conditional, covenant.

It is simply wrongheaded to understand the human covenant of marriage to be as unilateral as the Abrahamic covenant. Moreover, it is both hasty and dangerous to argue from the fact that God has chosen unilaterally to make his relationship to Israel or the Church permanent to the requirement that spouses must unilaterally remain in legal bonds of marriage.

If marriage is a covenant, and if covenants involve conditions, exactly what are the conditions? Are they the same for both men and women, or do they differ? Where does the Bible talk about all this? These are a few of the questions that this discussion engenders. Answering them is not an easy task. It is also a controversial project—much more so than I once imagined.

Simply put, the Bible warns a person against the breaking of the conditions when, in the seventh commandment, it says, "You shall not commit adultery" (Exod. 20:14). Though at first one might be inclined to think of this word only in sexual terms, the Deuteronomic comment on this command makes it clear that far more than sexual purity is at stake.[11] In a section spanning from 22:1 to 23:14, we find that the major value behind the command is "integrity" of relationships. Different types of relationships are addressed: social (22:1–14), sexual (22:5), natural (22:6–7), architectural (22:8), agricultural (22:9–10), customary (22:11–12), marital (22:13–29), lineal (22:30–23:8), hygienic (23:9–13). Looking at this list, it is evident that integrity *in general* and not merely sexual integrity is understood by Moses as entailed by the warning against "adultery." Deuteronomy says positively what Exodus put negatively. Deuteronomy says that the life of the Israelite is to be lived in purity and integrity. Exodus warns us not to adulterate that integrity.[12]

The Essential Commitments in the Covenant

Looking specifically at the section on marriage, we may note that responsibility is dealt with in regard to both the woman and the man. The admonition to each is interwoven with that of the other. The woman is enjoined to keep herself pure from any willful sexual relations with men other than her pledged one (cf. Deut. 22:20, 22–25).[13] For his part, the man is required not to ruin the reputation of a woman of Israel (22:19, 24–29). I will sum these up under the following heads: the man is to *protect* the woman; the woman is to be *monogamous*. But we are already a bit ahead of ourselves; let us turn back now to Exodus and see these same responsibilities as they appear in the first giving of the Law.

THE MAN'S RESPONSIBILITIES

Provision for the Wife's Bodily Needs

> *He may not reduce her food, clothing, or conjugal rights.*
>
> *(Exodus 21:10)*

After the statement of the general obligation not to commit adultery, the Law picks up in the following chapter the theme of covenantal relations. The implications of Exodus 21 to our discussion are not to be underestimated. Unfortunately the chapter is seldom, if ever, brought into the discussion of marriage, much less of divorce, the reason being that the one-flesh relationship under discussion is one with concubines and not (at least not transparently) with wives.

THE RELEVANCE OF EXODUS 21

There are very good reasons for breaking with the traditional avoidance of Exodus 21 in discussions of marriage. First, a concubine is nearly a wife. Though a slave, she did have an ongoing "one-flesh" relationship with her master. She bore him children, and they were considered his (remember that most of the sons of Jacob were born to him by his wives' servant girls). Exodus 21 makes it clear that the concubine had been bought by a price, which must have functioned similarly to the bride price of a full wife (v. 7). Second, though she was a concubine, therefore a slave, slavery in Israel was unlike that in surrounding lands. Victims of chattel slavery were protected from being sent back to their masters if they escaped (Deut. 23:15), but the permanent servant girl was to be treated like a daughter (Exod. 21:9).[14] Third, though the term *wife* is *added* in the English text in 21:10, it would seem that the translators have been well advised to interpret it this way (rather than simply "another maidservant") insofar as the verse at hand closely approximates Deuteronomy 21:15, which deals with a similar subject, namely, the disinheriting of the children of an unloved woman/wife. The Deuteronomy text prohibits an attack upon an unloved wife by disinheriting her children; the earlier Exodus passage prohibits a man from refusing to give a wife the opportunity to have children. The passage in the second amends the first at a crucial point. What good would it do to prohibit a man from disinheriting his wife's children if he could simply refuse to give the unloved woman children (through whom she gained inheritance from him) in the first place? The laws function together, and both wives and concubines are, in all likelihood, to be included in both.

Fourth, and more important, since the Scripture elsewhere does not discuss similar rights of a full wife, it may be presumed that this text is designed, in principle, to set forth the rights of all women under covenant who have a one-flesh relationship with a man.[15] Philosophically, this sort of reasoning is called an *a fortiori* argument; that is, it argues from the lesser to the greater: if God cares this much for a one-flesh partner of a lesser status (i.e., a concubine), then he cares at least as much for a full wife (i.e., a companion). If the slave has certain rights, it is unreasonable to assume that the free woman has fewer.[16] That would suggest that a partner in a covenant of equality would deserve less consideration than a partner in a covenant of inequality. Certainly God felt no obligation to provide for the covenant partner (Israel) when that partner had failed to live up to its side of the covenant! The very point of the "cursing" section bears that out. Any who would suggest that being a full partner implies less privilege bears a heavy burden of proof!

The *a fortiori* argument assumes new importance when we consider that God is very concerned with the reputation of the full wife. In Numbers 5 and Deuteronomy 23, there are passages that assess great fines against a man who would tarnish his wife's reputation. Would it seem likely that God would care so much for the woman's reputation and care nothing for her body? A smear upon her reputation brought a hundred-month fine and the prohibition of divorce. Could it be argued that God does not care if the bearer of that reputation is battered and beaten to death? That is not likely. Is it not manifestly probable that God intends the concubine passages to be used to derive principles for the judges to apply to the case of abused covenant partners who were equals to the males?

In short, marriage being essentially a covenantal, not a mystical, relation, a covenant of equals, absolutely nothing would imply the lack of a privilege granted a partner in a covenant of unequals. The wife has her rights.

What are those rights, or, if I may put it backwards, what are the obligations of the man? Exodus reveals four. Three are found in 21:10, and the last is enumerated in verses 26 and 27.

THE NOURISHMENT PROVISIONS

The first three obligations are prefaced by the phrase "he may not reduce." The idea here is that the master may not cut back on the provisions stated in the contract held by the girl's father (cf. v. 7). Obviously, that contract stipulated a certain amount of each of the items that follow. But before we look at them in particular, note that in the case of a slave contract, the concubine's father is obviously in a poor bargaining position. In all likelihood he would only have been able to arrange for a minimal amount of provisions for his daughter. Had he been in a better position, he doubtless would not have sold her in the first place, for, rather than "another mouth to feed," such a girl would usually have been a helpful part of his work force. On the other hand, if the master had really liked the girl, he would have taken her as a full wife, not put upon her the status of a slave. Given these considerations, it is likely that, as a rule, the sort of promises made would entail *minimal* support; that is why *reduction* of the provisions is prohibited.

Just how serious the issue is can quickly be seen by considering the nature of the provisions in question: food, clothing, sex. The first two are most readily understood. If the girl was getting minimal food, reducing the amount would be life-threatening. She could starve. If she were ill clothed, her body could succumb to the elements. She needed minimal shelter. But the third obligation, sex—"conjugal rights"—is not so clear.[17] Why is sex an issue? Answer: the future security of the concubine depended upon her children. She received no inheritance from her master aside from what he was required to give to his children by her (cf. Deut. 21:15–17). If he died before she did, as husbands most often do, she could not count upon his extended family to care for her in her old age (when she would no longer be desired as a concubine). Her hope was in her children. Any man who would so attack that future security of the concubine by denying her the chance to have children was to be considered a scoundrel indeed. The Onan story (Gen. 38), though dealing with a levirate situation (marriage of a widow to her deceased husband's brother) and relating to a "full wife," nonetheless makes this clear in the Old Testament, and Paul's harsh words regarding the neglect of one's family (1 Tim. 5:8) show that God has not changed his mind in the matter!

Since a slave was an unequal partner, it stands to reason that a husband was expected to provide far better for his full wife. The slave could expect the minimum. The wife could expect better.

KAISER'S OBJECTION TO EXODUS 21

Consideration must be given here to the arguments by Walter Kaiser that the third provision in the list should be "ointments" rather than "marital rights."[18] Noting that the Hebrew word in question is a *hapax legomenon* (once-spoken word), Kaiser questions the propriety of following the Septuagint (the Old Testament translated into Greek around 200 B.C.), whence arises "marital rights," when similar, threefold lists of essentials from Sumer and Akkad (more contemporaneous societies) end with "ointments."[19]

Close examination of the facts surrounding the choice in question does not, however, favor Kaiser's conclusion. First, there is no assurance that because the similar lists are threefold and contain two common elements the third element is the same. The case would be stronger, of course, if the Exodus list was itself from Sumer/Akkad. Second, I believe that it is still preferable to follow the "authorized" translation of the Hebrew Scriptures by those familiar with the tradition than one that is based on inferences drawn from similarities.

Kaiser does admit in a footnote that those arguing for "marital rights" do have two plausible supports for their alternative. The first is a linguistic point. The Hebrew term, though a *hapax*, is very similar to a word translated "to humble by ravishing [in illicit intercourse]." The second point is a cross-reference to 1 Corinthians 7:3, where Paul admonishes the husband to show his spouse "due benevolence," which, in the context, certainly means to "grant sexual intercourse."

Why Kaiser rejects these supports virtually out of hand is puzzling. Though it is clear that the term cannot mean "humble by ravishing," or "rape," we must remember that the term in Exodus is slightly different. Perhaps the difference involves mitigation of the implications of humbling by force? In any case, the more evident linguistic elements do seem tied to sex rather than ointments. Second, though the cross-reference to Paul is less weighty, it does show that an Old Testament scholar of the early Church did see it as an obligation for the man to grant his wife sexual relations.

Given these points, it seems far less risky to follow the traditional translation of the *hapax* than Kaiser implies. For my part, I will presume that the traditional translation is preferred until better argument can be found than mere similarity to ancient texts.

Presence

A corollary to the responsibility of provision is presence. If the husband is responsible to provide nourishment and security—including sexual intercourse—his continuing presence would be required. This does not mean that he cannot be away from the home for valid reasons, but it does mean that he cannot willfully desert his wife and remain innocent of failing to provide. The implications of this provision are also important to the question of divorce. If a husband's divorce of his wife is a legal desertion, then it would be nothing less than a form of breach of the requirement to provide for his wife.

Protection from His Abuse of Her Body

> *If a man strikes the eye . . . and destroys it . . .*
>
> *(Exodus 21:26)*

The final requirement of Exodus 21 is consistent with the first three. If the male one-flesh partner was prohibited from passively attacking the well-being of his covenant partner, we may reasonably conclude that more physical aggression on his part would be a more grievous insult to the relationship. If we think so, we are not disappointed by the later verses of the chapter (vv. 26 f.):

And if a man strikes the eye of his male or *female* slave, and destroys it, he shall let him go free on account of his eye. And if he knocks out a tooth of his male or *female* slave, he shall let him go free on account of his tooth. (Emphasis added.)

Note that the abuse in question is not a simple slap or a raised voice, but a serious attack. Hebrew scholars suggest that the eye-tooth reference may be a *merism*, that is, a term-set that goes from the greatest to the least. The implication of a *merism* at this location in the text would be that if the contract partner sustains any lasting physical damage, the covenant has been broken.[20] Note, too, that the slave is a person under covenant or contract. Remember also that a concubine is identified in the previous passage as a slave and certainly would have been protected by this passage. Finally, if we employ the same line of *a fortiori* reasoning that we did earlier, we see that the rights of a wife will at least equal those of a slave woman. In fact, logic implies that if a slave may not be beaten seriously, a full wife may not be beaten at all. The cord is tied: the man may not abuse his covenant partner. Neither passive nor active abuse would be tolerated by the law.

Protection of the Wife's Reputation

> They shall fine him . . . because he publicly defamed a virgin of Israel.
> (*Deuteronomy 22:19*)

To these requirements of physical protection we are now prepared to add introductory comments about the reputation of the wife and the husband's responsibility not to defame her. Two passages are pertinent; first is Numbers 5. This is the so-called law of jealousy (v. 29). A man suspects that his wife has been unfaithful to him, but he seems to have insufficient evidence for a normal adultery trial. The text offers the somewhat risky option of securing final judgment from the Lord. The man takes his wife before the priest (the issue here is revelatory evidence), and the woman is put through a ritual. God speaks through the effects of the ritual to proclaim the guilt or innocence of the woman. There is nothing magical about the ritual; it is simply designed to be a means of revelation.

The public nature of the process is important. After all, the husband has made a public statement about his wife's loyalty and purity. It is, then, only fitting that the truth be a matter of public record, derived through a priest, not through a politician—that it be done by the hand of the omniscient God, not by the word of humans who err.

The wording of the results of the test is our immediate concern. If she is guilty, "the man shall be free from guilt." The man in question is not the man who has committed adultery with the woman, but her husband; *he* shall not be guilty. Obviously, if she is *not* guilty, the husband *is*. But the text does not go into further detail regarding the nature of his guilt or the penalty for it.

This situation in which the issues are left hanging must have created some uncertainty in the minds of the people. This is not to say that some judicious settlement could not be reached, but in a fallen world God must speak extra clearly. And that is why Deuteronomy 22:13–21 is so valuable. In this "second giving" of the Law, a similar challenge to the integrity of the wife is discussed. This time it regards a new bride, rather than a wife of longer standing. In Deuteronomy, the groom claims that his wife has had premarital relations, is guilty of "shameful deeds" (v. 17). Again, the matter of evidence is considered. This time the wedding-night sheets, in the possession of the bride's father (safe custody), stained with the consummative blood, would seem to be the proof required. And if the proof could not be produced, the girl was judged to be a harlot and was dealt with as such (vv. 20 f.). If not, the man was treated in a way appropriate to his guilt. The specifics of his punishment will be discussed in the next chapter, but here we wish to note the nature of his guilt: "he publicly defamed a virgin of Israel" (v. 19). This makes it clear that the husband had a legal obligation to do nothing that would ruin the reputation of his wife, at least as regarded questions of her loyalty to the canons of their marital covenant.

New Testament Statements

The New Testament reaffirms these responsibilities of the husband. In Ephesians 5 the husband is admonished to "love" his wife. This admonition to responsible, self-sacrificing regard for her is defined further as nourishing and cherishing her (v. 29). If anything, there is a bit of emotional involvement implied in the latter term (*thalpo*)—a certain tenderness—that was not legally binding upon the husband in the Old Testament. We shall have more to say about these "extralegal" responsibilities as they relate to the ending of the covenant.

THE WOMAN'S RESPONSIBILITIES

Sexual Fidelity to the Husband

If no man has lain with you . . .

(Numbers 5:19)

The major condition of the covenant for the woman was sexual fidelity. She was required to have no other sex partner than the man to whom she was pledged. Passages in the Law that defined sexual adultery made this very clear. Consider first Leviticus 18:20:

You shall not have intercourse with your neighbor's wife, to be defiled with her.

This is supported by the penalty clause in Leviticus 20:10:

If there is a man who commits adultery with another man's wife, one who commits adultery with his friend's wife, the adulterer and the adulteress . . .

In the "second giving" of the Law, the formula does not change:

If a man is found lying with a married woman . . . (Deut. 22:22)

If there is a girl who is a virgin engaged to a man, and another man finds her in the city and lies with her . . . he has violated his neighbor's wife. (Deut. 22:23 f.)

In each case, the woman is identified as *pledged* to another man. Her marriage might have been consummated or might still be in the betrothal stage, but in either case, for her to join herself physically to another man constituted "adultery."

This analysis bears out a conclusion of chapter 1; that is, the consummation of marriage by intercourse did not constitute the most important element of the marriage relationship or of the establishing of the marriage itself. More important than the consummation was the betrothal. This fact is easier to understand when you recall that, in Hebrew marriages, the only vows that were ever said, the only agreement that was ever made, was made at the time of the initial betrothal. For them, the betrothal was not merely a sentimental statement of intention, as it often is in our society, but the very binding of the parties together by covenant. From that moment onward, the woman was considered the man's wife (cf. Deut. 22:24).[21] The heart of the covenant was not the one-flesh joining, but the contractual commitment.[22]

But though that marriage is not essentially sexual, it is to be remembered that the wife had the right to sexual relations with her husband (Exod. 21:10). She had the right to sex in order to grant her the possibility of offspring who could provide her future security. Sex was a *right of marriage* ("conjugal rights"), not an essential element in its establishment. Without the vows, no marriage exists. Without sexuality, the marriage has not been consummated. The consummation is like a man taking possession of property; he owns it before he takes it, but taking it makes the transaction final.

Deuteronomy 22:13 ff. presents us with a law that required the bride to be as pure as she presented herself to be. For her to claim to be a virgin but to have had previous sexual relations was a breach of covenant. Perhaps the thought here is that the girl had had those relations during the betrothal period, but no great effort is taken to determine the exact timing. She is simply said to have "played the harlot in her father's house" (22:21). This shows the seriousness with which the Law looked upon the purity of the bride.

An important distinction to make at this point is that the woman's responsibility with regard to marriage is put in the *negative*, whereas the man's is put in the *positive*. He must grant to her the act of sexual intercourse. She, on the other hand, was required only to refrain from having sex with anyone else. She was not required to have sex with him.

Protection from Her Abuse of His Body

Husband abuse of a physical sort is not directly mentioned in the Law. But it is indirectly. It is an implication of the same passages cited to prove that a woman's husband may not abuse her (Exod. 21:26 f.). If slaves could be free of their master if beaten, what must we conclude of a master beaten by his servant? The Law might have justified death for the slave in those cases (cf. Exod. 21:15 for how the striking of authorities was treated), but we can be satisfied with no less a conclusion than that such abuse would have ended the master's responsibility to provide for the dependent servant. The implications for this in marriage are obvious.

Presence

Though it is rather easy to see the need for the husband to remain available for the wife, it is harder to see an essential requirement for the wife to remain in the home. But such is the implication of the Law. Ending a contractual covenant was a matter of ransom, or transfer of ownership. And a ransom was not always allowed in the Law. Thus, a woman slave was not allowed to leave the master's house, as the male slave was (cf. Exod. 21:1 ff.).[23] In other cases ransom or redemption was allowed. In the case of a girl rejected as a bed-partner a process of redemption was required (Exod. 21:8). The rejected war bride of Deuteronomy 21 even needs to have an ordinance to permit her to "go out." And the divorced woman of Deuteronomy 24 needs the writ. All of these passages, and others, speak of the fact that a woman may not simply walk away from her husband. If she did, that would doubtless have been seen as a statement that she was repudiating her covenantal agreements.

New Testament Additions

The New Testament, of course, goes beyond the legal requirements for the woman by adding responsibilities for her to "submit" (Eph. 5:22/1 Pet. 3:1 ff.) to her husband. The term for this means to "order yourself under" someone else. This means that the woman chooses to place herself under the hierarchical control of her husband, in the same way volunteer soldiers choose to place themselves under the general. The text goes on to tell the wife to obey (1 Pet. 3:1) and reverence (Eph. 5:33) her husband.[24]

The New Testament also accommodates the increasingly exclusive monogamy of its hearers. In 1 Corinthians 7, Paul admonishes the wife to give her body to her husband. As we noted above, this was not required legally of the wife under the Law: if the woman withheld her body from her husband, he could simply take another wife or concubine. But when only one covenant was culturally permitted, the apostle needed to "require" reciprocal giving of the body to the spouse to provide a moral alternative to fornication.[25]

THE "LEGAL" STATUS OF APOSTOLIC ADDITIONS

The mention of these apostolic "admonitions" regarding both spouses gives rise to another question: since certain conditions or vows of the marriage covenant go beyond the essentials, what is the status of those conditions that might be added to the "essentials" by apostles or by the marriage partners themselves? What if the man should vow to be monogamous or the woman vow to obey? Are such "unnecessary" conditions valid? If so, are they the sorts of conditions that, if broken, damage the covenant as much as a breach of the "canons" or essential vows of covenant would?

First, let it be said that if an apostle adds something to the essentials, we may feel confidence in including those elements in present-day vows.[26] But if we have no inspired source for the additions, only the well-intentioned ideas of the couple themselves, we are justified in suggesting caution. Such additions could be dangerous. If God had thought it wise to include other conditions, he would surely have done so himself. He is omniscient. Where he has been silent, there must be reasons. Immediately, some will retort that the Bible itself makes some noteworthy additions, such as that requiring the woman to obey her husband (e.g., Eph. 5:22) or the husband to love his wife (Eph. 5:25). Without trying in any way to detract from the important nature of these "additions" to the Old Testament "canons of covenant," it is a point worth pondering that such items should be understood as being like apostolic admonitions, binding as the words of the master to the disciple but having no intended *legal* status. If this is the case, then to have broken them would not be to have broken the covenant. But, of course, this fact is somewhat irrelevant when such additions are commonly added to the canons when the vows are publicly stated. It is one thing if an apostle admonishes a couple to do something, it is another if the couple has made the admonitions a public troth.

Moreover, when we consider the extent to which the canons can be amended, this question becomes quite thorny. Some men have vowed to "obey" their wives. Some couples have been encouraged to vow to each other that they will never use divorce as a means of settling marital problems. What is the status of such vows? If the canons are God's minimum, the rest are human conditions. But, as Paul notes, human conditions once ratified are not to be changed or set aside (Gal. 3:15). Two alternatives present themselves: First, the additions are of equal status with the canons. On this interpretation, if when the canons are broken the covenant is understood as morally ending, the same would obtain if any other vow were broken. Thus, if the husband did not "cherish" his wife, or if she did not obey a certain command, the marriage would be morally over, just as if she had had intercourse with another man.

A second way of seeing things would be to judge such additions as *not* equal to the canons. On this interpretation, if the wife does not obey her husband, she has offended the covenant, but not in a manner that would morally end the marriage. And if the discipline for breaking a canon of covenant be divorce, the discipline for breaking an addition would not be divorce but something less. Though this second interpretation seems the more reasonable, remember that the husband's vow of monogamy fits into this category as well. This means that if he is unchaste, his wife may not divorce him, though he may divorce her for that same reason! Although this may not seem to be a totally happy interpretation, it is still likely that the second interpretation is preferable to the first, insofar as the first would seem to significantly change the canonical status of the essentials by making them equal to nonessentials.

Most difficult of all is the addition of a vow not to divorce. Such a vow is either unnecessary or improper. If it is saying only that the two never *intend* to end their covenant by divorce, then it is unnecessary—in the sense that all marriage covenants imply intended permanence. To say "for better or for worse" is to say the same thing. Clearly, the Bible does not support *sundering* a marriage by divorce. But what if unfaithfulness to the vows occurs during the marriage? Does *divorce* end the marriage in that case? It may end it legally, but it was the *unfaithfulness* that ended the moral obligation and sundered the organic union. Divorce then simply states publicly what has happened privately. Divorce then may be a divinely prescribed disciplinary action. If a vow not to divorce be interpreted as prohibiting divorce in such cases, then it is contrary to God's word. Shortly we will see how this vow is contrary to biblical teaching, insofar as it potentially inhibits the disciplinary action proscribed by Scripture and is contrary to the example of discipline set forth by God's action against his "bride," Israel.

Assuming for the moment that this is true, what then? Is a vow not to divorce invalid *ab initio,* or is it to be honored like the unfortunate vow Joshua made with Gibeon (a vow that should not have been made but, once made, should be kept)? One cannot be dogmatic here, but the latter does not seem likely. In the case of Gibeon, Joshua had been given a rule that was clearly understood but was applied wrongly. Those who vow not to divorce clearly do not understand the biblical mandate.

RECIPROCITY OF COMMITMENT

As a footnote to the study of responsibility in marriage, we may consider the question of reciprocality of the partners' responsibilities. Does the woman have an obligation to provide for her husband or, at least, to not defame him? Does he have the right to have relations with another woman? I believe that only two of the responsibilities are reciprocal: presence and no physical abuse. I do not find sufficient biblical warrant for reciprocity on the other matters. The most questionable aspect of this conclusion relates to matters of the husband's sexual fidelity. Readers interested in further argument regarding this matter should read appendix B.

THE RESULTS OF COVENANT KEEPING OR BREAKING

The Blessings of Keeping Covenant

The third element in a covenant is results. By this is meant the results of keeping or breaking the vows or conditions. In the next chapter we will consider the results of *not* keeping the vows. At this point we will consider the results of keeping them.

Specifically, what are the blessings of keeping one's marriage covenant? The first blessing of marriage is ready fulfillment. We are reminded that God created the woman expressly for the purpose of ending Adam's loneliness. By himself, he had no way to express himself to a peer. Many of his social skills were dormant. In addition, many of his psychological needs could only be fulfilled by receiving what the woman's personality could supply. The beauty of marriage is that the marriage partner is "ready at hand." Each does not have to spend anxious moments wondering if there is someone "out there" for them. Even when friends are numerous, marriage provides the potential for the greatest quantity and quality of "time together."

Along with this social and psychological fulfillment is physical fulfillment. In contrast with the man who takes his pleasure from a woman who is "common property," there is the married man, who may enjoy the body of his own wife, without the worry of whether she will be too busy with others to be available to him. And if a couple have taken care to cultivate a loving relationship, they may be assured that they give themselves to each other physically in love and respect. The bliss of sexual love is expressed in the Scriptures in the Song of Solomon.

As we have noted, this blessing is meant to be limited to marital relations. Premarital sex was considered fornication, and extramarital sex was considered adultery (unless an act of rape). Since fornication and adultery are sins, we can readily see that pleasure in the sexual act performed under those circumstances will bring no lasting joy, but only judgment, perhaps by the conscience, but surely someday by God. Guilt-free sexual pleasure is a blessing of marriage.[27]

It should be mentioned as well that sexual expression *aside from the intention to bear children* is blessed. As Geoffrey Bromiley has pointed out, marriage in Genesis is complete without children.[28] Nonetheless, children constitute the third blessing of marriage. Since with the Fall came death, human beings can experience the fulfillment of many temporal goals only by the extension of their own life in those of their children. Even in this life, the elderly often find that they need the support of their grown children. Thus, the Bible speaks accurately when it says,

Children are a gift from of the Lord;
The fruit of the womb is a reward.
Like arrows in the hand of a warrior,
So are the children of one's youth.
How blessed is the man whose quiver is full of them.

(Psalm 127:3–5a)

Since children are the product of sexual union, and since such union should only be in marriage, it may be said that children are a blessing of marriage. Until modern times a child born outside of marriage was considered an indictment against the biological parents. Consider the implications of the slur against Jesus in John 8:41.

Finally, if it can be said that children help their parents achieve temporal goals, it is sure that the same point can be made about each spouse with regard to the other. Genesis 2 tells us that God made the woman to be a helper (2:18) for the man. As we have already had occasion to mention, the idea here is not of a servant but of one called to be alongside another—a partner. Without negating the role of the man as head, it may be said that the terminology here implies that they will do things as a corporate venture. That would include decision making. Though the man may be the one responsible for the ultimate decision, and though God may have gifted the male to do the sort of directive thinking required in leading a social unit, for him to fail to take advantage of the wisdom of his wife is surely folly. She adds a dimension to decision making that a man often cannot supply, a certain wholistic sensitivity, without which the decision is often cold and unloving.[29]

Failure in the Covenant

All these blessings make marriage a very desirable institution, and it is little wonder that most people throughout history have taken advantage of the union. But not all who have done so have realized the blessings. For many, marriage seems like a trap. Consider the following verses, undoubtedly spoken from experience:

It is better to live in a corner of a roof
Than in a house shared with a contentious woman. (Prov. 21:9)

He who troubles his own house will inherit wind. (Prov. 11:29a)

Fortunately, the failure to find joy in marriage has not led most people to abandon marriage, to seek to obtain its joys by affairs outside of the marriage bond, or to strike out viciously against the marriage partner. Many have realized that it is far better to attempt to work out their problems honorably than to set themselves against the Witness (i.e., God) of their marriage vows. In brief, keeping the marriage vows is what enables the partners to experience the blessings of a good married life—in Genesis 1 and 2, personal fulfillment and a lack of anxiety. It enables the couple to do the work that God has set before each. Of course, the couple's happiness is not assured simply because they fulfill the minimum conditions set forth. A providing husband and a faithful wife might still hamper each other in attaining personal fulfillment. Love and happiness are, however, impossible when the vows are not fulfilled. One can only say that friendship and mutual fulfillment are *possible* when these conditions are met. Romantic love is not sufficient basis for fulfillment where the basic conditions are ignored or broken.

THE SANCTIONS AGAINST COVENANT BREAKING

The final element of a covenant is security. This refers to the agency that stood behind the vows to make sure that they were kept. The Bible clearly teaches that God himself is the security of all valid marriages. Proverbs 2:17 informs us that to commit adultery is not only to offend the human partner but also to break covenant with God. This is not to say that the covenant of marriage is a divine covenant in itself, as if the people of old made the marriage covenant with him, but rather that the human covenant was insured by God, who was its witness. God was the guarantor, which is to say that he will hold the partners accountable for the breach of their vows. This should strike fear in the heart of any thoughtful person; the very God who was powerful enough to create the whole universe will punish lapses. It is doubtful that most who commit adultery think of this while they are sundering their marriages. Practical atheists abound at such times![30]

On the other hand, it is possible to misunderstand this whole issue of security and think that the covenant itself is "divine." When the Scripture speaks of the covenant as being a covenant with God, that is simply another way of referring to God's being a witness of the human covenant. In biblical times, most, if not all, public covenants were secured by calling upon God (or the gods) as witness of the sincerity of the covenanters. One might aptly speak of all covenants as being "cultic," or religious. The religious nature of covenant is revealed by the action involved in covenant making. For example, in Genesis 15:18, the idiom *to cut* is used. The idea here is that a sacrifice accompanied the making of the covenant. The animals are *cut*. This act calls upon God to observe the agreement. A passage in Malachi makes this clear: "The Lord has been a witness between you and your wife" (2:14). It is in that regard that the covenant may be said to be a covenant "with your God" (Prov. 2:17). Marriage is a human covenant, with divine sanction.

The New Testament also speaks of such matters. Paul says, "Brethren, I speak in terms of human relations: even though [you may be speaking] of only a man's covenant, yet when it has been ratified, no one sets it aside or adds conditions to it" (Gal. 3:15).

Paul is drawing distinctions between human covenants and those made between God and human beings (i.e., the Abrahamic covenant). Human covenants regulate human relations. They are made between people; the vows are spoken by one person to another. Divine commands are spoken by God to humanity. Whatever part God may have in insuring the human covenant of marriage, marriage is still a human covenant.

This does not, of course, mean that God sanctions every marriage. In a subsequent chapter we will mention one very important kind of marriage that he does not sanction; here, we need only enumerate unsanctioned "marriages": incestuous (Lev. 18), homosexual (Lev. 18), and interfaith (where the believer willfully married the unbeliever in disobedience to God's Law, Ezra 9, 10). Marriage is human and conditional.

SUMMARY OF THE ESSENTIALS OF THE COVENANT

Marriage is a conditional covenant, insured by God, wherein the husband promises to provide for the essential needs of the wife and to do nothing to seriously injure her body or stain her reputation, while the wife promises to be physically faithful to her husband and to do him no bodily harm.[31]

The reader must be careful not to confuse the biblical idea of covenant with the prevailing laws of the nations. The prevailing laws may allow "marriages" not permitted by the biblical concept of the covenant of marriage. For example, the prevailing laws of Israel in the days of Herod Antipas permitted him to take his still-living brother's wife. But John proclaimed that Herod's marriage to Herodias was not lawful. John, of course, meant unlawful in terms of the biblical covenant. The same could be said of modern laws that might allow homosexual marriages. They may pass the bar of custom, but they fail at the bar of the Bible.

Thus, we see three levels of relationship in marriage:

Level 1:   The Legal Level   (The prevailing laws—contract)
Level 2:   The Moral Level   (The biblical covenant obligations)
Level 3:   The Organic Level   (The "one-flesh" union in marriage)

Throughout this book, our real concern is largely with the implications on level 2 of the act of divorce, which takes place on level 1. It is unbiblical activity on the legal level that must be brought into accord with the biblical-covenantal level. Thus John tells Herod that he must put Herodias away, that is, divorce her, end the legal relationship. So, too, Ezra insists that the immoral marriages with the women of the land be ended (see chap. 4). The mere existence of level 1 does not mean that there exists a proper relationship on level 2.[32]

We are not unconcerned with activity on level 3—the level of intimacy. The existence of a level-3 relationship may or may not entail a relationship on one of the other levels. Sometimes the existence of a relationship on level 3 precedes one on the other levels and may or may not call for a relationship on one of those other levels to be established.

This chapter has focused upon the sorts of obligations of covenant (level 2) that must be a part of the public agreement (level 1) in order for the social contract to be considered biblically acceptable. Some of these obligations are reciprocal (i.e., presence, no physical abuse); some are not (i.e., provision, sexual monogamy). In any case, the continued moral obligation to fulfill one's obligations is conditional upon the fulfillment of the spouse's obligations. Marriage is a *bi*lateral, not a *uni*lateral, covenant. Understanding this, we are prepared to consider what the Law of Moses, which sets forth that covenantal relationship, had to say about the act of divorce, an action on level 1 that speaks of a breach on level 2. This will be the subject of the next chapter.

CHAPTER 3

Termination of Marriage According to the Law

The last chapter dealt with the positive results of marriage, of keeping the marriage covenant. In this chapter we must, unhappily, consider the curses of breaking it.[1] For, indeed, many people have dealt treacherously against the spouse of their youth, making it necessary for the laws of nations to resolve such cases. Before turning to the Law of Moses to see the divinely established legislation, let us consider the pre-Mosaic practice as evidenced by the Book of Genesis.

PRE-MOSAIC TREATMENT OF COVENANT BREAKING

Sarah and Abimelech

The first instance is very significant, for in it we find both the failure of the husband to properly care for his wife and the potential violation of a married woman by another man. Both sides of the covenant are, therefore, in question. I refer to the time when Abraham tried to secure his own safety by presenting his wife Sarah as only his sister.[2] This deception Abraham repeated some years later in Gerar, where he concealed the true nature of his marital relations from Abimelech, its king. Abraham's son Isaac showed us how the sins of the parents can be visited upon the children when Isaac copied the deception to fool another Abimelech.[3] In each case the husband failed to properly secure the integrity of the wife. It is clear that the impropriety was on the part of the husband, though the kings' chief concern was with the adulterous relationship that could have occurred (12:19; 20:9; 26:10).

The New Testament may be referring indirectly to these incidents when a wife is told to remain submissive, even to a disobedient husband (1 Pet. 3:1–7). For we read the following inspired illustration:

Thus Sarah obeyed Abraham, calling him lord, and you have become her children if you do what is right without being frightened by any fear. (1 Pet. 3:6)

The exact referent is surely Genesis 18:12, where Sarah said to herself: "After I have become old, shall I have pleasure, my *lord* being old also?" This is the only canonical instance of this word from Sarah's lips.

But since this thought of hers offers no aspect of submission, we are left wondering at what point that submission went beyond words to reality. One option could be the submission necessary in having physical relations with him, but there is no conclusive evidence that her calling him "lord" is to be tied to the sexual act necessary to conceiving the child of promise. Indeed, that connection seems strained, to say the least! But if "giving in" to having sexual relations with her husband is not the point of the passage in 1 Peter, what is? It must surely be her general approach to doing the will of Abraham.

Therein lies a problem, however, for the one story that dominates the Abraham cycle is the account of the coming of the child of promise. Since Sarah exhibits much independence in this material, the reader must look elsewhere for expression of the sort of submission mentioned in 1 Peter. My own suggestion is that Sarah's submission is to be found in the two incidents just mentioned. The context of the Peter verse is a "disobedient husband." This surely fits the activity of a man who, out of fear, puts his wife's integrity into jeopardy. This must have been disobedience to the "word" of God's law instinctively known (Rom. 2:14), as there was no written scripture at that time.[4]

When the deception placed the wife in unjustified jeopardy, God acted to inhibit the king from mating with the wife. In the first story the king's house was plagued. In the second, Abimelech's life was threatened. The second story is the most instructive, for in it God actually speaks to Abimelech and tells him that he is a "dead man" for having another man's wife (20:3). This forcefully reveals what God thinks to be a proper punishment for adultery. Abimelech's plea in response is not that death is not a proper punishment for mating with another's wife, but, rather, that he has not done so. This supports the idea that the propriety of execution for adultery was instinctively known. Further reinforcement for this idea is found in the response of Abimelech in the third story (about Isaac), when he threatens to kill anyone who dares to touch Rebekah (26:10–11).

What we learn from these stories is that the breakup of marriage is so significant an event that death is thought appropriate for the person who would sunder the relation. The difficulty with the stories is that the "offending" parties are ignorant of the marriage and unwilling to sunder it. This latter fact may give room for some to say that the stories are irrelevant, insofar as our study is concerned with the question of willful breach of marriage vows. I believe that such a conclusion is too rigorous, and that the principle of death as punishment does arise from the stories and does apply to our study.[5]

Abraham and Hagar

Interesting, as well, is the story of Abraham and the release of Hagar (Gen. 21:8–14). According to the story, the mockery of the child of promise, Isaac, by the child of the slave woman, Ishmael, led Sarah to insist upon the putting away of Hagar. Abraham was reluctant to do this, out of love for Ishmael. When God gives Abraham permission to release the pair, he is clear to say that it is all right to do so, and that he will provide for their welfare. This provision is then set forth in the rest of the story.

Whether or not Abraham was concerned for the fulfillment of his obligation to provide for Hagar is hard to say, but I believe that God's words most likely promote that conclusion. He does not want Abraham to be distressed for the welfare of Hagar and Ishmael. God wants to affirm that the obligation of Abraham to care for Hagar is relaxed insofar as God himself will be a husband and father to them. This story implies that divorce, because it entails a failure to fulfill an implied vow to provide, is therefore wrong and only permissible where God himself releases the husband from the vow. Groundless putting away is a radical failure to live up to marital duties, a breach of covenant.

Tamar and Judah

Significant is the story involving Tamar and Judah (Gen. 38); in it, Tamar is an example of the childless widow, since her first husband, Shua, was so wicked that he was killed by God before he and Tamar could have children. Following the "law of the husband's brother" (the levirate), Tamar was then given to a younger brother, Onan. Onan wished to use the woman for his sexual pleasure but refused to culminate his gratification so as to give Tamar a chance to conceive a child (cf. 38:9). Because of his abuse of Tamar's rights, God took Onan's life as well. The story goes on to tell how Tamar's father-in-law, Judah, sought to defraud her further in a misguided attempt to preserve his last son, Shelah—as if the death of the others were her fault! Tamar then resorted to deception in order to gain her rights of progeny. In the end, Judah recognized her deception of him as more righteous than his defrauding of her.

There are several messages embedded in this story. The first is that no man has the right to abridge the woman's right to security in progeny, a point discussed in chapter 2. Second, and more to the point here, when such abridgment does occur, the woman has the right to be freed from such a one in order to establish a relationship in which the right will be observed. Finally, we learn that the prohibition to remarry (i.e., Shelah), out of whatever misguided motivation, is not righteous, but rather a defrauding worse than fornication.

These conclusions will meet with objections, of course, and the objections will center around the fact that remarriage in these cases occurs only after the "former" husband has died. But that objection misses the point. God ended the marriage of Onan in order to free Tamar to remarry. Though it is true that the means was death, the more important principle is that marriage may be ended when rights are abridged.[6] And, we note, those rights did not involve the usual sort of sexual unfaithfulness (i.e., adultery as promiscuity).

Joseph and Potiphar's Wife

In view of what was said about the story of Abraham and Sarah, it may seem a bit contradictory to see how Joseph was dealt with in the story of Potiphar's wife (Gen. 39:1–23). Rather than have Joseph killed, Potiphar sought recompense for the (alleged) attempted rape by sending Joseph to jail (v. 20). But remember, Joseph did not actually complete the rape, even according to the wife's lie. Perhaps Potiphar would have had Joseph killed if he thought that Joseph had accomplished the act. In any case, it is unwise to conclude from this story that death was *not* understood as a proper punishment for adultery.[7]

THE "END OF MARRIAGE" ACCORDING TO THE LAW OF MOSES

The End of Marriage and a Woman's Rights

THE FREEDOM FROM AN ABUSIVE HUSBAND (Exodus 21:10 f., 26 f.)

The Law of Moses contains several passages that relate to the question of when marriage ends. The first is Exodus 21. Comments on the propriety of using this passage in regard to "full" marriage (insofar as the passage speaks of servant girls) may be found in chapter 2. Our concern here is to note how the text relates to the ending of marriage.

Recall that the main focus of the chapter is on the rights of the woman. Two sorts of rights are discussed: the right to adequate physical provision (vv. 10 f.)[8] and the right not to be seriously abused (vv. 26 f.). Breach of covenant in either case justified the nullifying of the legalities (written or unwritten) of the covenant. Where the passive abuse occurred, the text tells us that "she shall go out for nothing, without payment of money." In the context (vv. 2–7) "go out" clearly entails a full release from contractual commitments. The one who has gone out (or at least her father, in this case) owes nothing to the former covenant partner. And where aggressive or active abuse of one partner by the other (vv. 26 f.) has occurred, the refrain continues: "go free." Further, we note that whenever the covenant is nullified the aggrieved partner has the understood privilege to contract a new covenant with someone else.[9] Put negatively, the aggrieved partner has no encumbrance from the former relationship that would inhibit a new covenant from being entered into.

The following conclusions can be drawn from these verses: First, when the husband, who owes provision to his mate, intentionally fails to produce that provision, his claims over his mate are thereby nullified. The fact of (moral) nullification precedes the legal recognition of it. Second, the legal release is the right of the offended partner. Third, the released offended party is free to establish a new covenant of the same sort with a new partner. (Or, put simply, the old marriage in no way precludes remarriage.)

The question may now arise as to why this passage was not more explicitly discussed as a divorce passage by the rabbis in the days of Jesus. Two suggestions present themselves. First, the text may well have been thought not to apply to marriage per se, insofar as it deals, prima facie, only with concubinage. Second, the chief concern in the day of Jesus was to find a passage giving the husband a right to divorce the wife; in this text, the right of the wife to force a divorce from her husband is the prime concern.[10] In other words, this text did not satisfy the social context of Jesus' day.

Another point to stress is that the marriage responsibility of the woman is put in the negative. At no point in the Law is she required to have sex with her husband; rather, she was required *not* to have sex with any other. Since her marital bond was to be sexually exclusive to her husband, freedom from it *must* entail the release to have sexual relations with another, although, obviously, the exercise of such freedom would have legally required the contracting of a new marriage, or "remarriage."

I am convinced that the failure of the Church to integrate this passage from Exodus into the theology of divorce is the single most significant reason for our failure to present a harmonious and reasonable doctrine of marriage/divorce. As we shall see, the principles that arise from this text establish a basis for Paul's teaching that "departure" is grounds for considering the marriage completely ended and for allowing the deserted partner the freedom to remarry (1 Cor. 7:15). In fact, understanding the Exodus passage enables us to understand the meaning of "free" in the Pauline teaching. A similar comment could be made with regard to the teachings of our Lord himself (cf. Matt. 5:32 f., et passim).

THE FREEDOM OF THE DIVORCED WOMAN (Numbers 30:9)

The freedom of the divorced woman from her former husband is also apparent from a consideration of the law of vows, found in Numbers 30. The topic of discussion is to what degree a "dependent" woman has the right to make and the responsibility to keep a vow that she herself has made. The point of law is that the man over her (viz., husband or father) has the right to veto the vow because she is under his authority (and probably because the objects promised were primarily his possessions, vv. 3, 5). However, the law did hold the woman responsible to keep the vow if the man in authority over her had given at least passive agreement to the vow (vv. 4, 6).

Special consideration is given to the matter of widows and divorced women (vv. 9–12). The rule is that, if the vow was made when they were under authority and the one in authority gave passive agreement, then that vow, *like that of such a woman made after she had been severed from her husband,* would stand.

Note that the widow and the divorced woman were categorized together. Both were equally free from the encumbrance of an authority. They had, in the matter of vowing, equal right to make a covenant with God. Both were no longer "under the man." This is quite significant in view of those New Testament passages that would seem to give to widows the right to remarry. Given this Old Testament material, it may be presumed that the New Testament would give tacit approval to a divorced woman to remarry as well. At the least, anyone who argues that the New Testament withholds this right bears the burden of proof.[11]

Nor will it do to suggest that the freedom to make a covenant (i.e., a vow) with God should not be generalized to include the covenant of marriage, as if we were committing the fallacy of undistributed middle, that is,

Widows' rights include the right to vow to God.

Divorcées' rights include the right to vow to God.

Therefore divorcées' rights are widows' rights (including the widows' right to remarry).

What we are saying is as follows:

Freedom from a marital authority (*a*) entails the right to make covenants (*b*). (The *principle* entailed is the right to make vows to God.)

The right to make covenants (*b*) entails the right to remarry (*c*).

Therefore, the freedom from marital authority (*a*) entails the right to remarry (*c*).

The grouping of the divorced and the widowed together by the Old Testament supports the conclusion (not so popular these days) that the New Testament encompassed the divorced in its discussions of the freedom of widows to remarry (Rom. 7:2 and 1 Cor. 7:39).[12]

FREEDOM FROM FORCED MARRIAGE (Deuteronomy 21:10–14)

Another law that affirms the rights of the woman and relates to the subject of divorce is Deuteronomy 21:10–14. This law is embedded in the section of that book that, according to Stephen Kaufman, is structured under the sixth commandment (murder) and, according to my understanding, is in a subsection of that commandment that relates to the rights of the descendants of the dead.[13]

According to this law, a woman who was taken as a spoil of war, may, under certain conditions, be made the wife of an Israelite.[14] The first part of the law sets forth the conditions under which the marriage may be contracted, and the conditions seem a bit unusual.

The nature of the conditions stated seems to reveal a concern for the treatment of the woman. The man is not allowed to take her on the field of battle. He must wait until he returns home and allow her a full month of mourning for her (presumably) dead parents. It might be expected that he would want her when he was away from his home and the warm embrace of his wife, but would he be as willing to have the woman if he had to wait and have her in the context of his home and his other wife? He then must do to her some things that might dull his interest in her: shave her head and trim her nails. Since he was probably first attracted to her beauty, this provision of the law seems designed to ensure that his interest goes more than skin deep. Of course he wanted her when she was good-looking, but would he still care for her when her looks were less captivating? And finally, he is required to "remove the clothes of her captivity." Thus he could no longer think of treating her as a spoil of war. He must now consider her a covenant partner.

Why all these conditions? Because the woman had no parent to speak for her in the making of the covenant—no one to protect her rights in the usual way. Even the slave girl (Exod. 21) had a parent who was a party to the contract. But this foreign woman's parents were dead, and thus God spoke on her behalf.

The first part of the law ends with the man fulfilling all the conditions and taking the woman to be his wife. But in verse 14 we read, "If you are not pleased with her, then you shall let her go wherever she wishes." This apodosis or conditional clause is interpretable in at least two different ways: first, that the marriage is consummated and at some subsequent time the man decides he is no longer pleased with her and therefore decides to put her away, or, second, that this decision comes at the end of the waiting period, before the consummation. Its similarity in approach to Exodus 21, another passage that concerns a disadvantaged woman who is intended as a bed partner, would lead us to decide for the second option.[15] Where the consummation is not completed, the Exodus law requires the master not to "sell her." It is the same here in Deuteronomy 21:14. And just as the master is told to treat her as a daughter in Exodus 21:9 (when he chooses not to mate her to himself), in Deuteronomy he is told not to "deal tyrannically" with her.

Ambiguity enters into the decision, however, with the inclusion of the reason the man is not to sell her. The text says that he has "humbled" her. This term has a certain breadth of meaning. On the one hand, it can refer to sexual relations (cf. Gen. 34:2 and Deut. 22:29, where the action involves rape). On the other hand, the term is often used of the ill-treatment by oppressors of a slave (cf. Gen. 16:16, Sarah's misuse of Hagar; Exod. 1:11–12, Egypt's misuse of Israel). Thought it is tempting to opt for the latter idea, it is difficult to see in the application of the protective conditions (i.e., shaving hair and trimming nails) mistreatment of the kind implied by the term in slave contexts. But then is it any easier to see this as a case of rape?

Perhaps so. For we must remember that this woman is a foreigner who did not ask to be taken to Israel and treated thus by this man. His people had killed her parents and had prevented her from having a normal marriage among her own people. The momentum for this Israelite marriage is all from his side. It is not beyond reason to suppose that the woman has rejected his attempts to consummate the marriage as best she is able. In other words, the consummation might have amounted to rape.

What then is the most probable interpretation? Presumably, the one that sees first his successful consummation of the attempt (v. 13) and then allows for an unsuccessful attempt (v. 14), which leads him to take the wiser path of allowing the woman to be free of him. Her spurning of him, in the second instance, is probably the reason for the caution to him not to treat her in a harsh or tyrannical fashion. Allowing her to go where she wishes, in turn, implies that she does not wish to stay with him. Thus, the crucial "divorce" section of the law actually deals with a sort of annulment, an occasion when a woman does not give consent to the marriage. If we are correct in so concluding, then the passage really has little to do with a "right to divorce," at least on the part of the husband. It is more an allowance for the woman's sake.

FREEDOM FROM UNJUST DIVORCE (Deuteronomy 22:13–21)

The protection of the woman's rights is also in view in a law that *prohibits* divorce. Deuteronomy 22:13–21 deals with the case of a man's challenging the purity of his bride. We will deal with the instance of a true charge when we discuss the protection of the husband's rights. But for now let us look at the perplexing instance in which the charge is proven false (vv. 17–19).

The result of a false charge is stated as twofold. First, the man was fined one hundred shekels of silver by the father of the bride (to be held in trust). This was a tremendous fine, amounting to about one hundred months' wages for the common man. Surely most men would have to sell themselves into slavery to acquire such an amount, and the effect of imposing such a fine was surely to inhibit the defaming of a virgin of Israel. But the fine was not the only penalty the defamer sustained. He was also prohibited from ever divorcing the woman (v. 19).

It seems most reasonable to assume that the direction of this law was to prohibit him from himself initiating a divorce. It is unreasonable to assume that it prohibited the woman from forcing a divorce at some subsequent time on the grounds of mistreatment (cf. Exod. 21); it is unreasonable because the whole direction of the law is to protect the woman from further abuse at his hands. To prohibit such a wife-initiated divorce would be contrary to this direction.

The reason for prohibiting the divorce on the man's initiative is that, according to the situation as presented in the Law, the man would want to end the marriage, perhaps have the woman executed as an adulteress. After such a charge as the man has made, even if the woman is cleared, it would still be difficult for her and her family to contract a suitable marriage for her, because of the stigma of the whole affair. Thus the Law appropriately sought to protect her from what would amount to abandonment. The man wanted to be rid of her and attempted to have her executed, and it is likely that, failing that, he would want to be rid of her by divorce. This the Law would not allow.

Of course, one might object to this line of reasoning: Why would not the man then simply resort to wife abuse and force *her* to initiate a divorce procedure (Exod. 21:10 f., 26 f.; see our earlier arguments)? The reasonable answer is that he might, indeed, try such a tactic. After all, some men are so unscrupulous that they will try any means to achieve their ends. If such a man were to try this, however, the Law stood ready to free the woman from that abuse. The man would then lose all indirect use of the forfeited one hundred shekels that might accrue to him as a result of his continued relationship to her and himself have to bear the additional stigma of being a wife-beater (cf. 1 Tim. 5:8 to see how at least New Testament believers evaluated such behavior). The Law cannot keep people from doing sin; it can only inhibit sin by threat of an appropriate punishment.

The perplexing aspect of this law centers around the assumed right of the man to divorce a wife at all, but I shall reserve comment on this matter until we arrive at a discussion of the man's right to end the covenant.

FREEDOM FROM DESERTION (Deuteronomy 22:28–29)

In the same Deuteronomic comment (viz., on the seventh commandment) and within the same chapter, there resides another command that protects a woman from legal desertion by prohibiting a man from divorcing her. In 22:22–23, we read of a man who has raped a virgin. The prescribed treatment for this offense is, first, fifty months' wages and, second, no divorce. Though the fine is less (apparently because there was no covenant broken), the prohibition on initiating divorce is the same.

The rationale behind the prohibition of divorce in this case differs from that of the preceding case. Though he is like the man in the previous case in not wishing to be bound by a covenant, this man sought to enjoy conjugal rights without covenant. The law responds by making him marry the woman without the option of ending the relationship. Again, legislation concerning divorce is supportive of the woman's rights.[16]

The End of Marriage and a Man's Rights

FREEDOM FROM AN UNFAITHFUL WIFE (Exodus 20:14)

The clearest right of a man to end his marriage appears in the adultery laws. Beginning with the statement of the seventh commandment itself, and proceeding through the casuistic procedures for the treatment of (sexual) adulteresses, it is evident that the practice of sexual adultery was intended to lead to the execution of the offending (female) spouse and her (male) lover. The laws may be categorized into two divisions: laws that apply when the offense is clear and those that apply when investigation is needed to uncover the facts.

The first category is represented by Leviticus 20:10:

If there is a man who commits adultery with another man's wife, one who commits adultery with his friend's wife, the adulterer and the adulteress shall surely be put to death.

This law is supported by similar laws found in Deuteronomy 22:22–27, where *pledged* women are executed with their lovers.[17]

The second category is represented by two laws, the first in Numbers 5. In the "law of jealousy," a wife found guilty was to "bear her guilt" (v. 31). Presumably this means "die"; at least, that is what it means in other cases in which adultery is known to have been committed (see above). Some have questioned this interpretation on the grounds that sufficient witnesses were not present to satisfy the stipulations of the "due process" law (cf. Deut. 19:15), but final confirmation may be found in the second passage dealing with allegations of impropriety on the part of a pledged woman: Deuteronomy 22:13–21. There, another test that does not literally fulfill the multiple witness law produces a clear call to execute (Deut. 22:20 f.). Moreover, even though the second case involves a new bride's purity on entering the marriage state, it is to be remembered that from the beginning of the betrothal onward she is considered the wife of the man, not just some half-bound woman.

Less often appealed to, but equally clear in their implications of the marriage ending, are those other laws that called for the execution of the woman who was pledged to a man—specifically, those dealing with the purity offenses of incest (Lev. 20:14), homosexuality (Lev. 20:13, by implication), and bestiality (Lev. 20:16).[18] Though the spouse might not initiate legal proceedings in all of these cases (the law might), the result of the action is the same.

But what if, for one reason or another, the execution commandments were not followed? What recourse had the innocent spouse to be free from a treacherous spouse? I defer discussion of that possibility until we discuss the time of the prophets, when such situations did occur and were provided for by divine mandate.

FREEDOM FROM A DESPISED WIFE (Deuteronomy 24:1–4)

Without a doubt, the most celebrated text on the subject of the husband's right to divorce his wife is Deuteronomy 24:1–4. By the time of Jesus, it was very nearly the only passage being discussed in this connection. Actually, the passage is of little value if used to that end, for its aim was to protect the woman from an abusive and hard-hearted husband. It provides no moral "right" to divorce, but only a legal provision for divorce to protect the interests of the wife.

As is usually noted today, the law is one long sentence stating certain conditions and the resultant response of the Law. It is easiest to analyze this law by breaking it down into its separate parts and considering the most important of them. First, some undesirable condition obtains in the wife. Second, the condition comes to the notice of the first husband. Third, he divorces her because of it. Fourth, the wife covenants with another man. Fifth, the second marriage ends (as a result either of the death of the spouse or of divorce). Sixth, the law prohibits the woman from going back to the first husband (though it does not prohibit her from marrying a different man). Seventh, such a return to the first spouse subsequent to remarriage to another is said to be an "abomination," because, eighth, she is said to have been "defiled" by the second marriage.[19]

Problem Phrases or Words
THE "NAKEDNESS OF A THING"

Historically, most of the argument surrounding this passage involves the first point: what was the nature of the woman's condition that gave rise to the husband's desire to divorce her? Most of the answers involve some sort of *offense* on the part of the woman. The offenses suggested range from "adultery" (Shammai's School) to "anything the husband found offensive" (Hillel's position). Let us consider the possibilities in order.

Adultery

This was the view of the School of Shammai. Whatever sense this view seemed to make in the days after the ending of the capital punishment laws and privileges in Israel, however, it is unlikely that adultery per se was intended by the words: "the nakedness of a thing" (the literal translation of the words in question). Kaiser summarizes Murray's objections, which are classic:

(1) The Pentateuch prescribed death for adultery (Lev. 20:10; Deut. 22:22; cf. 22:23–27);

(2) Numbers 5:11–31 even cared for cases of suspected but unproven adultery, so that could not be the intention of this provision;

(3) Deuteronomy 22:13–21 also covered the case of a bride who was charged with previous sexual promiscuity and who vindicated herself; so that could not be the alternative meant here;

(4) Deuteronomy 22:23–24 treats the cause of a betrothed virgin and her husband-to-be who voluntarily defiled themselves and hence the sanction was death for both;

(5) Nor can the "unseemly thing" of Deuteronomy 24:1 be a matter of coercing a bride-to-be to have sexual relations, for Deuteronomy 22:25–27 exonerated the virgin and put the man to death;

(6) Nor was it a matter of premarital sex between unbetrothed man and woman, for in that case the man must marry her and never divorce her (Deut. 22:18–19).[20]

This sort of reasoning seems conclusively to rule out simple adultery as the meaning of the words.

Unseemly Behavior Short of Adultery

The second option is that these words stand for some behavior that is unseemly but is short of adultery. This was the view of Shammai himself.[21] The majority of modern commentators seem to side with this option.[22] Like Shammai, they include in this category such things as immodesty of dress (e.g., going out without a veil) or of action (e.g., spinning yarn in the streets, an activity of prostitutes awaiting their next client).

In favor of this view is the use of *nakedness* in the Old Testament as an offense-term and a term with sexual connotations (cf. Exod. 20:26; Lev. 18; etc.). Additionally, the only other use of the two terms is in Deuteronomy 23:14, which is in the immediate context of poor hygienic practices (i.e., improper toilet hygiene).

The "nose-count" of authorities aside, however, there are several good reasons for doubting this opinion is correct. First is a consideration that arises from the context—the structure of Deuteronomy. I suggest that the breaking point between the Deuteronomic comment on the seventh commandment and the eighth is between 23:14 and 23:15. This division raises two noteworthy points for our consideration. The "other" exact use of the two terms comes in a concluding verse to the seventh commandment material. I believe that it is better to identify 23:14 as a summarizing comment stretching back over the whole of the seventh commandment material rather than simply to refer it to the rule on excrement. The key is the word "since," which begins verse 14. Does this mean that since God walks in the camp they must cover the excrement so that he does not step in it? Or does it mean that no unholy thing should be found in the camp since God is in the midst of the camp? Surely the latter. But if we so separate the walking from the excrement, how far back does the reference go? At least far enough back to include "nocturnal emissions" (v. 10). But since nocturnal emissions are *involuntary*[23] how can we suggest that "nakedness of a thing" necessarily means something that is immodest?[24] And, since the key terms follow the summarizing phrase, "your camp must be holy," it does not seem at all farfetched to suspect that perhaps most of the Deuteronomic comment on the seventh commandment might be implied by both these sets of terms. If that is so, then we have more options to choose from than simply immodesty. (I will specify them more precisely later.)

The second contextual matter centers around the nature of the section in which Deuteronomy 24:1–4 appears. It is the comment on the eighth, not the seventh, commandment; it is concerned with property, not adultery. This should caution us from too quickly expecting to find sexual offense in the key terms.

Out of this observation arises another perhaps more important: in each of the subdivisions of the material on the eighth commandment, the chief purpose of the law is to protect a disadvantaged party from abuse by an advantaged one. Observe the flow:

23:15–16	Slave is protected from master.
23:17	Children are protected from potentially abusive parents.
23:18	[The treasury] is protected from defiled offerers.
23:19–20	The poor are protected from usury.
23:21–23	[The treasury] is protected from truants, and people are protected from the idea of forced offerings.
23:24–25	The poor are protected by requiring those with food to give it.
24:1–4	*The Divorce Law*
24:5	The newlywed is protected from unreasonable military service.
24:6	The poor are protected from unjust holding of a crucial pledge.
24:7	The innocent are protected from unjust personal seizure.

From this survey, it can be seen that the function is to define the limits of property rights, with the view of protecting human beings from being considered pieces of chattel property. Note also that in no case is the person who the law seeks to protect *guilty* of anything immoral at all. If anything, the text seeks to identify what makes that person disadvantaged.

Embarrassing Conditions

In light of these elements of context, I am prepared to suggest that "the nakedness of a thing" refers to some fact about the wife that has made her undesirable to her husband. Her status as a wife, of course, plays into the need for her to be protected from an angry husband, but that status alone is insufficient to explain what the initial problem was. The most we can learn from the immediate context is that her problem is not an act of immorality.

The likelihood is that "the nakedness of a thing" is intended simply as a catchall term for something strikingly embarrassing that is true of or has happened to the wife. What might that be? Looking back to the context—the seventh commandment—we are led to suggest (backwards but respectively): accidental, but indecent, exposure (23:12–13); irregular menstrual periods (23:9–11); impure lineage (23:3–8); illegitimacy (23:2); sexual mutilation (23:1); rape (22:22–27). The only contextual element definitely not open to incorporation into the terms would be defamation by the husband (22:13–21). Standing against this interpretation would be that it would seem most reasonable for a man to seek to divorce his wife for suspicions of her purity (however ungrounded in fact). But, of course, since the text of Deuteronomy 22:19 has explicitly prohibited divorce in such cases, it is clear that "nakedness of a thing" cannot be construed to include it, and, in fact, the prohibition found there is given to preclude such an understanding. Yet, since the prohibition to divorce in 22:19 is for the woman's protection, and we are arguing that the permission to divorce in 24:1–4 is being presented as a protection of the wife, some harmonization needs to be offered. We will do so shortly.

In spite of this difficulty, this option is preferable to that of Shammai; it is also preferable to that offered by Hillel, that is, "anything the husband finds unacceptable." If Hillel were correct, one would expect the law to simply say that she (the woman) finds no favor in his eyes. The inclusion of the questioned clause seemingly intends to narrow the field of grounds to something or a category of somethings. But it must be admitted that Hillel's position is stronger than is sometimes imagined. It may well be that the text simply should read, "When a man takes a wife and marries her, and it happens that she finds no favor in his eyes because he has discovered something embarrassing about her . . ." The exact nature of what is embarrassing is left up to the husband. It is clear that any of the things in our previous list, if found true of a wife, would certainly have lowered her worth in the eyes of a husband who had any inclination toward hard-heartedness.

That leads to our next comment on the verse, namely, that despite the implication of Hillel's school any husband who would seek to dismiss his wife for any of those reasons would be breaking his covenant to provide for her. In other words, any man divorcing his wife without better cause was guilty of unfaithfulness or (nonsexual) adultery. In fact, the very permission in the text allowing her to be divorced is not presented as a "concession" to the husband's will per se but as an unnecessary action that God permits in order to protect the woman from this sort of man. This explains why our Lord speaks of this law as being for the "hardness of your hearts" (Matt. 19:8; Mark 10:5). Jesus means that God is allowing the divorce, not in order simply to accommodate hard-heartedness, but to provide for the wife in the face of a husband's hard-heartedness.[25] Thus, the text of Deuteronomy 24:1–4 does not intend to present us with a "right" of the husband to divorce his wife but, rather, with a discussion of how God intends to care for the wife in the face of a man who wills to wrongly divorce her. The concession that releases the woman from such a man is not the only protection, or even the primary protection, envisioned by the law at this point, however. The woman, being freed from her first husband, was then able to contract a marriage covenant with another man. The text later says that in doing so she has been "defiled." Does this mean that the second marriage is a state of adultery? Again, several interpretations have been offered.

"She Has Been Defiled."

CEREMONIAL DEFILEMENT

First, there are some who would see the defilement as purely ceremonial. It is true that the root of this word is a common one in the Old Testament, and that it refers to a varied collection of pollutions: ceremonial, religious, and moral. But John Murray is convinced that a purely ceremonial interpretation of the word in this case is not proper, since in the other Old Testament uses where ceremony is involved, some form of purification procedure is prescribed. In places where moral pollution is involved (e.g., Lev. 18:20), no such procedure is set forth, because none is possible.[26] Therefore, Murray is sure that some moral defilement is in view.

MORAL DEFILEMENT

This second view, moral defilement, is the one most commonly accepted by those who comment on the word. Murray notes the strength of the word when used in moral contexts by citing its usage in incest passages like Leviticus 19:20.[27] He goes on to argue that some "gross abnormality" has occurred by the second marriage. Yet Murray is reluctant to identify the second marriage as "adultery," because the defilement only seems to be taken into account with regard to the first husband—when the issue is of a remarriage to that one, after a marriage to another has occurred.[28]

This view, though appealing, is not without problems. First, Murray is misleading when he presses the strongest moral implications of the root of the word. For instance, the root is used of the pollution of Dinah by Shechem in Genesis 34:13. Although the rape is surely a morally offensive act (recall Deut. 22:28 f.), it is just as surely not on the level of incest. Second, it is hardly logical to argue as follows:

Gross immorality is defilement without purification procedure.

The defilement in Deuteronomy 24:4 is without purification procedure.

Therefore the defilement in Deuteronomy 24:4 is gross immorality.

Additionally, though a raped woman is said to be defiled, we must remember that she is an innocent party to the act; the resulting stigma does not impugn her integrity. If the woman were married, it would be no sin for her to resume relations with her first husband. If she were single and her father refused to give her to the rapist,[29] she might marry another man without fear of defiling him. The "defilement" of the woman reflects upon the rapist. So too, we note that the stigma of "defilement" of the woman in Deuteronomy 24:4 does not so stigmatize her that moral guilt hangs about her marriages to men other than her former husband. The stigma instead reflects back upon the man who caused the problem, that is, her first husband.

Actually, "defiled" is more difficult than such "root" analysis reveals. Kaiser notes that the verb is a *Hothpa'el,* which he typifies as "reflexive passive." That may not be exactly the right typification (why must a verb that is reflexive be passive as well?), but it may very nearly convey the point. Actually, the exact form of the verb is a *hapax legomenon;* that is to say, this word, in this exact form, does not appear elsewhere in the Old Testament. In fact, the *Hothpa'el* form itself appears only a couple of times in the whole Old Testament. Thus, we had better be careful about arguing from the form. This is especially true when the verb could have been put in a form that is clearly reflexive or another that is clearly passive. Moses went out of his way to make this form unusual!

"PROSCRIPTIVE" DEFILEMENT

My suggested solution is as follows: The husband does indeed commit adultery against his wife when he divorces her without grounds (i.e., takes advantage of the "Mosaic concession"), but a certain personal defilement of the woman does not take place until she marries another man. The text is trying to convey that the first husband is responsible to come to his senses before the second marriage occurs. That he does not underlines the offensiveness of the first husband's character. The man was so hard-hearted that he cast the woman from himself. Then, he was so unrepentant that he allowed her to be sexually coupled to another man. Thus, in a sense, the second marriage did defile the woman, but that fact stands not really against her character but against the character of her treacherous first husband. This explains why it is possible for her to be involved volitionally with the defiling action without incurring a specific statement against her character, and perhaps, a call for punishment of her for adultery.[30]

"That Is an Abomination."

We turn finally to the issue of the seventh point: the typification of the remarriage to the first husband (subsequent to her remarriage to others) as "abomination." The difficulty of interpreting this matter is not so great. The law was trying to head off any attempt of such a hard-hearted man to further abuse his wife by taking her back to himself for marital use. Such action amounts to "wife swapping." The man casts her from himself to be used by another and then takes her back again for his own use. This is to treat her like a piece of chattel property; it is a main concern of the eighth commandment section to prevent a human being from being treated like chattel.[31]

The Interpretation

The major interpretations of Deuteronomy 24:1–4 appear to be six in number. First is the implied interpretation of the AV, ERV, and ASV that the passage wishes to regulate divorce by requiring the first husband to formalize it by giving a writ of divorcement. The "defilement" and "abomination" sink into the background. Second, we have the interpretation of Murray that the passage is designed to discourage divorce. This view places the burden of guilt on the first divorce, holding the first husband responsible for defilement that occurs when the first marriage is restored after subsequent marriages.[32] Third, P. C. Cragie interprets the text as intended to inhibit remarriage (especially remarriage to the first husband subsequent to the wife's remarriage) after divorce. He makes much of the fact that the text identifies subsequent marriages as "defilements."[33] Fourth, there is R. Yaron's posture that the text is designed to inhibit the social tension of love triangles that would occur were the wife to remarry her first husband after marrying others.[34] Fifth, Wenham suggests that the text means to stigmatize as incestuous remarriage to the first spouse after subsequent marriages.[35] Heth and Wenham highlight the implication of several of these positions that the reason for the stigmatization of remarriages rests in the assumption that the bond of the first marriage still exists, that is, that marriage is indissoluble.[36] Finally, there is the interpretation offered in this book that the text intends to protect a stigmatized woman from further abuse by her offending first husband.

In deciding among these possible interpretations it is well to remember criticisms of aspects of the first five views presented earlier. The first is defective because it does not give full weight to the grammatical construction, though it correctly notes that a divorce writ is proper. The second view is correct in seeing the first divorce as the primary offense and the first husband as the chief offender, but it is wrong in attributing offense to the wife and in presuming that the bond with the first husband still exists. The third view is correct in its main contention that the text wishes to prohibit remarriage to the first husband, but it is inadequate in its underlying assumptions about incest and a continuing bond. The fourth position has little to commend its unique contention concerning "love triangles" but has some merit in stressing that aspect of the passage that seeks to preserve social stability. The fifth position, as well, has little to commend its primary conclusion—that the text wishes to prohibit remarriage to the first husband because a continuing bond with him still exists.

In defending my own interpretation I have offered a number of contextual matters, stretching from the non–morally offensive nature of "the nakedness of a thing" in Deuteronomy 23 to Jesus' statement that it was the husband who was hard of heart. At this point, I add the consideration of another biblical "commentary" on Deuteronomy 24: Jeremiah 3:1.

God says, "If a husband divorces his wife,
And she goes from him,
And belongs to another man,
Will he still return to her?
Will not that land be completely polluted?
But you are a harlot with many lovers;
Yet you turn to Me," declares the Lord.

We shall further discuss this text in the next chapter, but for now, it serves to note that God was trying to get the people of Judah to reflect on how his relationship to them contrasted with the situation behind Deuteronomy 24:1–4. The questions are, to a large degree, rhetorical. We are not, however, to find this dissimilarity in the fact that Judah had not yet been officially divorced by God, for if that difference is the major point, then the whole analogical argument, with its intended contrasts, evaporates. The same thing holds true for the fact that Judah had not officially married another.

Rather, the text wishes to have us focus on the two other differences:

God is not like the man who puts away his wife in Deuteronomy 24:1; Israel is not like the woman put away. Whereas in Deuteronomy the husband only found something embarrassing about his wife, in the text of Jeremiah 3 Judah was a public harlot. Thus, God was not like the hard-hearted husband against whom the Law acted to protect the wife but like the righteous Joseph (Matt. 1:19), who wished to serve his wife notice that the blessings of marriage are not available to a covenant-breaking spouse.

There is nothing wrong with a disciplining husband taking back a straying wife (even if another marriage has been contracted in the meantime). The text wishes to put strictures on an immoral husband, not a righteous one. The harmony of these passages underscores the view that Deuteronomy deals not with a sinning wife but with a sinning husband.

Conclusions Concerning Deuteronomy 24:1–4

Deuteronomy 24:1–4, then, is a provision for the woman. It is so in several regards. First, it permits her to be divorced from a husband who is set on ceasing to provide for his covenant partner. This permission makes it possible for her to be provided for by another man. If the first husband does allow this chain of events to occur, the Law steps in to forever prohibit him from taking her back as a man would a piece of furniture that had been used by another. The "concession" grants no moral option for the man to end his marriage, but the act of divorce, which he means for evil, God means for the good of the woman.

It remains for us now to harmonize this passage with those in the section on the seventh commandment, which sought to protect the woman from a hard-hearted man by *prohibiting* his ever divorcing a woman whom he had defiled. First, we note that the divorces that these laws forthwith prohibited were undoubtedly those relating to "the nakedness of a thing" (Deut. 24:1). Second, and important, it seemed to be the intent of the Law to prescribe a punishment that fitted the crime. In the case of the defamation law, the man had tried to get rid of the woman by execution. Even if the charges were untrue, there was a direct and public stain upon her character. It was in the nature of the case that it would be difficult for her to find a new partner when a charge of infidelity hung over her, even though the evidence had proved her innocent. The Law therefore provided security for her future by freeing her (to a certain extent) from the worry of how this undeserved bad reputation would affect her future marital relationships. In the case of the rape law, the man had sought to use a woman's body without continued obligation to provide for her. In doing so, he had stained her pure reputation. So the Law prescribes that such a one should always have to provide for her. Note that what is common to both laws is the idea of a stain upon the woman's reputation. In the fornication law, it is the reputation of a virgin; in the other, it is the reputation of a married woman. We conclude, then, that the direction of the "no-divorce laws" is to protect the woman whose reputation has been stained. The man who stained it must care for her indefinitely. He is being told that, since *he* has embarrassed *her*, he is not allowed to put her away if she simply does something embarrassing.[37]

The direction of the protection of the woman in the Deuteronomy 24:1–4 law is markedly different. I do not refer to the aspect of that law that protects her from returning to a hard-hearted man, but to the concession of the divorce itself. The 24:1 "permission" to divorce seeks to "head off" the sort of abuse of the woman that is cared for in Exodus 21:10–11 (and perhaps Exod. 21:26 f. as well). In other words, a man who is hard-hearted enough to divorce his wife simply for something he finds embarrassing is permitted to do so, except when he has already stained her reputation in such a way that it may be hard for her to contract a new marriage. But if the man who has stained a woman's reputation tries to abuse her physically, she still has recourse to the law, which allows her to force him to divorce her.

To this it might be objected that that is precisely the goal of the man in the first place, so does not the law here encourage, rather than discourage, the man from abusing her? As stated earlier, I think that the stigma attached to a "wife-beater," not to mention the possibility of the avenging of her by her family, would serve to inhibit most men from taking that route to marital release.[38]

Summarizing again, Deuteronomy 24:1–4 was a law that conceded that treacherous divorce would occur and allowed it as a way of protecting the woman. Primarily, however, it protected her from being passed back and forth between men like a piece of chattel. The law is not concerned with presenting a "right" for the husband to divorce his wife. Nor does it imply that an indissoluble marriage bond exists between the first, divorcing husband and his wife.

SUMMARY: TEACHINGS ON THE END OF MARRIAGE IN THE MOSAIC CODE

The following list summarizes the teachings of the Law of Moses regarding the "end of marriage":

1. Since marriage is a bilateral covenant, the covenant is truly broken when one party fails to keep the vows.
2. Implied in this "breaking" is that the moral obligation of the "innocent" party to keep fulfilling his or her side of the agreement is technically ended.

3. This "technical" ending should lead either to the restoration of the agreement (i.e., the offender renewing the vows and keeping them) or to the legal ending of the marriage contract.

4. In the case of the wife not keeping her vows of monogamy, no restoration is permitted, and the legal ending of marriage occurs with the execution of the wife and her lover.

5. In the case of the husband not keeping his vows to provide for the minimal support of his wife, court action is possible, with the outcome being either the restoration of provision or a forced divorce, which allows the woman to contract another marriage (if possible). If more active abuse is the grounds, the same recourse is possible. We may presume that a "husband-beating" wife could be divorced by her husband, in the same manner that a master-beating slave would be separated from the master.

6. The Law provides for the wives of hard-hearted husbands by allowing their husbands to separate from them. This provision does not imply that the husbands are guiltless, rather that they are guilty. The only time a husband is allowed morally to initiate a divorce is in the case of a woman who is forced into the marriage and continues to reject his advances. Husbands who stain their wives' reputations by slander or premarital sex are prohibited from initiating divorce proceedings against their wives (thus inhibiting the occurrence of such offenses).

7. Men are permitted to take second wives (since polygamy is morally permissible). Under the provisions of the Law, divorced women are morally permitted to remarry, though they are considered stained by the divorce (thus unfit to marry a priest) and defiled by the remarriage (thus off-limits to the hard-hearted man who unjustly divorced them). These stigmatizations, however, are not to be interpreted as moral offenses on the part of such a divorced woman.

8. All marriages are to be "in the Lord," in the sense of being between members of the confessing community of Israel and not between Israelites and heathen.

CHAPTER 4

Divorce in the Prophets: Discipline or Adultery?

INTRODUCTION TO THE PROPHETIC LITERATURE

It is not known to what degree the laws protecting the marriage vows were enforced. It is clear from the numerous passages in the Proverbs that speak of the adulteress or strange woman that that marriage vow was breached, and we may infer from the persistence of her presence that by the time of the United Monarchy execution for such an offense was not readily practiced. But these are all only inferences. As for the intentional failure of a man to provide for his wife, the text says virtually nothing, although it may surely be assumed that some of these offenses occurred as well.

What is clear is that by the time of Jesus, the death penalty was seldom if ever used for the offense of adultery. This is clear not only from a consideration of the Shammai-Hillel debate, wherein both schools presume that adultery would be grounds for divorce, not death, but from a consideration of the fact that Israel was a dependent nation and had to function under the laws of the overlords. Rome, at least according to the Julian Laws, did not recognize adultery as a capital crime, except under the most rare circumstances.[1] It may well be that something similar was the case under the prior overlords back to the times of the separate deportations of the Northern and Southern kingdoms.

Further light is shed on this matter by a consideration of several of the writings of the prophets. One of the most significant indications that adultery did not usually lead to execution but to divorce is found in Jeremiah 3. In this passage, dealing with an oracle given after the fall of the Northern Kingdom and before the fall of the Southern, God states that he has divorced the Northern Kingdom for their adulteries. He threatens the Southern Kingdom with the same treatment if they fail to be faithful. Such a discussion presumes that divorce is a customary treatment for unfaithfulness. But whether such language accommodates a prevailing practice, or whether it bespeaks a new dispensation of divine law is not clear. Usually, the former is assumed by commentators. (And this is my conclusion as well.)

But we are getting ahead of ourselves. In this chapter we will seek to uncover the two major marriage/divorce themes of the prophets. The first of these is the idea of divorce as a discipline for the sin of adultery; the second is the idea of groundless divorce as the sin of adultery.

THE DISCIPLINE OF DIVORCE

Divorce as a Step to Restoration from Adultery (Hosea 1 and 2)

THE PROPHETIC BACKGROUND

As noted earlier, at some point prior to the deportation of the Southern Kingdom, execution for adultery was at least partially displaced by divorce.[2] This fact plays into a very interesting analogy (or figure) found in the prophetic literature of how God's relation to Israel is like a man's relationship to his adulterous wife. God's treatment of adulterous Israel is similar to how a man treated his unfaithful wife: divorce. Let us look first at the marital analogy, then consider the disciplinary aspect of the analogy. Both elements are necessarily present in the two major passages we will consider: Hosea 1 and 2 and Ezra 9 and 10.

The presentation of Israel as the betrothed or bride of Yahweh does not arise until the times of apostasy just prior to the deportation of the Northern Kingdom.[3] Nonetheless, in reading the prophetic writings, we are clearly made aware that God has understood his relationship to Israel in those terms. In Jeremiah, for example, we read:

"Behold, days are coming," declares the Lord, "when I will make a new covenant with the house of Israel and with the house of Judah, not like the covenant which I made with their fathers in the day I took them by the hand to bring them out of the land of Egypt, My covenant which they broke, although I was a husband to them," declares the Lord. (Jer. 31:32)[4]

It is easy to see why the parallel should be drawn. For not only is marriage the prototypical covenant (hence its clear connotation in the form of the seventh commandment, which protected valid covenants) but also Israel's legal responsibility to God is put in similar terms. Consider, for example, these verses found in Leviticus 18:

And you shall not have intercourse with your neighbor's wife, to be defiled with her. (18:20)

Do not defile yourselves by any of these things. (18:23)

The idea here is that for Israel to have practiced any of the abomi-
nations of the gentile nations would be for them to have dirtied themselves in a way similar to how a wife is defiled by an adulterous relation
with a man other than her husband.

Even more striking is the Deuteronomical Law treatment of the first
commandment. In Deuteronomy 7, we read of the possible social in-
terrelation of Israel to the Canaanites:[5]

You shall make no covenant with them and show no favor to them. Furthermore, you shall not intermarry with them; you shall not give your daughters
to their sons, nor shall you take their daughters for your sons. For they will
turn your sons away from following Me to serve other gods. (7:2 f.)

Echoing this, Joshua says:

But you are to cling to the Lord your God, as you have done to this day [a
day of reaffirmation of the people to the Mosaic legislation]. . . .
So take diligent heed to yourselves to love the Lord your God. For if you
ever go back and cling to the rest of these nations, these which remain among
you, and intermarry with them, so that you associate with them and they with
you, know with certainty that the Lord your God will not continue to drive
these nations out from before you. (Josh. 23:8, 11 ff.)

We note that the word *cling* here is the very term used in Genesis 2:24
of a man cleaving to his wife. When Israel is told to cleave to God and
not to cleave to others, it is not a far jump to the marital metaphor of
the prophets. This is especially true when the method of infidelity
mentioned is "intermarriage" with the peoples of the land.[6]

Sadly, Israel did not keep the vows to God. The first breach had
already occurred, and that involving culpable ignorance. Back in
Joshua 9, the story is told of how the Israelites foolishly made a covenant with the Gibeonites, who had deceived them into believing that
they were from afar, peoples with whom Israel was allowed to make a
covenant. Because of the culpability that Israel bore in not clarifying
the exact origin of the Gibeonites, God made the Israelites keep the
covenant to them. And, later, in the days of Saul, when the covenant
was not kept with the Gibeonites, God judged Israel for being unfaithful.[7] But the later infidelity was intentional. The chronicler (perhaps
Ezra) writes:

But they acted treacherously against the God of their fathers, and played the
harlot after the gods of the peoples of the land, whom God had destroyed
before them. (1 Chron. 5:25)[8]

What is only alluded to earlier is, however, very explicit around the
time of the pending exile of the Northern Kingdom. Recording God's
oracle given to that people some thirty years before the fall of Samaria,

Hosea presents us with a striking illustration of the God-Israel, husband-wife analogy.

ISRAEL AS THE UNFAITHFUL WIFE OF YAHWEH

God wastes no time in the oracle getting to the point. Says he,

"Go, take to yourself a wife of harlotry, and have children of harlotry; for the land commits flagrant harlotry, forsaking the Lord." (Hos. 1:2)

Obediently, the prophet marries Gomer, who promptly bears what may have been their only legitimate child, for the text does not use of her subsequent offspring the telltale "bore him" as it does of the first. Nonetheless, Hosea names the next two children upon the command of the Lord. The name of the last child speaks of the nature of the relation between God and Israel: "*Lo-ammi,*" literally, "not my people." By this name God wishes to tell the Israelites that "you are not My people and I am not your God" (v. 9).

But lest any think the analogy does not come into the story, that is, that the rejection will only be God of Israel, and not Hosea of Gomer, the second chapter makes the matter clear. Hosea, apparently speaking to Jezreel (the legitimate firstborn), notifies Gomer:

Contend with your mother, contend,
For she is not my wife, and I am not her husband;
And let her put away her harlotry from her face,
And her adultery from between her breasts,

Hosea continues to speak of the things he plans to do to Gomer:

Lest I strip her naked
And expose her as on the day when she was born.
I will also make her like a wilderness,
Make her like desert land,
And slay her with thirst.
Also, I will have no compassion on her children,
Because they are children of harlotry.
For their mother has played the harlot. (1:3–5a)

Therefore, behold, I will hedge up her way with thorns,
And I will build a wall against her so that she cannot find her paths. (1:6)

Therefore, I will take back My grain at harvest time
And My new wine in its season.
I will also take away My wool and My flax
Given to cover her nakedness.
And then I will uncover her lewdness
In the sight of her lovers,
And no one will rescue her out of My hand.
I will put an end to all her gaiety. (1:9–11a)

And I will destroy her vines and fig trees. (1:12a)

And I will punish her for the days of the Baals
When she used to offer sacrifices to them . . .
And follow her lovers, so that she forgot Me. (1:13)

Clearly, these adversities are intended to make the erring wife come to her senses and return:

Then she will say, "I will go back to my first husband,
For it was better for me then than now!" (1:7)

And she will come at the first husband's invitation:

I will allure her, . . .
And speak kindly to her. (1:14)

Taking the literal interpretation of this section of the Book of Hosea, we are faced with the fact of Gomer's husband's discovery of her infidelity, his stated rejection of her, his intention to make her see the error of her ways, and his attempt to restore the relationship. On the allegorical interpretation, this section speaks of the relationship of God to Israel and perhaps has nothing to do with real events in the life of Hosea. I prefer to combine the views and argue that God really had Hosea marry and go through the pain of Gomer's infidelity, and that Hosea did, in fact, reject her for that infidelity, stating his intention to treat her in such a way as to make her come to her senses. I hold that chapter 2 is largely anticipatory of actions that Hosea did in fact take, but the historical actions themselves are not recorded. Chapter 3 resumes the oracle at a point subsequent to Gomer's realizing her true state. That chapter tells of how Hosea regained Gomer's companionship.[9]

ISRAEL AS THE DISCIPLINED BRIDE OF YAHWEH

It is more difficult to discern when and if Hosea, in rejecting Gomer and her behavior, actually went through a legal divorce. Some argue that he did not. Representative of them is Francis I. Anderson, who thinks that Gomer (representative of Israel) has deserted Hosea (cf. 2:7 vis-à-vis 2:15) and committed adultery. Accordingly, Anderson believes that "you are not my wife and I am not her husband" simply means that they are no longer living together.[10] But this is hasty. It seems clear from the fact that children two and three are "children of harlotry" (1:2), *yet named by Hosea* (1:6, 9) that Gomer was, at the point of 2:1–2, living with him. Moreover, it is clear that Hosea's threats (2:2–6) are then yet future. If so, then one would imagine that the pursuit of lovers (2:7) should also be considered future rather than present, and 2:7 is so translated. In addition, 2:7 states that she will not "overtake" the lovers. But having two illegitimate children by them at the time of 2:2 certainly speaks of her having been overtaken at that point! It is more reasonable to assume that her lovers are *predicted* to abandon her, at some point in the near future. But, if future at all, then Anderson's point about a present desertion fails.

Arguing further, Anderson says that no simple dissolution of the covenant can be intended by 1:9, because

the covenant nowhere makes provision for such an eventuality. Covenant-breaking on the part of Israel (unilateral withdrawal) calls for severe punishment. Israel cannot opt out by no longer acknowledging Yahweh. The punishment is not an expression of a broken relationship. On the contrary, it is enforced within the relationship; punishment maintains the covenant. Similarly Hosea's threats of punishment are proof that his marriage continues. The corrective discipline expresses his authority over his wife, and his continuing claim upon her. The husband does not take any initiative to dissolve the marriage. That, rather, is what the wife has already done by her conduct.[11]

This is a strange collection of statements. Anderson seems to have lost track of the analogy altogether. For though it is true that the Law made no provision for a legal release of an adulteress from her covenant, it is to be remembered that the Law did require the execution of the adulteress (Lev. 20:10). It made no provision for an adulteress to be punished by some means that involved her staying alive "within the relationship." Clearly it will not do to refer to the terms of the covenant, if by that we mean the prescriptions of the Mosaic Constitutions. It is far preferable simply to refer the matter to the practice of marriage/divorce in the days of Hosea and see the oracle as using these practices to speak of how God now intends to relate to Israel.

But what were the practices of Israel at that time? It is here that Jeremiah 3 enters the picture to support the view that Hosea really did divorce Gomer. For it is about the same events spoken of in Hosea 2 that Jeremiah's oracle speaks:

Have you seen what faithless Israel did? She went up on every high hill and under every green tree, and she was a harlot there. And I thought, "after she has done all these things, she will return to Me"; but she did not return, and her treacherous sister Judah saw it. And I saw that for all the adulteries of faithless Israel, I had sent her away and given her a writ of Divorce. (Jer. 3:6–8a)

The "treacherous departing" (Jer. 3:20) is within the covenant, not a desertion that is physical. And the rejection by the husband of the wife is a legal writ.

Anderson is, of course, familiar with Jeremiah 3:8:

Jeremiah 3:1–14 shows that Yahweh saw no difficulty in overriding such legalities in order to remarry his divorced Israel. Since Jeremiah 3 shows the influence of Hosea, its clear statement that Yahweh divorced Israel (Jer. 3:8), the northern kingdom, could be used as evidence that Hos. 2:4 is the declaration embodied in the bill of divorce. Isaiah 50:1 contains another tradition; it implies that there never was a divorce.[12]

The verse that Anderson has in mind reads:

Thus says the Lord,
"Where is the certificate of divorce,
By which I have sent your mother away?
Or to whom of My creditors did I sell you?"

Anderson forthwith adopts the "Isaiac tradition" against that of Jeremiah. In other words, he resolves the apparent dilemma by arbitrarily eliminating Jeremiah from consideration in interpreting Hosea.

But is this choice really necessary? I think not. There are several other factors that deserve discussion before such a radical approach is taken. First, we should remember the audiences of each of the books in question. Hosea prophesied to the Northern Kingdom about thirty years prior to its fall. His oracle speaks of and to that kingdom. Isaiah, though contemporary with Hosea, speaks his oracle to the Southern Kingdom of Judah. Accordingly, Isaiac materials should not be brought into contrast with the Jeremiac materials, since they refer to different kingdoms at different times. Anderson implies that the divorces referred to in Jeremiah and Isaiah are the same divorce. They are not. Only Jeremiah's comment should be seen as a commentary on Hosea. And according to Jeremiah, at the time that the Northern Kingdom was divorced, the Southern was not but should have learned the lesson.

Thus, Jeremiah's comment regarding divorce does correlate to Hosea's oracle. If it does not, then Hosea's oracle somehow completely missed the divorcement that Jeremiah says occurred to the Northern Kingdom at the time when "she" was sent away. It would seem rather strange to think that a divorce did occur (so Jeremiah) that Hosea's oracle did not predict. Of course, if we are inclined to see these as mere human writers, uninspired by the Holy Spirit, such a position would be possible. We would then simply imply that Jeremiah "reinterpreted" the prior divorceless tradition. I do not accept that view of the text.

But to conclude that Isaiah's oracle does not refer to the divorcement of the Northern Kingdom, though it does harmonize the passages, does not really solve all the logical problems. For we still have to ask whether Isaiah's understanding of divorce (speaking of the Southern Kingdom) logically agrees with the Jeremiah-Hosea understanding (when it speaks of the Northern Kingdom). Specifically, does Hosea have God saying that he rejects divorce as a way of dealing with a wayward covenant partner, whereas Jeremiah and Hosea see divorce as a proper divine discipline of such a partner? I do not think that it will do to suggest that God arbitrarily deals with one kingdom in a way different than he does another. So what may we say to resolve this logical dilemma?

I believe the solution rests in realizing that Isaiah 50:1 does not deny, but rather affirms, the divorcement of Israel. Consider again Isaiah 50:1. Adding the latter part of the verse to the part quoted earlier we have:

A: "Where is the certificate of divorce,
  By which I have sent your mother away?
  B: Or to whom of My creditors did I sell you?
  b: Behold, you were sold for your iniquities,
a: And for your transgressions
  Your mother was sent away."

Now, does this verse mean to tell us that the mother was not divorced and they not sold? That is one interpretation. To wit: there is no certificate, and therefore the mother should not act as if she were free. But why does the text say that the mother has been sent away and the child sold? Well, the argument runs, Israel is in slavery and they have been temporarily separated from God.[13] But that is not the more natural reading of the text. The key is in the second part of the verse. Just as it is not out of bad debt that God had to sell Israel (B) but because of their iniquity (b), so too it is not out of petty hard-heartedness (A)[14] that God has cast Israel away like a piece of property; they were divorced because of their own adultery (a). It is difficult to see how "sent away" could mean anything other than divorce, except to a people such as ourselves who have a concept of legal separation from "bed and board" without a complete cessation of the legal relationship.[15] Thus I conclude that Isaiah 50:1 does not reveal an alternative view to divorce for adultery but harmonizes completely with the material in the other prophets. They all see divorce as God's discipline of the wayward spouse, Israel.

But if we are right about the divorcement of the Northern Kingdom, how can we answer Anderson's formidable objection that a man who has divorced his erring wife has no right to treat her as Hosea intends? Indeed, Anderson further objects that if we see Gomer as having become married to another (cf. Jer. 3:1),

her relationships would no longer be adultery against Hosea. The original husband would have no grounds for disciplining her or for unmasking her lovers. This is the main obstacle in the way of identifying the statement in 2:4a as an act of divorce. That would be the end of the story. There would be no basis for all that follows. But in 2:6–15 the lovers remain "lovers." Hos. 2:9 suggests that the "first husband" [2:7] was still her husband. She had deserted him, but he had not renounced her. Her amours continue to be adultery against him; 2:4–15 treats her as an adulterous *wife*, not simply as a promiscuous woman.[16]

This sounds impressive, but there is more thunder than rain here. The fact is that God *did* divorce the Northern Kingdom and *did* continue his claims on it. Some other explanation needs to be found.

Several possible solutions present themselves. Either the fact that she is the guilty party makes the difference,[17] or the "adversity" mentioned in Hosea 2:6–15 is another way to speak of the implications of the act of divorcement. We prefer the latter, that is, that 2:6–15 is simply a way of speaking of the social and economic *results* of divorce. This is to say, by legally divorcing her (2:2) he now has the legal right to take back the clothing he has given her (2:3, 10) and the materials of his field by which she can make more clothing (2:9), to disinherit her children (2:4), to block her out of his house (2:6), to cut her off from the food and drink that she shares in his house (2:9) as well as the crops from which she could get sustenance (2:12),[18] and in general to cut her off from the way of life that she enjoys—that *he* has made possible. Thus, when she comes to realize that she has been simply *used* by her lovers, who will not be impressed by her without those husband-provided luxuries (2:7, 10), she will repent and return.

All this parallels exactly the *facts* of God and Israel. When God ceased to support Israel, "she" lost all "she" had and was no longer treated "respectfully" by "her" lovers. The loss of the husband-provided goods was, in that case, mediated by the hand of the "lovers" (e.g., Babylonia), but that fact is not detrimental to our solution. We simply need to point out that after the divorcement (the time of Hosea) there were social and economic losses (the deportation) and that a similar experience of divorce and loss apparently occurred in the life of Gomer. It was not so much that God pursued Israel in Babylon, but that he abandoned Israel to Babylon, and, that while "she" was there, he spoke kindly to "her" and called "her" to return. The same can be said for Gomer. Hosea divorced her, abandoned her to her own devices, which she found to be insufficient, and then lured her back to himself.

One other point in the Hosea passage needs consideration. In 3:1 we read:

Go again, love a woman who is loved by her husband, yet an adulteress, even as the Lord loves the sons of Israel, though they turn to other gods.

Is it proper to speak of Gomer as an adulteress, loved by her husband, if Hosea has freed her by divorce? In fact, what are we to make of the same sort of idea found in a number of places? For example, Isaiah 54:5 says, "For your husband is your maker. . . . For the Lord has called you, like a wife forsaken and grieved in spirit, even like a wife of one's youth when she is rejected." Or again, there is the NIV rendering of Jeremiah 3:14, which says that God is still "married" to the Northern Kingdom that he has just divorced (v. 8). In each of these instances a divorce is more or less certain, but the language of *existing covenant* is employed. How can this be?

First note that, in the case of Isaiah 54, the text is a prophetic projection into the time of the return, when Israel has been remarried to

Yahweh. Thus it is appropriate to use the language of existing covenant. But it is not possible to use this sort of argument for Hosea. One
possibility is that the text is employing a figure of speech (i.e., *heterosis*),
where sense of the English present tense is employed, though the severance is complete, to emphasize the offense to the legal covenant then
sundered and past. But this is not the most sophisticated way to understand the text. In fact, Hosea 3:1 is more complex than the translations reveal. First, the words for "wife" and "husband" are ambiguous.
"Wife" may simply be "woman," and the term used for "husband" is
actually more commonly translated "friend." Additionally, the friend
is not identified as "her" friend, but only as "a" friend. Thus, the text
may be saying nothing more than, "Go love a woman loved by a friend."
This rendering would hardly imply an existing marital relation. The
fact that the text does say that she is an "adulteress" complicates this
analysis, but does not ultimately defeat it. We should also remember
that an unrepentant offender is still known by his or her offense-term,
even if not continually practicing the offense at a later time.[19]

The Jeremiah 3:14 text is also more problematic than the translations
reveal. The term the NIV translates "married" is actually the verb *bâ'al*.
Though this word can be translated that way, it could also be translated
less maritally, and more politically, "have dominion." Additionally, it is
the preterite perfect, a form used of this verb only here and in Jeremiah 31:32. Such a form is not clear as to time. The dominion is completed action, but that dominion may or may not extend to the present.
In Jeremiah 31, the presumption is that it does not. In Jeremiah 3 the
translators have chosen to translate the exact same word as if the dominion does continue in the present. Should we take 31:32 as meaning
that Israel broke the covenant while bound to the Lord (as they still
are), or chapter 3 as meaning that God calls the apostate sons back to
himself—reminding them that they initially went astray while he had
legal rights over them (though that dominion is now technically removed by the divorce writ of the same chapter)? As for the grammar
itself, we can only be sure that dominion once existed.[20]

Recall, too, that in neither case (31 nor 3) are we assured that the
"dominion" in view is connected with the marital metaphor. After all,
the Israelites had a son-slave relationship to the Lord before they even
ratified the Mosaic covenant—that covenant bearing the weight of the
marital metaphor. Could it be that the *Ba'-a-li* and related words have
predominately political rather than marital overtones in the Prophets?
For example, in Hosea 2:16, where the noun form is used, the context
before and after strongly implies that marriage does not exist when
Israel calls God its master. In 1:9 God says Israel is not his people. In
2:19 he tells Israel that he will betroth them in some future day. *Ba'-
a-li* rests chronologically between these passages.[21] Thus, subsequent to
the divorce, Israel is not considered the marriage partner of God, but

merely a runaway slave. They revert back to the position of Israel before Sinai—a people redeemed out of Egypt with a strong arm.[22]

In any case it is ill advised to base a theology of marriage upon the words and verb tenses of these questioned passages. Their significance to this subject remains moot. It seems preferable to follow Hosea 2:2, which denies in strong terms that a marital relation exists past the divorce. The Hebrew there employs the term of factual negation (*lō*), which rules out the existence of the condition under discussion (i.e., marriage).[23] Hosea is saying that he no longer considers Gomer to be "his" (possessive suffix) "woman" or "wife" (standard term for a full partner).

What, then, may we learn from such books as Hosea, Ezekiel, and Isaiah? We learn that divorce is used metaphorically of God's discipline of Israel for their adulterous activities against the covenant. The linguistic thread that links the use of God to the husband and Israel to the wife is the idea of "adultery"—an adultery that, in the case of God and Israel, is sexual only metaphorically but actually an instance of unfaithfulness to the covenant. In other words, adultery is at root, or in principle, not essentially a sexual term, though it connotes sexual infidelity. Its essential definition is "breach of covenant, unfaithfulness, treachery, infidelity." A definition such as this shows how the idea of sexual infidelity on the part of the wife, in an Old Testament marriage, parallels the breach of covenant on the part of a husband who fails to keep his pledge to provide for his wife. There will be further discussion about this relationship at the end of this section, but first we must look at another prophetic treatment of the wife's infidelity to her husband: the intermarriage between Israelites and the women of the land in the days of Ezra the scribe.

Divorce as an Ultimate Solution for Adultery (Ezra 9 and 10)

The harlotry of Israel brings forth yet another and different treatment of the divorce issue in the Book of Ezra. In the ninth and tenth chapters, we read of Ezra's discovery of marriages between the returned Israelites and the women of the land (Samaritans?). The text tells how some of the princes approached Ezra and told him of this intermarriage (9:1) and of the extent to which the evil had gone—even the princes and rulers were involved (9:2). In fact, we are later informed that even the sons of the priests had gone into apostasy in this manner (10:18). The fact that the people brought the matter up to Ezra shows their sensitivity to the teachings of the Law on this matter, a sensitivity that preceded any evident reading of the Law to the people by Ezra.[24]

Much of what we are reading here is supportive of what we have already seen in this chapter regarding the *non*sexual aspects of the meaning of the word *adultery*. The unfaithfulness of Ezra's time only seems more sexual than that spoken of in the time of the pre-exilic prophets, in that marriage, which involves sexual relations, was a part of the facts of the case. But to stress the physical side of the unfaithfulness unduly is to miss the center of the passage. For it is the idea of *covenanting* with the "enemy" rather than simply *coupling* with them that is the problem. Or, to be more precise, the problem is that, in establishing legal marital relations with the women of the land, they had broken their "marriage" covenant with God. It would not have been unfaithfulness for them to have married Jewish girls, or even to have taken women of the land as concubines; sex with a human being was not the issue. It was the breaking of one of the rules of the Mosaic covenant wherein lay the offense. There is also in this account a reaffirmation of the important point that divorce, though a substitute for the Mosaic corrective of execution, is a necessary and acceptable means of discipline. For first the people (10:3) and then the prophet (10:11) understand separation/divorce as being "God's" way for the matter to be resolved. "But," one may properly ask, "was this really God's will, or only their own thought?" After all, neither of these statements is presented as an oracle. But that is only an academic point.

First, it is clear that the prophet thought it was consonant with revealed truth. This should not be minimized. Remember that it was a grave offense for a prophet to speak as from the Lord something that God had not said (Deut. 18:20–22).[25] For God's prophet to have advised immorality in God's name and not have been corrected by God is difficult to accept.

Second, in those passages where *preventive* separation (i.e., antecedent separation from the Gentiles) had been enjoined upon Israel, the principle that evil must be *removed* from the land (e.g., Deut. 7:5) is also taught. The putting away of heathen wives is a rather plain and reasonable application of that principle. The historical incident of the covenant with Gibeon (Josh. 9) shows that the people of Israel were able to apply the principle to instances of covenants with people of the land—in that case, however, the culpable negligence of the people in making the covenant in the first place called forth God's requirement of them to *retain* the covenantal relation, as a sort of punishment. The case of the people in Ezra's time differs from the Gibeonite case in that the marriages in Ezra involved rebellion rather than ignorance. Thus, I believe that the correct understanding of a basic principle was what led to the valid application of it suggested by the people and Ezra in their day.

Third, I hasten to mention, as well, that Israel's past times of apostasy had often been ended by days of repentance and revival, in which God blessed Israel for their *putting away* the things of evil to which they had clung. Read, for example, 2 Kings 18:1–7 or 2 Kings 23, which recount national renewal that sounds strikingly like that recorded in Ezra 9 and

10, since both the Kings materials and Ezra use the language of "making" or renewing the covenant. There are also a number of other prophetic passages that explicitly call the Israelites to "remove" evil deeds from among them. Since intermarriage is an evil deed, to remove it would be to divorce the heathen women (cf., e.g., Isa. 1:16).

The major difference between the Ezra incident and prior applications (viz., Isaiah, Hosea, and Jeremiah) of the principle of divorce as discipline is that the other prophets all apply the principle that divorce is a discipline for adultery by speaking of the putting away of the adulterous spouse, whereas in the Ezra case it is the spouse of the adulterer that is to be put away. But our discussion of the history of divorce as a discipline in previous revelation reveals that this "new" application is really clearer in the (older) Law (as contrasted with the Prophets) than the application of divorce as a punishment for the offender. Actually, the putting away of the offender (Isaiah/Hosea/Jeremiah) was similar in net effect to the putting away of the spouse of the offender (Ezra), in that in all cases the putting away had a strong chastising effect. It brought sorrow to the offender. In the former case it deprived the sinner of the blessings of covenant with the spouse (God) and led to the abandonment of the sinner by the partner in crime (the nations); in the latter case it deprived the sinners (the men of Israel) of their partners in crime (the women of the land) and led to the abandonment of the "blessings" or pleasures of the covenant with said partners.[26]

Thus, we conclude that there is nothing really new or unusual in the treatment of the apostates in Ezra's day. The admonition to divorce the women as a "fruit of repentance" was implicitly set forth in the Law and the prior Prophets. As an instance of correcting an "adulterous marriage," it set a precedent for dealing with later similar cases (Neh. 13) and anticipated the judgment by John the Baptist of Herod (Matt. 14:3).[27] As an example of Jesus' implication that there were some who were *not* joined together by God (Matt. 19:6b), it gave rise to the question of whether or not new believers should divorce their wives (cf. 1 Cor. 7:12 ff.).

The question, then, is not whether the Ezra corrective is unique,[28] but, rather, since it is not unique, but a strongly grounded moral principle of correction, whether it is to be applied in a similar way today. Some commentators contend that it should not be so applied. Laney, for example, cites three reasons for rejecting it:

1. Ezra was concerned for the preservation of the Jewish people as a separate and distinct nation. . . .
   God does not seem to be similarly concerned to preserve the racial or ethnic purity of Gentile peoples during an age of grace (cf. Gal. 3:28).
2. In the Old Testament period we see that intermarriage would lead to idolatry. . . .
   No such consequences are stated in the case of a mixed marriage between

a Christian and a non-Christian. . . . The presence of the believer in the home sets it apart. . . .

3. . . . to make application . . . to modern marriages . . . would contradict the clear teaching of Paul in I Cor. 7:12–13.[29]

These points, however, fail to convince. Ezra may have thought of ethnic purity, but the text makes it clear that his chief concern was with the spirtual apostasy that the interfaith marriages implied. Indeed, it is the interfaith not the interracial aspects that are the clear concern of the Old Testament. Was not Rahab in the Lord's line? She was a woman of the land. But she was a proselyte; her faith in Yahweh made the difference. It is still the case in the New Testament that moral/ spiritual purity proscribes intentional interfaith marriages (cf. 2 Cor. 6:14).[30] It would be presumptuous to suggest that when the principle of separation is restated in the nonethnic realm, the principle of correction should be considered obsolete. One would expect moral continuity unless there were specific New Testament annulment of it. Laney and others break this hermeneutical rule by presuming discontinuity.[31] In short, intentional interfaith marriage yields just as spiritually damaging consequences in the believer's life today as in Old Testament times. And though it is true that the "believer sanctifies" the unbelieving spouse, it must be remembered that Paul's context was Corinthian intermarriage, which was not a species of apostasy but the result of conversion. This latter point enables us to see the error of Laney's third argument: Paul is dealing with a different sort of interfaith marriage. But I will reserve full comment on Paul's teaching till a more fitting place in the discussion.

I conclude, then, that the principle set forth in Ezra—that divorce is a morally proper corrective for apostasy—abides, unless evidence can be found in further revelation for its abrogation. I believe that none such can be found.

THE ADULTERY OF DIVORCE (MALACHI 2)

One of the first passages appealed to by popular writers on the subject of divorce is Malachi 2:16. The verse often functions as a sort of absolute veto, and the appeal to it is thought to summarily end the discussion. What could be clearer than the express statement of Scripture: " 'For I hate divorce,' says the Lord, the God of Israel"? Paul E. Steele and Charles C. Ryrie call this text "one of the most profound texts in the scripture on the subject of marriage permanence" and move quickly to the conclusion that God despises divorce.[32] Laney tells us that "God's attitude toward divorce" is summed up by his statement here.[33]

The essential argument of these men is apparently as follows: since in the clause quoted divorce is rejected with no qualification at all, we should reject divorce absolutely. This argument is risky, to say the least. Though I would admit that the burden of proof rests with those who argue for an acceptable kind of divorce, we should surely wish to be allowed to consider context, near and far, in deciding the issue. Indeed, one does not have to go far to see that Malachi's oracle is spoken with only a certain kind of divorce in mind. This fact, tied to our previous discussions of proper divorce, places the burden of proof back upon those who would argue against all divorce. They still lack a text.

I hold, with most scholars, that the problem facing Malachi was a complex one. First, there were some people who had broken God's covenant by marrying women of the land (2:12).[34] This is a repetition of the sin mentioned in Ezra and Nehemiah, though we do not know the exact relation in time of the Malachi events to those in the other books. Second, some of the Israelites had divorced their wives (2:14–16). It is not stated that only those who had married the foreign women had done this, and it is a bit unexpected to find the charges in the order they are presented in the text. We would have thought that the order of offenses would have been reversed: they divorced and then remarried. Probably, the prophet knew of cases of men who had married who had not divorced Hebrew wives, and of some who had divorced Hebrew wives who had not remarried foreigners. As stated, the oracle catches all classes of sinners!

In any case, some had divorced their wives, and the association of the two complaints suggests that they had intended to marry women of the land—double offense. Indeed, the difficult verse 15 probably means us to draw this connection by alluding to Abraham's refusal to divorce Sarah in order to take Hagar, a woman of the land, as his concubine.[35] In other words, the people of Malachi's day have not been faithful to God as Abraham was; though he sinned by seeking to gain holy seed (Isaac) by the bondwoman (Hagar) he nonetheless remained true to God's law by not putting away his lawful spouse (Sarah). By contrast, men of Malachi's day had put away their legal wives in order to marry women prohibited by God's law (Deut. 7:3).[36]

In view of the context, namely, the unjustified divorce of legal wives, is it proper to suggest that *all* divorces are some species of treachery? Certainly not! Simply, if divorce per se is treachery, then God is treacherous and Hosea is treacherous when they divorce their "wives" according to the biblical record! It is not that God hates divorce because it is treacherous but that he hates treacherous divorce. And the sort of divorce that is treacherous is, for instance, divorce grounded upon nothing more than the desire to be monogamously devoted to another woman.

Laney suggests that the oracular statement that such men have "covered their garments with wrong" may be a colorful way of underscoring the treachery of these divorces. He points out that in Ruth 3:9 and in Ezekiel 16:8, the prospective husband spreads his garment over the woman to show his intention to protect her.[37] To say that his divorce has covered his garment with wrong may mean that, whereas he was to cover the woman with his (unstained) garment, he has instead covered his garment with the stains of violence, the divorce being a violation of the woman's basic rights and a sundering of the covenant.

It is at this point that we find our previous discussion of the man's obligations in marriage underscored. Recall that I argued earlier that for a man to fail to provide for his wife was for him to rend the covenant. What is groundless divorce but the same rending of the covenant, albeit with the trappings of legality and the illusion of morality? To deprive a woman of her right to bodily support while keeping the marriage a legal entity is a sham. To divorce her is a legal sham. Both are treachery. Both end the obligation of the woman to live up to her vows. God hates all such treachery, and he has made provision for the women in such case: remarriage, preferably to the offender, who comes to his senses as a result of the oracle of the Lord, but to another if he does not. To argue that she does *not* have the right to remarry has the burden of proof, insofar as the right to remarry is clearly stated earlier in the case of a woman deprived of what a husband should provide in marriage. Exodus 21:10 f., 26 f. states that right (Exod. 21:11).[38] Recall also that Deuteronomy 24:1–4 provided for the woman's well-being by allowing her (the victim of divorce on insufficient grounds by a hard-hearted husband) to marry another.

Though the text does not explicitly say so, it certainly implies that such divorce is adulterous. It is called treachery, and since it is treachery against the covenant partner, it may be presumed to be a form of adultery, as is any breach of the marital covenant. The man promised to continuously care for this woman, and now he has, by legal writ and without legal grounds (i.e., his wife's sexual adultery), declared that he will no longer do so. He has been unfaithful, and adultery is marital unfaithfulness.[39]

Finally, we note that semantic confusion is once again possible in these verses because some translators have chosen to speak of the treacherously divorced woman as a companion and covenant partner, in spite of the clear fact of prior divorce. This gives the impression that, after legal divorce, some legal relationship or existing covenant continues. This in turn gives rise to the idea that marriage continues in spite of divorce. A careful look at Malachi 2:14, however, reveals that those who translate 2:14 "though she *is* your companion and your wife by covenant," have not rendered the Hebrew in the preferred way. First, remember that in Hebrew verbs are not so much concerned with point of time as with completeness of action. Second, as in Greek, it was common for the writer to omit verbs altogether when the action had the effect of the English present tense. Though they had a particle that could convey the idea of the present, they more often than not omitted it and expected the reader to supply it. Third, supplying the present tense in a verbless clause is inappropriate if the previous clauses convey the sense of another tense. Fourth, the Hebrew "perfect" (i.e., completed action) is as close to the English "past" as one could expect. Though the action could have ongoing implications, the stress is on the fact that the action is finished.

Combining these grammatical elements and applying them to the text of Malachi 2:14, we note that "is your companion and your wife" is a verbless clause, without the particle, but in the context of a prior perfect (i.e., "you have dealt treacherously"). Thus, the translation of choice would be "though she *was* your companion and your wife." This matches quite nicely with the concept of relation subsequent to divorce in Hosea 2:2: "she is not my wife, and I am not her husband."[40] Divorce ends the legal relation; hence it is not strictly correct to speak of the former partner as still one's companion or wife.[41] Divorce (whether morally grounded or not) signals the end of the covenant.[42]

SUMMARY OF OLD TESTAMENT TEACHINGS

In short, the Old Testament taught that marriage was intended to be a permanent, convenantal relationship between a man, who was to protect and provide for his wife, and a woman, who was to remain monogamous to her husband. Marriages between legitimate partners were insured by God, before whom such were contracted.[43] The Law called for the execution of a woman who broke her marital vow, and when that admonition was disregarded, divorce became an accepted substitute, an act of discipline. When the man failed to live up to his side of the bargain, either by depriving his wife within marriage, by aggressive abuse in marriage, or by dissolution of the marriage, the Law provided for her protection by permitting divorce. The Law required the actively or passively abusive husband to release the wife, if she sued via the courts, though the husband technically did the filing for divorce. The innocent woman who had been divorced was permitted to remarry. The man in those cases (the "guilty" party) was permitted to marry, since polygamy was permissible, but the Scripture had especially strong condemnation ("adultery") for a man who divorced solely for the purpose of devoting himself to another woman. Thus, divorce could either be a discipline or an act of treachery; the grounds in view determined which it was. Remarriage was presumed to be a right for the guilty husband, as well as innocent parties, though the guilty party was clearly identified as an offender (in the prophetic literature). Guilty males, we presume, showed the fruit of repentance by remarrying the severed partner (along with the new spouse). Guilty wives, however, were not morally free to remarry.[44] The fruit of their repentance was to put away their subsequent partners and return to their rightful spouse.[45] Thus, a reestablishment of the broken marriage may be presumed to be the proper way to rectify the sin of divorce. But if an innocent partner married again in the intervening time, that subsequent union—even of a wife—would be morally permissible.

These, then, are the general teachings of the Old Testament regarding the issue of marriage/divorce/remarriage. They form the context for the New Testament teachings. Let us turn now to the teaching of Christ and his followers to see if they changed the Old Testament teaching.

CHAPTER 5

The Teachings of Jesus on Divorce
(Matthew 5:31–32a)

THE HISTORICAL CONTEXT OF JESUS' TEACHING

It is ironic that there should be so much controversy over the import of the teaching of Jesus on divorce/remarriage. In his great Sermon, Jesus explicitly sets about to rectify contemporary ethics, which he sees as debased by Pharisaical Scripture-twisting (Matt. 5:17 ff.). He saw his job as one of clarification, and a summary look at the state of divorce ethics in the days of Jesus shows that clarification was indeed needed! Unless Jesus was wrong in his profession of loyalty to the Scripture, we should expect to find that his teachings are entirely consonant with previous revelation. (And, I hope, with the conclusions set forth in the earlier chapters of this book.) As for the Pharisees, if Jesus was right, the meaning of the Old Testament had been eclipsed among them in the intertestamental period, such that divorce was no longer understood as either an act of sinful treachery or a discipline painfully applied with the appeal for restoration always in view. To the Pharisees, the ending of a marriage was the husband's *right*. The Deuteronomic provision for the wife of a hard-hearted husband (protecting her from his treacherous intentions, Deut. 24:1–4) was turned upside down to favor the husband, and the Pharisaical schools argued back and forth over what had to be *wrong* with the wife before the husband could exercise his *right* to put her away. The liberal school of Hillel thought that a man had the right to end his marriage if his wife did something he found distasteful. The conservative school of Shammai thought the man's right to divorce was limited to the case of a wife who had committed adultery. Both schools were concerned for the rights of the man and had little concern for the woman, thus reversing the concern of the Bible.

The Herods were egalitarian about divorce. During the days of Christ's majority, the son of Herod the Great, Antipas, had an affair with his half-brother Philip's wife, Herodias. Together, Herod and Herodias divorced their covenant partners in order to devote themselves to each other. They cared little for the rights of either men or women who got in the way of their lust. Members of the religious establishment were too satisfied with their economic and political position to raise much objection to this transgression of the Law. Only the prophet John ("the baptizer") dared to rebuke the erring house of Herod with Holy Scripture.

Out in the deserts whence John had come, there were ascetic, religious people who were not personally interested in marriage, rejected polygamy, and certainly opposed divorce and remarriage—the Essenes. They codified their ethical teachings on the subject in the so-called Temple Scroll. It contained their interpretation of the difference between the Masoretic and Septuagintal (LXX) texts of Genesis 2:24. They argued that the inclusion of "two" in the Septuagint (or a text similar to it) properly conveyed the sense of the original. God had intended that only two should be married. This would prohibit both polygamy and remarriage, practices necessary, so we have seen, to a full application of the Law and the Prophets.

Clearly, the ethics of divorce/remarriage were in a state of disarray in the days of Jesus. And into this morass of ethical confusion Jesus stepped, spoke a few words on the subject, and, we may presume, in the minds of his disciples eventually cleared up the issues. But we, his latter-day disciples, have taken those few words and produced from them our own pharisaical controversies. We are not even sure which of his statements on the subject came first; nor are we agreed upon whether all the statements attributed to him in the texts of the Gospels are his, as opposed to interpretations by the evangelists or even the early Church.[1]

It is unlikely that this book will end those controversies, but the continuing confusion calls for new ways to resolve them. With that aim in mind, we look chronologically at the teachings of Jesus.

THE TEACHING OF JESUS IN THE SERMON ON THE MOUNT (MATTHEW 5:31–32)

Jesus' Teaching on Groundless Divorce (Matthew 5:31–32a)

CONTEXT OF THE TEACHING

The Distant Context: "I Have Not Come to Abrogate the Law"

Any understanding of Jesus' divorce teaching in the Sermon on the Mount must be grounded upon a more general understanding of what

Jesus is about in the Sermon as a whole and of what he is about in the section that includes the divorce teaching. Regarding the first point there is a great deal of disagreement among scholars. Some hold that Jesus is altering the Old Testament Law. They see this in his quoting of certain commandments and in his immediate "correction": "but I say unto you . . ." Others respond that Jesus is merely trying to clarify certain popular misconceptions about Old Testament Law, pushing his listeners toward a fuller understanding of that Law than was being taught by the religious leaders of his day. There are a number of other views; it is not possible for us to go into this disagreement at any significant length, but I do need to make it clear where I stand on the issue.

Two things stand out in any cursory reading of the Sermon. First, it emphasizes things that were not the primary emphasis of the Old Testament Law. The Law, being a standard to be used by the judges in settling communal disputes, emphasized the sorts of actions that the civil authorities could resolve by evidence and expedite with civil action. But the prophets make it clear that, though such externals were stressed in the Law, God was also concerned with the attitudes of the heart ("circumcision of the heart"). Jesus, in stressing internal attitudes and nonlegal interpersonal relations in the Sermon, is picking up the theme of the prophets and expanding upon it greatly. In the Sermon Jesus clearly states, "Unless your righteousness surpasses that of the scribes and the Pharisees, you shall not enter into the kingdom of heaven" (Matt. 5:20). He is concerned that his disciples not limit the holiness of God to fastidiously kept rules that relate only to the outer, legal life.

The second thing that stands out is that Jesus is loyal to the Old Testament Law. In verses 17–19 he tells his listeners that he has not come to abolish the least of the Old Testament rules, but that they shall stand until "heaven and earth pass away." It seems clear, then, that Jesus means to recover the Law in all its fullness, *not* to make changes in it that would negate the least of its principles. This leads us to conclude that Jesus intends to clarify misunderstandings.

The Near Context: "You Have Heard . . ."

The structure of the Sermon is simple but subtle. Its introduction includes the Beatitudes, which inform the listening disciples of the inter- and intrapersonal nature of the words that follow. It also includes the Salt and Light statements, which give structural direction to the body of the Sermon. The believer is to affect the world like salt and like light. But these are no mere empty illustrations to be filled by the imagination of Church preachers. Reversing the similes, Matthew 5:16–6:34, Jesus tells the disciples exactly how the light should and should not shine.[2]

The subsection 5:21–48 is a discernible unit identified by the celebrated phrase "You have heard . . ." (5:21, 27, 33, 38, 43). Within this section there are six distinct sayings, some of which seem to relate to the Ten Commandments. In fact, they would seem to be comments on the last six of the commandments: murder, 21–26; adultery, 27–30; theft, 31–32; false witness, 33–37; coveting and defrauding, 38–42; and parents, 43–48.[3] The weakest element in this interpretation of the structure of the subsection rests in the fact that the crucial thirty-first and thirty-second verses are missing their "you have heard," giving rise to the suggestion that Jesus intended to include them with the teaching on adultery (vv. 27–30). I do not deny that there is a definite correlation to the adultery commandment, but I do feel that Deuteronomy 24:1–4 is best interpreted in its own section as a comment on the eighth commandment,[4] not the seventh.[5]

What I am saying is that Matthew 5:31–32 is, like Deuteronomy 24:1–4, not primarily trying to define adultery so much as trying to prohibit the treatment of the covenant partners as if they were chattel property.[6] Seen in this light, the text is certainly not trying to teach a new doctrine about marital relation—that is, a doctrine that differs from that found in the Law.

But, some will protest, does not Jesus quote the Law and alter it with his own teaching?[7] The answer is no. Jesus does on several occasions in the subsection quote Old Testament material, but he has served notice that he is correcting Pharisaical misinterpretations of the Law. It is as if he were saying, "You have heard the Old Testament quoted and explained in the following way, but let me explain to you its true and full meaning." In other words, the very quoting of the Law evoked in his listeners' minds the aberrant teaching that Jesus intended to correct. He does not intend to annul the commandment, only its interpretation.

A final structural point is that in each of the first three sayings (unlike the second three)[8] the "you" is assumed to be guilty of some offense that Pharisaical teaching had missed: in the first instance, murder; in the second, adultery; in the third, abuse of the wife as property. It is a foreboding refrain:

You think you are innocent, but you are guilty.
You think you are innocent, but you are guilty.
You think you are innocent, but you are guilty.

In each case they had been led to believe that they were avoiding guilt by the limited nature of their action. But they were wrong.

Summarizing what we have learned to this point from structural analysis: Verses 31 and 32 are a clarification of an Old Testament Law, a correcting of a wrong interpretation. The disciples, thinking that the action discussed is permissible, are served notice that God's righteousness finds it morally deficient in some way. In the case at hand, the disciples had been led to believe that the action of legal divorce *as taught by the Pharisees* was morally permissible; Jesus informs them that it is an abuse of the wife that in some way connects with the adultery commandment. Let us now devote ourselves to a careful consideration of each of the clauses in this saying.

The Immediate Context: "And It Was Said . . ."

As noted earlier, the omission of the "you have heard" clause seems to draw attention to the preceding saying. The point is not that the previous saying corrects the Pharisaical teaching while this one corrects the Mosaic, but rather that the third saying borrows that clause from the preceding saying. Jesus is still correcting Pharisaical misinterpretation. The connection, doubtless, is the concept of a broadened understanding of the adultery offense, but the entrance of the structure into the domain of the eighth commandment (theft) is not meant to be blunted. The offender of the property command is guilty of the offense of adultery as well, and so the third saying will state.

But if Jesus is still correcting Pharisaical misinterpretation, exactly what interpretation is he correcting? There were, after all, significant disagreements among the Pharisees on the issue of divorce. Rabbi Shammai thought that a man was justified (perhaps morally obligated) in legally severing his marital relation if the woman was guilty of some impropriety tantamount to adultery.[9] Hillel, on the other hand, thought a man justified in divorcing his wife on any grounds, that is, for any reason that came to him.

Though it is not necessary (and indeed is improper, Matt. 23:2, 3) to prove that Jesus opposed every teaching of every Pharisee, there are still several points that the Pharisees had in common that are candidates for Jesus' correction. We properly look for such points because Jesus was unlikely to make a general criticism where notorious differences were existent. His hearers might not be party to the teaching of only one Pharisaical school and might think that Jesus was being unfair to at least their rabbi. First, all the rabbis centered their discussion upon the very verses that Jesus quotes, Deuteronomy 24:1–4. Second, they all interpreted that passage as a provision on behalf of *the husband*. By so doing, they all presupposed that the Deuteronomic Law was setting forth a right of the husband and identifying a problem with the wife that justified the husband putting her away. Third, the Pharisees seem to have held that it was morally obligatory for the offended husband to put the offender away.

THE TEACHING ITSELF

"Whoever Divorces His Wife, Let Him Give Her a Certificate of Divorce"

John Murray, in his classic treatment of divorce, is quite fair in pointing out that, although the wording employed by Jesus is not a precise quote of either the LXX or the Hebrew text, this may simply be a proper paraphrasing of Deuteronomy 24:1–4. He goes on to point out that the Deuteronomy passage itself does not imply

1. That the Israelites had a right to put away their wives.
2. That in certain circumstances [they] were under obligation to do so.[10]

Later, Murray reaffirms his point that Jesus' teaching in this passage does not oblige a person to divorce his wife, even on the grounds of adultery.[11]

Though Murray is quite right respecting the implications of Deuteronomy 24 regarding these points, it is most unfortunate that his book gives so little attention to the strong Old Testament teaching that divorce is a discipline that, as a substitute for the previously mandatory execution, *is* morally obligatory. That Jesus agrees with this teaching is to be drawn, first, from the Sermon teaching that he does not wish to annul the least of the Old Testament commands, second, from the principle implicit in his general teaching on the treatment of unrepentant sinners, as recorded in Matthew 18, and, third, from the logical proximity of the Joseph and Mary case to the exception clause in Matthew 5 and 19. But we are getting ahead of ourselves. Suffice it to say that Deuteronomy 24 is wrongly interpreted to imply a right or a responsibility to divorce. And, we may expect that Jesus, in correcting Pharisaical interpretation, will deal with such inferences.[12]

"But I Say to You . . ."

The first clause, "but I say to you," again, signals a correction of Pharisaical misinterpretation regarding the right of an Israelite man to divorce his wife and remain guiltless before God.

"Whoever Divorces His Wife . . ."

The second clause, "whoever divorces his wife," should stir up memories of Malachi 2. For Jesus is now moving on to the biblical teaching of divorce. And, though Deuteronomy 24 was a law that emphasized the provision for a woman who was the victim of her husband's treachery, the Malachi passage centers upon the sin of that same husband.

"Except for the Cause of Unchastity . . ."

We arrive at the first instance of the celebrated exception clause, "except for the cause of unchastity." Many an exegete would wish that it could simply be dismissed and thereby render null whole sets of problems it seems to raise. One thing is certain, and that is that it cannot be excused as a textual variant. J. Carl Laney, one of the most conservative scholars to have written on the subject, writes:

While some would argue that these exceptive clauses are not part of the genuine teaching of Jesus but represent either an adaptation by Matthew or an interpolation by the early church, there are no sound textual arguments against the genuineness of the clauses.[13]

I agree with Laney that hypothetical alternative readings must be denied in favor of alternatives in the manuscripts. Resting on Bruce Metzger's *A Textual Commentary on the Greek New Testament*,[14] Laney notes the simple fact that there are no Greek manuscripts that omit the exceptions.[15]

In dealing with our subject we shall find it helpful to break it down further into a study of the concept of exception, and then a study of the meaning of *porneia*, the Greek word for "unchastity" or "fornication."

"EXCEPT"

There are five major views of this part of the clause.

INCLUSIVIST INTERPRETATION

The first is the "inclusive" interpretation. Heth and Wenham describe this view's interpretative translation as "not even in the case of unchastity."[16]

The idea here is that *all* divorce is rejected by Jesus, even divorce that is grounded upon *unchastity*. Heth and Wenham also report several journal articles that criticize this view.[17] The criticism is that this translation is ill advised. Though it is possible in Matthew 5:32, D. A. Carson notes that such an interpretation plays havoc with the Greek in the Matthew 19:9 parallel, where the preposition (*epi*, "of" or "for") is preceded by a negation (*me*, "not"). That structure, "not for fornication," is the natural way of introducing an exception.[18] If the two Matthean exception clauses are intended to teach the same point (and we know of none who disputes this point), then the latter text is sufficient to help us make a choice against the "inclusivist" interpretation of the clause in Matthew 5:32.

PRETERITIVE VIEW

A second interpretation is a part of a broader interpretation (of the whole clause) that is known as the preteritive view. This school of thought, associated with Augustine in ancient times and with Bruce Vawter in our own,[19] is sometimes called the "no comment" view. It holds that Jesus skirted the Shammai-Hillel debate by refusing to comment on the offense-term in Deuteronomy 24:1. He simply used "unchastity" as a synonym for the argued "uncleanness" in the Old Testament passage. Thus, "except" has the effect of saying "and I do not get into the matter of *porneia*." Vawter, in effect, has Jesus being cryptic in an effort to avoid the paradoxical criticisms of the Pharisees.

After presenting the case for this view, Heth and Wenham reject it for grammatical reasons. Centering their discussion, as they consistently do, on the Matthew 19:9 teaching, they question whether the grammar and context will allow the clause to be interpreted parenthetically. To this they add that in Matthew 5 it is highly unlikely that Jesus is trying to be cryptic, insofar as he is here trying to *clarify* Pharisaical misinterpretation.[20]

SEPARATION VIEW

The third view sees the exception as permitting separation of the couple, but not divorce. Q. Quesnell supports this view, as do G. J. Wenham and J. Dupont.[21] D. A. Carson's critique is telling: the key verb (*apoleo*) is used twice in the Matthew 19 parallel. In verse 3, it has the undoubted meaning "to divorce." "It is unwarranted to understand the same verb a few verses later in some other way."[22]

OFFENSE-CLARIFICATION VIEW

The fourth view argues that the purpose of the exception clause is to clarify when the sin of adultery has taken place. There are actually two species of this position. The first is offered by John Kilgallen. To him, the except clause informs us that some divorce, that is, divorce based upon *porneia*, is not adulterous, for the adultery was already present in the *porneia*. The divorced woman will not then be "made to be an adulteress" by subsequent remarriage, because the fornication has already rendered her an adulteress.[23] D. A. Carson rejects this conclusion for grammatical reasons. The passive infinitive, he replies, does not say the remarriage causes her to *be* an adulteress but to commit adultery. Carson adds that Kilgallen's interpretation will not work in Matthew 19:9, the parallel construction, because there it is the man, not the woman, who will commit adultery.[24]

Carson's first rejoinder is debatable; some would argue that Carson's own rendering is unfaithful to the *passive* voice of the infinitive (his translation is active). Kilgallen might reply that in both verses the same point carries. In 5:32a the husband will not be guilty for making his wife be or commit adultery in remarriage, because she already is an adulteress by reason of her prior fornication. In 19:9 the husband will not be guilty of committing adultery in his own remarriage, because of his first wife's prior fornication. In each case the issue is when divorce (and remarriage) will be accounted as adultery to the husband. In each the answer is only when the first wife has not committed fornication prior to their divorce. Recall that, even in 5:32a, the issue is not the guilt of the wife but of the divorcing husband. I consider this a possible interpretation, but still question Kilgallen's assumption that remarriage of the wife may be assumed in 5:32a.

Heth and Wenham take a similar position. They argue that the exception clause may only mean that the "divorce of an unchaste woman would not make her an adulteress, for she probably is already an adulteress."[25] But whereas Kilgallen removes the judgment of adultery from the divorce, Heth and Wenham do not necessarily do so. We later learn that, to them, *porneia*-based divorce is not to be considered adulterous, but it is still a moral offense unless the husband was forced by his culture to put his unchaste wife away.[26] The problem with this view, however, is that it argues from silence. What is the offense of divorces not grounded in *porneia*? Why allege fault where none is stated by the text?

PERMISSIBLE DIVORCE

The fifth view is that Jesus hereby signifies an exception to the general rule—no divorce. This interpretation is by far the one preferred by scholars, but there agreement ends, for they differ widely over the meaning of the crucial offense-term: *porneia*.

"PORNEIA"

Steele and Ryrie provide a rather nice table of the five interpretations of this word *porneia*.[27] From it we draw this list:

1. The Betrothal (engagement) View: *Porneia* means a preconsummational breach of chastity. (Isaksson)
2. The Consanguinity (incest/illicit marriage) View: *Porneia* means *incest*, as in Leviticus 18. (Laney, Steele and Ryrie)
3. The Preteritive ("no comment") View: *Porneia* means "whatever *uncleanness* means in Deuteronomy 24:1–4." (Vawter)
4. The Patristic (early fathers') View: *Porneia* means *adultery*. (Heth and Wenham)
5. The Erasmian (Erasmus's) View: *Porneia* means *adultery* or some other sexual offense. (Murray, Duty)

The great question that must be asked in response to each of these views is, What is the support for this definition of the term? We must be especially careful to interrogate views that intentionally delimit or expand the term beyond the lexicon. We must consider both the lexicon and the prior biblical context in deciding the issue. We shall start with the more restrictive of the views and work toward the more expansive.

CRITIQUE OF THE BETROTHAL VIEW

The betrothal view is one that holds that Jesus employs *porneia* in a technical sense, restricting its use from its usual broad meaning to betrothal unfaithfulness. (Mary's alleged offense was thought by Joseph to be an instance of *porneia* in this sense.) The most able defender of this view is A. Isaksson, who did a noteworthy linguistic study of *porneia*.[28] Though the study contains much valuable information, Isaksson does not make his case. He cannot show either that *porneia* ever incontrovertibly means *betrothal unfaithfulness* or that *porneia* must be so limited in the Matthew texts.[29]

He is nearer to showing the former than the latter, however. For though Heth and Wenham controvert his use of the Joseph and Mary incident, their objection rings hollow. These authors press the fact that the Matthew 1 verses do not, strictly speaking, use *porneia*, though the technical term for "divorce" is used.[30] But if these critics are correct, why did Joseph seek to put Mary away? If Jesus' teaching agrees with the Old Testament, then whatever Joseph thought Mary had done to find herself pregnant must be a species of *porneia*. It is difficult to think of Joseph imagining anything other than that Mary had been unfaithful. Insofar as virgin births were unheard of, betrothal unfaithfulness must have been his best guess! Is it not most reasonable to believe that Joseph felt that unrepentant betrothal unfaithfulness *should* lead to divorce?[31]

Another odd thing about Heth and Wenham's criticism of Isaksson is that in several pages of "fair-play" support for that position they note the seriousness with which Eastern cultures view such unfaithfulness,[32] but these two Westerners never seem to consider adequately that in the Old Testament both pre- and postconsummational unfaithfulness were considered the same offense (Deut. 22:22–27). The language is the same: the neighbor's "wife" or "woman" has been "violated." In short, betrothal unfaithfulness is, according to the Old Testament, a kind of adultery.[33]

Because adultery was to be dealt with by divorce (since execution was not practiced), Joseph, "being a righteous man," sought to "divorce her." Thus, the betrothal view seems to be correct in arguing that betrothal unfaithfulness is intended by *porneia*. But this view unfortunately continues to argue that such betrothal unfaithfulness is the only kind of unfaithfulness entailed in *porneia*. If the proponents of this view were to include postconsummative unfaithfulness the view itself would be destroyed. The integrity of the view depends upon limiting the meaning of *porneia* to the betrothal period. Of course, they might argue that only betrothal adultery is in view in Matthew, but the reference in Matthew 1 is not strong enough to sustain that. The mind of the listener would have included more in the meaning of *porneia* than the betrothal view allows, given the common usage of the word, so the burden of proof rests upon the betrothal school. And they cannot bear it.

CRITIQUE OF THE ILLEGAL MARRIAGES VIEW

It is clearer to divide the illegal marriages posture into two distinct schools: those holding that *porneia* primarily means *incest*[34] and those who think it primarily refers to interfaith marriages.[35]

We shall critique each species of this view in turn.

INTERFAITH MARRIAGES

First, let us look at the idea that *porneia* means interfaith marriages. According to this opinion, Jesus wishes to exclude from moral condemnation divorces to end marriages between Jews and Gentiles or between Christians and unbelievers. There are, of course, biblical precedents for both these alternatives. The Law forbade marriage between the people of the covenant and the people of the land (Deut. 7:3, et passim). The Ezra incident shows that legal severance of interfaith marriages was a proper corrective for such breaches of the Mosaic Law. I do not believe that Jesus would disagree with the prophet (and therefore, the Scriptures). Since the Ezra incident was relatively recent (in the whole history of the people), and insofar as Jesus often underscored the teachings of the prophets, it is not at all farfetched that Jesus wished to include such righteous, disciplinary divorces in the category of those that were not offensive.

Heth and Wenham, however, controvert this use of Ezra by casting doubt over the validity of interfaith marriages. Their point is that the exception clause deals with *real marriages*, whereas interfaith marriages were possibly seen as only *fornicating relationships*. They highlight the fact that Ezra uses rather unusual terms for the "marriages" of the apostates and for their forced "divorces."[36] Ezra, they tell us, was a very exacting scribe, and his rejection of the standard terminology should not be passed over lightly. I agree, but the conclusions they draw are hasty.

It is to be expected that Ezra would disparage the marriages of the apostates. If these relationships were offensive enough to cause him to tear his clothing, it is probable that he would tear at the relationships verbally. After all, as pointed out in the earlier section concerning Ezra, the marriages were anomalies. They were marriages; that is, they had been contracted in the very way that acceptable unions were. But these "legal" marriages of the apostates were unacceptable to the Mosaic legislation. Thus, they were at once legal and illegal. They were legal according to prevailing law, but illegal according to God's Law. Since they were legal according to prevailing laws, it would not do to simply ask the men to stop acting like husbands to the women of the land. Ezra's corrective could not have been simply along the lines of Paul's in 1 Corinthians 6:18: "flee immorality." No, the quasi-legal bond must be dissolved. And that dissolution was, according to prevailing law, a valid divorce.[37]

But to say that the historical context reminds us of illicit intermarriage between Jews and Gentiles is one thing, to suggest that Jesus is, in the Sermon, trying to continue mere ethnic purity is another. For although all his disciples were then Jews, it is presumptuous to suggest that our Lord did not, in his clarification of the standards of holiness, provide for disciples in all ages.[38] In view of the important New Testament teaching that in Christ there is neither Jew nor Greek, is it wise to suggest that Jesus continued the division?

Some would suggest yes, insofar as Jesus professed to have come only to the lost sheep of the house of Israel. But I see such exclusiveness as only a tactical move on his part, much the way Paul, the Apostle of the Gentiles, seems to have gone first to the Jews in each of the cities of the dispersion, regarding them as the most likely candidates to receive the gospel. But just as Paul "turned to the Gentiles," so too Jesus in his ministry also went to the Gentiles (Matt. 15:21 ff.). Doubtless the words and ideas of the Sermon were rhetorically designed for Jewish disciples' ears, but we should guard against making Jesus say things contrary to the teachings of his disciples, to whom he promised the Holy Spirit to "lead them into all truth" (John 16:23) and to whom he gave the task of discipling the nations, "teaching them to observe all that I taught you" (Matt. 28:20).

Some might suggest that Jew-Gentile intermarriage might have been proscribed as a concession to the Jewish community. Though at first seemingly supported by the Council of Jerusalem's dictates (which appear to have a similar design), this is unacceptable. Such a concession more closely parallels Peter's avoiding gentile fellowship in order to impress his Jewish friends (cf. Gal. 2:11 ff.), and such compromises are clearly condemned in the New Testament by the Apostle Paul. It is one thing to ask Gentiles to forgo certain forms of behavior so as not to offend Jews. It is quite another to tell Jewish believers to refrain from marrying Gentile unbelievers so as not to offend Jews. In the first case, Gentiles are asked to act like Jews so as to break down the wall dividing them; in the second, Jews are being asked to preserve the wall.

With regard to intermarriage between Christians and unbelievers, Paul, in his second letter to the Corinthians, does apply the Old Testament principle of separation to the people of the new covenant. Perhaps even this early on in the spreading of the kingdom message Jesus wanted his disciples to know that interfaith marriages were unacceptable to a standard of true discipleship. But is Jesus referring in the Sermon to sinning disciples who need to have their lives straightened out by disciplinary divorces?

Though it is true that each of the first three sayings in the Sermon implies the disciple is a sinner, a careful reading of verses 31 and 32 shows that the sinner is only a sinner *when he divorces*, not prior to the divorce. The saying seems to assume that the divorce is only valid if the wife is guilty of *porneia*, not the husband! In my view, then, though a divorce that aims at being a "fruit of repentance" would not be adulterous (because grounded upon the adultery of the marriage itself), we cannot see that this is the primary meaning of Jesus' words in Matthew 5:31.

INCEST

Besides interfaith marriages, another species of illicit marriages would be those that are incestuous. A leading proponent (in America) of the "incest" interpretation of *porneia* is Carl Laney. Arguing for another technical definition of *porneia* in the exception clauses, Laney offers several points for our consideration.[39]

First, *porneia* as "incest" is a New Testament usage. Borrowing from F. F. Bruce, Laney analyzes the structure of the definition of the Council of Jerusalem (Acts 15:20, 29) to determine the usage there of the word *porneia*. The Council's reordering (Acts 15:29) of James's list (Acts 15:20) of requirements for the Gentile believers evidences a thinly veiled dependence upon the "holiness code" of Leviticus 17:8–18:18 as a source for the suggestions. Assuming the Leviticus material to be ceremonial in nature, Laney argues that since *porneia* means "incest" in Acts 15 it could mean the same in the exception clauses.

Second, *porneia* as "incest" is a first-century Jewish usage. It is used that way in the Qumran materials (the Damascus Document), according to Joseph Fitzmyer.[40]

Third, *porneia* as "incest" fits the Jewish context. Here Laney presents his form of the "ethnic calculus": the holiness code is a Jewish concern, and that is why *porneia* is found in Matthew and not in Mark or Luke.

Fourth, *porneia* as "incest" fits the historical background. Here Laney ties the context of the Herod-Herodias affair to the exception clause in Matthew 19, arguing that restricting *porneia* to incest in that passage is all that is needed to give sufficient meaning in light of the historical context. Moreover, a pronouncement by Jesus would have been needed, since "incestuous marriage was obviously rather popular among the political leaders of Palestine in the first century" (citing not only Herod Antipas, but also Archelaus and Herod Agrippa II as evidence). Laney sums up these arguments by saying that "Jesus seems to be [saying] that it would be better for a couple to separate and end an illegal marriage than to continue an illicit sexual relationship."[41]

The major problem with this form of the illegal marriages view is that, like the forms already criticized, it fails to show that what is doubtless *a kind* of *porneia* is the *only kind* intended by Jesus in the questioned passages. Even if we grant all Laney's arguments, the definition of *porneia* may still be properly considered *in*clusive rather than *ex*clusive. Moreover, some of the arguments themselves are flawed. For instance, Heth and Wenham, by rather thorough analysis, show that the attempt to limit *porneia* in Acts 15 to a "holiness code" item, relevant only to ancient Israel, is fraught with problems. It could well be that the list in Acts represents the "Noaic Constitutions," that is, universal prohibitions against idolatry, blood drinking, and fornication or, as the Western Text has the list in Acts 15, idolatry, fornication, and murder. Either of these latter lists involves "essentials," to use the wording of Acts 15:28.[42]

Similarly, Heth and Wenham point out that Leviticus 18 itself does not seem to be dealing with matters of Christian liberty. They ask if believers are free to practice incest today.[43] Of course not, and realizing this leads the critic to inquire further into Laney's use of the Acts/Leviticus tie. Why, one may ask, does Laney limit the Leviticus reference to Leviticus 17:8–14(16) and Leviticus 18:6–18? Why does he skip Leviticus 18:1–5 and 18:19–30? Since these sections too are a part of the "code," one would think they would be relevant. The apparent reason for the arbitrary exclusion is that the banished portions show two things that are destructive to Laney's thesis:

1. Leviticus 18:1–5 and 24–30 show that the *porneia* equivalents found therein are the gross sins of the *Gentiles,* which caused God to remove them from the land; they are not a list of ceremonial rituals at all. Thus, Laney's effort to direct the discussion to something peculiarly Jewish, that is, a "holiness code" matter, backfires.
2. Leviticus 18:19–23 includes other offenses that would logically have to be classified as *porneia* equivalents: adultery, homosexuality, bestiality. But the whole effort to restrict *porneia* to a technical use is vitiated by expanding the list to include these. Adultery, especially, is a concept that Laney is at pains to exclude from the meaning of *porneia.* Again, the effort defeats itself and actually supports a quite broad definition of the questioned term.

Though Laney has failed to make his point, reviewing his material is helpful in establishing a broader definition of *porneia.* More will be said about that when we analyze the views of the patristic and Erasmian schools. But first we must return to the preteritive view's idea of *porneia.*

CRITIQUE OF THE PRETERITIVE VIEW

Since this position has already been criticized in other regards, here I merely point out that, if Jesus did intentionally avoid controversy regarding the meaning of "uncleanness" in Deuteronomy 24:1, *porneia* could mean anything. It really does not matter. Although a particular definition might be correct for *porneia/*"uncleanness," it is of no consequence to our understanding of the morality of divorce and remarriage.

CRITIQUE OF THE PATRISTIC AND ERASMIAN VIEWS

Some might see the patristic and Erasmian views as limiting the meaning of *porneia* to "adultery," but their proponents generally define that word "sexual infidelity."[44] Though they argue long for the inclusion of adultery in *porneia*,[45] they would also include the other sexual offenses, such as homosexuality and bestiality, probably including them and incest as forms of adultery. The support for such breadth comes in part from the lexicon. Guy Duty lists most modern lexicons up to his writing (1967) and adequately shows the standard definition of *porneia* to be "sexual immorality in general."[46] This holds true for the Hebrew parallel term *zānâh* and the use of *porneia* in the Septuagint.

What then could be the complaint against this definition? Laney offers the following:[47]

1. *Porneia* is not the normal word for "adultery." The normal Greek word is *moicheia,* which is much narrower in scope. The two terms should not be equated.[48]
2. The words are found in the same verses, which indicates that they are not intended to be synonyms (cf. Matt. 15:19; Mark 7:21; 1 Cor. 6:9; Gal. 5:19; Heb. 13:4).

Several responses are in order. First, it is true that *porneia* is not the normal word for "adultery"; however, no one really argues that it is. Rather, these schools believe that *porneia* includes *moichos.* This Laney himself seems to admit when he says that "*porneia* can be used in a broad sense in the New Testament to refer to any kind of unlawful sexual activity."[49]

Second, the passages that include both terms retain a sense of the distinctiveness of each when you presume the concentric nature of their definitions. For instance, careful consideration of Matthew 15:19 reveals the overlapping nature of terms:

For out of the heart come evil thoughts, murders, adulteries, fornications, thefts, false witness, slanders. These are the things which defile the man . . .

Note that, in this series, no less than four times a more *limited* concept precedes a *broader* concept that (linguistically) encompasses it:

1. "Things which defile" includes all previous items on the list.
2. "Murders, adulteries, fornications, thefts, false witness, and slanders" all include "evil thoughts," for the text tells us that it is "from the heart" that such things come.
3. "Slanders" include "false witness," although sometimes slander might include truthful witness.
4. "Fornication" includes "adultery" but also other unseemly things, such as homosexuality, bestiality, and incest.

As may readily be observed, the narrower term(s) comes first, immediately followed by the broader term(s). In this list, Jesus goes from the specific to the more general, so as to catch up other evils not implied by the narrower term.

As for the other passages, Mark 7:21 (a parallel text to Matt. 15:19) does not have the poetic structure of its parallel, but the obvious overlap is present. Would Laney wish to argue that "coveting" is totally distinct from "thefts," or that "pride" and "foolishness" are mutually exclusive? First Corinthians 6:9 yields the same analysis: is "theft" separable from "coveting"? As for Galatians 5:19–21, is there not linguistic overlap between "strife" and "outbursts of anger, disputes, dissensions, factions"? Only Hebrews 13:4 does not allow such a comparative analysis. But that does not mean that the writer is not using them as synonymous parallelisms: "fornicators even adulterers God will judge."[50] Laney is far from making his case against the *general* sexual meaning of *porneia*.

I would suggest, however, that there are two moot issues in the definition of *porneia* held by these two schools: First, should *porneia* be limited to the realm of sexuality? I am not trying to suggest that sexuality is not the marked *connotation* of *porneia;* rather, in view of the Old Testament understanding of "spiritual" *porneia,* might not one leave open the possibility of *porneia* being defined in principle as "activity against the covenant"? Although this would readily seem to be far too broad, I shall presently give evidence that a broadened definition of *moichos* (implicit in *porneia*) was indeed the intention of our Lord, and that, when that meaning was fully understood by the Pharisees, they sought to challenge him on the matter, namely, in the Matthew 19 incident. We shall discuss the matter in greater detail in chapter 7.

A second point, and one that is far more questionable, is whether Jesus intended *porneia,* as a grounds for legitimate divorce, to include male "unfaithfulness," in the sense of "sexual infidelity." We must remember that in the ancient world it was never the case that a man's sexual activities outside his relationship with his own spouse would be considered "adultery" against her. The practice of polygamy and the definition of the fornication laws in the Bible preclude any interpretation of such activity as adultery against her. Even his adultery against another man's covenant (i.e., his sexual relations with another man's wife) would not have been considered adultery against his own wife.

Such activities would, however, have been considered *porneia*, not against his wife, but against God (cf. 1 Cor. 7:2). Yet there is a very good reason for not interpreting a husband's *porneia* as being grounds for his wife divorcing him. In the first place, the Old Testament at no point made it such. Second, Jesus' comments on the point specifically speak of the man divorcing his wife on the ground of *porneia;* the comments make no reference to her divorcing him on such grounds. But can we not simply assume that the exception clause may be reversed? After all, does Jesus not reverse the condemnation of a woman who divorces her own husband (Mark 10:12)?

I believe not, and for the following reason: Jesus makes it a point to note that a woman who divorces her husband is guilty of adultery. This is to say, where the difference in sex of the spouse is relevant, he notes the reciprocity. Lest any think that a woman may divorce her husband without bearing the onus of adultery, Jesus makes it clear that that is not the case. But Jesus does not offer *porneia* as grounds for the woman to divorce her husband. Had he intended that, we may presume that he would have made a statement to that effect. Neither does Jesus deny that a woman may legitimately divorce her husband for his intentional failure to provide or for his abuse of her. If he had, he would have been abrogating a right given in the Law. Jesus is silent about such matters, because he is not discussing the woman's right to divorce but, rather, the man's rights and responsibilities.[51]

Remember that Jesus is trying to clarify the meaning of the Law of God. That Law needed clarification on the point of the woman's unfaithfulness, insofar as the execution strictures (Deut. 22; Lev. 20, etc.) were no longer and could no longer be exercised and the marriage ended in that way. But on the point of the woman's grounds for putting away her husband for abuse, the Law was still clear and relevant (though often ignored by the rabbis). For Jesus to have allowed for a woman to put her husband away for *porneia* would have been for him to have introduced an application not in accord with the Law, to have introduced a custom not arising from previous biblical principle.[52]

Finally, we must ask whether Heth and Wenham are correct in seeing the effect of the exception clause as only freeing from the stain of adultery a man who is forced by his culture to divorce an adulterous wife. On this view, the definition of *porneia* remains as the broad Erasmian position asserts, but effectively ends up in the place of the preteritive view, which denies that the exception clause has anything to do with the prohibition of divorce. The divorce is still wrong, but the guilt for it is charged to the woman's account.[53]

This view is inadequate for three reasons. First, I believe that the Old Testament (Jer. 3:1; Isa. 50:1; and Hosea 1 and 2) and the New (Matt. 1:19; 18:15 ff.) are united in their approval of divorce as a discipline. For Jesus to go against this tradition would be for him to abrogate the penalties for adultery. He denies that he intends to do any such thing (Matt. 5:17 ff.).[54] Second, it is highly questionable to interpret Matthew as saying, "He who divorces his wife is guilty of adultery unless he is forced to do so because his wife has committed adultery, in which case she is responsible for the sin that such divorce instances." About the best that can be said for this interpretation is that it would be in harmony with the absolute prohibition of divorce already held to by Heth and Wenham. Finally, this view creates an interesting ethical dilemma. How is it possible that a culture can force a man to divorce his wife if he refuses to do so? Would we not hold such a man responsible to stand against his culture and uphold the ideal of God?

Does God accommodate culture in that way? Daniel and his three friends would surely have adopted a different stance if they had had Heth and Wenham to advise them! But Daniel and company were not slow to stand against immoral culture; they refused to compromise their standards. And God is no more to be bullied than they. Was his divorce of Israel a result of cultural pressure?[55] In short, I find this variation ethically sub-biblical.

"Makes Her Commit Adultery"

AN ADULTERESS OR A STIGMATIZED WOMAN?

The clause "makes her commit adultery" appears to fly in the face of the entire doctrine of marriage that I have been setting forth in this work. It seems to controvert the idea that a divorce ends the marriage relationship, for, if the woman who is presumed innocent and is divorced by her husband is still liable to being classified as an adulteress when she remarries, then one can only conclude that her marital union still exists in spite of the legalities. Even Murray, who holds to the view that the innocent party may remarry, says,

The evil of putting away (for any other reason than that of adultery) is viewed from the standpoint of what it entails for the woman divorced. The man "makes her to be an adulteress." . . . The man is not said in this case to commit adultery; his sin is rather that he becomes implicated in the wrong of adultery on the part of his dismissed wife.[56]

Like almost all the scholars who comment on this clause (and a surprising number simply ignore it when it comes to detail), Murray accepts two questionable points in concluding as he does.

1. The aorist infinitive (*moikeuthanai*) is properly translated as an active "to commit adultery." Says Murray, "It is apparent that the sense is active and means, "to commit adultery.""[57]
2. The act of adultery is not the divorce but the remarriage, which is envisioned in the next clause ("and he who marries a divorced woman commits adultery"). Murray: "The wife does not become an adulteress simply by being divorced. . . . It is necessary, therefore, to envisage some subsequent action in which the woman is involved as drawn within the scope of this expression 'Makes her to suffer adultery.' "[58]

Murray was aware, however, that R. C. H. Lenski had previously challenged this traditional interpretive framework. In 1943 Lenski argued the following points:[59]

1. The woman of 5:32a is innocent of wrong. It is her husband who has destroyed the marriage by the divorce—rendering her unable to fulfil her marital commitments. It is improper grammatically

to find the responsible agent for her "adultery" in a second, hypothetical husband, for the causal agent of an infinitive must precede it.

2. The "adultery" relating to the wife is said to occur at the time of
the divorce, not in some subsequent marriage; 5:32a and 5:32b
are independent clauses.

3. The woman is said to "suffer" the adultery, not "commit" it. The
infinitive is passive not active, and no one has shown that it should
be translated actively.

4. Therefore, it seems better to interpret this verse as condemning
the woman's husband for stigmatizing her as an adulteress.

Murray attempts to do the missing study Lenski laments. Murray
first notes that the passive of *moikeuo* occurs only two other times in
the New Testament, once in the parallel saying of Matthew 19:9 and
once in John 8:4. But he goes on to point out that the former is unhelpful, since it is in exactly the same saying, and the John 8 passage
is textually doubtful, though he adds that those verses are "helpful in
determining the meaning of the passive, if *moikeuomena* [the form in
John 8:4] is regarded as passive rather than middle."[60] Murray's discussion of this text actually appears on the next page in the continuation of the note. There he argues that it has the sense of active if
passive, but could be middle. Few, if any, would regard the form in
John 8:4 as other than middle. In fact, the context of John 8 demands
that the woman be identified as the actor because it comes in a statement of charges against her. The Pharisees are reported as saying,
"This woman has been caught in the act *herself* committing adultery"
(emphasis added).

Murray then considers evidence from the Septuagint and finds but
one "possible" instance of the passive of *moikeuo* in the canonical books:
Leviticus 20:10. Actually, the verb form *moikeusatai* appears twice in
that verse. He forthwith identifies that form as aorist subjunctive *middle,* translating the Hebrew imperfect *Qal* construction of the verb. He
then states that it should be translated in the sense of an active verb
form ("to commit adultery"). Thus far, this is not very impressive, as
the middle form is usually translated with an active sense, and the verse
in Matthew 5:32 is definitely not a middle but a passive. Then Murray
enters upon a long discussion of how the Greek noun (*moikeuomena*)
translated "the adulterer" and "the adulteress" is itself a translation of
the Hebrew active participle ("committing adultery"). But here, too,
Murray is blocked by the fact that *moikeuomena* (a noun, which arises
from the more basic verb form) may arise from the middle (indicative)
rather than the passive form of *moikeuo*. Given the context of the word
in Leviticus 20:10, this is by far the most likely choice. But Murray

drives onward with an "if" argument that I leave to the reader's discretion to pursue.

A passage from Sirach (23:23) is then discussed. The form of the verb here is aorist passive (*hemoikeutha*). The wording could be either of the following:

And, thirdly, she commits adultery in fornication and brings in children by a strange man.

And, thirdly, she is made to suffer adultery in fornication and brings in children by a strange man.

Murray finds the former the more "natural,"[61] but argues that in either case the context shows that the woman is guilty of actively committing the offense of adultery.[62] It is true that the woman is known to have been guilty of actively committing adultery, but it is not clear that we know that from the verb in question. We know it from verse 23, which tells us that she "leaves her husband and brings in an heir by a stranger." This is not a case of divorce (as the woman could not initiate that except in the case of her husband's abuse—which the context seemingly excludes) but of desertion. In other words, we may choose the second option and still see within it the offense of adultery—because of the context, not because it is necessary to translate the verb actively.[63]

But is this not the very point to be raised concerning the Matthean passage, namely, that the context there implies *nothing of the kind?* The actor there is most definitely the divorcing husband. If, as Lenski insists (and concerning which Murray has nothing grammatically to say), it is improper to bring the subsequent clause ("and the man who marries the divorced woman") into the interpretation of the questioned clause, then Murray has not proven his point, but may in fact have proven what he intended to deny, that is, that the woman is the recipient of the stigmatization as an adulteress in the event of the divorce.

In spite of this shaky groundwork, Murray becomes emphatic:

In Matthew 5:32, therefore, it is not impossible to regard *moikeuthanai* as having an active meaning, namely, to "commit adultery." In this case the clause would be rendered, "he makes her to commit adultery." But whether this be the sense or not, it is not feasible to exclude from the word *moikeuthanai* actual involvement in the sin of adultery. Let the sense be active or passive, the woman is conceived of as entering into adulterous relations.[64]

It may be helpful at this point to get out of the exegetical swamp and try and find a hill from which we can get a better perspective on where we have come from and where we are. Murray's work at this point may create in the reader exegetical vertigo. He makes us feel that the burden of proof rests upon his opponent (Lenski) rather than upon himself. We must remember several grammatical points:

1. The verb form in the text of Matthew 5:32 is an aorist passive infinitive. The presumption is that the translation should reveal the action as *against* the woman, not as being done by her.
2. The exception to this basic rule is that deponent verbs may have this form and be translated actively, but ours is *not* a deponent verb.
3. The sense of the aorist tense is that the action occurred at some definite point in the past.
4. A passive aorist would normally be translated "I was _____ed." In the case of our verse, "She was adulterized."
5. An infinitive is a verb form that has a number of uses. It could point out either the purpose or the result of the main verb. The main verb in Matthew 5:32 is "causes" or "makes," which in turn is further defined by the first verb: "is divorcing."
6. Thus: "the one who is divorcing is causing his wife *to be adulterized*"—or simply, when he divorces her he commits adultery against her.

It would seem to me, however, that Murray has shown that in only one possible instance, namely, Sirach 23:23, does a definitely passive form of the verb "commit adultery" have a possibly active sense. And that sense is really determined by a context that is significantly different from the one in the Matthean Sermon. In Sirach 23:23 the woman is at fault because she deserted her husband and had relations with another man (all one sentence), whereas in the Matthew 5:32 passage the woman has been legally deserted by her husband and, for all that independent clause tells us, may *never* have had relations with another man (such a relation is mentioned in a second, independent clause). Murray seems to be skating on rather thin exegetical ice. Certainly it is not normal procedure to use such an exceptional point to overturn the standard rules.

Yet Murray concludes the argument in his note by engaging Lenski directly. His main argument centers upon Lenski's self-admittedly tentative translation of the passive as, "brings about that she is stigmatized as adulterous." Murray insists that

such an interpretation of the force of the aorist passive is wholly unwarranted. While it is true that some kind of passive force may have to be recognized, the passive cannot be forced into this kind of service. The idea of merely subjective judgment on the part of others is not inherent in the passive. And whatever strength may be given to the passive in this case, the woman is still viewed as implicated in adultery.[65]

One cannot resist a couple of rejoinders to Murray. First, though it may be grammatically unwarranted since not inherent, that is not to say that the context might not warrant such a translation. It is to be remembered that the Old Testament was quite concerned about the stigmatizing of a pure woman. Twice the Law spoke to such issues (Num. 5:31 by allusion, if she was innocent he will bear guilt; Deut. 22:17–19, if she was innocent he had to pay one hundred shekels of silver, or about one hundred months' wages). If a disciple is to divorce his wife only on the grounds of "unchastity," that is, adultery, but then divorces her without these grounds, what does the divorce imply about this woman? The watching world will see the divorce and assume that the woman is guilty of adultery. This in effect puts the sin of the husband upon the head of the woman! He broke his vow of provision by divorcing her (a nonsexual form of adultery or treachery; see appendix D) and framed her with the stigma of being guilty of the only grounds for divorce allowed in the kingdom: sexual adultery. Thus, the woman is treated like a piece of property that has received the stamp of defective, when, in fact, it is the stamper who is morally defective. Moreover, grammatically, if the idea of the infinitive as a purpose of the main verb is stressed, it makes sense to say that the aim of his divorcing her is to render her adulterized, or "as an adulteress." This might even be stronger if the infinitive were rendered as a noun: "He makes her an adulteress."

An "Adulterized" Woman

But the likelihood is that the adulterization that the text wishes to express is not his "making her out to be" an adulteress (so Lenski), but rather that his act of divorcing makes her adulterized. In other words, it seeks to identify her husband as an adulterer. After all, the chief problem with the prevailing Pharisaical teachings on Deuteronomy 24:1–4 was their implication that the husband was guiltless and the woman undesirable, perhaps for serious moral reasons. But as I have shown in chapter 3, the text of Deuteronomy intends nothing of the kind; it was intended to protect the woman from such a man. How ironic that Murray and others have preserved the exact Pharisaical mistake by insisting that the woman is "implicated in adultery." Rather, it is the husband who is guilty of adultery in Matthew 5:31 f.

The context bears this out:

Matt. 5:21–26   You think that you are innocent of murder, because you only did it in your heart? You are wrong. You are guilty of murder!

Matt. 5:27–30   You think that you are innocent of adultery, because you only lusted in your mind? You are wrong. You are guilty of adultery!

Matt. 5:31–32   You think that you are innocent of adultery, because you have a legal writ? You are wrong. You are guilty of adultery!

It would be as wrongheaded to suggest that the wife was complicitous in the adultery of 5:32a as to suggest that the woman of 5:28 was complicitous in the lust, or that the brother of 5:23 was deserving of the unjust anger.[66] No, the context draws us inexorably to the conclusion that the woman *suffers* the offense of adultery in the event of the divorce. Simply, "everyone who divorces his wife, except for the cause of unchastity, makes her to suffer adultery." This is exactly what the Old Testament Law says in Malachi 2. The man who has divorced his wife solely to marry somebody else is guilty of treachery against her.

But if this is so, why does not Jesus simply say "everyone who divorces his wife, except for the cause of unchastity, is committing adultery against her"? Why does Jesus make a point of using the difficult passive form? My suspicion is that, as Lenski suggested, there is an issue of stigma in such cases. But the stigma is not the only issue, or even the most important issue, at hand. Lenski was wrong in making stigma the primary idea of the clause in question. It is a secondary point, but one that the text does not want to miss. I believe that only the aorist passive infinitive is able—in as few words—to convey the idea of both Malachi 2 and Deuteronomy 22:19.[67]

It is indeed interesting to compare Matthew and Deuteronomy on this matter of difficult verb forms. In each case, the biblical text has made it hard on us by choosing a verb that in one way or another is nearly *hapox* (used in the Bible only once). The Hebrew translated "she has been defiled" is without parallel in the Old Testament. Even the verb form is nearly once-spoken. The commenting passage in Matthew 5:32 flashes at us another unusual form. And it is difficult to know whether to use Deuteronomy to interpret Matthew, or Matthew to interpret Deuteronomy. Should we translate "suffers adultery" as "adulterizes herself" because the Hebrew has a seeming reflexive/passive idea, or should we translate the Hebrew "she has been defiled [by her husband who cast her to another man]"? Should we use the fact that only when the second marriage occurs does Deuteronomy declare the woman defiled (thus perhaps implying that the union remains) to suggest (after all we have said) that, in Matthew, the clause following the questioned infinitive *does* give the cause to the infinitive? Or, should we allow the sufficiency of the stigmatization-in-the-divorce of the treacherously divorced woman help us infer that it is the husband (in Deuteronomy) who allows his wife to contract a marriage with another man who is the defiler? Or perhaps we should not see the two as synonyms after all; perhaps it is that the woman who suffers adultery becomes defiled (i.e., morally "off-limits") with regard to her hard-hearted husband when he allows her to marry another rather than seeking reconciliation.

My own feeling is that we should allow the Matthew passage to inform the Deuteronomic one, because that is what Jesus is trying to do in the Sermon at that point. There was misunderstanding regarding the Deuteronomic passage, and Jesus is trying to clear the problem up. The Pharisees regarded the husband of Deuteronomy 24:1 as righteous and the woman as guilty and defiled. Jesus reversed this to say that the man who took advantage of the Deuteronomic concession was guilty of adultery, and the woman was innocent of moral guilt, though stigmatized. Matthew is probably silent regarding the defilement of Deuteronomy 24:4 precisely because, having stated that the woman was put away with definite force (as if "once and for all"), it is not necessary to reaffirm the obvious, that is, if she remarries she may not return to the former husband. The Pharisees, after all, did not argue about that; nor did they misunderstand the rule in that respect. The main intent of both Deuteronomy 24:1–4 and Matthew 5:31–32 is to protect the woman from a hard-hearted husband who is treacherously inclined to treat her like chattel property. Deuteronomy 24 emphasizes the protection of the innocent wife. Matthew 5 emphasizes the culpability of the divorcing husband. Deuteronomy is not trying to exonerate the husband of the guilt of a form of adultery; Matthew is not trying to implicate the wife in adultery. Deuteronomy is not trying to offer a legal way out of a broken marriage; Matthew is not trying to prohibit the legal ending of a broken marriage. And by the same token, it is not the main purpose of Matthew to teach that legal way. The exception clause is only an aside to the main point: implicating the treacherous divorcer as an adulterer in the eyes of God.

A final comment on this difficult verse relates to the key verb in this difficult clause: *makes*. Some versions translate this verb "causes," and that raises an interesting contrast between this word and another, similar concept of causation in Matthew 5:29. The earlier verb is *scandalizo*, which means "cause, obstruct, or offend." Carson notes that its noun form is used "originally referring to the trigger of a trap (cf. Rom. 11:9)."[68] This verb is full of the connotation of indirect cause. The other person stumbles, but you caused it. This causation is one act becoming the occasion of another's volitional act of sin.

The verb in Matthew 5:32 (*poieo*), however, seems to imply more direct causation. It is the divorcing husband who makes the wife do or be something. Given the close relationship of these verbs in the context, one is surprised that the text would not have repeated *scandalizo* rather than using *poieo*. Conceptually, the traditional interpretation, "causes her to commit adultery," involves the idea of an act that becomes the occasion for the woman stumbling into adultery *when she remarries*. In other words, the divorce was a *scandalon* to her—the trigger to the trap that sprang shut upon her at the time of her remarriage. Later uses of *scandalizo* in Matthew (18:6, 8, 9) support this point. Matthew uses that word whenever he wishes to speak of one person causing another to sin. It is not clear that he ever uses *poieo* for that purpose. It is true

that *poieo* is sometimes used with the infinitive to show action that results from the initial "makes." One lexicon, under "*poieo*," cites Mark
1:17, 7:37b, Luke 5:34, John 6:10, Acts 17:26, and Revelation 13:13b.[69]
Of these, however, only Acts and Revelation associate *poieo* with a passive infinitive, and in each case, there is no volitional choice involved
in the action of the infinitive. In our verse, by contrast, we are asked
to believe that the woman is forced by the divorce to enter into an act
of adultery. Why should we suppose this? Cannot that innocent woman
realize that to remarry would be to commit adultery and remain celibate for the rest of her life—living honorably with her parents' family?[70]

Jesus' teaching on the sin of groundless divorce was not understood
by his listeners. Even his own disciples misunderstood. Thus it was
necessary for him to return to this issue at a later time (i.e., Matt. 19),
when certain questions had formed in his disciples' minds and in the
minds of Jesus' critics. We will deal with his expanded restatement in
chapter 7, but before that, we will turn to the next aspect of Jesus'
teaching: What of the morality of remarriage? The next clause in Matthew 5:32b, deals with that subject. Because of the obvious relation of
this final saying in the Sermon to the content of Luke 16:18, we will
treat them together in the next chapter.

CHAPTER 6

The Teachings of Jesus on Divorce, Continued
(Matthew 5:32b/Luke 16:18)

THE DIVORCE TEACHINGS OF JESUS IN THE SERMON ON THE MOUNT (CONTINUED)

The Sin in Groundless Remarriage

> *"Whoever marries a [divorced woman] commits adultery."*
>
> *(Matthew 5:32b)*

Treatment of Matthew 5:32b seldom exceeds a paragraph or two, even among scholars. This logion is overshadowed by Matthew 19, a longer passage, by Luke 16:18, which seems more complete, and by its proximity to the logion of 5:32a, to which it sometimes seems appended. As a result, it is not allowed to speak for itself and in its own context.

Nonetheless, by searching out comments here and there, it becomes clear that there are several possible interpretations of it that can be and are held. To facilitate analysis of them, we will note first what appears to be the most straightforward position, then move to others that attempt to modify it.

ALTERNATIVE INTERPRETATIONS OF THE REMARRIAGE SAYING

The saying is a conditional (subjunctive) statement ("If . . . then"), called by some grammarians a "probable future" (expressed with the conjunction *ean*). This does not mean that the event spoken of will probably happen but that, *granted* the action of the main verb, the event will in all likelihood happen. The main verb ("marries") is an active aorist (point of action). Thus: "If [and when] anyone [whoever] marries . . . , he is [in the process of] committing adultery."

The most basic interpretation of this saying is the one that takes it precisely as it stands. It identifies a man marrying a divorced woman as an adulterer. This has the effect of a prohibition. Moreover, it is probably near necessity to presume that since a man cannot commit an outward sin of sexual adultery by himself, the divorced woman with whom he commits adultery is also guilty of it.[1] No judgment is made regarding the morality of marrying a divorced male, guilty or not.[2]

We may presume that this primitive understanding of the text was soon abandoned by interpreters because the verse was overshadowed by the Lucan sayings (16:18) that seem to equally prohibit marrying a divorced male. However, if Jesus expected his hearers to understand that, it is difficult to imagine whence he expected that knowledge to come. On the other hand, one may rejoin that that is precisely why he made the later statements. In any case, this basic position is usually altered in one of at least four ways. First, some have sought to expand the meaning of this saying to include more than the man and the divorced woman. Second, others have tried to limit the statement to only certain divorced women. Third, some qualify it according to time. Finally, some seek to reinterpret the nature of the offense-term (*adultery*) itself. Since most of these views presume that a real offense of adultery has occurred, it may be well to consider the last first, to see if the passage really prohibits remarriage.

Remarriage Only Stigmatizes

THE VIEW EXPLAINED

The classic defense of the position that reinterprets the offense involved was written by the Lutheran and Greek scholar R. C. H. Lenski. We previously considered his theory of stigmatization of the innocent woman in 5:32a ("brings about that she is stigmatized as adulterous"). We did not rule out the possibility of stigma, noting that on several occasions the Old Testament Law prohibited the defamation of a "virgin of Israel" (e.g., Deut. 22:19). However, we concluded that stigmatization was only a secondary meaning of the offense-phrase. It was perhaps enough of an issue to rule out the clearer active, "commits adultery against her" but not enough to unseat the preferable "causes her to be adulterized."

Lenski continued his theory of stigmatization into the conjoined logion, interpreting its meaning by the translation "and he who shall marry her that has been released is stigmatized as adulterous."[3] He explained this view further by arguing that the participle ("she who has been divorced") is both perfect and passive, conveying the idea *both* that this woman was put away and that that procedure is final. This idea, then, Lenski related to the preceding saying: the first husband was unjustly putting away his wife, and now the divorce is a completed fact.

Lenski further argues that the second husband is not the agent of the "adultery" but the recipient of it. Thus, just as the woman of saying *a* was not guilty of sin, but suffered it, the husband of saying *b* is not guilty of adultery, but only suffers it. What he suffers is then interpreted as in the saying about the woman. The man has not sinned, but only become stained with the same stigma as was previously described as staining his present wife.[4]

THE STIGMA VIEW CRITICIZED

We may first ask if this view makes sense on its face. Whereas the sayings so far in this section of the Sermon seem to be identifying as an offender a man who thinks he is innocent, the idea that the second husband does not commit adultery runs the other way: some might think the husband is guilty of adultery, but God wants to reveal him as innocent! Of course, it might be rejoined that the text indirectly identifies the divorcing first husband as the offender. But why then is the first husband not more clearly brought into the saying? In the first saying, the treacherous man is brought to the forefront. In 5:32b, it is the second husband who is at the forefront.

Clearly, the stigma view presupposes at least two points that, if they are not true, render the position incredible. First, the woman in question must be innocent of adultery. If the woman is guilty of adultery, then the man may well share in her guilt. Lenski makes much of the point that both the woman and her new husband have nothing in either of their histories to justify a charge of actual adultery. Second, the new husband cannot be the agent of the verb *moikatai* ("commits adultery"). If he is not the *recipient,* then how could he be said to *suffer* stigmatization?

Considering the first of these, we understand Lenski to find evidence for the innocence of the woman in a combination of the tense and voice of the participle and the relation of the second logion to the first. The completion of a divorce procedure against her in saying *b* is identified with the process of divorce underway in saying *a*. The hypothetical innocent woman of the latter saying, then, is identified categorically with the woman of the former saying.

All scholars will grant Lenski that the participle is perfect as to tense. Most will grant that it is passive in voice. Many will agree that there is a relationship of identity between the women of the sayings. For my part, I question whether the participle is passive and deny that there is any identity between the principal women of the sayings. I offer the following reasons:

The relevant participle, *apolelumenan,* being in the perfect tense, could be either passive or middle in voice. Most translators assume the passive, but there is no reason this has to be the case. The form is the same in either case, and the context has to determine which is meant.[5]

Were the voice middle, the whole interpretative situation would be changed for Lenski. If middle, the woman would, in one manner or another, be implicated in the divorce process that has been completed. The nature of her involvement would depend on what sort of a middle it is, for there are three major ideas that may be involved in the middle: reflex, intensification, and reciprocity. Of the three, we may rule out the last, as it only occurs with plural subjects. An intensive middle underscores the producing *agent* rather than the agent's participation. The reflexive middle, which is the nearest to the basic idea of the voice, refers the result of the action directly to the one who did it, with an emphasis upon that person's participation in the action. The following translations would then be possible:

Reflexive middle: "she who has divorced herself"

Intensive middle: "she herself who has divorced"

In either case, the point to be noted is that the woman has been, not a passive object, but the causal agent. Lenski's interpretation cannot stand a middle.

But is it middle or passive? The context decides, but the near context could abide either. It could be the woman of the preceding clause (passive), or it could be a woman, who, like the sinning divorcer of the first saying, has herself ended her marriage (middle). The issues become complex.[6] Were the text to have stressed the woman by using a definite article, *she,* instead of merely putting the participle in the feminine singular, we would almost certainly have a grammatical indicator for tying this saying with the first and identifying this woman with the treacherously divorced woman in the first saying.[7] But the article is missing. This is just "a" woman.[8] At this point, let us simply say that Lenski may be leaning on a broken reed if he depends on the voice of the participle.[9]

Matters go from bad to worse when one considers the second assumption: the grammar of the crucial verb "commits adultery" (*moikatai*). Lenski insists that this verb, like the infinitive of the previous saying, is passive—that the second husband is the recipient of its action, not the cause. Lenski is surely in error. Though "causes her to be adulterized" (*moikeuthanai*) in the preceding saying can only be passive (being in the aorist), "commits adultery" (*moikatai*) in this saying, being in the present tense, has a form that can be either passive or middle. However, there is the added factor that the verb in question is deponent.[10]

Some basic grammar may be instructive. A deponent verb, though middle or passive in form, should be translated as an active in function. Deponent verbs are verbs whose active form has been laid aside in preference for the middle. The form changed, but the function did not. Following the grammar book, then, we would not side with Lenski, because the verb is deponent. Thus, the verb should be translated "he is committing adultery."[11] This makes Lenski's interpretation impossible. If the second husband is the agent of the verb, then the only way stigmatization can still be argued would be for the second husband to stigmatize an already guilty woman! It seems useless to go on, even to consider stigma as a secondary concept.

"Actual" Adultery Views

If Lenski's idea of mere stigmatization is inadequate, the only reasonable alternative is that actual adultery takes place when the remarriage occurs. But to say this does not solve all the interpretative problems. There are at least three major variations to this category (at least two of these are liable to variation themselves).

THE NO-REMARRIAGE VIEW

THE VIEW EXPLAINED

One position goes beyond the basic statement by absolutizing the prohibition. It says that all remarriage is prohibited by this saying.[12] The logic behind this expansion seems to be the following: remarriage is denied the divorced woman because the consummation of the second wedding defiles her bond with her first husband. (The presumption here is that the marriage bond is unbreakable.) Moreover, if she is still bound to her first husband, he must still be bound to her. If he is still bound to her, then he too is not free to consummate a relationship with another.[13]

The assumption here in the case of the husband is that polygamy is immoral.[14] This is a questionable assumption, given biblical passages up to this point in the text.

This no-remarriage view does not require any relationship between 5:32a and 5:32b. Generally, this interpretation is given in the context of such verses as Luke 16:18a and supported by the idea that for a man to divorce his wife and marry another is adultery.

THE NO-REMARRIAGE VIEW CRITICIZED

Concerning the support of this interpretation by verses identifying a divorcing and remarrying man as committing adultery, I shall withhold criticism until we analyze Luke 16:18. Instead, we here turn our attention to the two basic assumptions of this position: first, that a continuing bond is the only way to explain how the man can be said to commit adultery with the divorced woman when they marry and, second, that polygamy is immoral.

Taking the last first, we note that, if polygamy is moral, then for a divorced man to marry again would not be immoral per se. After all, he could simply have married the second woman alongside the first and been guilty of no offense. Only if polygamy is immoral can this view make way from the text of Matthew 5:32b alone.[15]

In line with what I have argued before[16] I would contend that in the time when this verse was spoken, polygamy was known to be moral—the Scriptures giving it moral sanction. Moreover, one must understand that if this point is conceded, the argument that a continuing bond exists between the husband and his first wife is rendered irrelevant. The morality of polygamy implies that a man may have more than one "one-flesh," covenantal relationship at a time. The divorced man may be faulted for the divorce of his first wife, but he cannot be faulted *simply* for marrying another. It is not clear that the logic of this verse *alone* requires us to include male divorcés in the condemnation of remarriage.

If we are correct in this criticism, then we are back to the basic position: divorced women may not remarry. And if expansion of the saying (to men) is out, perhaps some form of limitation could further clarify the prohibitions here.

THE NO-REMARRIAGE-FOR-THE-INNOCENT VIEW

THE VIEW EXPLAINED

The no-remarriage-for-the-innocent view, exemplified by Murray, is a part of the Erasmian position. The view holds that the union of marriage is not dissolved by the divorce, but by sexual infidelity. Erasmians hold that in 5:32b Jesus is presenting a saying limited to cases in which this bond has not been broken. The woman of that clause is the innocent woman of the preceding saying. Though legally divorced, she is still bound to her former husband. Until that bond is broken by an act of sexual infidelity on the part of either original spouse, each is morally obligated to remain celibate. A second "legal" marriage no more justifies its consummation than the legal divorce does. The verse does not mean to inhibit the marriage of an "innocent" spouse once the bond has been broken by the sexual infidelity of the "former spouse," but proscribes a marriage in which an "innocent" spouse who has been treacherously divorced becomes *guilty* of breaking their continuing bond by consummating a second marriage. Those guilty of groundlessly divorcing their partner are not for that reason guilty of adultery (that is a sexual sin), but *would be* guilty of adultery if they remarried (before their offended partner?).

Murray claims to have "good reasons" for limiting the logion to remarriage with a treacherously divorced woman. They are, first, guilty women are only the focus of a preceding parenthetical (except) clause, and second, the concern of the combined sayings is with the consequences of and wrongs entailed in unjust divorce. Jesus is silent on the status of the remarriage of guilty women, though he suggests that the force of the except clause may carry over and dissociate the second husband of such remarriage from the condemnation of adultery.[17] On the other hand, since this saying does not speak to the condition of disciplining divorcers (male or female), it is possible to teach that the innocent party in such cases is free to remarry. The reason for this is that the guilty party by the act of adultery has dissolved the marriage.[18]

THE VIEW CRITICIZED

Criticisms of the previous positions arise again. First, as noted under the discussion of the no-remarriage view, the morality of polygamy makes the egalitarian nature of this position suspect. To be most proper, it would have to speak of the innocent *female* divorcée. Second, as mentioned in the criticism of Lenski's view, Murray's presumption that there is an interpretive connection between 32b and 32a is questionable. His supposition that this woman is the innocent divorcée of 32a is wrong if the participle is a middle—thus rendering the woman the agent of the divorce and not the recipient of the former husband's action. Third, I believe that Murray's view is determined by his assumption that the marriage bond is broken only by sexual infidelity. I believe that assumption is ill grounded in the Scriptures. The divorce of the innocent woman breaks the promise of the husband to continuously provide for her (Exod. 21). To presume that the remarriage of such a woman is adultery flies in the face of Deuteronomy 24 in a way that no well-meaning dispensational argument can explain.

Another problem arises for Murray's view when he later admits that for a treacherously divorced woman to marry is adultery (Matt. 5:32b), whereas a deserted woman may marry without tainting her husband (1 Cor. 7:15). It would seem that if the "one-flesh" bond exists until broken by sexual infidelity (Matt. 5:32b, etc.), the deserted woman would not be free to remarry until her former husband remarried or committed fornication.

Murray argues valiantly to harmonize the two, trying to force Matthew 5:32b language solely into the category of 1 Corinthians 7:10–11, and not into any relation with 1 Corinthians 7:15. Remarriage for "putting away" by Christians is presented as a different item than "going away" in a mixed marriage. After all, does not Paul say that the two categories are different when he distinguishes between Jesus' teaching and the matters discussed in 7:15?[19] Ultimately Murray's effort is unconvincing. Unless some more significant distinctions between Matthew 5:32b and 1 Corinthians 7:15 can be given, it would seem that the disharmony will remain.

Seeing the no-remarriage-to-the-innocent-divorcée view as inconsistent and unlikely, we turn to a second variation of the limiting views.

THE NO-REMARRIAGE-TO-THE-GUILTY VIEW

THE VIEW EXPLAINED

The essence of the no-remarriage-to-the-guilty view is that 32b prohibits the remarriage of a treacherous spouse, in this case the woman who divorced her husband. Since it permits the remarriage of an innocent divorced person, this view must deny that the marriage bond lasts past the divorce. Like the previous view, it would most likely argue that whatever moral obligation exists in marriage ends with the offense that determined the guilty party to be such. The most consistent statement of such a position would argue that, if no moral grounds predate the divorce, the divorce itself becomes such grounds. This is not to be construed as saying that the innocent party will always be the one divorced, for sometimes the innocent party will be a disciplining divorcer. Guilt is determined by the unfaithful (not necessarily sexually understood) action of one spouse. When the innocent party divorces as a discipline, it is to serve notice that the moral bond, which the spouse has broken, must be restored by a renewal of the covenant before the offended partner will function as a spouse.

Such a view denies remarriage to the guilty party, not because some bond still exists, but because the guilty party has unfinished moral business, that is, repentance, including actions that are the appropriate "fruits of repentance." If the guilty party was the divorcer, as in the saying at hand, then that party should not marry another person but seek the forgiveness of the offended former spouse. The appropriate "fruit" would be to restore the marriage by recommitting to the marriage vows, if the offended will and can take the offender back. To marry someone else while repentance and restoration is possible is evidence of continuing treachery, in the same way as thieves remain thieves until they provide restitution, or prove they are still thieves by fencing the property they have stolen.[20]

THE VIEW CRITICIZED

An initial criticism of this view is that it presumes that the woman divorced her husband, a procedure not available to women in Palestinian society at that time.[21] But this criticism will not stand. First, Herodias did divorce Herod.[22] That made the statement relevant. Second, there is no doubt that Mark 10:12 includes the same point. We cannot deny the possibility of Christ here identifying the wife as a divorcer without denying the even more straightforward identification in Mark's Gospel.[23] Our interpretation harmonizes with Mark on this point. They are conceptual complements, each touching on a different side of the same issue: the remarriage of women who unjustly divorce.

A second criticism of this view is that it goes against the idea of an indissoluble moral bond that exists between marriage partners. If the view were further qualified to relate to guilty female divorcées(ers), then it would be criticized by positions that protest polygamy. However, since I have argued *against* such an indissoluble bond and *for* biblical polygamy, none of these criticisms damage the position.

A third criticism against this last qualification could arise out of the citation of such verses as Luke 16:18a, Matthew 19:9, and Mark 10:11. How can this interpretation be harmonized with them? Some of them would not seem to be harmonizable. I will answer this criticism when we discuss those texts.

Beyond these criticisms, there are two questions to ask this position regarding its focus upon the second husband. Why exactly is he singled out, rather than the divorcing woman? And why, if her marriage bond is broken, is he hung with the tag "adulterer"?

The answer to both is that the text at hand sees the second husband as an accomplice in the continuing rebellion of the guilty. Several matters support this suspicion. In the first place, remember that the Sermon was preached to the disciples, who were probably mostly men; Jesus spoke to the majority of his audience. Second, remember that the question of the right to end the marriage was one primarily of concern to men, since few women divorced their husbands. In one sense this fit the Law's plan for men to be the ones who led in family decisions. But this "lead" was a great responsibility, to be exercised in a manner designed to keep families together. In the days of Jesus (and in most days of history), however, men were behind the disruption of marriage. Jesus is trying to undercut this by speaking against male lust, male treachery in divorcing, and male treachery in claiming a woman who should be going repentantly back to her husband.

This latter progression brings up two matters that may explain why the man is singled out in the remarriage saying, and that may help us see the reasonableness of this interpretation. One is rhetorical, the other is historical. Consider again the connection between the three logia of Matthew 5:27–32. There is an interesting progression in the three cases in which men are guilty of adultery when they might at first seem to be innocent. The logical progression runs: thoughts of treachery with another's wife, treachery to rid oneself of one's own wife, and the treacherous claiming of the neighbor's wife. Lust, treachery, and duplicity.[24] But this progression may have more behind it than a common topic. To Jesus' listeners, Galileans, the progression would sound like a comment on the daily news scrolls. They spoke of certain aspects of one of the most celebrated cases of contemporary immorality in high places: that of Herod Antipas.

Remember the Herod incident. Luke 3 tells us that John preached against Herod's marital sins (3:18) before Jesus was even baptized (3:21). Jesus' Sermon certainly came after his baptism (cf. Matt. 3:13–17 vis-à-vis Matt. 5–7). The Sermon seems to have come near the beginning of his ministry with his disciples, as it lays down the ground rules of discipleship (Matt. 4:18–5:1). Thus, it is likely that the Sermon was preached while John was striking out against Herod, and it probably was preached in Galilee, Herod's domain. Furthermore, the Pharisees were notoriously silent about the case. Their silence might imply that Herod was not guilty of any other error than incest in his marital relations. Whereas John focused upon the incest, Jesus sought to strike at the more common sins of Herod.

The false impression that lust, treachery against one's wife, and treachery against one's neighbor are somehow passed over by God because the first is covered by the heart and the last two are covered by the prevailing laws must be corrected.[25] Herod's antics were in the minds and hearts of the people, and it is highly unlikely that Jesus' hearers would have understood such teachings as these without some reflection upon the biggest story in the "daily newspapers." We may presume that to some degree the Herod incident informed the saying. Let us see exactly how the history and sayings could relate.

Looking at the combination of all three sayings that relate to adultery, a rather interesting progression appears:

1. A man desires a married woman (5:28). (Remember that *woman* can be translated "wife," and, in view of the word *adultery* that is used in the text, "wife" is the preferable translation. Nor does the text specify that it is the *neighbor's* wife—thus neither tying it to the immediate vicinity of the lusting one's home nor eliminating the possibility of a kinship relationship with the husband of the woman).

2. A woman is divorced by her husband (5:32a). (Though the text mentions the possibility that the divorce might have been for adultery—the "exception clause"—the thrust of the passage is upon a man who divorces a woman unjustly.)

3. A man marries a woman who initiated a divorce that is final (5:32b). (The definite article is missing so as not to force us to think of this as the treacherously divorced woman or the innocent woman of the except clause.)

This series fits the case of Herod Antipas, who desired his brother Herod Philip's wife, Herodias, that is, lusted after a married woman. He then seems to have eloped with her (from Caesarea del Mare). At her insistence he unjustly divorced his own wife (the daughter of the king of Petra) and then married the divorced Herodias (upon receiving permission from Rome). In her case, Josephus informs us, Herodias herself did the divorcing, not Herod Philip.[26] Thus, the middle participle and the deponent passive verbs would seem to fit the historical facts nicely. Matthew 5:32b then reads: "And if someone marries a woman *who herself has divorced* he himself is committing adultery." This fits the Herodias case precisely. The stress upon the man who marries such a woman would put the blame upon Herod even more than upon Herodias—the man being seen as morally responsible for her divorce.

Of course, Jesus is not simply condemning Herod, but all who, like Herod, would aid in or instigate treachery against their neighbor. Then as now, it is usually the man who lusts, clears the way for his next love, and wrests the woman away from her commitments. And then more than now, few women (who were prevented from holding most jobs) would think of divorcing their husbands without having a new spouse waiting in the wings. In such cases, the "adultery" of the second husband is clearer yet. He was a party to the sundering of the first marriage—a clear instance of adultery according to the spirit of the Mosaic Law, though it might not be precise to speak of him as an adulterer until he actually took possession of her. Even were he not to have sexual intercourse with her before the legal divorce, he would not be free from the condemnation of One such as Christ, who could easily see when prevailing law was being used as a cloak for evil by such a trick. To have finally removed previous covenant (perfect participle) cannot fool God. The guilty parties are, in their remarriage, about the business of adultery.

Believing that Jesus is condemning those who, with their neighbor's wives, are treacherous against their neighbor, I do not agree that 32b is "unqualified." Jesus is not interested in introducing new legislation that prohibits the remarriage of every divorced female. Such an idea would contradict the essence of Deuteronomy 24 and Exodus 21. The interpretation that any remarriage is adultery or that remarriage to an innocent divorced woman is adultery is not a clarification of the law; it would annul several of them, and that is something Jesus specifically said he was not going to do (Matt. 5:17 ff.).

But this may not be enough qualification. If the concern of the saying, and of the Law that it seeks to clarify, is to promote the continuation of valid (first) marriages and to prohibit subsequent marriages that inhibit restoration, what do we make of a case in which the "guilty" divorced woman has seen the error of her ways and sought to return to her husband, only to find that he is unable or unwilling to take her back? Since the thrust of the saying is to satisfy moral strictures, not simply live up to mystical, ontic unions, what would Christ say to such a woman? Unfortunately we do not have an instance of this, but I suggest that he would not bind such a one by such a saying as this. For the saying is not designed to prohibit the marriage of the "subsequently" innocent (i.e., repentant woman) but of the "continually guilty."

My point here arises from general principles of Christian ethics, which we will consider in greater depth when we look at the context of the Matthew 19 divorce legislation.

Conclusions Concerning Divorce Legislation in the Sermon

The teaching of Jesus on divorce/remarriage in the Sermon should be understood in its proper perspective. Insofar as the subsequent words of Jesus on the subject are only supplemental to the Sermon, and uttered in spontaneous dialogue with his opponents and disciples, we must suspect that the positions set forth in the Sermon are topically complete when understood in the context of the Law and the Prophets. We have focused upon the Sermon sayings without recourse to the later ones precisely for this reason, while not expecting the later sayings to be in the slightest contradictory to what has been said to this point.

To sum up the "academic" teachings of Christ, the main teaching is that the Old Testament means what it says when it speaks of covenant breaking as treachery (Mal. 2). Treachery in the heart is adultery. Treachery in divorce is adultery. Treachery fulfilled in remarriage is adultery. Just not doing it in bed will not fool God. Just because the prevailing laws say a writ of divorce ends (moral) responsibility to the first covenant does not mean that God will fall into line. The prevailing laws and teachings be damned. The received teaching of the Old Testament is that divorce without grounds is treacherous. The only proper use of divorce is as a discipline for actions that by their nature breach the essentials of the marriage covenant. Since that is so, the man, who has pledged to provide for his wife, has committed adultery against his wife by divorcing her, has publicly spoken his treachery. No remarriage need take place for this adultery to occur, and Jesus mentions none nor alludes to none in Matthew 32a. Further, since divorce is only to be used as a discipline, the watching public may well suppose that the innocent woman was actually guilty. Thus, this man actually defames her with his own sinful acts—an offense specifically proscribed in the Law. In the first saying of the divorce couplet, Jesus is seeking merely to restore to their fullness Deuteronomy 22:13 ff. and Malachi 2:15.

Having said that groundless divorce is adulterous against the spouse in the case of the male, it is unnecessary to say it regarding a female, for any legal annulment of the vows is covenant breaking by definition. The woman who groundlessly divorces is also guilty of adulterizing her husband and stigmatizing him as guilty of breaking his vows to her. Those who don't realize that the law is reciprocal on this point need only listen to the nuances of Matthew 32b, when Jesus speaks of a woman who has ended her own covenant.

In the second saying, Jesus wished to point out that her compliance with prevailing law, which permits morally groundless divorce, does not free her from the sin of adultery. She intended to break her vow of monogamy. That is why she divorced her husband—she wished to have relations with another. The spirit of the Old Testament should not be difficult to discern in such a case, but there might be the need to pinpoint the adultery of her partner in the crime of vow breaking: the man who resultingly takes her. This point is the burden of the second saying.

In one sense, both sayings warn against the same form of the sin of adultery: legal adultery, because a divorce writ in itself does not relieve the partners of moral responsibility to fulfill their vows to each other— a point manifestly in harmony with the flow of the Sermon. The Pharisees taught that the divorce writ ended *moral responsibility;* Jesus denies this. In such cases the divorce writ is merely a cloak that covers evil.

But in saying thus have we rejected a position once accepted, namely, that marriage being essentially a covenant a divorce ends marital obligation? If it is over, why cannot the guilty party remarry at will? I answer that the legal obligations are indeed over, but the moral obligation to repent still exists. The woman who does not repent and become reconciled with her husband is still an "adulteress" in the same respect that an unrepentant murderer is still a "murderer" even though the event is in the past. The second husband is in the process (present tense) of making himself an accomplice to his new wife's continuing treachery to her past husband and, in all likelihood, was the adulterous target of the woman while her first marriage was on the books. The second husband's marriage to this divorced woman is part of an overall process of treachery against the first husband.

The thrust of Matthew 5:32b is similar to that of Luke 16:18. The latter passage also discusses adultery and remarriage; we turn to it now, to view it in its context.

THE DIVORCE TEACHINGS OF JESUS IN LUKE 16

The Customary Neglect of the Context

Most treatments of Luke 16:18 suffer from their failure to take the context into account. In fact, seldom is there a full treatment of this important verse in its own right. Usually it is appended in some way to the discussion of the Matthew 19/Mark 10 parallel. Laney, for example, has a whole chapter on the teachings of Jesus in Mark and Luke, but of the nine pages in that chapter, only one is devoted to Luke.[27] Murray, who also ties Luke 16 to Mark 10, never mentions the former without also mentioning the latter. His discussion centers around showing that Mark 10 and Luke 16 complement Matthew by discussing the adultery of remarriage where there has been no fornication.[28]

DISCONTINUITY WITH THE OLD TESTAMENT?

A Higher Teaching?

Those who do touch on the context differ quite radically over how it affects the passage. The *Pulpit Commentary,* for example, argues that

Jesus was telling the Pharisees that his teaching on the law of divorce-ment was more strict than the Old Testament—which earlier code will not pass away. It has Jesus saying:

"See," He said, "the new state of things which I am now teaching, instead of loosening the cords with which the old law regulated human society, will rather tighten them. Instead of a more lax code being substituted, I am preaching a yet severer one. My law of divorce is a severer one than that written down by Moses."[29]

Thus Jesus' teaching is pictured as different from the Law. The Law permitted remarriage, but "grace and truth" proclaim it to be adultery.

The Rejection of the Mosaic Concession?

Laney offers a less radical approach to Jesus' relation to the Old Testament doctrine. He suggests that Jesus simply distances himself from the Mosaic concession, harkening back to the original teaching of God in Genesis 2:24. This alternative, like that of the *Pulpit Commentary,* concludes that Christ is proscribing all remarriage.[30]

It is my suggestion that neither of these approaches to the context sufficiently grasps Jesus' meaning or that of the Gospel writer. I un-derstand Jesus as attempting to affirm the precise teaching of the Law and the Prophets, neither more nor less. To have done more or less would have undercut the strength of his criticism of the Pharisees.

CONTINUITY WITH THE OLD TESTAMENT

A serious consideration of the broader context of Luke presents, I believe, a different picture, one of continuity with the Old Testament. Analysis of the structure of the sixteenth and the (beginning of the) seventeenth chapters of Luke reveal the following closely related units:

1. The parable of the unjust steward, 16:1–13
2. The rebuke of the listening Pharisees, 16:14–18 (including the divorce saying)
3. The parable of Lazarus and the rich man, 16:19–31
4. The warning of the disciples, 17:1–4
5. The dialogue between Jesus and his disciples, 17:5–10

Analysis of the Lucan Rhetoric

THE PARABLE OF THE UNJUST STEWARD

The first unit sets forth the teaching that some people are so com-mitted to money and position that they would rob their master to en-sure their own ease. The steward in the story is a man at a crisis point in his life. His past is that of a thief. Having been entrusted with his master's affairs, he has mishandled them to his own advantage, often using his master's goods for his own gain. When discovered, he simply changes his tactics and uses his remaining authority as a steward to give his master's debtors a "cut rate." Though this does not at first seem to be to his own advantage, it really is, insofar as those on the receiving end of his injustice to his master now are indebted to him for cutting their debt in half. All this shiftiness causes the steward's master to comment on how wordly-wise and shrewd the man is. In other words, the wronged master "damns him with faint praise."

The point of the parable is that some people will break trust to further themselves. Surely this is a point worth remembering for the disciples, as they are, in a sense, the stewards of God's wealth—the kingdom and the gospel message (including the teachings of true discipleship). But the section that follows in the text shows that Jesus had a particular group in mind when he spoke of the unjust steward.

THE REBUKE OF THE PHARISEES

The second unit begins with the Pharisees laughing behind his back at Jesus' teaching. Jesus exposes their conceit and identifies them as the very stewards about whom he has been talking. In the structure of the Gospel, it is clear that Jesus was all along thinking of the Pharisees. It was no happenstance, no coincidence, as if Jesus were thinking of some abstract steward and then the Pharisees mumbled themselves into the picture, thereby giving him a chance to illustrate the principle in their own time. No, the Pharisees are the prime and intentional illustration. Jesus has "set them up," so to speak.

Says Jesus in 16:15, "You are the ones I'm talking about!" In what respect? They, like the unjust steward, love money more than they do their master. Who is their master, and wherein have they failed their stewardship? God is their master—they were supposed to be his spokesmen to his people. Their failure is identified as "justifying themselves in the sight of men." But exactly what does this charge entail?

THE DIVORCE TEACHING

It was at this point that Jesus became specific. "The law and the Prophets were proclaimed until John; since then the gospel of the kingdom of God is preached, and everyone is forcing his way into it." What did Jesus mean by this remarkable saying? Well, clearly, John preached like a righteous steward. He was a true spokesman for the standard of God. He served but one Master, whose message he proclaimed. We should expect from this part of the saying that Jesus is in some way suggesting that the Pharisees are a contrast to John. Jesus does not mean that John was the last to teach the righteous standard. Jesus himself continued to teach it, as the great Sermon clearly shows.

Jesus continued that the gospel of the Kingdom of God had been preached from the time of John. This is clearly a reference to his own ministry. But Jesus was not the first to teach about the kingdom, John was. Jesus does not mean to contrast himself with John, but to show that both John and himself added to that standard of Law the clear message of the gospel. There is in the time designation no criticism or abrogation of the Law. No, that message (the Law, v. 17) will not pass away. The message of the "good news" of salvation presupposes conviction wrought by the preaching of the Law. The Pharisees understood that before gospel comes Law, with its requirement to be a servant to the Master himself. And they were willing to identify with the movement toward the kingdom. But they wanted to define that service in their own terms. They wanted to be thought of as the custodians of the kingdom, while personally rejecting the inner change of heart that is the hallmark of a true steward. They wanted the blessings of the kingdom without bowing to the obligations. They did not want to get into the kingdom through the door, but through the window. Jesus understood full well such thieving hearts, and so did John. The Baptizer had refused the likes of the Pharisees entrance into the antechamber of the kingdom, telling them to go back home and produce the fruits of righteousness (Luke 3:7 f.). The Matthean parallel notes that it was specifically to the scribes and Pharisees that John spoke these words (Matt. 3:7–11).

The object of faith must be Jesus as Lord, not simply Jesus as national Messiah. Just as the steward in the parable was willing to count his master as master without any commitment to allowing him the rights he was entitled to as master, so too the Pharisees were willing to muster to the service of the kingdom as long as it didn't cost them anything. This is not the way to enter the kingdom. There is only one way to enter it: admit that Christ is the Way, the Truth, and the Life, and that there is no other way but him. To accept him as the Lord and Savior requires first a recognition that we have sinned and that only by completely giving our rights of determination to him will he give his life to us. But the Pharisees refused to acknowledge how woefully short of God's standard—the very Law that was their stewardship— they had fallen. They sought to excuse themselves and thereby enter the kingdom through the window—or, as Jesus puts it, upon having the door closed in their faces, they sought to batter it down with their formal religious "clout."

But what, we press, was the specific point or a specific point of their failure to be good stewards of the Law? Of course Jesus had identified a good number of things in the Sermon, but he takes the time to bring before them a charge of immediate note: the celebrated issue of divorce. Given the flow of his argument, for Jesus to have put any distance between himself and the standard of God, which was the overall stewardship in question, would have been for him to have undercut the argument. How inappropriate for him to have said that God said

X, but I say *X + 1.* Such a personal display would have been most out of place. Similarly, for him to have said, "God gave you a cut rate from the time of Moses, but I am returning you to the pure teaching of Genesis 2:24!" is, if anything, even more bizarre. It makes God to be the unjust steward who does not demand full rate.

I submit instead that Jesus was specifying one celebrated instance of the Pharisees' poor stewardship when he pointed out their failure to accurately represent God's teaching regarding the morality of divorce and remarriage. And rather than fish around trying to discern what in that regard he was referring to, I submit that the reference to John is doubly potent. For it had not been long before this saying that John, already identified as a just steward, had lost his head for refusing to offer Herod a "cut rate" regarding the Old Testament Law on marriage. According to Luke 3:19, John rebuked Herod "on account of Herodias, his brother's wife, and on account of *all the wicked things which Herod had done.*"

Note, please, that Luke 3:19 does not say that John rebuked him simply for the matter of incest.[31] That was only a part of the wickedness that Herod had done in taking to himself his brother's wife. As we noted earlier, beyond incest, Herod had divorced his lawful wife and contrived at the divorce of Philip by Herodias. About these sins, the Pharisees had been silent. Having doubtless themselves abused the divorce legislation in their own marriages, and having not taught God's doctrine of divorce—and having had this pointed out by Jesus in the Sermon—they proceed by their silence to side with Herod, God's debtor, giving him a cut rate, that is, no public rebuke.

THE PARABLE OF LAZARUS AND THE RICH MAN

The Lucan structure proceeds into the parable of Lazarus and the rich man. In view of the contextual discussion of the Pharisees' commitment to riches, it is nearly impossible to miss the point that the rich man in the story is a deceased Pharisee. His whole life he went about giving the debtors of God a cut rate so as to ensure himself a place in Israelite society, and now he realizes that such riches and status and such friends cannot "receive you into the eternal dwellings" (16:9). Upon finding that it is now too late to become a happy steward in the dwellings of the master (16:24 f.), he is stricken in conscience regarding the rest of the Pharisees back on earth. He wants this Lazarus to go back and warn his brother Pharisees that they must repent or they will end up in the place where he now suffers.

In the story, Abraham tells them that even the resurrection of a man named Lazarus (or any other—Jesus, for instance) will not convince them that they should mend their ways. For their god is their position and their wealth, and they have already rejected clear evidence of how to avoid such a tragic afterlife. The message is in the Law and the Prophets. The living Pharisees knew that there was a Master, they knew the Law, but they rejected it. Theirs was an unpardonable sin, insofar as they had rejected God and sided with his adversary while possessing full knowledge and experience of the oracles.[32]

THE WARNING TO HIS DISCIPLES

In the fourth unit, we see Jesus turning to his disciples and admonishing them to warn a stumbling brother. Just as John warned Herod, they were to rebuke the sinner. What? Herod, an Idumaean, a "brother"? Yes, in the sense that Herod claimed to follow the Law. We do not see John so addressing Roman authorities. They made no pretense of obeying the Constitutions of Israel. But Herod claimed to be the Jews' brother and to follow their standard. The disciples are told to rebuke such professors, for there is a chance that they will repent and become good disciples.

Of course, we know that that is not how it turned out in the case of John and Herod. John, like the Lazarus in the story, was then in his grave, basking in the bosom of Abraham! Was not Jesus sending them to their own graves? They can only cry: "Increase our faith!" And he seeks to bolster them by telling them that the requisite faith was not so much as they imagine, and that they should remember a faithful steward collects his reward after the work is done—just as John was then claiming his reward in Abraham's bosom.

Conclusions

What is the result of all this contextual investigation? It is helpful to repeat something similar to what was said at the close of our discussion of Matthew 5:32b. The significance of determining whether or not the Herod incident is behind the sayings of Luke 16:18 is that, if it is, we do not expect the text to inveigh against *all remarriage* but only against such as we see in Herod's case: treacherous remarriage. Herod's divorce of his rightful wife was sheer treachery, condemned by Malachi 2. His complicity in the divorce by Herodias of his half-brother Philip involved him in the treachery of a covenant-breaking and adulterous wife. He was a partner with her in the sin of adultery. The language employed here is a simple third person present active indicative: "he is committing adultery." There is no surprise here, no need for the use of the middle voice. The Pharisees knew they were giving a "cut rate."

But what of the voice of the participle in the second clause? In Matthew we noted that the woman *herself* (middle) divorced the husband. Does not Luke imply that the woman was divorced, and is this not different from the case of Herodias and Philip? Actually, the voice of the participle here is exactly the same as that in the Matthew passage, that is, either middle or passive. I, of course, take it to be middle—implicating the woman as the treacherous divorcer, while stressing the complicity of the second husband in the first divorce by centering the saying upon him.

But, one may well ask, how is a person today to have known enough of all this background to realize that "all who" is really "all who [like Herod]"? A straightforward reading of the verse seems clear enough: no remarriage! Have we not turned the verse nearly on its head by limiting it to cases like Herod's?

To this one must reply, with Walter Kaiser, people always want to "skip the exegesis and go straight to the blessing."[33] The references to John and the loyalty of Jesus to the Old Testament should have steered us in the right direction in the first place. Beyond this, the reader should have known that the interpretation of these verses as a proscription of all remarriages, though prima facie the proper one, has no support in the Old Testament, the very stewardship that Jesus and John sought so diligently to uphold, "every jot and tittle." For one thing, a study of Malachi and the polygamy passages should have led one to understand that a man taking a second wife was not *in itself* a moral offense. How then could remarriage for a man be adultery, unless predicated solely upon the desire to share himself exclusively with a new partner? Abraham took another woman to be his one-flesh partner, and he was not guilty of immorality for doing so. Why not? Because he did not in the process break faith with Sarah. So too, remarriage in itself is not a problem (at least for the Old Testament male). It all depends on the conditions upon which that second marriage is predicated: Was the divorce just or treacherous?

But we are getting ahead of ourselves here. The next chapter, on Matthew 19 and Mark 10, will return us to these crucial issues. But before I close this chapter, I need to stress that Jesus is not in Luke 16:18 simply taking a shot at Herod Antipas. The condemnation is equally devastating regarding anyone who, like Herod, remarries by a process of treachery. Or if you prefer, the passage warns against remarriage of or with the guilty party. Thus, the traditional "Erasmian" interpretation, which sees this text as not addressing the case of the innocent divorced person, is vindicated. However, rather than coming to that conclusion by saying that the verse states a general rule and pedagogically ignores the exception, I am saying that the text more directly rebukes the remarriage of the guilty party.[34]

CHAPTER 7

The Teachings of Jesus on Divorce, Continued
(Matthew 19:3–12/Mark 10:2–12)

THE MORALITY OF DIVORCE

"Is it lawful for a man to divorce his wife for any reason?"

Only with our previous discussions behind us do we feel ready to embark upon the crucial parallel passages found in Matthew 19:3–12 and Mark 10:2–12. Sadly, many studies of the teaching of Jesus so center upon these texts that they reduce all else to a footnote. Heth and Wenham's *Jesus and Divorce* is a prime example. It is a study of alternative views of the exception clause as found in Matthew 19:9. I believe that to understand these final teachings of Jesus on the subject of divorce, a person should already know clearly and fully the prior teachings of our Lord.

A Conflate Reading as a Solution to a Synoptic Problem

As to the passages themselves, a word needs to be said first about the celebrated differences between them, differences that have led some to believe that they are really two different accounts or are at least an example of one tradition altering the other for theological purposes. I believe otherwise. A great many studies make much of the fact that the readers or even the writers of the Gospels would only have had this or that block of material of the teaching of Jesus on divorce. Some would say that since Mark was written first and sent to a particular destination, its readers would hardly have had available to them the exception clause preserved by Matthew. Others presume that Matthew was written first and those who read it would surely have been surprised later to hear of the absoluteness in Mark or Luke. I consider all of this to be the sort of unanswerable speculation that profits little.

What seems fair to say is that the teachings of Jesus on divorce were spread abroad and known by Christians. Paul, who probably wrote his first letter to the Corinthian church before any of the formal Gospel accounts, repeats teaching that he did not receive firsthand. And, although we will not at this point do a complete exegesis of that Pauline passage, we might find it helpful to note that when Paul does refer to Jesus' teaching in 1 Corinthians 7:10–11, he specifies that the one addressed needs to be reconciled. Since no remarriage has necessarily taken place at that point, and since the one who needs to be reconciled is always the guilty party in biblical terminology, Paul is obviously speaking to a person who has divorced without the grounds of *porneia*.[1] It would seem to me that this use of language by Paul implies a knowledge of the material preserved by Matthew, and not simply that preserved by Mark or Luke. And why, I ask, should anyone who has all the words of Jesus in the parallel readings of Mark 10 and Matthew 19 presume that those who listened to Jesus preserved only the Mark 10 approach until Matthew saw fit to resurrect it at some point after Mark had written? This sort of groundless assumption, it seems to me, is dangerous to exegesis. It picks what it wishes to support and then creates a scenario that it then offers as evidence. There is not the slightest reason for thinking that the New Testament church did not know all of Jesus' words on divorce from the moment he spoke them.

We must remember that it was one dialogue between Jesus and the Pharisees that gave rise to the accounts preserved by Matthew 19 and Mark 10. Rather than speculate about traditions with limited memories, we would be well advised to try and construct the original from the preserved accounts. In doing so we should not be deterred by the fact that we do not have a unified written account of the complete dialogue. We have the parts, and, if we respect the integrity of the parts, and try and blend them, presuming the least amount of redaction (thereby employing a form of the principle of parsimony), we may arrive at a conflate reading that is the base common to the "traditions" and perhaps well known to everybody involved.

What follows here is such a reconstruction, with the material peculiar to Matthew in boldface and the material peculiar to Mark underlined. Where redaction has taken place, I have chosen the Gospel reading that I believe is the likeliest original and put the redaction in brackets.

And some Pharisees came up to him, testing him, and began to question him whether it was lawful for a man to divorce a wife, **saying, "Is it lawful for a man to divorce his wife for any cause at all?"**

And he answered and said to them, "What did Moses command you?"

And they said, "Moses permitted a man to write a certificate of divorce and send her away."

And he answered and said, "Have you not read, that he who created them [but] from the beginning of creation made them male and female, **and said,** 'for this cause a man shall leave his father and mother, **and shall cleave to his wife,** and the two shall become one flesh'? Consequently they are no longer two, but one flesh. What therefore God has joined together, let no man separate."

They said to him, "Why then did Moses command to give her a certificate and send her away?" [But]

Jesus said to them, "Because of your hardness of heart, he wrote you this commandment. **Moses permitted you to divorce your wives; but from the beginning it has not been this way.**

"And I say to you, whoever divorces his wife, except for immorality, and marries another woman commits adultery."

And in the house, the disciples began to question him about this again.

And he said to them, "Whoever divorces his wife, and marries another woman commits adultery against her; and if she herself divorces her husband and marries another man, she is committing adultery."

The disciples said to him, "If the relationship of the man with his wife is like this, it is better not to marry."

But he said to them, "Not all men can accept this statement, but only those to whom it has been given. For there are eunuchs who were born that way from their mother's womb; and there are eunuchs who were made eunuchs by men; and there are also eunuchs who made themselves eunuchs for the sake of the kingdom of heaven. He who is able to accept this, let him accept it."

Though the reading may seem a bit stultified at some points, it seems no more so than a great many other places where the text is unquestionably preserved in full. This running dialogue eliminates the question of whether Jesus brought up Moses or they did. The answer is that both did, though not at the same time. It also shows that Mark modified the primary document (Q? a hypothetical collection of the sayings and parables of Jesus) more than Matthew, but only by shifting some material around, while following his usual technique of eliminating whole topics for catechetical purposes. We shall learn more from this conflate reading, but let us do all things in proper order.

An Analysis of the Conflate Reading

We will first analyze these passages as a conflate reading, then consider the significance of their present condition in the separate Gospels.

THE OCCASION OF THE PHARISEES' TEST QUESTION

And some Pharisees came <u>up</u> to him, testing him, and <u>began to question him whether it was lawful for a man to divorce a wife,</u> **saying, "Is it lawful for a man to divorce his wife for any cause at all?"**

It is a point of interest to some exactly what the background was for this test of Jesus. Generally one of three alternatives is discussed:

The Hillel-Shammai Debate?

The Pharisees were trying to get Jesus to take sides with one or the other of the two Pharisaical schools: Hillel or Shammai.

According to this idea, the dominant Hillel group was trying to get Jesus to side with the more conservative Shammai group, thus discrediting him with the people, who were presumably favoring the more lenient position.[2]

This posture does not seem to me to be likely, for at least three reasons. First, the questioning Pharisees are not identified as being of one party or another. In fact, it is not clear that the distinction is significant to the New Testament. Jesus seems to lump them all together into a unit of misinformed moralists: Pharisees. Now if the Scripture doesn't draw such a distinction, why should we? This is not to say that we may not speculate about which group dominated the questioners; however, to understand the question as arising from partisanship does not seem to be the focus of the text. Second, and related to the first, what real profit would a group of Pharisees have obtained by showing that Jesus sided with another legitimate Pharisaical school? Would Jesus have lost face with the Pharisees by being identified with the distinguished conservative Shammai? Surely not. It is wholly out of character for the Pharisees to have tried to get Jesus to disagree with only one faction of their own religious community. Rather, it is their custom to show Jesus out of harmony with the Law of Moses. And this is precisely where the dialogue centers: upon the Law, not upon opinions about it.[3]

Third (and on the assumption that the questioners were Hillites), it is not at all clear that the people of Jesus' day did prefer the Hillite view. Such an assumption seems warranted subsequent to the fall of the Temple (A.D. 70), but J. Jeremias has shown that the divorce rate was probably close to only 4 percent, hardly an overwhelming problem![4] Assuming that the Pharisees were aware of the popular view as evidenced by the prevailing rate of divorce, and assuming that the Pharisees were aware of Jesus' conservative position on divorce as evidenced by the Sermon and by Luke 16, it would have been counterproductive to their goal of discrediting Jesus with the populace to have shown him to be conservative like Shammai. I cannot find much in favor of this opinion except that we have knowledge of the internecine squabbles of the Pharisees and believe that the New Testament must have recognized and spoken to them.[5]

The Herod–John the Baptist Affair?

The Pharisees were trying to get Jesus to speak out against Herod Antipas' marital affairs.

On this view, if the Pharisees could only show Jesus to be as outspoken as John, the word might get to Herod and Jesus might end up as John did—beheaded.

To be said in its favor is that the New Testament is expressly concerned with this matter in a number of locations.[6] Moreover, to have placed Jesus in jeopardy with Herod would have significantly endangered his ministry—exactly the goal of the Pharisees.

Nonetheless, there are good reasons for rejecting this theory as an explanation of the nature of the "test." First, Jesus had already spoken of this issue in the event recorded in Luke 16:18, at a geographical location equally risky relative to Herod. Also, Herod had already taken notice of Jesus in regard to preaching like John (cf. Matt. 14:1 ff.). It is unlikely that this new occasion would have contributed effectively to the stated cause. Second, it is highly doubtful that the Pharisees would be willing to talk about the John-Herod affair. Recall that when Jesus questioned them about the authority of the baptism of John, they were afraid to speak publicly against the prophet (Matt. 21:23 ff.). Would they be likely to risk asking a question that would challenge the teaching of that martyr? It is especially doubtful when they knew in their hearts that John (and presumably Jesus) was in accord with the Law. And, what about their own culpable silence in the whole affair? Had they not lost face with the people by their silence when that popular leader lost his head? I think it highly improbable that they would have dared to bring up the subject in any public place!

But there is a greater reason for doubting that the Herod affair was behind the test. The question asked is 180 degrees in the wrong direction from the one they would have asked. Had they been interested in Herod, they would have asked Jesus if there was any reason a man *had* to put away his wife. That was the rebuke voiced by John (Luke 3). Instead, they asked him if a man had the *right* to put away his wife, a question that did relate to the less-celebrated aspects of the Herod affair, but certainly not the sort of question that anybody would have construed as an unequivocal challenge to Herod. The question of the Pharisees concerns right to divorce, not responsibility to divorce. For these reasons I think it advisable to search for another explanation for the test.

The "Concession" of Moses

> *The Pharisees were reflecting upon the prior teachings of Jesus and thought they had found a place where he disagreed with Moses. They thus sought to drive a wedge between Jesus and the Law, thus discrediting him with the people and showing his earlier words rejecting abrogation of the Law to be empty.*

Such a ploy is far more characteristic of the Pharisees. The very next time we find them challenging Jesus it is over the matter of the authority of his teaching (Matt. 21:23 ff.), an obvious chop at any contention that that authority came from the Law. Later yet, when they made one of their final attempts to discredit him, they again questioned him about the Law (Matt. 22:34 ff.). Jesus, in his subsequent condemnation of them, sarcastically derides them for their failure to be proper stewards of the Law, though they had put themselves in the seat of its teachers (Matt. 23:1 ff.). This latter text would seem to imply that they saw themselves as the exegetes and protectors of the Law. This would agree with Jesus' reference to their rejecting Moses and the prophets regarding the divorce legislation in Luke 16. Granting that this is a correct analysis, it is easy to see that they would like to show Jesus' teaching to be every bit as alien to the Law as he claimed theirs was.

The conflate text gives two indications of what the Pharisees had in mind. The first clue comes from the Gospel writer Mark, who introduces the subject thematically: they were questioning him as to whether it was lawful for a man to divorce a wife. Note that they do not ask about remarriage; they do not ask about the meaning of "uncleanness"; they do not ask if it is ever necessary to divorce a wife. The fact that they are questioning him may indicate that it was not clear to them what he really did teach on this matter. After all, early in his teaching (the Sermon) he had spoken of the grounds of *porneia*. But in the most recent exchange (that recorded in Luke 16), he had offered no grounds. In other words, there may have been the same confusion among them that exists among our own scholars about what the real teaching was!

In addition, we must credit the Pharisees with knowing everything that we know about Jesus' teachings to date. Recall that in the Sermon he prefaced his teaching on ethics with a slap at the Pharisees, saying that if his disciples did not exceed Pharisees in righteousness, they would not enter into the kingdom. Doubtless someone, perhaps someone in the crowd, conveyed these remarks to the local Pharisees, and they in turn shared them with their brethren. But at first there was little that could be done—at least with regard to the divorce doctrine. After all, his teaching seemed to be similar to that of Rabbi Shammai. To have questioned him about grounds would, as noted earlier, have really gained them nothing by way of a crevice in which to drive a wedge between his teaching and the Law.

But his more recent slap at them, couched in the language of absolute prohibition of divorce (and remarriage), changed all that. After they had regained their wits from his blast at their stewardship of the divorce legislation, they sought to put together a probe that would discredit him. It was an all-or-nothing question. "Is it lawful for a man to divorce his wife for any cause at all?" If he answers yes, the very best they can hope for is a stalemate. Even they themselves could not agree upon exactly what the grounds were. Thus, they must be hoping that he would answer no.

Given the form of his most recent saying on the subject (Luke 16:18), they had good reason to believe that he would answer that way. Perhaps, they may have thought, he has "hardened his categories." If the latest teaching were reaffirmed, they felt they could drive the wedge between Jesus and the Law, for the Law certainly did give the man the right to put his wife away—at least for adultery!

THE SOCRATIC RESPONSE OF JESUS

And he answered and said to them, "What did Moses command you?"

This "Socratic" response was definitely not what they wanted to hear. Jesus sidesteps the no and tosses it back to the "self-proclaimed" experts on the Law. They must be very careful here lest they say too much and find themselves fighting each other over the exact nature of the grounds, so they cautiously respond that there are *some* grounds without specifying exactly what they ·re.

THE CAUTIOUS RESPONSE OF THE PHARISEES

And they said, "Moses permitted a man to write a certificate of divorce and send her away."

This was the only safe answer: Moses did allow divorce. But at this juncture they are close to having no further point to make. If they ask him if that contradicts his own teaching (Luke 16:18), he may simply say no, and the dialogue winds down. But that is the only direction that they can go; they must get him to say no to the original question. But in their cautious statement they speak better than they know!

Jesus then takes the initiative, for he discerns that their understanding about the whole matter is wrong. They start from the assumption that a man has a right by Law to put away his wife. They fight among themselves over exactly what this right of the husband is, whereas God desires permanence. To point out this crucial flaw in their thinking, he reminds them of another teaching of Moses:

THE TRUE MOSAIC CONTEXT FOR THE DIVORCE DISCUSSION

And he answered and said, "Have you not read, that he who created them from the beginning of creation made them male and female, and said 'For this cause a man shall leave his father and mother, and the two shall become one flesh'? Consequently they are no longer two, but one flesh. What therefore God has joined together, let no man separate."

They had been concerned with "when the man may walk away from his wife." Jesus points out that the design of marriage is not to see it end. The man and his wife were biologically designed to complement each other. One half of the complement is not enough. The two chose each other intending never to go back to their former ways of living—intending to permanently join together. Because of this choice they do not have the right simply to "walk away" but should see themselves as a continuing social unit. And it must be remembered that God himself is the guarantor of the covenant. No human being should think that he or she has the moral right to dissolve the covenant. The covenant cannot be dissolved without challenging the One who insures the covenant: God himself.

At this point we should pause in our flowing dialogue and note how inappropriate it would have been for Jesus to have interrupted his argument by making new or incidental points about the doctrine of marriage. This would not have been the time to adopt the Temple Scroll approach to polygamy, for example. By employing the Septuagint's "the two," he simply means to identify clearly that the two who once could turn and walk away from each other have by their choice eliminated the option of doing so.

As far as we are concerned, it seems inappropriate to read into the final statement ("What God has joined . . .") *permanence*. The verse teaches nothing of the kind. Jesus does not say, "Since what God joins together is permanent, don't get a divorce." To have said that would have been to say exactly what the Pharisees wanted him to say. It would have shown him to be teaching contrary to the Old Testament.[7] Jesus affirmed as strongly as possible (without abrogating any teaching of the Law) the obligation of marriage partners to stay married. He said that it is *immoral* to sever the marriage bond, not that it is *impossible* to do so. He does not say, "Since God insures marriage you should never get a divorce."[8] Jesus does not use the normal and technical term for divorce here, but instead uses the word *chorizo*, which is well translated "sunder." In all the uses of this word in the New Testament it never is used as a synonym for divorce. Jesus does not deny the right to *divorce a spouse*, he merely says it is wrong to *sunder a marriage covenant*.

What is not clear in this statement is exactly when such a sundering takes place. It could be at the point of divorce, or it could be at the point of *porneia* or even "uncleanness." Jesus had affirmed the basics of divorce, without giving the Pharisees anything to "shoot at."

But the Pharisees (like some of our modern exegetes) jumped to the hasty conclusion that by this saying Jesus implied that a man may not divorce his wife at all. And they are partially right, for from the context it is clear that some divorces might be categorized as sundering events! In any case, Jesus' response seemed to be exactly the sort of absolute, negative teaching they had hoped he would voice. The Pharisees therefore leaped to the offense:

THE FALSE COUP DE GRÂCE

They said to him, "Why then did Moses command to give her a certificate and send her away?"

This is truly a botched question, because nothing in what Jesus has said would logically deny that there might be a time to put away a person who, by unlawful actions in the marriage, has sundered the marriage bond already! But then, they doubtless thought they smelled the blood of victory.

Alas for their argument. Jesus now crushes it by showing how completely they have misunderstood the Mosaic legislation they cite.

THE TRUE COUP DE GRÂCE

But Jesus said to them, "Because of your hardness of heart he wrote you this commandment—Moses permitted you to divorce your wives—but from the beginning it has not been this way."

This statement rings like a hammer upon their feeble words.

Two Crucial Mistakes in Interpretation

And yet, it seems to me that most modern exegetes have enfeebled Jesus' words by making two crucial misinterpretations of Jesus' meaning at this point.

Is God Like the Unjust Steward?

The first is the incredible assertion that God himself is guilty of what Jesus identified as the Pharisees' unrighteous stewardship of eternal Law. The phrase "because of your hardness of heart" is interpreted as saying something like: "Well, God knows that divorce will take place, so he made a concession to you, allowing you to do what you wanted." This is giving the Master's debtors a "cut rate" (cf. Luke 16:5–7) with regard to divorce law. Can God condemn in human beings what he himself allows? That certainly does not sound like the Father of whom Jesus said, "You are to be perfect, as your heavenly Father is perfect."

However Jesus meant this "concession," it would be blasphemous to interpret concession as compromise.

What then? For whom is the concession? For the wives whom these hard-hearted men have been divorcing since before the days of Moses. It is "because" of their hard hearts, not "on behalf" of them. God has provided *against* the fact, not in favor of it. Knowing that they will be treacherous and turn their backs on their covenant partner, the wife of their youth, God has provided a law that will minimize the abuse. He will permit husbands to put innocent wives away so that these wives will be saved from their husbands, who would perhaps physically abuse them if forced to keep them. So the permission to divorce has nothing to do with condescending to wicked men, but everything to do with preserving innocent women.[9]

Is God Opposed to Moses?

The second mistake in interpretation is in seeing Jesus as abrogating this concession. This is done specifically in the exegesis of the next saying of Jesus, but the interpretation of that saying is determined by his words "from the beginning it has not been this way." Can these words be referring to the Mosaic concession? Most commentators say yes. But, we may ask, have not husbands been hard of heart since the beginning? Has not God been concerned for the well-being of wives from the beginning? Since Jesus has come, have hard-hearted men disappeared from the face of the earth? Have wives ceased to need such divine protection? How can we answer yes to any of these questions?

The grammar here is interesting; "from the beginning it has not been this way" does not mean from the beginning until a point in the past (i.e., the giving of the Mosaic "concession"). That translation would be clear had the text used the pluperfect. But it uses the simple perfect instead, which should be rendered "from the beginning all the way up to the point of my speaking these words." To be more specific, we take this verb to be an intensive perfect. That form is the "strong way of saying that a thing *is*."[10] In other words, Jesus is not trying to distinguish between a dispensation up to Moses and one beginning with his present teaching, but rather a continuing divine attitude that runs clear from the beginning of creation up to the point of the Lord's speech—right through the time of Moses and the exercise of the Law!

This raises an interesting consideration. Did God or did not God inspire Deuteronomy 24:1–4? Perhaps we should adopt an interpretation of Jesus' words that drives a wedge between God and Moses. "From the beginning God had it one way, but then Moses gave another. And now I am going to restore the divine way." If God's character is changeless, then it must have been that Moses imposed his own ideas at that point in the Law. Perhaps Christ wishes to point this out by saying it was *only* Moses who compromised the true teaching to the desires of hard-hearted men![11] Certainly not! Jesus did not mean to divide Moses from God, and if he had, the Pharisees would have been the first to point it out—which they do not.

What, then, is the "this way" that has not been from the beginning? Even though the *this* is a Greek word that directs attention to a close reference (the grammar book would make it the "concession"), I believe that it is only defensible to make its antecedent the implied right to get out of the marriage that is behind the questions of the Pharisees. For them, Moses was, in Deuteronomy, granting the man a right to end his own marriage.[12] Remember their initial question: "Is it legal for a man to put away his wife for any cause at all?" Note as well their response to Jesus' Socratic answer: "Moses permitted a man to write . . . and send away." Jesus attacks their implication that marriage is an institution whose covenant is hedged in favor of spouses that wish to exit the relationship. Marriage is meant "for keeps," not for temporary association. It is the Pharisaical implication that has not been God's way from the beginning. Deuteronomy 24:1–4 had nothing to do with an alleged right to put away one's wife. Deuteronomy 24:1–4 was God's rule for minimizing the effects of treachery. Additionally note that the referent is, in a way, the close "concession"—not as Moses meant it, but as the Pharisees had interpreted it!

I believe that Murray and others are wrongheaded in suggesting that Jesus tries to correct a mistaken Pharisaical thought that when the woman commits adultery the husband must divorce her. I do not deny that some rabbis held to such obligation, nor that there was such an obligation, but there is not sufficient indication that that point was important to these Pharisees or to Jesus. Certainly Deuteronomy 24:1–4, which seeks to protect the woman from the abuse of a hard-hearted husband, finds it proper for her to receive a certificate of divorce, and, just as certainly, that text does not require a woman to be divorced for the sin of *adultery*.[13] As we noted earlier, there is no indication that "uncleanness" refers to any act of an immoral sort. As to the responsibility of a man to sooner or later divorce the spouse as a matter of discipline, I shall have more to say presently. But that idea is not only rabbinic, it is also the lesson we learn from God's treatment of Israel.[14]

CHRIST'S SUMMARY OF HIS TEACHING TO THE PHARISEES

Jesus then summarized for the Pharisees his previous teaching on divorce and remarriage to make the awesome point clear.

"And I say to you, whoever divorces his wife, except for immorality, and marries another woman commits adultery."

This, of course, is not at all what the Pharisees wanted to hear. By the most likely interpretation of the grounds for divorce implied by this saying, Jesus could be considered no more conservative than Shammai—and that ended the debate, as far as the Pharisees were concerned. They could go no further without arguing among themselves. Thus, Jesus turns away from them. He had no more interest than they in continuing the dialogue.

Nonetheless, there was within Jesus' words a rather shocking implication. Jesus was saying that the man who took advantage of Deuteronomy 24:1–4 and put away his wife was really guilty of the sin of adultery—sexless adultery![15]

But we are getting ahead of ourselves. For we must now take the time to dissect this statement to see exactly what Jesus is saying. We must carefully consider the exact grammatical structure of the sentence, lest we be charged with being ignorant of factors that others think prohibit such an interpretation as ours.

"Whoever Divorces His Wife, Except for Immorality and Marries Another, Commits Adultery"

The most extensive study of the syntax of this saying as it is presented in Matthew 19:9 has been done by Heth and Wenham. The facts they set forth are summarized in the following list:

1. The saying (thus far) is a conditional statement. If a certain condition is met, then a certain result will follow.
2. The statement of condition (technically, the protasis) is compound. It states two conditions: divorce and remarry.
3. The protasis contains a negated prepositional phrase placed *before* the coordinating "and."
4. Prepositional phrases are adverbial and normally qualify the verb they *follow*. That verb is "divorces."[16]

Along the way, however, they note three qualifications that are also significant to the discussion:

1. This construction may well be a *ha paux*. It is rare indeed to find a compound conditional with a negating prepositional phrase that comes after the first verb.[17]
2. "Greek word order is far less significant to the meaning of a sentence than the order of words in an English sentence."[18]
3. (Spoken with regard to simplistic appeals to the lexicon in determining the meaning of a word) "it is the context in which a word appears where it is used on the lips of a particular individual with a given meaning he intends to convey—all of this indicates to the reader how a word is being used." (I would add that the same warning is even more appropriate where syntax is involved—since syntax often involves higher level interpretation than the mere meaning of a word.)[19]

THE PLACEMENT OF THE "EXCEPTION CLAUSE"

The major point of controversy, as far as Heth and Wenham are concerned, is the precise location of the negating prepositional phrase (i.e., the celebrated "exception clause"). They note that it could have been placed in any one of three locations in the protasis:

Whoever (1) divorces his wife (2) and marries another (3) commits adultery.

1. Between *whoever* and *divorces*.
2. Between *the wife of him* and *and marries another* (which was Matthew's choice).
3. At the end of the protasis (i.e., after *marries another*) and before the apodosis (i.e., the result, *commits adultery*).

The first option would, they feel, make divorce for fornication "mandatory." The second would make the *combination* of groundless divorce and remarriage adultery. The third would permit remarriage after groundless divorce.[20]

Heth and Wenham are especially set on disproving any use of this verse to affirm the right to remarry after divorce, a right denied by early Church Fathers. The first major (modern) proponent of the view they reject was Erasmus, the sixteenth-century Christian humanist; hence they identify the position by his name: the Erasmian position. The modern spokesman for this view is John Murray, late theologian of Westminster Seminary, and it is largely Murray's work that they criticize. At this point they object to his statement that the number 2 position can properly support what they fancy only the number 3 could. By using the principle that the prepositional phrase modifies the verb that precedes it, they object strenuously to any attempt to make it modify both parts of the protasis. They stop short of denying that it is possible for both parts to be modified, however.

As for their own explanation, they feel that the Greek structure present in the verse may only properly be interpreted in their way, which later they refine to say that "putting away for reasons other than unchastity is forbidden; and remarriage after every divorce is adulterous." This latter statement arises from their opinion that "we are dealing with two conditional statements, one that is qualified and one that is unqualified or absolute."[21]

Just how sound are their conclusions? I do not feel that they will bear the weight of analysis. First, their conclusion that the complex conditional is properly delineated as two conditional statements is highly strained. The verse does not contain two independent statements, only one. They artificially separate the first from the second condition. They have done this, it seems to me, simply to stress the alleged independent nature of the second condition. They wish to say that remarriage after every divorce is adulterous. But the verse does not say this. The negating clause does indeed modify the first condition, but it is logically suspect to separate the qualified idea from the second condition, which is syntactically tied to it. Or maybe we should put that the other way around: it is improper to interpret the second condition independently of the negated first condition.

Heth and Wenham start with humility, but lose it when they first admit that the construction is unique and then dogmatically deny that the second condition can in any way be qualified by the qualified first condition. They cite the frequency of such negating prepositional phrases modifying what comes before rather than what comes behind, but happily forget that there are perhaps no other instances quite like this one (a complex conditional with the negating phrase interrupting the conditions). Thus, I believe that they are hasty in their conclusions.

Moreover, it is doubtful that the except phrase would have been put at any other point in the sentence. As Heth and Wenham note, such phrases do not precede the verb they modify unless the phrase is intended to be the emphasis of the statement.[22] By all accounts, the phrase is not intended to be emphatic, and that is the only reason I can see why it ever would have been put in the number 1 position. The exception is clearly not the point of the verse: it is an exception, pure and simple. Nor am I convinced that, had the exception been placed in the number 1 position, the saying would have required divorce if fornication had occurred in the marriage. It would far more likely have simply implied emphasis.[23] The number 1 position would certainly have been a grammatically confusing location for a nonemphatic, negating prepositional![24]

The number 3 location is even more confusing grammatically and conceptually. Since, as these writers have noted, the negating prepositional phrase normally modifies the verb (singular) that precedes it, it would have given the impression that "he who marries another, except for fornication, commits adultery." But, what is "marrying another except for fornication"? This option is certainly grammatically harsh. In fact, whatever could the placement of the phrase there mean? Would it not give the impression that divorce resulting in remarriage would be adulterous *unless the reason for remarriage was "fornication"*? What does this mean? To say that the divorce was grounded in "fornication" clearly implies that the first wife was divorced because she was a fornicator. But who is guilty of the fornication in number 3? If the negating clause is tied only to the immediately preceding verb, *[re]marries,* and not to *divorces,* it is anybody's guess who is guilty of fornication—perhaps the husband, perhaps the second wife. Who knows? In any case, whoever it is would seem, by committing it, to have freed the husband of the sin of adultery, and that, of course, would be grossly immoral. It would negate the condemnation of adultery where treacherous divorce and remarriage had taken place—and *because* somebody had committed fornication in some way relating to the remarriage![25]

It is possible, perhaps, that the prepositional phrase could have been put after the apodosis: "he who divorces his wife and marries another commits adultery (except for fornication)." But this too is semantically confusing. The prepositional phrase should be closer to its verb than that. I see no reason to speculate further about this option, which is not mentioned by Heth and Wenham.

That leaves us only with number 2, exactly where the Gospel writer put it. But what are the logical implications of this location? It would seem that they may be summarized as follows:

1. The negation is not emphatic. It is an aside from the major point: the husband does not have a right to end his marriage.
2. The negating phrase modifies the previous verb: "is divorcing." Unchastity is a concern regarding the divorce, not the (re)marriage. It is valid grounds for divorcing. Grammatically, the negating value of the phrase would still obtain even if there were no second condition.
3. The apodosis cannot be alleged to obtain unless all the conditions that precede it obtain also. Thus it is improper to say that all divorces that end in remarriage are adulterous. Rather, all divorces not grounded in fornication that end in remarriage are adulterous.[26]

In the end, it seems to me that something like the following is going on in the minds of these scholars: insofar as remarriage is always an indication of adultery and divorce is always a sin of at least some other sort, the syntax of the Gospels must be interpreted as saying this. In other words, Heth and Wenham have read their own conclusions into the syntax. Actually, the statements in Mark and Luke, when abstracted and considered out of their context, do prohibit all divorce and remarriage, but, when seen in their contexts and in the context of Matthew's exception clauses, they prohibit only divorces and remarriages that are ill grounded—an ill-grounded remarriage seen as one that is based upon an ill-grounded divorce, and an ill-grounded divorce seen as one not grounded in *porneia*.[27]

Conclusions

REMARRIAGE AND THE "INNOCENT PARTY"

Several reflections on these points are in order. First, Heth and Wenham's contention that the verse prohibits remarriage after *every* divorce cannot be conclusively proved by the grammar. The Erasmian view is still possible, as they admit.[28] Second, since the verse wants to make a point of the fact that groundless divorce involving a remarriage is adulterous, it is most reasonable to conclude that properly grounded divorce involving remarriage is *not* adulterous. To be sure, it would be clear that it is permissible to remarry in such cases had the conditional read: "only if a divorce is improperly grounded and remarriage occurs is adultery present." The absence of the *only* may be interpreted as casting some shadow of doubt over the remarriage of the righteous divorcer. But one who affirms that remarriage of the righteous divorcer is adultery bears the burden of proof, and the proof certainly cannot be obtained from this saying or an abbreviation of it (as is certainly the case in Mark's rendition, since he is relating only part of the conflate reading).

Third, the passage does not speak at all to the matter of the treacherously divorced person remarrying. That issue is never brought up, and conclusions concerning this matter must be supported from other locations in the biblical text. I believe that the Scripture permits such remarriage in two ways:

1. The man could always marry another woman, as long as she was a valid marriage partner, for example, not a "woman of the land" or a "blood relative." Thus, the morality of polygamy affirms the right of the innocent man to remarry.[29]
2. The woman who was treacherously divorced could remarry without moral stigma, according to Deuteronomy 24:1–4.[30]

REMARRIAGE AND THE "GUILTY PARTY"

What, however, should be said about the guilty party? Does this teaching completely eliminate the option to remarry for the divorcing husband who groundlessly puts his wife away? Our answer is in one sense yes and in another no. Were Jesus to completely eliminate a right to remarry, he would have to abrogate the Old Testament doctrine of morally permissible polygamy. And, we note, this would not at all be what we would expect from the nature of the dialogue at hand. It is not to his dialectical advantage; nor would it be consistent with his profession to *not* abrogate the least of the laws; nor does it fit into the flow of the dialogue for him to have implied that remarriage for an unjust man was adultery. We cannot jump to the hasty conclusion that Jesus is completely condemning the second marriage.

But what then does the presence of the second conditional mean in the overall condemnation of adultery? Perhaps at this point it is worthy of note that a textual problem exists with the second conditional. These important words are omitted in some significant manuscripts of Matthew.[31] However, since they are present in Mark, and since we are examining the conflate reading, we need not busy ourselves with this matter until we come to a consideration of the particular omissions and inclusions of the Gospels considered separately. Beyond this, the textual support for the omission is not as strong as for its inclusion.[32] Thus, we have no right to ignore the combination of conditions.

I prefer to see the presence of the second conditional as an identification of the reason for the unjust divorce. It is the person who is divorcing and remarrying as a united action who is committing adultery. We might even say that the divorce has not been properly grounded upon occurrence of fornication in the marriage; this man has put away his valid wife *"for the purpose* of marrying another woman." This conjecture is supported by two considerations. First, this places it clearly in the category of the divorce situation that Malachi addressed, men divorcing their proper wives to marry others ("women of the land"). The only difference is that the specific objects of remarriage in Malachi's day were illicit per se according to Deuteronomy 7:3. As we noted in chapter 4, the reference to Abraham in the Malachi 2 passage affirms that these Hebrews could have taken these women as concubines (as Hagar had been), thus sort of half-wives, without moral stigma. The point of the Malachi passage is that the abiding sin is the rejection of the valid partner. This is to say, the problem is the divorce itself.[33] So too here, it is not the remarriage itself that is the problem. The immorality only occurs because the first wife has been unjustly divorced (a point that Matthew notes and the other Gospel writers choose to ignore).[34]

Second, it is not improper to find in the meaning of the connector "and" (*kai*) the idea of "for the purpose of."[35] And the idea of immediate connection seems clear in the combining of the conditions in the protasis that precedes any moral condemnation in the apodosis. The condemned action is again like that of Herod. He divorced his valid partner to marry Herodias. And so it often happens, especially where men do the divorcing. They wish to devote themselves to only one woman (or more commonly the woman wishes the man to so devote himself), and so they treacherously put away the partner by right to achieve the desired monogamous relationship. It is the case that, since the man promised to continuously provide for his valid partner, this putting away is itself adulterous.[36] This is doubtless Paul's point in 1 Corinthians 7 when he instructs the treacherous partner to remain unmarried or be reconciled.[37]

Thus, we cautiously conclude that remarriages that are not the goal of the divorce, that is, a part of the combined action of divorcing and remarrying, may be permissible—all other things being equal. Against this one might argue that the presence of the exception clause between the conditions spreads the two apart. But I do not think this is a proper evaluation. As we have noted earlier, the present location of the negating prepositional phrase is the only one reasonable, and it is parenthetical. Therefore, I do contend that the divorcing and remarrying are historically united in the hypothetical wrongdoing.[38]

CLARIFICATION TO HIS DISCIPLES

Their Questioning

And in the house, the disciples began to question him about this again.

With this saying Jesus has properly and completely answered the test question of the Pharisees. They wanted to know if a man had a right to put his wife away and, if so, for what causes. Jesus corrects their orientation, turning it from the idea of how they can get out of marriage to the eternal design of marriage: union. And he righteously affirms the right of the offended party to discipline the erring spouse. But his own disciples were apparently not clear on the divorce teaching. For when he turns aside and goes into a house, they question him further: What does it mean? His response is not as detailed as that already given. He simply summarizes the major point of the teaching:

Male Treachery

And he said to them, "Whoever divorces his wife, and marries another woman commits adultery against her."

The only point omitted is the exception clause. He omits it because what he now says is what he wishes to leave with them, that is, what adultery is: the sundering of the vow to continuously provide for the valid marriage partner. Marriage was intended to be permanent. The marriage bond cannot be broken without the sin of adultery taking place. This explains how the saying, as I interpret it above, fits with the section that stresses the sacredness of that bond. When the covenant is broken by an action such as "fornication," the divorce does not "sunder" the bond, the action itself has. If there is not such sundering then the legal divorce is itself the sundering—is a treachery, is adultery.

Heth and Wenham make a serious mistake at this point when they hasten to imply that, since marriage is not sexual union, the Erasmians err in suggesting that fornication (while the covenant is operative) breaks the bond.[39] These authors hold that illicit sexuality does not break the bond, and that that is why the sexuality of the remarriage is adulterous. They hold that the couple whose marriage is legally and even properly ended[40] still have a marriage bond with each other until one of them dies. Thus, a remarriage constitutes adulterous sexual activity.

They have sadly failed to comprehend the covenantal and contractual nature of marriage. It is *not* the simple fact of extramarital sex that constitutes the sundering of the bond, but the intentional engagement in acts that are counter to the canons of the covenant. The woman who intentionally has sex with another man sunders her marriage. The sundering does not take place because sex has occurred—the marriage is not sundered when she is raped—but when she is willing to engage in an act that she promised in the covenant not to do. For the man, his sundering of the relationship rests, not in his having sex with another woman—polygamy was morally permissible—but in his forsaking of his covenant partner simply to devote himself to another bed partner. The bond is broken *when the covenanted promises are not kept*.

This does not mean that every breach of the covenant must lead to a legal divorce. If the covenant can be restored without such severe disciplinary action, that is permissible in an age of "grace." God shows us the example to follow when he attempts for some time to get his "wife," Israel, to see the error of her ways. Only after that attempt does he "put them away." Nor does such a disciplinary action mean that reconciliation is impossible without a *formal* remarriage to the same partner. It is enough for the erring partner to reaffirm the intention not to further break the covenant. So Israel did in their times of national revival.

The Reversal Clause

"and if she herself divorces her husband and marries another man, she is committing adultery."

This addition might seem only applicable for disciples who would soon be "discipling the nations, teaching them whatsoever I taught you." However, the Herodias case, in which she divorced Philip, certainly made this saying relevant to Jewish ears even at that point. Nonetheless, women divorcing men was rare in Israel, and for Jesus to have brought this point up in front of the Pharisees would only have put the subject off on a sidetrack. The point would have been clear to such teachers, but they would likely have been scrambling for "debater's points" after being so thoroughly silenced by Jesus.

The Disciples' Evaluation

The disciples said to him, "If the relationship of the man to his wife is like this, it is better not to marry."

This is the only substantive response of the disciples to the saying of Jesus. It is a sober response, but there is in it no hint of the "astonishment" mentioned by some teachers.[41] Laney voices the feelings of many commentators when he suggests that the disciples must have thought Jesus' teaching more strict than the teachers they were accustomed to hear. The only explanation that Laney can see for such a comment is that the teaching of Jesus must not have allowed for any divorce.[42] But this view simply cannot stand up under examination. For as we have seen, Jesus in fact did allow for divorce on the ground of *porneia*.

Yet Laney will not be disposed of so easily. His own idea is that *porneia* means "illicit marriages, incest," and, therefore, the exception clause simply permits an illicit marriage to be legally ended. The parties involved in the marriage alluded to are unfit for each other. Thus, no legitimate marriage may be morally broken by divorce.

There is a certain consistency to this approach, but it will not wash. The term *porneia* decisively includes more than incest, and the incest itself might not be with the marriage partner but another family member—promiscuity. Indeed, any attempt to limit the crucial word to the perversion of incest will sooner or later end up showing the careful Bible student that incest was grouped with adultery, homosexuality, and bestiality as gross forms of *porneia*.[43]

In the end, we are justified in saying only that the disciples were sobered by Jesus' teaching that divorce is not a right to be exercised by the man but an exceptional disciplinary action to be taken only if the spouse has already broken the covenant, and that any attempt to divorce a wife simply out of a desire to devote oneself to another woman is the sin of adultery. Such teaching was not held by any rabbi. Even Shammai, who permitted a man to divorce his wife if she had committed an act tantamount to adultery, does not go on to call a divorce without such a ground the sin of adultery. In effect, the Pharisees knew of nothing such as Matthew records Jesus as teaching: that adultery need not involve sex, that it may be constituted simply by a man breaking his vow of continuing provision for his spouse (even if the breaking is done with legal sanction).

The Eunuch Saying

> But he said to them, "Not all men can accept this statement, but only those to whom it has been given."

Two problems arise in the interpretation of Jesus' response. First, to what "statement" does he refer, and, second, who are the men to whom that statement had been given?

TWO IDENTIFICATIONS OF THE "STATEMENT"

D. A. Carson succinctly points out the options:

Either *ton logon touton* (lit., "this word"—regardless of whether *touton* is original, since *ton* can be a mild demonstrative) refers to Jesus' teaching (vs. 4–9) or to the disciples' misguided remark in v. 10. We will look at them in reverse order.[44]

"STATEMENT" EQUALS THE DISCIPLES' REMARK

Carson continues that

NIV's "this teaching" (v. 11) favors the former; but this is unlikely, for it makes Jesus contradict himself. After a strong prohibition, it is highly unlikely that Jesus' moral teaching dwindles into a pathetic "But of course, not everyone can accept this."

Accordingly, Carson suggests that "it is better to take 'this word' to refer to the disciples' conclusion in v. 10: 'it is better not to marry.' Jesus responds that not everyone can live by such a verdict, such abstinence from marriage."

Heth and Wenham, in the unpublished manuscript of their *Jesus and Divorce,* stated reasons why this identification is unlikely. First, the term *this statement* "is a significant unit in Matthew's Gospel . . . and elsewhere it *always* refers to the words of Jesus which He has just finished delivering."[45] Second, they observe, with Quesnell, that it is not customary in Gospel writings for the disciples' responses to Jesus' teaching to be positively received by Christ.[46] In the published version of *Jesus and Divorce* they altered this section. Stressing that on the "traditional" view verse 11 would seem to speak of two classes of disciples ("not all" vs. "only those"), they strongly reject the idea that Jesus' teachings on divorce and remarriage could be for only one group and not another.[47]

"STATEMENT" EQUALS JESUS' TEACHING

It seems preferable to identify the "statement" with Jesus' previous teaching. However, to interpret the retort as sarcastic ultimately yields the same general result as that offered by Carson. The "ironic" approach has Jesus saying that of course there are some who do not need to pay attention to his teaching: eunuchs. The net effect is that, since few men desired celibacy, they would choose to get married and, by that choice, place themselves under obligation to follow the rule set forth by Christ for the married, that is, stay married until death or *porneia.*

WHAT IS THE SIGNIFICANCE OF THE "EUNUCH SAYING"?

"For there are eunuchs . . ."

At present there are three major interpretations of the "eunuch saying" that follows Jesus' dialogue with the Pharisees and comprises his response to the reaction of his disciples.

THE RENUNCIATION-OF-MARRIAGE VIEW

These verses advocate the renunciation of marriage. In them Jesus is promoting celibacy for the sake of the kingdom.

This view, called "traditional" by Heth and Wenham, is advocated by W. D. Davies and D. R. Catchpole.[48] According to this view Jesus is agreeing with the disciples and issuing a "call to celibacy." In other words, celibacy is elevated as a valid option for those who have not been given the gift of marriage (cf. Matt. 19:12). But Heth and Wenham object that such an interpretation is wrong for just that reason, as noted earlier: in the Gospels, Jesus seldom agrees with the disciples. To this, they add that Matthew omits all similar apparent depreciations of the marriage state included in other Gospels (Luke) and rather elevates marriage in the wedding feast parable.[49] Finally, they submit Paul's introductory comment to his own elevation of celibacy as proof that Jesus had not previously taught that celibacy is preferable. In 1 Corinthians 7:25, Paul says, "I have no commandment from the Lord," just before he launches into a discussion of the virgin state.

Carson softens the interpretation by suggesting that Jesus "freely concedes that for those to whom it is given 'it *is* better not to marry'; and 'That one who can accept this should accept it.'" In other words, Jesus admits that marriage is not intended for those who have the gift of celibacy.[50]

This is not as bad as speaking of "elevating celibacy," but I still feel uncomfortable with it. Does the text itself, aside from the questioned passage, suggest that celibacy is a "gift"? Hardly. Celibacy is seen as imposed by hereditary deficiency, by mutilation by others, and by one's own choice.[51] Without a clear teaching of the "gift of celibacy," it seems preferable to suggest another interpretation altogether.

THE CELIBACY-OF-THE-DIVORCED VIEW

The verses refer to the husband whose wife has been put away, requiring him to consecrate himself to a celibate life (at least until his former wife dies).

Proponents of this view, in addition to Heth and Wenham, include Q. Quesnell, J. Dupont, Hermas of Rome, and J. D. M. Derrett.[52] On this view, the referents of "not all receive this saying" are the Pharisees, who reject the words of Jesus, whereas "those to whom it has been given" are the disciples of the kingdom.[53]

Support for this position is drawn from the account of the rich man, which follows the divorce passage. It is pointed out that when the rich man turns away and Jesus tells them the "hard saying," that it is difficult for rich men to get into heaven, the disciples voice astonishment ("Who then can be saved?"), which is met by Jesus' comment, "With men this is impossible, but with God all things are possible." In this case, the "this" reaches back to the "hard teaching," not to the words of the disciples. The argument then runs: just as the two groups of receivers in the rich man story are unbelieving men and disciples, so in the divorce legislation is the division the same.[54]

Though this all sounds tempting, this view's major drawback is that it commits a logical fallacy. In effect, its proponents are saying:

In A there is a formal pattern Y with content Z.

In B there is a formal pattern Y with content $?$.

Since Y is the same in A and B, the content "$?$" must be Z too.

This is a form of the fallacy of the undistributed middle. Just because A and B are alike in the stated formal respect Y does not mean that they are alike in the material respect Z. Beyond this, it seems to me that the stories are not the same at crucial points. Although the second story does contain a saying, it is not the saying to which the "this" refers, but salvation itself. By the nature of human beings as fallen, salvation is beyond them, unless God acts. In the divorce legislation, the "this" refers to the rules of marriage, which any who marry are expected to observe; there is no indication anywhere in the Bible that the ability to keep essential marital vows is a "gift," unless it is a gift with which even fallen humans are born.

It seems to me that the proponents of this view have made a mistake that goes beyond bifurcating disciples; they have bifurcated humanity in such a way that God seems to demand behavior according to one set of rules for disciples and another for the lost. Though this distinction may work regarding "house rules" for the Church, it is destructive of ethics when it is done in the domain of basic morals. We have returned again to the idea that God is a Pharisee who does not demand full morality of his debtors (those created in the image of himself and for whom his Son died). If it is wrong to attempt to break the covenant of marriage (by remarriage), then it is wrong for both the saved and the lost.

This interpretation does commend itself for insisting upon a connection to the saying of Jesus rather than the response of the disciples, but there is no reason to assume that the connection drawn is correct. My own opinion is that these expositors have missed one of the more humorous texts in the New Testament. Jesus has laid down the rule of marriage in his saying. That rule is: marriage is designed for keeps. The husband cannot raise some alleged right to exit the institution aside from his wife's previous breach. Since, we may suppose, adultery was uncommon in those days, this has the effect of saying that, if a man enters into the "bonds of matrimony," it is for keeps. To this the sobered disciples reflect that if marriage is that binding one should exercise the option of celibacy.

The disciples' response is, on its face, ludicrous. How incredibly shortsighted to forgo the pleasures and profits of marriage simply because it is nearly impossible to get out of it! How would you respond to such a foolish statement? Proverbs 26:5 tells us to "answer a fool as his folly deserves, lest he be wise in his own eyes." This is, I think, exactly what Jesus does.

He tells them that his saying about marriage (which, note, is not limited merely to the discussion of remarriage) is intended only for those to whom it is given, or, put otherwise, it only applies to those to whom it applies. If a person wishes to be celibate, then, of course, he or she needn't pay attention to Jesus' words. They are not intended for the unmarried, but for those who are or wish to be married.

The disciples have spoken of a man who, fearing the intended permanency of marriage, cuts himself off from marriage; Jesus goes into detail denoting the groups of people who do not have to worry about his saying: congenital eunuchs, forcibly castrated men, and those who remain celibate by choice, for religious reasons, it is presumed. All these need not worry about marriage. But the others, those who are in possession of their genitals and wish to use them, must adhere to the saying. In short, Jesus is saying: "If you have the plumbing, and you intend to use it, you must follow the rules!"[55]

The alternative then presents itself:

THE RULES-OF-USING-THE-"PLUMBING" VIEW

The saying informs the disciples that his teaching on marriage is only intended for those who get married.

This interpretation of the eunuch saying does identify the referent of the "this statement" with his own teaching. Jesus does not agree with the surly reflection of the disciples. They were suggesting that celibacy should be standard behavior, and Jesus points out that celibates are exceptions. He does not attack celibacy—had he, Paul would have had a very different response in 1 Corinthians 7:25! This view does not reflect negatively upon the institution of marriage. It shares this with the celibacy-of-the-divorced view, but has the benefit of being simpler. The celibacy-of-the-divorced view presumes that Jesus reflects only upon the remarriage of the divorcing husband. That is, at best, only one aspect of the complex conditional saying of Jesus. This third alternative can be seen as commenting upon the entire pronouncement at its most general level. Jesus has been trying to affirm the sanctity of marriage per se. It is most appropriate that the eunuch saying address the same level of teaching. The third alternative does so, and thereby is the alternative that presumes the least. This adherence to the "principle of parsimony" gives it the edge as the preferable interpretation.[56] Jesus simply informed his disciples that his straightforward teaching that marriage cannot be broken by the man without his committing the sin of adultery does not apply to those who are by birth, force, or choice not using the "plumbing." Conversely, his saying *is* for those who choose to use it and care about the morality of that use!

Significant Differences Between Gospel Accounts

So far, we have been considering the pronouncements of Jesus on divorce in the parallel texts of Matthew 19 and Mark 10 as a conflated reading, believing that Jesus did confront the religious leaders and spoke words from which the different Gospel writers selected their accounts. It is appropriate at this point to note the differences between the accounts. In doing so, we wish to understand the message of each Gospel account in its own right and thereby understand why each included or omitted material from the original, longer reading. In this section we need to finally put to rest the issue of why Matthew includes the exception clause and Mark omits it.

The major differences between the two Gospel accounts vis-à-vis the conflate reading seem to be four in number:

1. Matthew alone contains the exception clause.
2. Matthew alone contains the eunuch saying.
3. Mark alone contains the reciprocal clause "and if she herself divorces . . ."
4. Matthew's account has the Pharisees make Moses command divorce, whereas Mark has them note that Moses permitted divorce.

WHY MATTHEW ALONE CONTAINS THE EXCEPTION CLAUSE

The first difference in this list is the most celebrated. As noted in appendix C, some have sought to explain the distribution of this clause to Matthew on the basis of an "ethnic calculus," whereby Matthew is supposed to have directed his Gospel to a more Jewish audience and therefore included for them an exception to the general rule against divorce and remarriage that fit their culture. This exception is variously defined as relating to Jewish betrothal customs or the Levitical "holiness code." This explanation we found wanting.[57]

My own explanation for the inclusion of the clause in Matthew and the exclusion of it in Mark revolves around two major poles. The first, granted by all scholars, is that Mark is a short Gospel, designed that way, in all likelihood, so that it may function as a sort of catechetical tool, a manual of the teachings of Jesus. His Gospel being a sort of "primer" focusing upon doctrinal issues, Mark considered the larger body of materials that were available to him and the other Gospel writers and edited out whatever material he thought superfluous to his task.[58] It is my belief that Mark eliminated the exception clause for the sake of brevity.

I anticipate that someone who is adept at mathematics will object that the exception clause contains far fewer words than the reversal clause. But this is to miss the point. It is not the mere number of words that is at issue. The exception clause in Matthew 19 must be seen in its relation to materials present elsewhere in Matthew's Gospel; I refer to that large section in the latter half of Matthew 18 that deals with discipline. Note carefully that the entire section Matthew 18:15–35 is missing in Mark. The prior material (Matt. 18:5–14) is paralleled by Mark 9:33–50. Careful consideration of these inclusions and exclusions reveals the following: Matthew and Mark include material concerning self-criticism, but only Matthew expands this to discussion of the criticism of others, that is, discipline of the brother. Mark ends the section that precedes the divorce legislation with the idea of putting your own self in order and living at peace with others. Thus the flow of his Gospel is self-criticism and keeping the peace.

Matthew, on the other hand, includes a large section on discipline. In that section he mentions confrontation of the other who has offended you. And after laying down a certain process by which charges are to be brought, he notes our Lord's harsh teaching that the unrepentant sinner is to be excluded from the fellowship of the brethren. But that is not the end of it. He goes on to note that the purpose of discipline is restoration—forgiveness. Jesus does not demand that forgiveness be given, or that the offended wait forever to hear a confession in order to get about the activities of everyday life. Some sinners should be thrown in jail until (if ever) they come to their senses. Matthew precedes his divorce section with the words, "so shall my heavenly Father also do to you, if each of you does not forgive his brother from your heart" (Matthew 18:35).

In Matthew's context, it is only natural that he should reflect upon this general teaching in the section he strings together with it. How appropriate that the call for forgiveness from the heart should move on to two cases of hard-heartedness: unjust divorce and the hindering of children. And in the first case, how appropriate that Jesus should utter the exception clause, since that clause succinctly captures the whole Old Testament doctrine of (righteous) divorce as discipline of an adulterous and unrepentant spouse!

It is worthy of more than a footnote here to say that the fact of discipline, and its hope of success, does not forever determine the marital status of the righteous divorcer. Though it is true that God, in his infinite patience and aseity, waited for divorced Israel to return to him, and though Hosea shows us how successful the divorce and restoration process can be, it is faulty logic to go from the "is" to the "ought" by concluding that the righteous divorcer (the innocent party) should wait indefinitely for the repentance of the spouse. Human beings are not like God. God may choose whether or not to be alone, but it is not good for human beings to be alone. And though that aloneness may be assuaged by friendships, we must remember that Paul notes that it is better to marry than to burn. The innocent party is under no obligation to wait indefinitely for the return.[59] Guilty parties have forfeited the right to expect consideration. Theirs is the task of repenting and being reconciled as quickly as possible. Remember, too, that some will never willfully repent. Those should not be forgiven and restored. To do so would be to make a mockery of divine justice. On the other hand, to fail to receive back a repentant spouse when the disciplinary divorce is effective is a dangerous misuse of the doctrine of grace and forgiveness, as Jesus makes clear in the unforgiving steward parable. To fail to forgive and restore certainly releases the guilty party from an obligation to "remain unmarried," because it puts the guilty shoe onto the other foot. The guilty becomes the innocent, and the innocent becomes the guilty. All these points seem implicit in the disciplinary discussion found in Matthew.

To return to our subject, note that for Matthew to have included the exception clause is to be expected. For Mark to do so, when he has edited out the matter of discipline, should not be. It is more than a matter of word count; it is the tip of a large iceberg. Mark simply did not want to get into a discussion of the discipline of others. His context is judgment of oneself, not judgment of the other. His is a context of *keeping* the peace if possible. The inclusion of exceptions to the general rule of no divorce—don't try and legally end your marital relationship—is most inappropriate, for restorative as divorce is intended to be from God's perspective, it is still legally and emotionally disruptive. It is the hard path of "tough love."

THE MATTHEAN EUNUCH SAYING

The second Matthean passage omitted by Mark is the eunuch saying. Again, it is simply because Mark is a selective Gospel. The majority of the private teaching of Jesus to the disciples is more or less redundant to that spoken before the Pharisees. Perhaps for this reason Mark omits it. The important point in it, that is, the reversal clause, he retains. And, being concerned with location, he mentions the house. Matthew, focusing upon the teaching, does not mention where the discourse with the disciples took place. And the fact that the Lord has shifted his attention to them is clear.

THE MARKAN REVERSAL CLAUSE

The third difference, the reversal clause, seems an oddity. Since Mark's custom is to omit material found in Matthew and Luke, why is his Gospel expansive on this point? Believing in Matthean priority, as I do, part of my explanation is that Mark did not wish that bit of Q material to be lost—as it was not included in either of the other two finished Gospels. But there are other considerations as well. For one thing, Matthew emphasizes the chauvinism of the Israelite males. He includes the clause "you to divorce your wives." Mark omits this clause. In the flow of the Matthean account comes across an emphasis on the guilt of the men, notwithstanding the inclusion of the exception clause. At no point is this more evident than in the eunuch saying, where the chauvinism of the disciples is quite pronounced. It is also evident in the harshness of the Pharisees' summation of Deuteronomy 24:1–4 ("Moses command[ed] to give her a certificate and divorce her"). It may also be reflected in the inclusion of "cleave to his wife," with which Jesus pricks the male conscience of the Pharisees. He is stressing that they were the ones who had committed themselves to the women. There may be more indications of this rebuke of the celebrated male superiority that pervaded the Israelite community in Matthew's Gospel, but I believe that these are sufficient to make the point that Matthew was highlighting this aspect of the conflate reading by his selection.[60]

DIFFERENT PRESENTATIONS OF MOSES?

Perhaps what I have said so far helps to explain the fourth of the points of significant difference: the different representations of Moses. The statement found in Matthew is harsher, and its inclusion there fits the flowing antichauvinism theme, whereas the milder statement fits better the more irenic flow of Mark's Gospel.

SUMMARY

Let us summarize this section by stating that although both Gospels contain the same general material, each has its own emphasis. Matthew is more specific and inclusive as a rule. Continuing a prior theme of disciplinary action, he includes the exception clause, and emphasizing the rebuke of Jewish male chauvinism, he omits the reciprocal clause, while including aspects of the original dialogue that entail that matter. Mark, on the other hand, is more general, omitting material extraneous to his catechetical approach. The differences are not disharmonious in the final analysis. And it is to that matter, that is, the harmony of Gospel sayings on divorce, to which we now turn on a grander scale.

CONCLUSIONS—THE HARMONIZATION OF THE WHOLE

What, then, is the full teaching of Jesus on divorce and remarriage? Simply put, it is the same as that of the Old Testament as expressed in the Law and the Prophets. It is true that Jesus tends to emphasize what the Old Testament did not, but then that is characteristic of him. The Matthew 5:31–32a passage clearly teaches that divorce, when it is groundless, is the sin of adultery in the eyes of God. Since the issue here is substantially that taught in Exodus 21, we see nothing unique or new about this aspect. Matthew 5:32b and Luke 16:18b affirm that any man who is a party to a woman's unjust divorce of her husband is guilty of the sin of adultery.[61] The fact that treacherous divorce by the woman is for the purpose of taking another man obviously places it in the category of standard sexual adultery as set forth in the Law (e.g., Lev. 18 and 20; Deut. 22:23 ff.). In this case, the fact of a legal divorce does not displace the overall judgment that this woman and her new husband are taking a man's wife (i.e., herself) for sexual purposes.[62]

Luke 16:18a, Matthew 19:9, and Mark 10:11 all reflect the Malachite oracle against unjustly divorcing a wife in order simply to marry another woman. And Mark 10:12 admits of the reciprocity of the application of the principle at this point. Further, the celebrated exception clauses are merely an application of the principle stated in the Old Testament Prophets that divorce is a tragic means of discipline to make the offending spouse come to his or her senses and be reconciled. Finally, the Old Testament permission for the innocent party to be remarried (explicit in Deut. 24:1–4 and implicit in Exod. 21:11, 26 f.) is not blunted by anything said by our Lord. Even the guilty party who repents but is not forgiven is not to be identified with the divorce/remarriage prohibited by Christ. Old Testament permission for such a one is most evident in the nexus of polygamy passages.[63]

Jesus does not speak explicitly to the propriety of a woman divorcing her husband on the grounds of his mistreatment of her. Jesus passes over this Old Testament instruction (Exod. 21:10 f.) without a word.[64] And his words should not be used to construe that he is expanding the moral grounds for a woman to divorce her husband to include the husband's sexual infidelity (*porneia*). The exception clause is only used in the context of the wife's unchastity, not the husband's. This does not exonerate the husband from the onus of sin, but only from the penalty of divorce. His *porneia* is to be dealt with like any other non-canonical marital offense, that is, confession and repentance or ultimate excommunication from the fellowship of the Church.

CHAPTER 8

The Teachings of the Apostle Paul on Divorce

(1 Corinthians 7:1–24)

INTRODUCTION

The writing of Paul on the subject of divorce is probably limited to one passage in his letter to the church at Corinth. However, since his teachings on marriage are found in a number of passages, we will find it necessary to look at them as well, though they only bear upon the subject indirectly. We will look first at 1 Corinthians 7. We will devote chapter 8 to his admonition to married persons, covering his words both to Christian couples and to Christians in mixed marriages. His advice to single people will be treated in a separate chapter (9) along with his "marital analogy" in Romans 7. Our final treatment of apostolic materials will be in chapter 10. Considering that chapter as sort of miscellany, we will group together a number of teachings that I am convinced do not really inform our discussion. I deal with them because many popular writers think that these passages indirectly decide the case regarding the propriety of divorce and remarriage. In that chapter we will deal with the "love" teaching of Paul in 1 Corinthians 13. There we will attempt to show how our previous conclusions can be harmonized with that Christian virtue. Then we will consider the apostolic teaching on "submission," the teaching of Paul (Eph. 5) and Peter (1 Pet. 3). Finally, we will deal with the "qualification of church leaders" material in the pastoral Epistles.

The order set forth here is not lightly chosen. It is a continuation of the concern for reading and understanding the biblical text approximately as it was chronologically written.[1] It does, I think, make a certain difference whether one starts with Romans 7/1 Corinthians 7:39 or 1 Corinthians 7:10–28. As in the Gospels, if one starts with the more absolute sayings against divorce and remarriage, one is disposed to explain away the more permissive words. Contrarywise, if Paul has already granted certain permissions concerning divorce/remarriage, it is rather easy to interpret absolute negations as pedagogical overstatements or general rules. Of course, since Paul's writings are, I hold, consistent, the reader should ultimately be able to come to the same conclusions either way, but it seems wiser to follow the writer through in his own order.[2]

THE EXPLICIT TEACHINGS OF PAUL ON DIVORCE/ REMARRIAGE

The Antecedent Context

"There is immorality among you. . . ."

(*1 Corinthians 5:1–6:20*)

It is appropriate that the first words of Paul on the subject of divorce should be a repetition of the teachings of our Lord. The explicit reference to Jesus' teaching in 1 Corinthians 7:10 functions as a hinge in our exposition. Paul freely applies the messianic teaching with no qualms about its relevance.[3] He then proceeds to give further, but non-contrary, applications of the abiding principles in a manner relevant to the struggling church at Corinth.

The teaching itself is, of course, but one word of advice to a church plagued with problems of all sorts. Paul knew of some of these problems from the reports of a family identified as "Chloe's people" (1:11); of the rest he was informed by letter from the church itself (7:1). These sources seem, in part, to divide the letter into two sections, though that division does not seem to be as important as the thematic developments noted in most outlines of the book. The marriage/divorce material comes at the head of the second division, at the beginning of the treatment of questions sent by the church. And yet there is no great break between the final matter in the Chloe section and the divorce material. Paul seems to have structured his response to Chloe's report so that it logically leads into the subject of marriage and divorce.

COMMUNION WITH (SEXUAL) SIN(NERS) PROHIBITED

The thematic development evident in the book offers us a starting point for our discussion in 5:1. Paul deals with an unfortunate occurrence of incest involving one of the church members. Noting that such behavior is reprehensible even among unbelievers (therefore not even needing a reference to its condemnation in the Law), Paul prescribes harsh discipline—excommunication from fellowship. He concludes this matter by telling the church to prudently judge their own public sins, rather than try and discipline the immoral actions of outsiders.

RECOURSE TO THE COURTS FOR "DEFRAUDING" PROHIBITED

The second matter mentioned relates to their treatment of their brethren before public courts of law. Apparently some church members were airing petty and private matters before unbelievers, thus bringing the fellowship into bad repute. If any group should not need recourse to courts for such matters, it should be Christians, who were to be known by their love and harmony. Paul's admonition is, again, to judge such matters as a fellowship. These passages reveal a sad state of affairs still with us today. The church was permissive when it came to major matters (incest) but harsh (individualistically speaking) when it came to small issues.

This section does not mention exactly what those petty grievances were. By omitting this fact, the section underscores the need not to take *any* such small matters to the civil courts. But it is not farfetched to suggest sexual matters lingering in the background. This conclusion arises not only from the previous section, which discusses the gross fornication of incest, but also from a consideration of the predominately sexual and marital matters that quickly follow in the text (6:9–7:40). And in those subsequent sections, one of the more crucial terms of the litigation section is repeated: *defraud*. In 7:5, Paul admonishes married people not to deprive the spouse of sexual relations. Could it be that just such a deprivation was one of the "small things" taken before the civil courts?

Consider this possible connection: Paul points out to the Corinthians a gross sexual problem that was infecting the church. Though incest was not commonly practiced "among the Gentiles" (5:1), such a sin was doubtless committed in this instance in the context of a sexually permissive and defiled Corinth. This general context, and such grossness, in all probability led some sensitive souls, upon conversion, to completely reject sex itself as sinful and desire to live lives of celibacy (cf. 7:3–7). It is not stretching the matter too far to see behind this "party" of ascetics the influence of Greek philosophy that saw the body as itself undesirable and "immoral." Be that as it may, when such purists happened to be in existing marriages, their views would have produced an obvious problem for their spouses, who might well have had other ideas about the desirability of continued sexual relations. It might be that these deprived spouses were seeking legal support at the courts—an embarrassing suit, to say the least![4] It is to such a group of offended "suitors" that the apostle writes. He remands the cases to the church court. He does not, at this point, agree with the direction of the depriving group. In fact, his very use of a word like *deprived* (v. 7) is rather obviously a taking sides with the nondepriving group. But he gives no specific condemnation of depriving one's spouse of sexual relations, only the implied rebuke that the church court should deliver. Is this progression too speculative? Let us continue consideration of the sections.

RECOURSE TO PROSTITUTES PROHIBITED

The next section (6:9–11) proceeds to detail a catalogue of sins that will inhibit entrance into the kingdom of God. At the forefront are the sexual sins. Why this list, and why in this location? A definitive answer may not be available, but it is reasonable to see this as Paul's point of agreement with the would-be celibates who are reacting to the evils of the city around them. There is also in this catalogue of sins a preparation for the rebuke of another problem, which surfaces in verses 13–20: consorting with prostitutes.

But Paul is not in complete agreement with the ascetically minded church members of Corinth. Verse 12 rebuts the contention that "things," such as bodies, are intrinsically evil. It is not the things but the use to which the things are put that is evil and rejected by God. It is the uses mentioned in verses 9–10 that must be avoided, and marital sex is not found in the list! Again, Paul underscores his point. In verses 13–20, Paul takes one of the sins of the list and points out wherein it is "unlawful."

But the question of context arises again. Why would a Christian go to a prostitute? The traditional answer is that the promiscuity of the city led to this practice. Doubtless this is correct. But could it not also be that these were not only unmarried men seeking sexual experience but also married men, deprived of sex at home by an ascetically minded partner? How many times have we heard the threat, "If I don't get it at home, I'll get it somewhere else!" And Paul, by inhibiting the spouse from legally forcing (if that can be done!) his wife to have sex with him, seems to have played into this kind of thinking. So Paul anticipates this response to his blocking of litigation by blocking recourse to extramarital sex.

Moreover, for good reason, sexual relations imply union into a team. But the vocation of a prostitute makes her an illicit choice for a partner. To be teamed with her is to be joined with one whose commitment is contrary to the will of God. To become a member of her body—to become one flesh with her—is to defile one's own body, which is the temple of the Holy Spirit. We are one flesh with him. What fellowship can God have with the Devil?[5]

DEFRAUDING IN MARRIAGE PROHIBITED

All this makes it very hard on relatively *innocent* spouses who have simply found themselves married to some soul who misunderstands God's view of sexuality. Though Paul has begun the message to that ascetic spouse, that is, the body is not bad, and implied that the church should correct such deprivation, he has really said little to admonish such spouses to give themselves in the sexual act. Paul achieves balance on these subjects as he turns to answer the questions that church members have raised to him.[6]

He begins with the statement that it is good for a man not to touch a woman. There is a certain enigma in this statement. Is this the first statement of his principle that singleness is a virtue insofar as single people can be devoted to God's service? Or is it a restatement of his prior points about fornication?

Gordon Fee, in his excellent study of the first verse of this chapter, argues that Paul is advising marriage to those who find it difficult to avoid the sin of fornication. Fee suggests that, rather than start off with a preference for celibacy, which is then withdrawn for those who are troubled by their passions, Paul is reminding the married Corinthians that their own marriages are the answer to their passions (vv. 1 and 2).[7] Fee's main point is that the normal meaning of *ma aptesthai* is "not to touch," not "not to marry," as the elevation-of-celibacy school prefers.[8] The question from them that he initially answers is, then, something like: May I go to the prostitutes if my wife isn't satisfying me at all times? (Prov. 5:19).[9]

The next three verses oblige married persons to give their body to their spouse. And by saying thus, Paul balances the ledger. The man must not go to the courts to force his wife to have sex (6:1–8). He must not seek sex outside of marriage (6:9–20). The wife must not withhold herself from her husband, thus pressuring him to fall to Satan's temptation to seek sex outside marriage (7:1–6). The latter saying provides the judgment for the church in its own attempts to adjudicate the argument between the ascetic spouse and the sexually active spouse.[10]

Of some interest is verse 6. Paul states that his prior admonition is not a command but a concession. What exactly does he mean by this? Several options exist. First, since such a "this" usually refers to something immediately said, he could be referring to the resumption of sexual relations after the temporary denial. But this seems to contradict the main thrust of the admonition in verse 5. Second, he could be referring to the whole of his advice. This would mean he has no command to require people to satisfy their sexual drives by means of their spouse. But this would imply that immorality is a moral option. That would be absurd.

A third option is that the entire saying (v. 5) is the concession. Against this is that the husband's having sexual relations with his wife *was* a matter of command (Exod. 21:10 f.). On the other hand, there was no Old Testament requirement for the wife to have sex with her husband. If she refused, he doubtless would simply have taken another wife to fill that need. Perhaps this element should be highlighted, giving us a sort of variation of the third option. That is the very reciprocality of his admonition not to deprive one's spouse. Though the Old Testament did not require such reciprocality, the cultural monogamy of the Greeks required such a concession in order to accommodate the customs in place. We must note that such a bilateral admonition would not have been needed in Old Testament times. This latter interpretation also has the benefit of helping to make sense of the next major section of the letter, which presumes that the woman is the one depriving her husband (cf. vv. 10–11).

The final option, however, which seems to make the best sense of the data, is that the concession is the temporary option to defer sexual relations for a season of prayer. Though at first this might seem strained—why would he call occasional prayer a concession—Fee suggests that it is a concession to the ascetically minded Corinthians.[11] This option makes even better and more direct sense of what follows. In order to avoid the conclusion that Paul disdains celibacy, he hastens to note that singleness, after all, is preferable to marriage if and only if passions can be contained. This is Paul's first clear statement of the principle that singleness and marriage are both gifts of God, and that he commends the gift of celibacy. There is no disparagement of either gift in the final analysis—both are from God. We note also that Paul does not explain the rationale for this desirable celibacy at this point. That waits for verses 25–35. He concludes this section by stating that it is far better to disregard his affirmation of celibacy (for the unmarried and widows) than it is to burn with lust. This parallels his reasons for getting married (v. 2) and for sexual deprivations in marriage to be temporary only (v. 5).

The Teachings

TO CHRISTIAN COUPLES: GROUNDLESS DIVORCE DENIED

"To the married I give instructions, not I, but the Lord."
(1 Corinthians 7:10–11)

The Corinthians' Question

Now come Paul's teachings that directly relate to the matters of divorce and remarriage. The question behind these teachings must have been somehow related to the first question. Perhaps it was, May a couple who cannot agree upon the need for sex in marriage simply end their marriage and form another with a believer who is of like mind? It is hard to believe that they want to know simply if a marriage partner can walk away from the marriage or if divorce and remarriage are proper. The teachings of Jesus doubtless had been spoken to them (e.g., the Sermon on the Mount). After all, had not Jesus ordered the evangelistic program to teach whatsoever he had taught the disciples? Certainly the divorce teaching in its pristine form was already known to those at this church, where Paul had spent eighteen months. This is why we suspect some wrinkle in the question that reaches past the elementary teaching that it is wrong for a spouse to divorce with no other reason than to find a more desirable mate.

Recourse to the Answer of Jesus

But if this is the case, Paul surprises them by reminding them of that very basic teaching. He tells them that to divorce without grounds is improper, and that if they have done so they are not to strike a second covenant but to seek reconciliation with their (former) spouse. This advice has the benefit of tying the final knot in the rope he has been working on. To spouses who seek to circumvent his admonition to give their body to their spouse by getting rid of the spouse and finding a more congenial partner, he rejects separation, that is, the sundering of the marriage. Of course, the prohibition works both ways. To the spouse who might desire a new mate who would be less demanding with regard to sexual relations or to the spouse who might desire a mate who would desire more in the way of sexual relations, his advice is the same: "stay married."

THE IMPLIED "EXCEPTION"

Now, one might react somewhat negatively to my loose paraphrase of verses 10 and 11. One might wish to stress, especially, that Paul does not speak of an exception to a no-divorce teaching of Jesus, but absolutely rejects divorce and remarriage.[12] But I believe that, although this is technically true, the evidence nonetheless points in the direction of an implied exception. First, note that Paul refers to the teaching of Jesus, which *did* include the exception clause. We have no right to presume that Paul was unfamiliar with the exception. It was spoken on both of the occasions wherein Jesus taught on divorce, that is, the event of the Sermon and the event recorded by Matthew and Mark. Since neither Matthew's nor Mark's Gospel was as yet written,[13] it is presumptuous to suggest that Paul only knew of the nonexception clause form of the teaching. In fact, since Mark in all likelihood knew of the exception clause but excluded it only for purposes of abbreviation, even if Paul obtained his understanding only from the Markan tradition he still would have received the exception along with the rest of the tradition.

But however this speculation about the sources of Paul's knowledge of Jesus' teaching might turn out, there is another indication in the text that the exception is implied. It is the word *reconciliation* (v. 11). This term, though used theologically of both the guilty and the innocent parties in a dispute, is more limited in biblical usage. The term is *never* used of an innocent party. God is never said to be reconciled to us, but only we to him. Since this is the case, it is clear that Paul sees this person who has divorced the spouse as guilty of some offense. Since he refers to teachings of Jesus, we must ask who Jesus considers to be guilty of any moral offense in marital breakups. It is relatively simple to prove that Jesus disdains divorce for improper grounds, and though it may be argued (wrongly, I believe) that Jesus rejects remarriage for any grounds, it is nowhere evident that Jesus prohibits all divorce for whatever grounds and apart from the issue of remarriage. It is far easier to understand Paul as simply prohibiting groundless divorce with the aim of remarriage—which he blocks—and admonishing reconciliation. At least, we may say that, given the exception clause in the teachings of Jesus, the burden of proof rests with the person who would affirm that Paul (reflecting the teachings of Jesus) holds a person guilty of sin for divorcing a spouse on the grounds of *porneia*. I suggest that this is a burden that that position cannot bear.[14]

"SUNDER" VERSUS "DIVORCE"

We should note, as well, that Paul does not say that a woman should not *divorce* her husband. He says that she should not *sunder* her relationship. The Greek term is *chorizo*, not *apoluo*. Heth and Wenham point out that these two terms are synonyms in the papyrus literature of the day and doubtless would have been thought such by the Corinthian readers.[15] Nevertheless, these authors argue that we should not be compelled to see them as synonyms. Their reason is that both the terms as synonyms implied a full divorce with the right to remarry. This is contrary to their own view, and they must distance the text from this legal usage of the papyri terms. I understand their desire to keep the biblical usages harmonious, but my own search for harmony leads me in a different direction. Having not found warrant for their idea of divorce without the right to remarry, I do not feel a need to argue as they have. Rather, I wish to keep the terms that Jesus used true to his own apparent distinctions between them. Remember that Jesus does use both terms, but restricts his condemnation of a given divorce as adulterous to where there were no sundering grounds.[16] This is to say that the terms are not perfect synonyms. And what language is so broken down that there is such a thing as a perfect synonym? There are always nuance differences. It seems to me that in the teachings of Jesus *chorizo* emphasizes the moral severing of the existing valid bond or covenant. *Apoluo,* on the other hand, was Jesus' way of referring to legal and complete divorce, without regard to grounds. Both terms refer to ending the marriage, but the former is an offense-term, and the latter is a descriptive term. Jesus teaches that *divorce* (descriptive term), when it does not involve the sundering offense of fornication, is itself *sundering* (moral offense term), and the nature of the offense Jesus identifies as the sin of *adultery*. This does not mean that the readers of the Corinthian letter had to stretch to understand Paul's usage. In fact, since in this instance the sundering certainly did in fact involve legal divorce, the use of the terms in the papyri of the day is quite in harmony with my suggestion.[17] Even in the case of the Gospel passages (Matt. 19:6; Mark 10:9), it is clear that *chorizo* connotes divorce. But I contend that *chorizo* is implied as the essence of *fornication* in the exception clauses. Thus, one may sunder one's marriage either by fornication in marriage or by groundless divorce. Such a statement is entirely in harmony with the teaching in Matthew 19. Now, if our analysis of these terms and their use is proper, I feel that it is another indication that Paul is here dealing with cases where there were no sundering grounds, but where the divorce itself was the sundering.[18]

THE LIMITS OF PAUL'S PROHIBITION

As such, divorce becomes grounds for the moral freedom of the innocent party. This is to say that the aggrieved are given implied permission to remarry, insofar as Paul prohibits only remarriage of the sundering or guilty party. The reason that he permits the guilty divorcer to stay divorced (v. 11) is that it may be impossible for the divorcer to be reconciled to the former spouse.[19] Actually the language may simply mean: "If you got a groundless divorce, don't run out and get remarried to a more desirable partner, but instead be reconciled to your wronged former spouse."

This latter reading would even permit remarriage of the guilty partner at some *future* time, for we believe that Paul's admonition here is dealing with an immediate problem. Someone has put away a spouse without grounds, probably in order to marry a "better" partner. Paul is trying to stop it. I do not believe that he wishes to block all future possible remarriages in the event that the guilty party attempts to reconcile and finds that this is now impossible.

For example, do we wish to say that the prohibition of remarriage of this guilty party extends beyond the lifetime of the offended former partner? Probably not. But Paul does not specifically say here that such a conclusion is overextended. What if the "innocent" party refuses to be reconciled? Is the "guilty" party doomed to celibacy, or has the moral "shoe" been put on the "innocent" partner's foot? Perhaps the order of Paul's final words is significant. He does not say, as we might have expected, "Be reconciled or remain unmarried"; he says it the other way around, "Remain unmarried or be reconciled." I see in this the advice applying as long as reconciliation is a reasonable option. It deals with the immediate, not the long-range. Thus, Paul's advice to the troubled married here need not in the slightest disagree with our previous conclusions.

TO THOSE IN MIXED MARRIAGES

"If the unbelieving one leaves . . ."

(1 Corinthians 7:12–24)

The Nature and Origin of the Corinthians' Question

Paul now moves to another question. It is a question similar to the preceding one in that it deals with the severing of the marriage relationship. But, whereas the former question dealt with the *right* to put away a believing spouse (to avoid the sexual relation), the latter question deals with the *obligation* to put away an unbelieving partner. We may imagine that the question was phrased something like this: Is it proper to remain married to a spouse who is not in the faith?

Whence arises such a question? It is easy to see Paul's connection with his prior admonition: "You should flee fornication, that is, a one-flesh relationship with an unbelieving prostitute. If you become one body or one flesh with her, you defile the temple of the Holy Spirit. Instead, be married to a Christian, who can fulfill your marital needs (i.e., sex) except when you both agree to forgo sexual relations in order to pray." From such admonition, it might be possible for a careless reader to suspect that Paul disdains mixed marriages of all sorts as contrary to Christian purity. But this only shows us part of Paul's logical progression. It does not explain the origin of the Corinthians' question.

Perhaps we may gain some understanding of what lay behind this question by considering a certain mistaken notion prevalent among the believers. In 5:10, Paul speaks of a previous letter in which he had admonished the believers "not to associate with immoral people." The Corinthians had misunderstood that admonition to mean not to have relationships with nonbelievers. Since he is correcting this misunderstanding in the present letter, it is probable that some of the people receiving it thought that it was proper to separate themselves from unbelieving spouses. This second misunderstanding needed to be corrected as well. With this sort of misunderstanding lingering in the background, it is understandable that the question should arise in their midst about the propriety of leaving an unbelieving spouse.

Another probable element (aside from the comment of Paul in his prior letter) may have been earlier teachings of Paul during his stay with them. Though we may only speculate about what exactly he taught them, we must believe that Paul, following the example of the disciples, followed the instruction of the Lord to teach the nations what he had taught them. Part of the teachings of Jesus regarded the consequences of becoming his followers. Jesus taught that belief in him would divide families (Matt. 10:34 ff.). He went on to say that a person who left house and family for his sake would be rewarded (Matt. 19:29/Mark

10:29–30). Perhaps the Corinthians had missed the point that in none of the relations mentioned was there the slightest indication that a spouse should "leave" his or her partner, that is, that a valid covenant should be sundered. Thus, again, the Corinthians might well have wanted clarification of the teaching.

A final, yet more speculative possibility is that Paul had previously taught them that grand Old Testament doctrine of separation. That, after all, was behind the very teachings of Jesus just mentioned. That doctrine had over and over been stated and exemplified: Do not make binding covenants with the unbelieving people of the land. If you have, break them off. This was the stern message of Deuteronomy 7:3 and Ezra 9 and 10. Perhaps it is not too hard to see these people, many of whom doubtless were Jews learned in the Law and the Prophets, reflecting upon the message of Ezra and wondering if it pertained to their own situation.[20]

Paul's Advice

However many of these points may have informed their question, we know that they asked it and that Paul sought to provide them a righteous answer. He does not pretend that he has a made-to-order citation from Jesus or from the Old Testament. He says to them that his admonition comes from his own sanctified reason.[21] Such reason was informed by his understanding of God's justice and holiness.

How to Handle Acceptance by the Unsaved Spouse

Paul's main point is simply and quickly put: "Do not separate." This negative response to the question is in line with his prior admonition in 5:10 not to "take yourself out of the world." It is also in line with his just-spoken admonition to the spouse of a believer not to separate from a spouse on inadequate grounds (7:10 f.). Separation may come, but it should not be initiated by the believer. Behind this advice is a principle, or a couple of them: first, that valid covenants are binding and, second, that simply being married to an unbeliever is not in itself a sin of disloyalty to God.

HARMONIZATION WITH THE PRIOR CONTEXT

Here we must pause and explain how these principles can be harmonized with the teachings mentioned earlier. First, note carefully that when Jesus mentions division of a family never once is it the division of a husband and wife. The relationships mentioned are not covenantal. When a child comes of age, he or she may have to break off family relations because of belief in Christ. But the sayings do not sanction breaking covenant. And insofar as the situation envisioned by Christ relates to postconversion discord, this omission of husband-wife relations is very significant to the problem as it arose in Corinth.

HARMONIZATION WITH EZRA

The problem in Corinth was quite different from the one that Ezra encountered in post-exilic Israel. Ezra was rebuking those who, knowing the Law, had married *proscribed* persons. Their marriages were, from Moses' point of view, illicit. They may have had the sanction of prevailing legal custom, but they were against the Law. By contracting the marriages these Israelites were committing adultery against God. Thus, the only fruit of repentance that the scribe could accept had to include the discipline of putting the illicit (i.e., unbelieving) partners away. This was not at all the situation in Corinth. These believers had been married *before* they were converted. Paul is at pains to make this point in 1 Corinthians 7:17–24. It is not illicit for two unbelievers to covenant in marriage. Since they had contracted covenants under these conditions, they are to realize that the covenants were and are still licit and should be kept. There was no hint of spiritual disloyalty on their part in such unions.

It is thus a mistake to see in the admonition of Paul a negating of the moral disposition of Ezra. It is wrongheaded, for instance, to suggest that the harshness of the Old Testament has been superseded by the softness of the love ethic of the new dispensation. Neither Jesus nor Paul take it upon themselves to clean up Yahweh's ethics or the ethics of his prophets. The Old Testament had taught that it was wrong to be willfully and rebelliously yoked to an unbeliever. Paul explicitly agrees (2 Cor. 6:14).[22] Paul even quotes the Old Testament to show what correction is necessary for those who fail to keep separate: "Come out from their midst" (Isa. 52:11). It would seem that that is essentially what Ezra forced upon the intermarriers of his day. Certainly at no point does Paul suggest that Ezra was wrong or that Ezra's corrective is not still the proper disciplinary action.[23] Thus, we may presume that even in our own day believers knowingly marrying outside God's will must show the fruit of repentance, which is the dissolving of the relationship.[24]

How to Handle Rejection by the Unsaved Spouse

Now, although Paul clearly replies to the supposed question in the negative, he is not so naive as to think that conversion might not lead to the sundering of marital covenants. For, although the relationship with a believer offers some special consideration by God of an unbelieving spouse (1 Cor. 7:14), it is still possible that the Evil One might put it in the heart of an unbelieving spouse to initiate separation. It is as if Paul is now repeating Jesus' warning that conversion will bring persecution and the separation of families. And it is regarding this possibility that Paul's controversial words concerning the resulting "freedom" of the forsaken spouse are spoken.[25]

We need not assume here that *desertion* without a valid divorce is the only leaving in view. The exact term here is *chorizo*, "to sunder or separate." This is the same term used in verse 10. In the former verse it quite obviously entails legal separation or divorce, because remarriage is prohibited. In all likelihood legal sundering is anticipated here as well.[26]

THE "PAULINE PERMISSION"

In any case, Paul states that a forsaken believer is free from bondage in such cases. Exactly what this means has occasioned not a little spilled ink. Is Paul saying that the forsaken one is free to remarry, or only free from the need to fulfill marital obligations, or free to not pursue the departing spouse?

FREEDOM TO REMARRY OR NOT?

Heth and Wenham present us with no less than seven reasons why they believe that the free-to-remarry option is incorrect. Since this is the major point at issue, we will consider each of their arguments and see how convincing their stand is.

First, they make their stand upon the fact that marriage is a creation ordinance and an indissoluble union according to Jesus.[27] I believe that I have previously shown that Jesus does not teach that marriage *is* indissoluble but only that it *ought* to be.[28] They have made the common mistake of confusing moral statements with ontological ones. As for the "creation ordinance" idea, I believe that I have shown that in addition to the rather theologically speculative aspects of these terms, nothing in Genesis 1:27 or 2:24 implies ontological permanency for marriage.

Second, these authors insist that the idea "free from the bonds of marriage" is out of harmony with Paul's admonitions in verses 10–16. With Plummer and Robertson they argue, "All that *ou dedoulotai* clearly means is that he or she need not feel so bound by Christ's prohibition of divorce as to be afraid to depart when the heathen partner insists on separation."[29] To this they add, third, that the rejected interpretation is contrary to the nature of marriage as a creation ordinance recognized by Paul as binding in 1 Corinthians 11:2–26 and 1 Timothy 2:12–15.[30]

Against this it must be stated that the contextual disharmony to which they refer arises from their failure to correctly understand verses 10–16. Paul has not said in verses 10–11 that all divorced persons should not remarry, but only the guilty party (i.e., the ones who need to be "reconciled"). The believer is told not to divorce the unbelieving spouse for the reason that that spouse has a valid marriage covenant and has committed no sundering offense. As to the verses cited from Paul's writings, they seem to me to be irrelevant. The fact that Paul recognizes the headship of the male (husband) over the female (wife) and that he anchors his thoughts in the Genesis account has nothing transparently to do with the issue of the permanence of marriage.

Fourth, Heth and Wenham see the freedom to remarry as contrary to the "hope of conversion" in verse 16. Siding with the early Church Fathers, they connect verse 16 with verse 13; they reject the modern commentators who connect 16 with 15. The significance of this is that connection with 13 favors a hope for the conversion of the forsaking spouse, if the forsaken remains available for reconciliation. The connection with 15 prognosticates little hope but rather suggests that it is futile to remain available, hoping against hope that the conversion will take place. Modern translations are mustered to show the difference:

NEB: "Think of it: as a wife you may be your husband's salvation; as a husband you may be your wife's salvation."

NASB: "For how do you know, O wife, whether you will save your husband? Or how do you know, O husband, whether you will save your wife?"

Heth and Wenham's customary attention to detail in matters grammatical is missing in their support of the NEB-Fathers reading. They only note that the "if" in verse 16 will allow for it, and "contextual congruency favors it."[31] Against their view stands the rather detailed work of R. C. H. Lenski, who points out that the "for" (*gar*) points neither to the subordinate clause of verse 15 (the matter of peace) nor to the sanctification of the spouse in verse 14 (nor, we would add, to the mandate to the believer not to leave the spouse in 13), but rather to the major point in verse 15: the believer is not bound. He regards connection with 13 or 14 or a subordinate clause in 15 to be grammatically artificial (as I do) rather than "contextually congruent."[32]

The one reason that a forsaken spouse might not experience peace centers upon the hope that by continuing to remain bound in some way, at least in the mind, there is hope for the former spouse's conversion. The forsaken believer worries that allowing a complete ending of the marriage will somehow hurt the former spouse's chances of coming to the Lord.[33] Paul brushes this false sense of responsibility aside. It is the Spirit who has the ultimate responsibility to see conversion to its conclusion. Such a guilt-ridden, forsaken believer is brought back to reality by Paul. "How do you know" (adverbial accusative) God intends to use you in your former spouse's conversion? Lenski ends by pointing out that the "if" has the sense not of "if you won't" but of "if you will." Paul is not asking the forsaken one, "How do you know that you *won't* contribute to the former spouse's salvation?" but "How do you know if you *will* contribute to it?"

The textual congruence stands against Heth and Wenham, not for them, for it is their interpretation that refuses to release the forsaken ones from bondage, keeping them bound under the lingering hope that by restricting themselves to a life of "limbic" chastity they preserve the hope of another's salvation. A greater form of bondage than this is hard to imagine! If the submissive spiritual condition of the convert led to the ending of the marriage, is it reasonable to suppose that acting as though still married will lead to the salvation of the lost?

The fifth argument centers around the Greek words employed for "bondage" or "bond" in 1 Corinthians 7:15, 27, 39, and Romans 7:2. The authors point out that the term for "bondage" in verse 15 is *douloō*, whereas verses 27 and 39 (and Romans 7:2) have *deo*. The former, they insist, is never employed with regard to the legal aspect of marriage; Paul uses the latter term for that. And, they continue, even if the terms were the same or even if the same term were used, it would not make any difference, because all that would be implied is that the believer "is not under obligation to pursue the unbeliever to keep the marriage together if the unbeliever wishes to leave."[34]

These arguments are, in my estimation, strained, to say the least. First, although Paul may not use *douloō* specifically to speak of the legal bonds of marriage, he uses it in its common sense of "the bondage of slavery." Paul uses it in Galatians 4:3, where being in "bondage" to the "elemental things of the world" (v. 3) is parallel to being "under the Law" (v. 5). Is this not to suggest that *douloō* involves legal bond? To argue that *douloō* involves *legal* bond, but is improperly applied to a *marriage* legal bond seems like straining at a gnat. Whatever the difference between the two words, the clear legal implications of the crucial *douloō* make it far more akin to *deo* in usage than to the artificial interpretation of "freedom only from bed and board, without the right to remarry" offered by Heth and Wenham. In all likelihood, *douloō* is a harsher term than *deo*, the former stressing *forced bondage* (1 Cor. 9:19, though there it is forced upon himself by himself) and the latter stressing *chosen servanthood* (cf. 7:23; Rom. 6:17–20).[35]

Given this significance, as attested by contextual use, Paul is simply saying that no one should keep this woman in forced allegiance to her marriage bond. But this is precisely what Heth and Wenham have presented Paul as doing—keeping her bound to her covenantal obligation not to have sexual relations with another! Herein lies another great mistake of the no-remarriage school. They have been myopically focusing upon the apostolic concession of reciprocal right to the spouse's body, rather than on the specifics of the Old Testament marital bond of the woman. In the Old Testament God does not require the woman to have sex with her husband but, rather, not to have it with anyone else. Were her obligation simply put in the positive—have sex with your spouse—their case might be made to the point that those who think otherwise have the burden of proof. However, since her moral obligation is consistently put in the negative—you can't have sex with another man while married—to be freed from that bondage is to be free to remarry, if done properly and "in the Lord."

Their sixth argument is an appeal to the early Church Fathers. They point out that it is not until the fourth-century father Ambrosiaster that a writing father permitted a deserted spouse to remarry.[36]

About this I have little to say. It does not seem to me that an exegetical case can be made simply by an appeal to the Fathers. In the first place, not many Fathers of the first centuries wrote on the subject. Most of the restrictive Fathers are separated from Paul by time and temperament. But beyond this, I have little patience with those who reject the "situation in life" of the hearers of Paul and the papyri on the grounds that we must, after all, let Paul speak for himself but quickly appeal to the hearsay teachings of ascetically minded Fathers of later centuries. This is not exegesis but historical proof-texting.

The final argument mustered by Heth and Wenham is that verses 17–24 reveal Paul's commitment to keeping the mixed marriages together. As they put it, "Believers should remain in the same situation in life in which they were when they became Christian because Christ demands of His 'slaves' sole obedience to Him not a shared allegiance to other masters."[37]

This is rather poorly stated as regards the main point at issue and, on the face of it, seems rather irrelevant to the question of whether or not a forsaken believer has the right to remarry. It may well answer another question: "What if I was divorced *before* becoming a Christian?" But that is not the problem at this point. We are speaking of people who were divorced *subsequent* to becoming Christians. Heth and Wenham would have done better to suggest that Paul is, in 17–24, urging the Corinthians to remain in the state in which they were when converted, namely, married. But this idea, though a logical possibility, seems strained. After all, these believers are no longer in the same state in which they were called. They were legally married when converted, and now, through no fault of their own, they are forsaken, probably legally. It is as if to suggest that Paul really does not understand their situation. In reality, it is Heth and Wenham who do not understand their situation. For, throughout their work, it is evident that they are under the mistaken impression that the marriage bond is not really broken by legal divorce, and thus, they fall back into the unbiblical view that marriage is not essentially covenantal but essentially mystical and sacramental.[38] If that supposition is removed, 1 Corinthians 7:10–16 makes perfectly good sense as affirming the right of the innocent party to remarry. The reason that guilty parties do not have an immediate right to remarry is that they have unfinished covenantal business. They have a *moral*, not a *mystical*, obligation to reconcile.

Before we leave this material it is necessary to touch upon one point that these authors have made that we hurriedly passed over in our response to their criticisms of the right-to-remarry school. Recall that they stated that becoming a Christian does not make any difference in marital obligations. By and large, I agree with them. If Paul is saying anything, it is that conversion does not negate one's vows to another human being. It is not the interfaith marriage itself that is grounds for the right to remarry; it is the forsaking by the unbeliever. That forsaking is a breach of the minimum in marriage vows. It is adultery. Thus, this unbeliever is in exactly the position of the man who divorces his wife and, thereby, commits adultery against her in Matthew 5:32a. The forsaken believing spouse, on the other hand, is in the situation of the ill-treated woman of Deuteronomy 24:1–4 and has that woman's right to marry another. Paul is correct in saying that the case at hand is not directly commented upon by our Lord, but that does not mean that he is not completely in accord with him and the Law and the Prophets that he did not abrogate.[39] Of course, none of this is to say that the former spouse is likely to take the believer back. The conversion experience is likely to have the reverse effect. It will give the unbeliever just one more reason to want to remain free from this person. Even where the unbeliever fought the divorce, the conversion may stand as a stumbling block to the reestablishment of the marriage. In any case, the convert should make an effort to seek the forgiveness of the offended one and reestablish the covenant. If the convert is rejected, he or she is free indeed.

CONCLUSION: FREE TO REMARRY

It is thus my conclusion that when the unbeliever severs the marriage by legal (i.e., divorce) or illegal (i.e., desertion) action, the Christian spouse is free to remarry. This conclusion is also consistent with our previous findings.

It should be clear then that I do not see 1 Corinthians 7:15 as offering another "exception" of a different kind than *porneia,* but rather a nonsexual instance of the same kind of moral offense, that is, unfaithfulness to the essentials of covenant. Breach of covenant is the only grounds for righteous divorce, and that is an act that is against the very warp and woof of the (marriage) covenant itself. *Porneia* (by the wife) is a sexual application of such breach.[40] Whether the abrogation of marriage vows is sexual (by the female), physical (abuse by either, or neglect by the male), legal (divorce), or illegal (desertion by either), the point is the same: the marriage has been sundered by such actions.

Having concluded thus, how can these interpretations of Paul be harmonized with what appears to be the clear teaching of the apostle (i.e., that marriage is "till death do you part") in 1 Corinthians 7:39 and Romans 7:2 ff.? It is to those verses that we now turn.

CHAPTER 9

The Teachings of the Apostle Paul on Divorce, Continued
(1 Corinthians 7:25–40/Romans 7:1–12)

THE NONEXPLICIT TEACHINGS
Paul's Advice to the Unmarried (Corinthians)

> "... as long as her husband lives."
>
> *(1 Corinthians 7:39)*

There are in the writings of Paul two passages that do not directly mention divorce or "putting away" but do discuss the duration of marriage. They are 1 Corinthians 7:39 and Romans 7:2–3. These verses are often quoted as veritable "showstoppers" with regard to permission to divorce and remarry. It is our task in this chapter to dissect them and, by close analysis of their contexts, to see if it is possible to harmonize them with the view already set forth in this book, a view that does permit some divorce and remarriage.

GENERAL INSTRUCTION TO THE UNMARRIED

> "*Now concerning virgins . . .*"
>
> *(1 Corinthians 7:25–35)*

In our previous chapter, we followed Paul in prohibiting the guilty party from remarrying (at least until reconciliation attempts have been exhausted) and in releasing the innocent party to remarry. Both issues involved the already married. In the second half of chapter 7 of First Corinthians, Paul turns to another matter broached by the people of Corinth: Is it advisable for the unmarried to become married? or, Is marriage expected?

The Structure of the Section
His advice is broken into several parts:
I. Advice to single people, vv. 25–35

A. Prologue: the source of the advice, v. 25
B. Basic advice: sociological stability is preferable at this time (emphasis on singleness), v. 26
C. Consideration of the moral options, vv. 27–28
   1. From the man's side, vv. 27–28a
     a) those married: stay married, v. 27a
     b) those subsequently single (probably inclusive of divorce): stay single, v. 27b, "but . . ."
     c) moral permission to remarry, v. 28a
   2. From the woman's side, v. 28b (virgins)
II. The underlying principles behind the advice, vv. 28c–35 (this section reaches backward to part I and forward to part III; it is somewhat parallel to 7:17–24)
A. Sparing them trouble (emphasis on singleness), vv. 28–31
B. Keeping them undistracted, vv. 32–34 (basic principle: be in the state that is most conducive to leaving time for serving the Lord)
C. Summary: practical nature of the above, v. 35 (leaves room for needed marriage)
III. Advice to those responsible for single women, vv. 36–40
A. Consideration of the moral options, vv. 36–39
   1. From the Guardian's side, vv. 36–38 (virgins)
     a) the need for the ward to marry, v. 36
     b) no need for the ward to marry, v. 37
     c) summary; implied general principle, v. 38
   2. From the ward's side, vv. 39 f.
     a) those married: stay married, v. 39a
     b) those subsequently single (widowhood): stay single, v. 39b, "but . . ."
     c) moral permission to remarry, v. 39b
(B. Implied, immediate need for sociological stability)
C. Epilogue: the source of the advice, v. 40 (emphasis on singleness, v. 40a)

Concerning the prologue and epilogue there is little that we need to say. Paul notes as he has before (v. 12) that his advice at this point does not come explicitly from a previously revealed command, but instead from his sanctified reason. The basic advice to preserve social stability ("remain as you are," maritally speaking) repeats his previous advice to the married (v. 24).

Controversy arises in the next section. In the process of giving advice, Paul tells some people that if they marry they have not sinned. Who are they? Are they virgins, widows, the divorced, or all of these? If the divorced are included, then the permission to marry is a permission to remarry. Remember that there is no term for "remarry," as opposed to "marry," used by Paul. For example, it is clear that the topic of 7:11 is, in part, the propriety of remarriage. But Paul does not say, "Don't *remarry.*" He says "remain *unmarried*" (*agamos*). This latter term is simply the negation of the normal word for marriage (*gamos*). Were there a specific term used by Paul in this context for "remarriage," it would be relatively easy for us to decide if Paul means to stress the right of the divorced to remarry in verse 28. Such specific terminology might also incline us *not* to see remarriage in verse 28, *if* the simple term for "marry" were used in that location. Since such terminology is not found at this point, we will have to argue the case from another vantage point, that is, the terms used identifying the personal objects of the advice.

Who Are the "Virgins"?

The identification of the "virgins" is a matter of dispute. The positions include the following:

1. The widow in a levirate marriage.[1]
2. A couple who have set up house together for economic reasons, but who have agreed to live a celibate life—a sort of "spiritual marriage."[2]
3. An engaged couple (or the female therein).[3]
4. A virgin daughter who is at or beyond marriageable age.[4]

Often, the specifics of these views do not come clear until authors directly consider verses 36–38.

LEVIRATE MARRIAGES

Of these positions, I believe that we may safely dismiss the idea of a levirate marriage. There is little to commend it to us; there is no indication that the levirate law was practiced in Corinth.

CELIBATE COUPLE

As for the idea that these are a celibate couple, two considerations speak in its favor: the term *virgin* is used figuratively of the pure men in Revelation 14:4, and we do know that in Corinth there were some who wished to live as married without sex (cf. vv. 3–5). There is, however, more to condemn than commend this alternative. First, the figurative usage in Revelation does not refer to a couple, only to a group of pure single persons. And in that text there is a striking reversal in the use of *virgin* for the idea of sexual purity. The men in question are said not to have had relations with a woman. Elsewhere the term almost always refers to females who have not known a man or to unmarried women (cf. Matt. 1:18, 23; 25:1, 7, 11; 2 Cor. 11:2; Luke 1:27; Acts 21:9).

Second, if this couple did not have a marriage covenant at all, Paul surely would have clearly blasted them for giving the appearance of the evil of fornication. Given the evils and temptations of fornication as they existed in Corinth, such an arrangement would have provided an example to salve the consciences of non-Christian fornicators, who would not have believed such celibacy possible. Nor were the temptations to be taken so lightly by those celibates who thought they could stand. Had not Paul warned men in chapter 6 that they should flee fornication? And had he not in earlier verses warned a couple not to tempt themselves by abstaining from sexual relations for a prolonged period of time? I cannot see a shadow of a chance that this position would have met with anything but the harshest condemnation by the apostle. Yet at no point does he speak out against it (unless that is encompassed somehow in verse 36). Indeed, such a position would have to see Paul commending such a risky relation, for which there is absolutely no moral precedent in the Scriptures. For Paul would be saying to them, "He that stands steadfast in his heart . . . who has power over his own will . . . does well" (v. 37).

ENGAGED COUPLE

Heth and Wenham side with J. K. Elliot in supposing that this is an engaged couple who are now reconsidering the consummation of their marriage so that they may serve the Lord. The most explicit support for this idea is that the term *virgin* is used of betrothed girls in a number of New Testament verses.[5] But I cannot agree with their use of this fact. Though it is true that the virgins of the texts cited were betrothed, that is not known from the term at hand but from the context. There is no compelling reason to believe that the context of 1 Corinthians 7 supplies that information. These scholars might appeal to the fact that verses 36–38 in part seem to imply that the man addressed may marry the virgin (esp. v. 36—"let them marry"). But other parts of the section seem to lean the other way. For example, verse 38 may credibly be translated, "He that gives the virgin in marriage does well." A fiancé does not give the woman away.

Additionally, this view suffers, I suspect, from a rather modern and Anglo-American understanding of betrothal. Paul, we must remember, was a Hebrew of the Hebrews, a man learned in the Law. What was the Law's view of betrothal? It was tantamount to marriage. The fact of betrothal called for the consummation at the time of the wedding feast. The vows to become one flesh were stated at the time of the engagement. It would seem to me that by affirming a breakup of this relation in 1 Corinthians 7:38 or 26, Paul is encouraging the breaking of the intention to marry, if not the vows themselves. Nor will it do to suggest that the couple agrees on this matter. In verses 2–5 it is presumed that at least one member of the couples spoken of feels defrauded. And in verse 36, it appears quite clear that the woman feels inclined to make the union. Would Paul say that the man can do "what he wills"? True, it goes on to say, "Let them marry," but what if the man decides not to will that but to insist on *not* fulfilling the promise of engagement? Paul's words would support that as well, on this view, and I cannot see that this would be moral given the ninth commandment (much less the seventh).

Some have suggested that what we have here is not really an engaged couple but an unengaged couple anticipating engagement. On this view, they are thinking of "calling the whole matter off" to remain pure.[6] But, again, this strikes me as more American than Corinthian. The text speaks of the woman as "his." It does not use the simple genitive but a more possessive indicator, *autou,* "his." Would such be said of a "girlfriend"? And why is she so old—"if she be of full age"? Such would hardly seem so common in the ancient world as to call for a lengthy comment.

SINGLE WOMEN

It falls, then, to seeing (with Lenski, et al.)[7] the "virgins" as single women (though perhaps men are included, at least in subsequent verses). What hinders the acceptance of this view? First, and perhaps foremost, is the statement in verse 36: "Let them marry." Since the command is given to the "he" whose virgin this is, it would seem this is tantamount to suggesting incest, the man marrying his virgin daughter!

But this is only a seeming necessity. I agree with Bauer, Arndt, and Gingrich in seeing this passage as suggesting that a father or guardian is being allowed to let his daughter marry a man who, doubtless, is the object of his daughter's (or ward's) affection and who has raised this dilemma for him.[8] In spite of strenuous argument to the contrary by Elliot and company, it still seems best to suggest that this man is being told that it is moral to have the dependent given in marriage or withheld from it.

Supplementing this view, I suggest that Paul's admonition to single persons actually breaks down two different parts: first, a section addressed to the single persons themselves (vv. 25–35) and then a section addressed to the father or guardian of a marriageable virgin woman (vv. 36–40). The former section has as its aim suggesting the principle of beneficial celibacy to persons who are considering marriage; the latter tries to direct guardians, who may or may not have to administer to single women wishing to be married, in spite of the apostolic "general rule" to remain single in order to maximize service to the Lord. Let us look at each section in turn.

The Origin of Singleness

Verses 25–35 are directed to the unmarried. They are a complement to verses 1–24, which is primarily a message to currently married persons. Verse 25 begins by speaking to "virgins," which word I interpret in the normal way as unmarried females. I believe that Paul then brings forth his basic principle: "remain in your present marital state." However, since this dictum is worded "it is good for a *man* [*anthropo*, masculine singular] so to be," Paul flows with the thought and begins to speak of single men. He speaks of them regarding the origin of their singleness, and in this regard, the section balances a similarly digressive discussion of the origin of the married state in verses 2 and 8.

WHO ARE THE "RELEASED"?

The origin of singleness is not only virginity. Singleness also comes to married persons. Thus, Paul asks, "Are you bound to a wife? Do not seek to be loosed." In saying this he is not speaking to every married man, because for most men, that would be rather unnecessary advice. It would be like suggesting that the man hopes his wife will die, commit adultery, or desert him—all rather surprising thoughts. I suspect in saying this he is merely referring back to his advice in verses 10 and 12; namely, try and keep the marriage together rather than hoping for its demise. "Have you been bound at some point in the past, with the result that you are still bound today? Don't go seeking for a way to get out of the marriage relation." Of course, some forms of seeking would be downright immoral. And it would be less than noble to hope for the spouse to breach the covenant or die. What, then, is left? Either instances where both might seek to end the marriage by "common agreement" (no-fault) or even where there were grounds. I consider the former more likely, but the latter would still be a valid way of saying it even to an "Erasmian." The goal of the discipline of divorce is not the single life, but restoration of the marriage!

Then, Paul entertains the possibility that the person has been released at some time in the past with the result that at the point of admonition the person is still in an unmarried state, this is to say the person has been divorced; or perhaps the divorce was out of righteous motives but the goal of restoration has not been achieved. To this group, Paul suggests a continued state of singleness but adds, significantly, that if they do get married they have not sinned. We may presume that this remarriage could be either to the former spouse (unlikely in view of the perfect tense of "have been loosed") or to another.

This sort of statement obviously implies that remarriage is morally permissible and does not limit it to the first spouse. And that, in turn, is unacceptable to some exegetes who are set against remarriage. Again, taking Heth and Wenham as examples, let us look at several arguments that they bring to bear to block this sort of interpretation.

NOT THE DIVORCED?

First, they suggest that the context prohibits seeing these loosed ones as divorced in the first place. They argue that the section is referring to "virgins," whom they believe cannot include the divorced. The perplexing thing is that alongside "virgins" is the word *unmarried* (*agamos*), and this word is used in verses 8 and 11 to refer to persons previously married—"separated" or divorced. They feel that they must somehow show that the use of "unmarried" in 27–28 is nuanced differently than in the others, else it might be argued with the traditionalists that these verses digress into a discussion that permits divorced people to remarry. They berate the Erasmians for careless interpretation and misunderstanding of how one word has shades of meaning determined by the context.[9] This apparent motivation leads to rather manipulative efforts.

Essentially their argument comes to this: if it can be shown that the term means *XY* in one verse, *XZ* in another, *XAO* in a third, and *XAP* in a fourth, then it is highly unlikely that it would mean *XZ* in a fifth. Of course they feel that very sophisticated contextual exegesis is required in order to derive the exact nuance in each of the verses.

In verse 8 they seek to limit the relevant meaning of "unmarried" to "widowers." Their argument supporting this is a purported logical parallelism between "unmarried" and "widows" in that verse.[10] But this is woefully weak. How do they know that the two words connected by "and" are logically parallel and exclusively complementary? They admit themselves that there is a Greek word for "widower" that Paul did not use. But they attempt to turn this into an argument on their behalf. They imply that Paul intentionally avoids this word, and that his custom is to use *agamos* in its place. It is far more natural simply to say that "unmarried" in verse 8 includes the broad range of single persons, virgins and divorced, and that Paul then underscores the group widows by mentioning them specifically. Perhaps he felt it necessary to mention the widows specifically to Corinth because of the problems peculiar to them (cf. v. 26). After all, his advice to the women in Timothy's church would be different (cf. 1 Tim. 5).

As for "unmarried" in verse 11, Heth and Wenham allow the word here to mean "divorced"; they imply that the word is limited to divorced here. That is true, but they seem to be playing a semantic game. Though it is clear that the word here is used only of divorced or separated persons, they imply that that is the *meaning* of the word here. That is not quite correct. The context does not tell us that the "unmarried" are "divorced" but that the "divorced" are "unmarried." The meaning of "unmarried" is not limited, but the meaning of "divorced" further defined.

In verses 32 and 35, they point out that the gender of "unmarried" in 32 shows that it refers to a man, whereas the gender in verse 35 reveals that it speaks of a woman. Both verses they limit to engaged people, presumably because that is their interpretation of the direction of the admonition in that section.

Again, I must protest. Aside from the matter of whether that section

is primarily *aimed at* the engaged—I prefer to speak of those anticipating marriage—there is not the slightest contextual reason for *limiting*
those words to the engaged.[11] Paul is simply making a statement of
principle concerning those unencumbered by marital commitments.
Again, it seems that these authors have allowed their modern view of
engagement to determine their interpretation. Since the ancients saw
engagement as a marital commitment, the males of verse 32 and the
females of verse 35 most decidedly *cannot* be considered engaged. Paul
cannot mean that men who had already made their covenantal commitments but had not taken possession of their pledged ones have no
concern for their "woman" or that women who had agreed to marry
a certain man "undistractedly" (v. 35) serve the Lord. No. The adjective
unmarried may be distributed by gender so as to agree with its noun,
but it may not be made to refer to engaged, as opposed to other "unmarried" persons.

I cannot see that Heth and Wenham have shown that the meaning
of *unmarried* is not univocal throughout the chapter. And, since the
only specific group to which the term is specifically applied is people
who are divorced, I cannot see how they hope to exclude them from
those deserving the term in verse 27.[12]

With such weak arguments to support them, it disturbs one to read
how Heth and Wenham chastise C. Brown for using "divorced"/"unmarried" in verse 11 to illuminate verses 27–28.[13] Brown argues that
verses 27–28 include but are not limited to the divorced, and he allows
this conclusion to affect his translation of "virgins" in verse 25 to read
"unmarried[s]."[14] I suggest that his treatment of "virgins" is hasty, but
I find no fault with his thoughts regarding verses 27–28. Since "unmarried" is used only in this section in the New Testament, and since
one of the four uses there clearly includes the divorced, the burden of
proof is on Heth and Wenham to show why they cannot be included
in verses 32 and 34 as well as being implied in verses 27–28.

Heth and Wenham seek to rest this burden on the back of Paul's
"structural" indicator ("Now concerning virgins") in verse 25, suggesting that having ceased to speak exclusively to the married and previously married he is turning exclusively to advice for the never married.[15] To support this, they cite extensively from Gordon Fee's
rhetorical criticism of 1 Corinthians 7:1–9.[16] His argument that verses
1–7 consistently refer to married people is seen as undercutting any
appeal to verse 8 as a reference to the "previously unmarried." Their
own interpretation of the "unmarried" of verse 8 is those "who were
at one time married and therefore can only be widowers."[17] The admonition to the previously unmarried does not begin until verse 25.

This sort of argument seems overbearing. Even if the major section
of 7:1–9 is addressed to the married, why is it improper to suggest
that "unmarried" in 7:8 has its normal meaning: anyone not currently

married, including single people, widowed [men], and divorced persons?[18] I know of no legitimate way to exclude virgins from the parenthetical verses 8 and 9, and no matter how you care to argue, the major section 7:1–14 is written to those currently married, with the exception of verses 8–9. If that section has a parenthetical digression, so may the section to those who are never married (7:25–35). Heth and Wenham have turned a structural indicator into a "Berlin wall" to exclude the interpretation they cannot accept.

Another argument used against the inclusion of divorced people in verses 27–28 is the purported contradiction this would produce with regard to verse 11b. Paul says, "Do not get remarried," then permits it.[19] But these authors simply suffer here again from their faulty interpretation of the earlier verse. Verse 11b refers to those who do not have grounds for divorce. Verse 27b refers to those who were either themselves divorced or who had grounds for divorcing their spouses. At least this interpretation harmonizes the passages.[20]

Finally, these authors suggest that the word for "having been released" is not Paul's customary term for legal divorce. The word is derived from *luo*. If Paul had meant divorce, he would have used *chorizo* or *aphiemi*, as he does elsewhere in chapter 7. They interpret *luo* as released from the bonds of betrothal. They note that this verb (or a form of it) is used of divorce in the Gospels, but they imply that this is not Paul's term, at least in 1 Corinthians 7.[21]

But this is not impressive when we recall that the terms Paul does use for "divorce" in this chapter both imply *offense* on the part of the divorcer. *Chorizo* (vv. 10, 11, 15) implies the sundering of the valid bond. Doubtless divorce is the primary mode of sundering intended (though there is no sound reason for thinking that desertion would not fall under this admonition as well). Jesus uses it in the same way, as we noted earlier. To Paul, *aphiemi* means "leave" (vv. 11, 12, 13) and may well imply divorce. But here again, its primary meaning is not divorce, but to leave. In the context, that leaving is illicit. It is improper to take these two instances of terms that are close in meaning and imply divorce in context and state dogmatically that they are Paul's words for divorce. Rather, it is wise to admit that these terms do not essentially entail divorce, but that when the context brings across that implication, they imply treacherous divorce. The more common term for divorce in the New Testament is, like its counterpart in the Old, not an offense-term, but a morally neutral term, that, absent a negative context, may be used of morally acceptable divorce. Thus, Paul in verse 27 is likely simply referring to a treacherously divorced (or innocent) spouse, or a man who has divorced his spouse as a moral discipline, or a widower.

Heth and Wenham stress that "released" is not Paul's term for divorced, but they do not tell us how "released" can refer to engaged couples—their own view. Presumably Paul is telling them not to seek to break off their engagement. This may not be as helpful as these authors suppose, however, for engagement in the ancient world—especially to Rabbi Paul—would be tantamount to a marriage covenant, and its breach probably a sin like adultery. This means that the advice Paul gave here would likely work for fully married persons as well, and his permission to those who are released to marry again would apply to the divorced also.

Conclusion

It seems proper, then, to say that in his general treatment of the never married, Paul digresses to speak to the formerly married a point of advice that equally applies to all who are properly unmarried, however they came to be in that state (i.e., death or divorce). His advice, in the round, is to be in the state that maximizes one's service to the Lord. He does not wish to make a major teaching to the divorced and widowed at this point, any more than he did in verse 8, but, as in verse 8, they are worth being mentioned in the context of people with another marital status.

Highlighting the theme of this book, note that there is simply no sound reason not to take verses 27–28 in a normal sense of presenting a (treacherously) divorced person with the moral right to remarry, while suggesting the worthy option of kingdom celibacy. If the person chooses celibacy, good choice! If the person chooses to remarry, that's OK too! The presumption is that such a one will wisely choose based upon a knowledge of which state will ultimately allow more time in service for the kingdom. Remaining unencumbered with a spouse theoretically will make time for the kingdom. But without the gift of celibacy, a person will spend time burning and might end up making time for Satan—by falling into fornication.[22]

INSTRUCTION TO THOSE OVER VIRGINS

"A wife is bound as long as her husband lives . . ."

(1 Corinthians 36–40)

If Paul on two occasions in chapter 7 permits (divorce and) remarriage of the innocent (vv. 15, 28), what are we to make of his statement in verse 39 that a wife is bound to her husband as long as he lives?

Various Interpretations

Several options present themselves:

1. The statement in verse 39 insists that marriage is a state that cannot be broken; therefore, even though a formal divorce may be obtained, such a severance is not recognized by God, and therefore, no remarriage during the lifetime of a person's (former) spouse is permissible. (Heth and Wenham)

2. Verse 39, when taken literally, represents only one way that a marriage may be broken and remarriage contracted. However, since death and divorce are in the same category to the biblical mind, remarriage after divorce, as after the death of the spouse, is presumed. (Murray)

3. Verse 39 is advice primarily designed for widows, specifically allowing for their remarriage.

4. Since this section is exhortative to the indecisive person who has "control" over his "virgin," it is intended only to serve him notice that his choice to have her marry is "till death do them part." It affirms the necessity to *intend permanency*, and it does not wish to speak to the propriety of divorce and remarriage. (Erasmus)

In my estimation, the fourth view is correct, although there may be something to the second as well. The first alternative seems impossible, if (*a*) the Scriptures are consistent and (*b*) our interpretation of the earlier passages is correct. I will not argue either of these points here. The first is a primary assumption of this work; the second is argued earlier in the book. Our previous conclusions, I believe, will stand on their own merits.

The question concerning the second view is stated by Heth and Wenham. They believe that this idea presumes a "legal fiction," the idea that the adulterer should be treated *as if he were dead*. These authors object to the implication that

Jesus substitutes one form of the letter of the law (death for adultery) for another form of the letter of the law (divorce), rather than giving the spirit of the law, with its much higher standards of forgiveness and reconciliation, as Jesus does in Matthew 5:21–48. If it is true, that the "one flesh" bond of marriage taught in Genesis 2:24 is indissoluble during the lifetime of the spouses, then no "legal fiction" can change that fact.[23]

As I have noted earlier in this work, I believe that the Scripture indeed recognizes and uses the clearly historical fact that divorce was used by the ancient Hebrews as a substitute for the death penalty.[24] The points are clear: first, the death penalty was prescribed for cases of sexual infidelity by the wife; second, Gomer, though guilty of sexual infidelity, was not executed but was divorced; and third, God used this "substitute" treatment of the guilty wife as illustrative of his judgment of his wandering wives Israel/Judah. The conclusion I draw is that divorce is an *acceptable* substitute for the death penalty.[25] Thus, both with regard to the legal system of Israel and with regard to God's just evaluation of penalties, divorce seems to be an acceptable substitute for death, so that it is proper to say that death and divorce are in the same category. This is further supported by our previous study in Leviticus,[26] where we noted that widows and the divorced were categorized together regarding their responsibilities to their former husbands and their present vows. About this I will have more to say.

Actually, it is not quite correct to say that the woman divorced for being unfaithful should be treated "as if she were dead," but, rather, that her marital obligation to her first husband is the same as if he were dead. In neither case does the former husband have a right to expect the woman's marital fidelity to him. The issue is not whether or not the divorce renders his "ontology" moribund but how death or divorce affects the covenant. I, at least, am not suggesting that God or society actually holds a trial for the guilty party in which that one is found guilty, sentenced, and executed. But I do imply that the covenantal effects are the same as if that had happened.

The second point in Heth and Wenham's response I also find inadequate. Genesis 2:24 does not teach that marriage is indissoluble but that the covenanters should enter into marriage intending to make it permanent.[27] The fact that marriage was intended to be permanent before the Fall does not logically imply that it was after the Fall. One cannot jump from intentionality to ontology.

But, though I do find the second view adequate, I think that it is better to see 7:39 in the light of its own context. Some understand the context to be the intermediate context (v. 8), where widows are mentioned. On this view, Paul is tying up the loose threads. He is providing advice for the disposition of marital status of widows, as he has not specifically given them the right to remarry.[28] But would this be necessary? Would not that have been known by all his readers in Corinth? After all, the law of the levirate certainly presupposed that widows could marry. The only thought to be corrected by that law was that it would be incestuous for the husband's brother to marry the widow. The law protects against the charge of incest, not against some law prohibiting the remarriage of widows. There must be some better reason for the presence of these verses.

Who Are the Keepers of Their Virgins?

My own feeling is that verse 39 is meant to connect with verses 36–38. In these verses Paul has been addressing someone who is undecided about the advisability of marrying (off?) a virgin. As noted earlier, this may be a man and his fiancée, a boy and his girlfriend, a father and his daughter, or a guardian and his ward. I think it likely that the latter is the best and includes the father-daughter combination. To the man, Paul says that it is morally permissible to choose either way, to marry or not to. Previously, in his advice to the virgins, he has given a reason not to marry, that is, so as to be able to spend more time in devotion to the Lord. That advice is, in turn, qualified by his previous advice that it is better to marry than to burn. Burning is probably behind his words in verse 36 about acting unbecomingly toward the virgin. It is explicitly expressed in verse 8, where widows and, we presume, other single people, are mentioned regarding a reason to marry. So the virgin in question wishes to marry in order to properly care for her biological urges. For her guardian to block this outlet for her is unbecoming. It could set her up for undue temptation. Or, it may be that she wishes simply for the sort of security that a husband could provide. For him to deny her this is unbecoming. In either case, the choice to marry or not to marry is not a moral choice, but a practical one, with points of argument on either side.[29]

But in all of this advice Paul may well feel that he has dulled the important point that marriage once contracted must be honored. It is permissible not to enter into marriage, but it is not permissible once the covenant has been made to simply back out of it. The time for a decision to quit the marriage is before the vows. Such advice is parallel to Jesus' point in Matthew 19:11 ff.: "If you want to get married, you have to follow the rules."[30]

On this account, Paul is not, at this juncture, trying to teach the whole theology of the breakup of marriage. He is not trying to entertain the matter of divorce, because that is out of sight and mind. This marriage is not even contracted yet. Why talk now of some future, hypothetical breach of covenant? For now, Paul merely sets before the indecisive guardian the moral limits of his ward's marriage from her perspective. It would have been correct to have added that she is also free to re-marry if the husband ever sins so grossly that the marriage bond is sundered, but why repeat that when both Jesus and Paul have made that point clear in their previous teaching? For now, what is needed is a reminder about the seriousness of marriage. Paul speaks of a decision for permanence, not a permanent decision.[31]

What Is the Bondage That Remains Until Death?

There is another point to ponder in the wording of the text. We note that the text speaks of the two as being legal partners. They are bound to each other. In other words, the admonition is directed to two, or concerning two, who are legally and morally bound to each other. Can as much be said of the parties in the case of a divorce? If there is a divorce, they are no longer legally bound to each other, but what of the moral bond?

Heth and Wenham hold that the bond in this verse is legal. Thus, the text is saying that the woman is legally bound to be her man's wife until he dies. They reject efforts employed by Erasmians (and myself) that seek to interpret this bond by the freedom-from-bondage passage in verse 15. They point out that there are two different words used by Paul. In verse 15 the term is *douloō;* in verse 39 it is *deo.* They belittle efforts showing that the two words have a common root by labeling them the "root fallacy" or the error of etymoligizing ("giving excessive weight to the origin of a word over and against its actual semantic value in a given context").[32] For their own part, they doubt that the words do have a common root and argue that Paul never uses *douloō* to refer to the legal aspect of marriage. They conclude by saying that even if *deo* had been used in verse 15 the context would still keep it from being understood in the same way *deo* is used in verse 39.

I shall not quibble with them about the origins of the word. I disagree, however, with their conclusion that there is no relationship between verses 15 and 39. In the first place, it is clear that Paul does use *douloō* with regard to marriage in verse 15. I previously rejected their improbable interpretation that the Christian spouse is simply free from responsibility for the divorce. The text is not referring to the agent responsible for the divorce; that the separating unbeliever is the responsible agent was never in question. Paul is trying to relieve the rejected one of thoughts and feelings of obligation to the departed spouse. He would, of course, have had no moral right to do so if the legal aspect of marriage were not settled. To tell the rejected woman that she is not in the position of a subordinate one (*doulos*) is to deny that her former husband is her leader (*kurios*). But the relationship of a woman who is "under her husband" (*hupandros*) in the legal bond (*deo*)[33] of marriage *is* one of *doulos/kurios*, at least according to the view of the Apostle Peter (1 Pet. 3:6). Heth and Wenham simply cannot keep these two words from bearing logically upon each other. If the woman of verse 15 is free from her position as a *doulos* it must be because she has no *deo* obligation. If she retains a *deo* relationship till death (v. 39) even if separated from her husband, then she must still consider herself a *doulos* and feels that obligation properly; Paul would have no right to tell her she is free (v. 15). Heth and Wenham cannot have it both ways. Either they have to qualify duration of verse 39, or they have to deny the freedom of verse 15. I prefer to interpret the thrust of verse 39 by previous teachings in verses 15, 27–28, and others.[34]

Supposing the husband to have committed some grievous offense against the body of his wife, I argue that she is no longer morally bound to reciprocate by keeping her own covenant obligations. For, by his actions, he has breached his covenant with her, releasing her from her moral bond. Were she to divorce him (end the legal bond), it would not be she who sundered the marriage, but he. In effect, his breach would have rendered her no longer under him or under the obligations of the covenant. Except for the legal fiction (the marriage writ), he ceases to be her husband. So, too, were he to divorce her treacherously, that is, without sufficient (sundering) grounds (i.e., *porneia*), she would not be under him either morally or legally. He could not be considered "*her* husband" or *her* man, nor she "*his* wife." And the admonition given relates only to a woman who still is, morally, at least, *under a man*.

A male guilty party would have had the moral right to marry, insofar as this action would not hinder him from restoring the first marriage (viz., because polygamy was morally—though not culturally—permissible). The apparent disharmony that this statement raises with regard to the teaching of Jesus and Paul is only prima facie. Jesus, in condemning the man who divorces and remarries (Matt. 19 and Mark 10) is not so much concerned with the remarriage as with the divorce. He abhors treachery motivated by the desire to marry another. The remarriage is a part of the continuing adultery insofar as it is tied to the divorce—it is the reason for the divorce. And did it (that is, the second marriage) not inhibit the restoration or continuation of the first marriage, it would not be considered adulterous at all.[35] It *is* inhibitive in societies that prohibit polygamy.

Paul, in 1 Corinthians 7:11, significantly omits the injunction "let *him* remain unmarried" when he reverses his words to the treacherous female divorcer.[36] And when he does proscribe the remarriage of the guilty female divorcer in that verse, he seems to so tie the remarriage to the immediate option to reconcile that a distant and relatively unrelated remarriage (even of this same guilty wife) is not in view but only one that is a part of the dissolution in the first place. By so viewing the remarriage of the guilty, we are actually back to what was said earlier concerning the teaching of Jesus. And, after all, Paul notes in these verses (i.e., vv. 10 f.) that he is simply reflecting the teachings of our Lord.

Conclusion: The Keeper Is the Guardian

Thus we find in favor of the fourth alternative, suspecting that Paul simply wishes to advise the guardian to measure his decision with the ruler of intended permanency. If he gives her in marriage, he may not go the next week and try and take her away from her husband. Saul did this when he sought to separate Michal from her husband to marry David. This "converted Saul," Paul, would not wish the behavior of the Old Testament Saul to become a precedent for the Church.

Paul concludes by reminding the guardian of his prior principle, based upon sanctified reason, that, for now, singleness for the virgin will be in the best interest of her happiness. Given the whole discussion of defrauding with which this section begins, with the likely ascetic influences and with immorality of the city constantly harrassing the married, we can understand his words.

Marriage as an Analogical Illustration of Freedom in Christ

"The married woman is bound to her husband while he is living."
(Romans 7:1–14)

We have not found in the didactic teaching of Paul on divorce in 1

Corinthians 7 any measure of support for a denial of the right to divorce and remarry (at least on the part of the innocent). It is, therefore, unlikely that such moral teaching can properly be derived from Paul's illustrative material in Romans 7:1 ff. In fact, it is almost a truism in hermeneutics that doctrine should not be based solely upon analogy and illustration. Yet often this passage in Paul's epistle to the Roman church is the first court of resort for those who wish to proscribe divorce and remarriage.

These well-meaning defenders of marriage make their appeal with such conviction that they seldom take the time to inquire Paul's purpose in using an illustration of the marriage state. In fact, he mentions marriage to illustrate what God has done for us in the substitutionary atonement. Far from trying to teach his readers that they are absolutely bound to their (physical) spouse till that spouse dies, he is, in fact, trying to tell them how to be free from their (spiritual) spouse to marry another while the abandoned spouse still lives. But let us set this forth in proper order.

THE "LAW" HIS READERS KNEW

"I am speaking to those who know the Law."

Paul begins to illustrate the precious gospel message that sin kills but Christ makes alive (6:23) by making a general point about the Law: it has its rights over the living, not the dead. In context, he is saying that spiritual law, God's law, demands its rights over the one under its jurisdiction. This is almost a tautology, but not quite. For it points out that a person who is dead is not under the Law. Laws are for the living. Paul is not trying to refer here to a person dead in trespasses and sins; that would be to mix his metaphors. Nor does he wish to overwork his analogy between spiritual law (cf. 6:15) and secular law (7:1). By this, I mean he does not wish to bring up that the law of a given land only concerns its citizens, not those of another nation. He does not broach the possibility that a person may become an expatriate and disavow citizenship in that land. He does not reflect on the condition of those banished from a given land. Paul is making a simple point: the people who live in a land are bound by its laws while they are living.

The exact nature of the "law" that these people know is not specified. I rather imagine that Paul does not care what particular law this statement evokes in the minds of his readers. What he says, as far as he goes, is equally true of Roman law or of Hebrew law. Law always functions in this way. Were his referent specifically the Mosaic Law, we would be advised to review our previous treatment of it in chapters 2 and 3. But it is sufficient here to simply think of the points concerning the relevance of law just mentioned.

THE TEACHING

The Wife's Dilemma

"For the married woman is bound . . ."

Paul now narrows the general rule to a specific application, one that enlivens the minds of his readers. He chooses the area of marriage. The person "under law" becomes the woman, the wife. This means that the legal obligation would be understood as her responsibility to keep herself to her husband. As far as I know, all the laws of the Roman peoples agreed upon the obligation of the woman to be loyal to her husband. Polyandry was not a practice accommodated by Roman rule; nor was it the policy of the peoples that made up the empire. As long as the man was her husband, as long as he lived, she was permitted to have sexual relations with him alone. Anything else was adultery. Had Paul gone beyond this point of unanimity, he would have had to be specific about the law in view, for the laws of the various peoples in the empire differed on the issues of divorce and of how to treat adultery.

Paul is careful in his choice of expressions. Only certain aspects of general marital relations will illustrate his point. Nor would it have been in his logical interest to entertain all the possible ins and outs of marital laws. His is the task of illustration, and the point that he intends to illustrate is how we may be free from our husband the law in order to belong to another, namely, Christ. This, needless to say, severely limited how he could apply his analogy, especially if the law evoked in the mind of his readers was the Mosaic Law, for according to the Old Testament Law, there were only a few ways for the woman to achieve release and remarriage.

Paul walks a thin line. In his illustration the woman is married. She has a husband, and he is alive. Only these assumptions will work, since (before we are joined to Christ) our husband, the law, is alive. These facts reveal that we are obligated to the law. But ours is a husband of death, for we are ourselves guilty of the grave offense of adultery against our husband. We have not been completely faithful to him. We have broken our vows to him. We have transgressed the law. We are worthy of the death penalty.[37]

Were we to be joined to Christ while still bound to the law, it would not be proper. Just as a wife cannot be joined to another man while her husband lives, so we cannot be (at the same time) both bound to the law and joined to Christ. We must be freed from the law. But how can that be? The Law of Moses knew of only a few ways that a woman could be free from her husband. First, she could be freed if her husband gravely offended the covenantal obligations. This is obviously an inappropriate line of reasoning, for our husband has not sinned against us ("Is the Law sin? May it never be!" 7:7). If union with Christ awaits the disloyalty of the law, we will never be joined to Christ. So any hope of our divorcing the law for treachery (Exod. 21:10 f.) is empty. And any thought that the law will intentionally cease to "minister" to us (i.e., put us treacherously away, Deut. 24:1) is vain as well.

Another theoretical possibility for release would be the death of the husband. But does the law die? No. "It is easier for heaven and earth to pass away than for one stroke of a letter of the law to fail" (Luke 16:17). God's law will not pass away. It is futile to expect our husband the law to die.

The only other possibility would be for us to be properly and intentionally released by the law. But what would this entail? Logically, either divorce or death. Paul's point is made only if he ignores the possibility of divorce as a *discipline*. For if we are divorced in this manner, as God divorced Israel (Jer. 3:8; Hos. 1:9 f.), then the only recourse for us is repentance and restoration (at least for as long as the husband is still awaiting our return). That idea is a beautiful picture of our release from and remarriage to *God,* but the implications are not so happy when the husband is not God but the *law.* For this reason, it is counterproductive to address this subject from the illustration of forgiveness found in the Prophets (e.g., Hos. 2:14 ff.). Would Paul wish us to repent and be reconciled to the law—still under its bondage? Certainly not!

The last option, death, seems even less happy. Our execution for breaking the law frees us from our husband, but a dead wife is unable to be joined to anyone. Thus, it seems that there is no escape from our bondage to the law. And since we have already failed to be faithful, a righteous husband—and the law is certainly righteous—is duty bound to see justice done.[38] According to Paul, the prescribed sentence is death. One way or the other, the wife must die.

The Solution

   "Through the body of Christ"

It is here that Paul surprises us with a unique solution. A substitute appears to take our place beneath the stones of justice. Our wished-for mate, Christ, takes our penalty on himself. We die in him. Thus, since we technically die in him, we fulfill the penalty and are no longer bound to the old husband. And since Christ not only takes us with him in death but also in the resurrection from the dead, we are alive to be subsequently joined to him as to a husband.

Any other way of telling the story—of illustrating the theological point—would have distorted that point. Divorce, though a theoretical option in two regards—by us or by the law—would totally ruin the progressing argument. Divorce had to be ignored as an option in order to present a workable solution—to get us completely free from our husband and joined to another while our husband still lived. An exceedingly clever illustration. An exceedingly "clever" God!

So, then, people expecting Paul to make anything (positive or negative) of the moral possibilities of divorce set forth in the Law and the Prophets show themselves to have missed Paul's thought in these verses. Divorce is irrelevant to the theological issue. And it is worth underscoring what I noted with regard to 1 Corinthians 7:39, that all these references to bondage only relate to a woman who is bound to a husband. They do not speak at all of a woman who is no longer morally bound to a man, who has sundered the covenant by actions that are themselves immoral, that is, unfaithfulness during marriage or at the point of divorce.

In closing this discussion, it is worth noting that, though the New and Old Testaments most often use general terms for "husband" and "wife," terms that could also mean "man" and "woman," respectively, there is a technical way of speaking of the woman who is bound to her husband, and that technical terms is used in this chapter. It is *hupandros,* "under the man." This term implies clear legal and moral obligation. But we have already noted that, according to the Old Testament in Numbers 30:9, a *widow* and a *divorced woman* are both in the same category. They are not bound to a man, but may bind themselves by oath. Just as the widow is not under obligation to the dead man, so too the divorced woman is free to contract a new oath to God. Her former husband has no rights over her. Morally she is no longer under him. She is on her own. It could not be said that the divorced woman is "under her husband." Like the woman to whom Jesus spoke in John 4:18, she may have had a husband, but this is only past tense after the divorce has taken place. Romans 7:2 speaks of a woman who is under a husband. This is not true of a divorced person. Divorce is essentially irrelevant to Paul's discussion, and any attempt to use these verses to disallow divorce and remarriage is a study in poor hermeneutics on several levels.

Miscellaneous Teachings of the Apostles

(1 Corinthians 13/Ephesians 5/ 1 Peter 3/1 Timothy 3)

THE NONEXPLICIT TEACHINGS OF PAUL (CONTINUED)

Paul's Teaching on "Love"

> *Love endures all things . . .*
>
> *(1 Corinthians 13:7)*

Often one finds people who are unhappy about all this technical analysis of legal passages. From them one hears of a simpler way to handle our subject: simply consider the apostle's treatment of love in 1 Corinthians 13. For love, we are told, cannot harmonize with such actions as divorce and remarriage. After all, does not the "ode to love" in that letter say in several ways that love would long endure the sorts of "grounds" that have been suggested in this book as morally adequate for divorce and remarriage? Specifically, how can the dissolution of marriage jell with statements that love "is patient, is not jealous, does not seek its own, is not provoked, does not take into account a wrong suffered, but rather bears all things, believes all things, hopes all things, endures all things . . . never fails"? Instead, divorce and remarriage show that someone has ceased to be patient, has made a self-serving response out of provoked jealousy, and has decided to take into account a wrong suffered because he or she has lost hope and refuses to bear more. One who divorces despairs of believing that it will pay to endure more and therefore considers the effort at continued loving a lost or failed cause.[1]

A proper response to such reasoning begins with the admission that many times lesser motivations and attitudes prevail in the tense conditions of a divorce and a remarriage. But these sorts of attitudes and motives are not commended in this book. They are an abuse of the biblical system, not a proper use of it. And as the saying goes, "Abuse does not prohibit use."

Second, I argue that, when approached from the biblical viewpoint, such motives and attitudes are not necessary as regards our subject. Proof is ready at hand and, at least in the case of divorce, is final: God is love (1 John 4:8), but God divorced Israel (Jer. 3:8). If divorce and love are incompatible, then the Bible is indeed confused on the subject, for it certainly attributes both to God at the same time, while arguing that there is no contradiction in him. But what harmonization is possible? Let us look in turn at each questioned phrase in 1 Corinthians 13.

"LOVE IS PATIENT"

Love is patient (*makrothumai*). God was long-suffering with Israel. For centuries, he put up with "her" infidelity. But there came a point at which no one could reasonably charge God with an unethical lack of patience for his discipline of the covenant partner. Patience overdrawn is coddling or stubbornness. Patience "gone to seed" shows evidence of condoning sin or of inability to act in a way that best promotes wholesomeness. God is guilty of none of these offenses. Neither is the person who chooses to act as God did to a spouse such as God had.

But, it is rejoined, God waited centuries, should we not be willing to wait throughout a short lifetime? No. In the analogy, both God and Israel are in the place of covenantal partners. The "centuries" may cover the lifetimes of individual members of Israel, but in the analogy, a thousand years is but a day. When God pictured the discipline of divorce in a real human time frame, that is, Hosea, he truncated the centuries into a far shorter time. Patience? Hosea was patient. His second and third "children" were not his but hers by harlotry.[2] He did not run out and file for divorce when he first knew that Gomer had broken the covenant. He was patient. But there was a righteous limit to his patience.[3]

"LOVE IS KIND"

Love is kind (*chrasteuetai*). The word implies that the lover is of service to the one loved. And though divorce may not seem to fit this idea, that is shortsighted. You must ask if it is kindness to allow an erring spouse to suppose that continued and unrepentant sin is not so bad as to require an appropriate response, a response aimed at restoring the fellowship that is only to be shared by partners in a properly functioning covenant. "Fellowship at any price" is evil. The Church, in kindness, is told to excommunicate the unrepentant from fellowship (Matt. 18). And we should remember that it is interpersonal offenses that lead to this excommunication. If it be subjoined that individuals should not cut off as the institutional Church does, we ask where this lesson is taught in Scripture? The divorce legislation follows the excommunication passage in Matthew, and that divorce legislation includes the "except" clause.

It must be remembered that one of the main functions of divorce is discipline. And though sentimental people often condemn discipline for showing a lack of love, the opposite is true. Discipline is "severe mercy"—"tough love." Kindness points out the speck in the other's eye because kindness does not want the speck to hinder the other's sight. It is manifestly unkind to allow the sin of the other to go untreated (cf. Luke 17:1 ff.). A lack of discipline is hate or rejection of the other at a most basic level. Joseph understood discipline. In kindness, as well as in justice, Joseph sought to put Mary away. His kindness was seen in his desire to put her away privately; his justice rested in the desire to divorce. But there is no evidence of unkindness to her.

"NOT JEALOUS"

God is revealed to be a "jealous" God (Exod. 20:5). But his jealousy is not like that condemned by Paul. There are actually two different terms used in the Greek. The one used in our present text is never used in a positive sense in the New Testament. It means "inflated" (*phusioo*), which implies empty pride and selfishness. But this is not necessarily true of the one who divorces. At stake are the words of covenant, not the empty claims of selfishness. To employ this word *phusioo* of the disciplining divorcer would be to presuppose no right of covenant to the thing envied. It is, after all, wholly improper to speak of a husband as being envious of his wife and her lover in a case of adultery. By vow the husband has the right to her fidelity; it is not a matter of envy or jealousy at all.

"DOES NOT ACT UNBECOMINGLY"

Paul is saying that love will not do anything that is "improper" (*aschemosune*). For some, divorce and remarriage are unbecoming actions. But I protest their definition. What is an "unbecoming" act? We want to be sure that we understand the meaning of the biblical writer, not the biblical interpreter. What does the Scripture count as "unbecoming"? That is precisely what we have been seeking to determine in this study. It is my conviction that some divorce and remarriage do not merit such an appellation. If the technical analysis does not condemn an action, we must withhold the term *unbecoming*. Certainly we are not permitted to speak of an action employed by the Holy God himself as "unbecoming." And God divorced Israel. Do we seek to be more holy than God?

"DOES NOT SEEK ITS OWN"

The idea here is that love is not *selfish*. And as was noted with regard to jealousy, it is inadmissible that a judicious response to convenantal infidelity be branded an act of selfishness. Is God selfish? Certainly not. Fidelity on the part of Israel was a matter of covenantal agreement; it was therefore a matter of reasonable and righteous expectation. Selfishness had nothing to do with the matter. Beyond this, disciplinary divorce is an act done out of love for the offending partner. Such divorce cares enough to place the offending spouse on notice that actions have effects and that those effects have a personal price tag on them. If the discipline works, then this "tough love" has saved the offender from continued offenses of the same kind.

"IS NOT PROVOKED"

This is telling us that love does not give way to "vicious outbursts" (*ou paroxunetai*), outpourings of bitterness and rage. One must admit that often divorce is associated with such outbursts on the part of the offended. But this does not have to be the case. Does the disciplinary concept of divorce necessarily have such behavior associated with it? Hosea and God responded in righteous indignation, but theirs were actions of love, with the aim of a loving restoration. Ezra responded in very forceful righteous indignation, but who would charge him with a "vicious" outburst?

"DOES NOT TAKE INTO ACCOUNT A WRONG SUFFERED"

Only if an evil is suffered and taken into account can a biblical divorce take place, so how can divorce not fail the test at this point? On the other hand, if divorce cannot pass, how can we remove the charge of an unloving attitude from God? Remember, God will eventually send evildoers to hell, if they have not trusted in his Son. Therefore, this phrase cannot mean that love *ignores* a wrong suffered. Rather, it means that it is always willing to forgive and will forgive if the conditions of forgiveness are met. Love notes wrong and calls the erring other to repentance (Matt. 18; Luke 17; Gal. 6:1). Anything less is not *agapic* love. Love is willing to forgive, but does not unless there is repentance. Otherwise, God would empty hell out of love. Love is willing to forgive seventy times seventy times, but not even once if repentance is insincere (cf. Matt. 18:23–35). Love does not hold a grudge, but it has a righteous memory. It does not count tit for tat, but it must forget on the basis of *righteous* forgiveness.[4] So "takes no account of evil [*ou logizetai*] done to it" must be understood in the light of the next phrase.

"DOES NOT REJOICE IN UNRIGHTEOUSNESS"

Love is "unhappy" (*ou chairo*) when it discovers evil in marriage. It does not ignore it, thinking it not important enough to expose as wrong. Divorce is a formal way of stating righteous indignation against the object of one's Christian love. One of the saddest failures in Church and home today is the failure of love to show its tough side—show it not in spite, but in grief. Love knows wrong when it sees it and cares enough to do what it can (nonhypocritically) to take the speck out of the other's eye.

"REJOICES IN THE TRUTH"

Paul is not speaking of a giddy attitude that ignores what is going on around the Christian. "Rejoices in the truth" refers to a joy (*sun-chairo*) that harmonizes with the facts. In the case of covenant breaking, love rejoices through the suffering with the knowledge that God brings repentance by discipline. Only when the pattern of righteous discipline is exercised can love be said to rejoice in the truth. Far too many believers "hang in there" acting and/or believing that the infidelity of their spouse was only a figment of the imagination. They have been deceived into thinking that a peaceful coexistence with sin is possible. To retain a "happy attitude" in a marriage full of covenant breaking is to "rejoice in error."

"BEARS ALL THINGS"

Now come the positive statements. Love "preserves" itself (*stego*) through unhappiness in marriage. It continues to do so as it puts away the loved one. And it keeps on loving though it countenances remarriage. Love suffers through. But love is also realistic. God suffered the sins of Israel. Hosea suffered the infidelity of Gomer. And when they put away the offender their love continued to bear up under the effects of broken covenant. For the follower of Christ, the issue is not whether love toward the offender will continue, but how it is appropriate to express love toward the offender. Part of bearing up is the "tough love" of divorce. Part of bearing up through the realism of remarriage is the continued willingness to forgive the former spouse. It is illegitimate to presume that all divorce and remarriage are incompatible with the preservation of Christian love.

"BELIEVES ALL THINGS"

Love is "confident" (*pisteuo*), but not credulous. It neither pays attention to rumors nor ignores clear evidence. God, Ezra, and Hosea did not believe rumors. They knew the sad truth that there comes a time when continuing to live in a broken covenant passes beyond confidence into self-deception and foolishness. Divorce, and even remarriage, comes as a result of knowing the truth. The fact that love is confident does not inhibit such actions.

"HOPES ALL THINGS"

Love is "trusting" (*elpizo*). It has favorable and confident expectations of the marriage partner, even the sinning partner. But, again, *agapic* love is not a blind passion. In divorcing as a discipline it hopes for the best: reconciliation. But, as time goes on, it may realize that the best that may be hoped for short-term is remarriage for the innocent, though it hopes for the repentance of the former spouse in the long-term. Love hopes for the day when *Christian* fellowship may be restored. It hopes all things, but it continues to live with its feet in the real world. It "hopes all things" in the *now*.

"ENDURES ALL THINGS"

Love "bears up courageously" (*hupomeno*). It bears up even during the trauma of divorcing the unrepentant spouse. Though remarriage to another takes place in the face of continuing failure of the disciplined one to respond, the nonsentimental love of the sinner endures. God is our best example of this. After divorcing Israel, his love of Israel endured during their continued rejection in exile. It endured even while he joined himself to the Gentiles. For humans, remarriage may preclude certain responses that love could make were the sinner to repent later on. But it does not end all responses, especially the most important of them: forgiveness.

"LOVE NEVER FAILS"

Love does not, on its own, fall into inactivity (*katargeo*). It is active, without being obnoxious. It reaches out with forgiveness to the offender, but it does not make the offender accept it. Love may take the "tough" role, trying to make sinners see the error of their ways, but whether by negative or positive means it perseveres. It may see marriages fall into inactivity. It may see covenants be legally abolished. It may see remarriages. But it is alive.

SUMMARY COMMENTS: WHAT IS "LOVE"?

In all these statements about how love behaves, one may miss what the Bible actually means by love. And without going into undue detail, we would serve ourselves by clarifying how the love that acts in these ways through broken covenants/divorces/remarriages differs from other attitudes. The word at issue is *agape*. Some incautiously speak of it as divine love or unconditional self-sacrifice, but we must understand this word (which the pagans also knew and used)[5] in less religious terms. It refers to an attitude of regard toward its object—the treatment of the object in a manner appropriate to that object. Because its behavior is not dependent upon the response of the object, it is thought to be unconditional. This is not quite correct. Its behavior is always determined by the nature and status of the object. For example, God loves the world, not because it acts positively toward him, but because it is made up of persons whom he in his sovereign will has created in his own image and likeness. He does not have the same regard for the lower creation, which has a different nature.

By the same token, God loves different groups of people differently. His regard for the Church leads him to behave toward it differently than he does toward those outside it. They have a different status. So, too, a given man has general obligations toward every woman but has special obligations to his covenant partner. He owes her no such regard until she becomes his wife. Technically speaking, he does not regard his wife because she treats him well or poorly but because she is his wife. It is her status, not her behavior, that determines his behavior.

Friendship (*philos*) is another matter. This term speaks of an attitude that is determined by response on the part of the recipient. It reaches out and gives of the self, but retracts its kindnesses if it is spurned. God loves all, but is the friend of few. Marriage demands love, but hopes for friendship. Nor should we suppose that the nature of this friendship is only cool affection. It may include passion. But if it is not requited, it dies. It would probably be a sin to fail to want to be the friend of one's marital partner—it is a sin to fail to want to be the friend of God. But to be a friend cannot be required, because it is dependent upon the condition of both parties at the moment.

The love Paul speaks of is the first kind. It responds appropriately to its object. It inquires who objects are and regards them according to their nature and status. To apply this to our discussion, we may say that the provisions of marriage (the essential actions pledged) need only be given to the covenant partner. Men need not provide food and clothing to every woman, and they should not provide sex to any woman who is not their spouse. Likewise, women need not promise a man to abstain from a sexual relationship with someone else unless the man is their husband. But the man who is in covenant with a woman must provide the essentials to her. She may be "unbearably" nasty to him. It does not matter. Those things she deserves because she is his wife. She, in turn, must be exclusive to him, whether or not he is nice to her. Monogamy is her due to her husband.

Does divorce not offend the nature of this sort of love? Not necessarily. If divorce is merely a statement that one will no longer keep one's side of the bargain, it is offensive to love's requirements. But if one of the two partners has intentionally broken the covenant, that partner has thereby changed status. The only regard subsequently due such a partner is that which must be shown to any other human being. Sin against the covenant removes the covenant partner's status. Covenant-breaking behavior is not like just any behavior. Just as the speaking of the initial vows established the covenant status, so the breaking of the essential terms of those vows ends that status.[6]

Paul knew that we owe it to any person to keep covenant. But if another has broken covenant, we then no longer owe the *special* obligations stated in that covenant. The obligations of love stated in 1 Corinthians 13 are *general* obligations, and, therefore, we still owe them and can give them to the (former) partner though divorce and remarriage have taken place.

A final comment is in order. Though love may be consonant with divorce and remarriage, a simple reading of this section will reveal that it will take God's power to love an offender through divorce and remarriage to another, or through forgiveness in marriage. But God is in that sort of business.

The Analogical Relation Between Marriage and Christ's Union with the Church

> *". . . as Christ also loved the Church."*
>
> (*Ephesians 5:22–33*)

THE ANALOGICAL ARGUMENT

Another passage that is often put to service in inhibiting divorce and remarriage of all kinds is Ephesians 5:22–33. Here is how Laney forges the argument:

The marriage union is designed to reflect the relationship between Christ and His church. Just as a union is formed in marriage when two people commit their lives to each other, so a union is formed when the believer is joined to Christ. Will Christ ever break the relationship between himself and His church? Absolutely not (Heb. 13:5)! Will Christ ever be "divorced" or separated from the believer? Never (Romans 8:35–39; John 10:28)! Since the marriage union is a picture of the permanent relationship between Christ and His church, the marriage union itself must be permanent. If marriage were a dissolvable relationship, it would be an inaccurate representation of the indissoluble relationship between Christ and His church.[7]

The clarity of this argument requires no further exposition. Its criticism does.

THE CRITICISM OF THE ARGUMENT

The Direction of the Analogy

Several assumptions and conclusions in this argument can properly be challenged. First, it is stated that marriage is designed to reflect the relationship between Christ and the Church. But is this true? Not really. For though it is true that the apostle uses certain similarities between marriage and the Christ-Church relation to enhance his ethical admonitions to both husbands and wives, it is not quite correct to say that marriage is designed to picture the relationship between Christ and the Church. It is an existing institution of marriage that is being discussed. There is no evidence of *design* except that the apostle designs to use the Christ-Church relation to illuminate ethics. Laney has turned the analogy around.

Theological Digression in the Analogy

A careful reading of the passage in the Epistle will reveal that the apostle begins by admonishing a spouse, sanctions his admonition by drawing attention to a similarity in the Christ-Church relationship, becomes "carried away" with the analogy, becomes aware of his theological digression, and returns to the subject of marriage. He does this on several occasions.

DIGRESSION ONE: SAVIOR OF THE BODY

The initial point is that wives should be subject to their husbands as to the Lord. This admonition is supported by the analogical argument that, just as the Church is subject to Christ, so wives should be subject to their husbands. Husbands stand in the place of Christ in the same respect that wives stand in the place of the Church. But then Paul rises into the theological skies, making the statement that Christ is the Savior of the body. Question: Is the husband the savior of the wife? Well the husband is to be the protector of the wife's well-being, but that is not the same thing as saying that he is her savior. And Paul admits the lack of analogy by saying, "*but* as the Church is subject to Christ, so also the wives ought to be to their husbands in everything" (v. 24).

Careful consideration of this pattern is instructive. It teaches us that there are limits to the analogical relationships that can be drawn between the pairs. Accordingly, it is dangerous to press the truths of the Christ-Church relation into the husband-wife relation. We must take care not to overdraw the analogy. We must limit ourselves to what Paul says.

DIGRESSION TWO: SANCTIFIER OF THE CHURCH

The second analogical relation begins with the admonition that husbands should "love their wives" (v. 25). Then comes the analogy: "Just as Christ also loved the Church and gave himself up for her." This is followed by the theological digression: "that he might sanctify her, having cleansed her by the washing of water with the word, that he might present to himself the Church in all her glory, having no spot or wrinkle or any such thing; but that she should be holy and blameless" (vv. 26 f.).

Again, it is noteworthy that the digression contains elements that simply are not true of the husband-wife relationship. Does the husband cleanse the wife? Does he present her to himself holy and blameless as a result of his own work in her life? Probably not, even though the husband is to be careful to preserve the purity of the wife[8] and has a Christian obligation to be a part of the cleansing of another Christian from his or her daily sins (John 13:1–17).

DIGRESSION THREE: MYSTERIOUS UNION

The third movement relates quite directly to the second. Admonition: husbands ought to love their wives. But the analogy becomes more complex. Paul inserts a different sort of analogy into the pattern: "as their own bodies. He who loves his own wife loves himself; for no one ever hated his own flesh, but nourishes and cherishes it" (vv. 28 f.). Then the pattern returns. Analogy: "just as Christ also does the Church because they are members of his own body" (v. 30). Then the interruption, a quote of Genesis 2:24, followed by the theological digression, "this mystery is great" (v. 32), with its analogical disclaimer, "but I am speaking with reference to Christ and the Church." This disclaimer is doubled by the disjunction "nevertheless," with which Paul concludes the entire discussion by restating the initial admonitions: husbands, love; wives, respect.

The Missing Analogue: Permanent Union

The question that now presents itself is, Where exactly are we to locate the alleged teaching that divorce and remarriage of human beings is impermissible insofar as the relationship between Christ and the Church is permanent? Clearly, the likely location would be in the discussion of love. But we have already seen that nothing intrinsic to love disagrees with the view of divorce and remarriage set forth in this book. Therefore, the point regarding love must center, not in its nature, but in the specific application of love in the Christ-Church relation. This is to say, with Laney, that since Christ would never divorce the Church, the husband should never divorce the wife.

The Ignored Analogue: Divine Discipline

But this is a conclusion—an analogue—*not* explicit in the text. And it is risky to consider it—not only insofar as Paul never broaches the subject, and therefore the point is analogically speculative, but also because such a conclusion seems based upon thinking contrary to explicit biblical teaching. I am referring here to a similar analogy drawn in the Old Testament that proves the opposite point. In Jeremiah, Hosea, and Isaiah, Yahweh is spoken of as the husband of Israel. And yet God does divorce his covenant people and marry another. In Hosea, the analogy is tight: Hosea is to Gomer as Yahweh is to Israel. Or, the human relationship is to be a picture of the relationship existing between God and his chosen bride, Israel. In that case, the analogy explicitly involves divorce, and it does so in a positive light.

The upshot is that where the discussion of divorce does occur in a divine-human analogy, far from implying a rejection of divorce, divorce is pictured as a righteous act—a disciplinary measure of love. We saw earlier that the detractors of divorce and remarriage simply dismiss the Old Testament analogy by saying that if we take it seriously we would also have to take polygamy seriously, since God is pictured as a polygamist in the same passages.[9] They do not take seriously the possibility that they are wrong about the polygamy, and they do not take seriously that, polygamy aside, their sort of critique at this point might just as well dismiss the discussion of Ephesians 5. After all, if such analogical discussions are not to be taken seriously with regard to human marriages, why take the New Testament seriously either? If metaphors are to be discounted because they are figures, then we must play fair and discount them all. And if it be argued that the God-Israel metaphor is never applied to human marriage, whereas the New Testament Christ-Church language is, we must stress that the Hosea case proves this rejoinder invalid. It is left then to try and argue that God-Israel is metaphorical and the Christ-Church relation is not. This will prove a very difficult alternative, because Christ is not a literal brain, and the Church is not a literal torso.[10]

Such discussions of the Old Testament are even more significant in view of Laney's textual support for his statement that Christ will never abandon the Church. Hebrews 13:5 speaks its promise, not to the Church, but to individual believers, and is a quote of certain Old Testament promises (Deut. 31:6, Josh. 1:5) that are made to Israel. In view of the conditional nature of such promises in the Law—the surrounding contexts deal with cursings as well as blessings—it might be well for Laney to search for a stronger text. Perhaps one can be found; in any case his point is not well made.[11]

Nor will it do to argue that although God might divorce his covenant people, he would never finally divorce and marry another. Does not God finally cut off those insincere ones in the Church (Heb. 6:4 ff.)? And did not God marry the Church before he fully restored his bride, Israel?[12]

An Implied Analogue: As Their Own Bodies

Also interesting is an analysis of the "intruding" analogy in movement three. Paul says that men should love their wives as they love their bodies. Does the love of the body imply that I will refuse to discipline it? Might I not find there to be circumstances in which an amputation of my arm might be necessary for the good of the rest of the body? Is it unloving to my body to remove a defective kidney and replace it with another? I do not wish to be flippant, but such questions prove that even here one cannot exclude the very ideas involved in our position. To be sure, Paul does not explicitly discuss them, but they are actually more relevant than seriously considering unstated theological analogues, when the text clearly sees similar digressions as irrelevant to the husband-wife relation.

Laney is not to be summarily believed when he argues that if marriage is not permanent then marriage is not a fitting picture of the relationship between Christ and the Church. The analogues fit as stated in the text. There is no reason to suppose that *dis*analogy in unstated matters disallows analogy in matters stated. It is simply wrong to argue that Paul intends marriage to be an "accurate representation" of the Christ-Church relation *with regard to permanency.* Paul argues nothing of the kind. He merely states that we ought to do X in the same way that Christ does X to the Church. Loving permanently and without recourse to divorce and remarriage is never stated as a value of X.

Mosaic Versus Abrahamic: Which Relation?

A final word needs to be said in regard to the relation of the Mosaic to the Abrahamic covenant. As we began to argue in chapter 1, the Old Testament analogy of God-Israel is a Mosaic discussion. In Ephesians the analogy seems to be Abrahamic. Could it not be argued that since the New Testament analogy is Abrahamic, and the Abrahamic covenant is unilateral and permanent, marriage is understood in the new covenant as unilateral and permanent? This is possible, but not likely. Marriage may be likened to either the Mosaic or the Abrahamic covenant, because both are covenants. Marriage may be like the Abrahamic or the Mosaic in *some* respects without being like either in *all* respects. The key to proper argument is sticking to the evidence. We are unjustified in drawing analogies that the text of the Scripture omits. Marriage is like the Mosaic covenant in divorce and remarriage. Marriage is never likened to the Abrahamic covenant in being unilateral in commitment and permanent in duration.

CONCLUSION

In summary, Ephesians 5 does not draw the analogical relation between Christ-Church and husband-wife on the point of permanence;

nor does it discuss divorce, human or divine. Therefore, use of this passage to affirm permanence in marriage or to deny the moral propriety of divorce/remarriage is simply overworking an analogical argument and should be shunned. If any discussion of analogy is proper on the subject of divorce/remarriage it would be one drawn between human marriage and God's divorce of Israel and subsequent remarriage to the Church.

EXCURSUS: THE TEACHINGS OF THE APOSTLE PETER ON MARRIAGE

"Wives be submissive to your own husbands . . ."

(1 Peter 3:1–6)

Just as Ephesians stresses the need for a husband to "love" his wife, and, as we have seen in our own discussion of 1 Corinthians 13, divorce and remarriage is not incompatible with "love," so 1 Peter 3:1–6 expands upon another theme in Ephesians: submission. The question is raised, How can a woman submit to her husband and divorce him at the same time?

"Be submissive to your own husbands"

As we have noted before, the admonition is to one's "own husband." The text is not addressing a woman whose husband has morally disqualified himself from the office of husband.[13]

"Even to them that are disobedient to the word"

Is it proper to assume that "even to them that are disobedient" includes those who breach the marital vows themselves? I think not. The man in the text has not disqualified himself from his office as husband, but only acted in a way that is disobedient to other commands in God's word. Such an interpretation sufficiently harmonizes this text with the view set forth in previous chapters, and this explains why she is admonished to "[win] their husbands without a word," rather than being admonished to feel free to divorce/remarry (1 Cor. 7:15). This man is hard to live with, but he has not broken the canons of the covenant. The husband in Peter's Epistle is obviously willing to remain with and provide for this wife—give the essentials of his marriage. His disobedience relates to other matters. Perhaps in view of the admonition not to adorn oneself with outward grandeur, we may suppose that his disobedience centers around his commitment to material things, which have perhaps displaced God in his life. This seems likely, because the focus of submissive behavior in the prior sections is designed specifically to counter a similar failure of an authority.[14]

"Thus Sarah . . ."

It is interesting that Sarah is used in this text to exemplify submissiveness. Wherein? Probably when Abraham put her chastity in jeopardy by presenting her as his sister in Egypt and Philistia. The husband was not to impugn her integrity without exacting evidence. In this, Abraham was not disobedient to his vows per se, but he certainly was playing on the edges of the vows. Or, perhaps this reference suggests that, like Abraham's, the husband's problem centers upon a lack of faith in God to provide for his needs. But, we must ask, is such a lack of faith a breach of the marital covenant?

In short, the woman of 1 Peter is not in the place of a woman whose husband had breached the marriage vows; therefore, Peter does not speak of or urge divorce but submission. The marital covenant is not sundered by unrelated problems in the husband's personal relationship with his God.

"Live with your wives . . ."

Husbands, on the other hand, are told to live with their wives in an understanding way (3:7). That seems to be euphemistic for sexual relations, so this woman does seek a physical relationship with her husband, uncharacteristic of a woman having an affair. The text goes on to speak of honoring her, a grossly inappropriate bit of advice if the woman were guilty of adultery. Clearly, then, the text is not discussing a woman who has sundered the marriage, but rather someone whose personal piety is lacking. The man is to see her or her role as "weaker," but not unchaste.

It is simply irrelevant to trot out this passage to inhibit "just divorce," when the passage does not hint at *porneia* as being involved in the circumstances. We have here, again, a misguided hermeneutic that would seek to understand such verses as disregarding unfaithfulness as legitimate grounds for the discipline of divorce and the right to remarry. In short, 1 Peter does not clearly speak against the possibility of divorce (or of remarriage).

THE NONEXPLICIT TEACHINGS OF PAUL (CONTINUED)

Divorce/Remarriage and Qualification for Church Office

> *"The overseer must be above reproach."*
> *(1 Timothy 3:1 f.; 12/Titus 1:6 f.)*

The final passages to be considered are found in the pastoral Epistles, in three sections dealing with the qualifications of church leaders

(1 Tim. 3:1–11; 3:12–13; Titus 1:6–9). Each contains a phrase (1 Tim. 3:2; 3:12; Titus 1:6) that is usually translated rather literally "the husband of one wife." It is the interpretation of this phrase that concerns us. Does it mean to exclude from positions of leadership persons who are divorced and remarried, or not? And does the fact that it is found in a section dealing with leadership mean to imply that its application is to be limited to that group? Let us look at the second issue first.

TO WHOM DOES THE QUALIFICATION APPLY?

There are rules in the Old Testament concerning the priests that only applied to them. In Leviticus 21:7, 14–15, the Levitical priest and the High Priest, respectively, were prohibited from marrying certain categories of women, namely, harlots, divorcées, and widows. The common people were not subject to these exclusions. Indeed, there are celebrated cases of the common people marrying such women: For example, Ruth, a widow, married Boaz, in a story that moves its reader with appreciation for the system of levirate marriage, which God himself implemented and sanctioned (Deut. 25:5 ff.). Or there is the case of Rahab, the harlot, who is usually thought to be the same Rahab in the line of Christ (Matt. 1:5). And David married the divorcée Michal (his former wife, who had been married to another just before he married her again, 2 Sam. 3:12–16).

Laney, who believes that the Levitical rules offer us a "precedent" for understanding the Pauline qualifications section,[15] nonetheless objects to understanding these qualifications as restricting only persons holding the office of elder or deacon. He expands the application to everyone who *functions* as if they were in those offices. Examples he gives of such functioning include church planting and teaching in a church or seminary.[16]

Strangely, however, Laney allows for persons not living up to at least the "husband of one wife" qualification to function in "evangelism, discipleship, counseling, and many other support ministries serving the local church and missionary groups."[17] The strangeness involved in this concession centers around the fact that all the allowed ministries would seem to involve the essential aspects of the forbidden group. Specifically, we note: spiritual authority (certainly involved in the tasks of elders and disciplers), teaching (for elders and disciplers/counselors), and the beginning of the Church in at least the lives of those evangelized. Indeed, was not the office of deacons in the Book of Acts specifically established to "support" the ministry of the elders (Acts 6:1–7)? It would seem that Laney is on the right track but does not go far enough, for there is no reason to believe that a person not meeting the qualifications should be allowed to function in *any* capacity in the Church.

But the application actually goes far beyond the matter of "functioning." This is evident by looking at the list. There is not a single qualification in the list that should not be enjoined upon each and every church member. What church would not send the elders to the home of a member whose life publicly exhibited the offenses proscribed?[18] The offenses include intemperance, insensitivity, disorderliness, inhospitality, drunkenness, hostility, contentiousness, avariciousness, carelessness about the order of the home, capriciousness about life in general, double-tonguedness, greediness, unjustness, unholiness, unrulyness. On the positive side, the qualifications include "aptness to teach." The women (wives?) mentioned in 1 Timothy 3:11 should avoid slander and unfaithfulness. Now, what Christian men or women should not have it said of them that they meet these qualifications, or that the Church should be obliged to correct them, even to the point of excluding the incorrigible from communion and other forms of fellowship?

What I am driving at is that God expects each member of the body of Christ to live up to all these qualifications. None of the qualifications are designed exclusively for the leadership in the local church. The function of these sections is to set forth a checklist of what it means to be a proper disciple, so that the Church may be especially careful to screen out persons from leadership who are not fit. But holding the list up to their lives does not imply that the list should not be a part of the normal discipleship of *every* follower of Christ. After all, persons qualified for leadership in the Church do not become qualified as the list is held before them; rather, having previously disciplined themselves according to such a list, their life now is revealed by checking against a formal list to be "approved." Thus, whatever "the husband of one wife" means, it is to be expected that every Christian meets that standard. One who does not should be disciplined by the church for failure to do so and brought into alignment with the standard on this matter of Christian ethics.

Thus, churches that simply exclude divorced and/or remarried people from leadership (on the basis of these passages) should also discipline them—even to the point of excluding them from fellowship if they do not repent and bring forth the fruit of repentance! To omit to do so is to reject the words of Jesus, who said: "Be on your guard! If your brother sins, rebuke him; and if he repents, forgive him."[19]

TO WHAT DOES THE QUALIFICATION REFER?

Several alternatives have been offered to explain what the qualification refers to. Carl Laney succinctly itemizes the standard options.[20]

The Alternative Views

1. Exclusion of *married men* from official offices: This refers to the Roman Catholic idea that priests and persons in orders should be celibate, since such persons should be "married" only to Christ and his Church, not to a human woman or man.[21]
2. Exclusion of *unmarried men* from such offices: The idea here is that only men who are married are qualified to counsel and lead the Church, as their experience in the marital and familial spheres is a testing ground for their experience in office.[22]
3. Exclusion of *polygamists:* Laney (and most others) consider such a practice to be exemplary of "immorality."
4. Exclusion of *digamists: Digamy* is a term referring to a person being twice (or more) married (legally). The category could be further divided into groups identified by the nature of the second marriage: remarried widowers, the divorced and remarried, those who marry the divorced.[23]

Criticism of the Positions

CELIBATE PRIESTHOOD?

Laney quickly identifies the problem with the first alternative, celibate priesthood. Says he, "This view . . . is refuted right in the context where we read that the elder is one 'keeping his children under control' (3:4)." He also cites other passages that affirm marriage (1 Tim. 4:3; Gen. 2:24; Heb. 13:4).[24]

MARRIED PRIESTHOOD?

The second view, married priesthood, fares almost as poorly with the context. Laney again: "Consistency of interpretation would mean that if the elder must be married, he must also have children (3:4), yet no expositor that I am aware of is willing to push the issue that far."[25] I underscore these remarks. Since the form of qualification is the same in both cases, if he may have at least one wife, then he must have at least two children. And that seems manifestly absurd. Paul himself had neither wife nor children; there is no evidence that Timothy was married; and history records that the apostle John was likewise wifeless and childless. Would one wifeless leader write to another wifeless leader requiring lesser leaders to have wives?

MONOGAMOUS PRIESTHOOD?

The third alternative, monogamous priesthood—the most sure on the face of it—is nevertheless improbable. Laney notes that Roman law forbade polygamy and that the Greeks (Timothy's father was a Greek) did not practice it.[26] All this raises the question of why Paul proscribes, in the position of greatest prominence (it comes immediately after the heading demand for blamelessness), an institution that was not even being practiced by the people whom Timothy was to check for qualifications.[27] Is it conceivable that a Church built upon the foundation of the prophets (Eph. 2:20) and blessed in Abraham (Gal. 3:29) could not allow David or Abraham to function in the position of a deacon? Some may insist upon it, but I cannot. And if I am correct in this matter, then, in turn, this truth would have ramifications for the discussion that follows, on the matter of remarriage.

A ONCE-MARRIED PRIESTHOOD?

AN UNBLEMISHED PRIESTHOOD?

The fourth view, a once-married priesthood, has numerous problems as well. First, if the subcategory of remarried widowers is considered, we again are compelled to note that this seems out of context with previous (i.e., Old Testament) permissions. Only the High Priest was prohibited from marrying a widow, and a priest who was a widower was not prohibited from marrying a second wife. Since the list of qualifications of a High Priest excludes only the marrying of a widow, anyone arguing that a widower priest would be ceremonially defiled by remarrying bears the burden of proof. Additionally, we may at this point object to the procedure of using the Old Testament Levitical system as a precedent for a discussion of New Testament office. For the Old Testament system also excluded handicapped priests, whereas the New Testament presents us all as priests ("a holy priesthood," 1 Pet. 2:5–10).[28]

In short, priests of the kingdom of God are to be spiritually pure, not ceremonially pure. The Old Testament priestly system is obsolete (Heb. 8:13). Nonetheless, I believe that we can say with assurance that if a practice such as remarriage of a widower priest is not seen as even ceremonially disqualifying under the old system, as concerned with social purity as it was, it is fruitless to suggest that same practice is prohibited of church leaders in the new covenant. Thus I also reject the idea that "husband of one wife" is meant to prohibit a church leader from marrying a widow.

But, of course, ours is not a study in ecclesiology per se. Our chief concern is with the subcategory of digamy, which sees this clause as excluding the remarried person or a person married to a divorced person from the office of overseer. What of this option? First, let us note that the phrase does not literally speak to the matter of marrying a divorced person. The emphasis is upon the status of the man, not the woman. Frankly, that which was the issue in the Old Testament would be reversed by this statement in the New. The Old was not concerned with divorced priests marrying another (specifically, because polygamy was permissible) except if to do so they had divorced their own wives unjustly.[29] The New Testament directs its qualifying statement to the male and ignores the status of the wife. And to argue that the New continues the practice of the Old on this matter is wrongheaded for reasons just stated concerning the obsolescence of ceremonial legislation.

As for the suggestion that the phrase refers to remarried widowers, we should keep the thought in the context of 1 Timothy 5:9. If the phrase in 5:9 is taken to exclude a second marriage after the death of the spouse, then, Robert Saucy notes, we have the anomaly of Paul telling young widows to marry again, whereupon if, after following this advice they are widowed again and fall on hard times, they find that the apostle has cut them off from perhaps desperately needed financial aid. For Paul excludes from church aid widows who have not been a "one-husband wife." This does not seem fair or likely.[30] But if 5:9 does not mean to exclude widows who have remarried, then it is not likely that 3:2 is meant to exclude widowers who have remarried. Kent asks the question pointedly: Was this the most serious moral problem in Ephesis or Crete?[31] Certainly not.

A NOT-DIVORCED/REMARRIED PRIESTHOOD?

This seems to leave only the digamists identified as being divorced and/or remarried. Laney actually deals with this group in two parts: the divorced and remarried, and the simply divorced. The divorced and remarried he faults for living in a state of adultery.[32] Since they are guilty of the sin of adultery, they should not be in positions of leadership. But this, of course, assumes that *all* divorced and remarried persons are guilty of adultery, and that the sin of adultery is a sin from which there is no complete restoration. The first presumption depends upon the thinking that it is the act consummating the second marriage that is adulterous. And with this point I cannot agree. I stand by the conclusions set out earlier that the primary offense in divorce and remarriage centers upon the breach of covenant, which occurs before the divorce, and therefore stands as its grounds, or is the divorce itself, which then sunders the marriage. I further feel that it has been adequately shown (chapters 5 and following) that at least the innocent party has the right to remarry if postdivorce reconciliation is unsuccessful. Indeed, since the divorce itself morally as well as legally severs the covenant where there are no moral grounds for the divorce, even the guilty party may remarry, though the guilty should only do so after attempting to restore the former covenant. The divorce ends the first marriage; therefore, the divorced and remarried man has only one wife at a time.[33]

But Laney is manifestly against any interpretation that would allow for the divorced and remarried to stand qualified. He belieoves that to broaden the qualification to allow for those who are married merely to "one wife at a time vitiates the value of the qualification, since virtually anyone could [then] meet the standard."[34] Laney reveals by such a response that his is far too quantitative an understanding of the clause. Had he a qualitative grasp of it, he would see that this argument is far from sound.

Laney's second argument is that such an interpretation is "refuted by the requirement that the elder or deacon [be] one who 'manages his own household well' (1 Tim. 3:4, 12). The disaster of divorce and remarriage would be evidence of the mismanagement of one's household."[35]

This is a "disaster" of an argument. In the first place, this argument is irrelevant to the issue of remarriage, which Laney (against Ryrie) says must be involved with the "husband of one wife" clause. It is, in fact, an abandonment of the "husband of one wife" clause in favor of another clause that is said to disqualify the divorced/remarried. And, in its own right, the "household management" qualification, at least as Laney details it, will not support disqualification of the divorced. For such analysis would imply that both God (who divorced Israel, Jer. 3:8) and Hosea (who divorced Gomer, Hos. 1–2) were poor managers. It seems overbearing to suggest that a Church based on the prophets could not have allowed one of them to serve communion, or that the God they worship in church could not have distributed food to the widows! We are forced to suggest that Laney has, again, read his prejudice against the divorced into a qualification. Nonetheless, it is profitable for us to consider this second qualification, for implicit in it is an argument for seeing some divorced people as eminently qualified to serve. For if divorce is a rebuke, then, far from revealing poor management, it may show control. It may be a sign of decency and order on the part of the person in question. Would not Eli have been exonerated by God had he rebuked his sons?

But we are getting ahead of ourselves, for this argument we are discussing really deals with the category of those persons who are simply divorced (irrespective of their subsequent marital status). Regarding this group, Laney resubmits the "management" argument, then shifts on the qualifications list to the heading statement that such leaders should be "above reproach." Says Laney, "the elder and deacon must be above reproach (1 Tim. 3:2, 10)—blameless! Although the circumstances vary, it generally takes *two* to make a divorce. A divorced man, though remaining single, would probably not be 'above reproach.' "[36] Later, Laney explicitly says that there is in a "real sense . . . no 'innocent party' in a divorce."[37]

To this it must be said, first, that "above reproach" is a heading, a structural form to be filled with what follows. The qualifications speak of what constitutes "reproach." Laney, whose previous use of the material qualifications has not proved the divorced/remarried are disqualified, cannot expect help from the term that summarizes the qualifications. Second, aside from the definition he gives to "reproach" in the passage and the general argument he makes from it, Laney has not proved from any other passage that all divorce/remarriage is sinful. Third, by arguing that in troubled marriages none are "innocent," Laney puts qualification beyond us all. For if *perfection* be the criterion for holding the offices, then they will remain vacant. Laney has not shown us that the divorcer is guilty of the sin of adultery, but only suggested that the divorcer must have done something that led to the divorce or omitted to do something that could have prevented the divorce. The Scripture, on the other hand, argues that no simple aggravations of a spouse justify divorce.[38] This seems to put Laney in the rather peculiar situation or arguing that there is no sin serious enough to justify divorce, but any sins that lead to a person being divorced are so serious that that person should be disqualified from functioning as a leader in the church.

And what about those who admit that the divorce was immoral and subsequently try unsuccessfully to reconcile with their spouse—or the person who treacherously divorced them before they became Christians? Are these, too, permanently disqualified? Laney: "It is important to recognize that while the guilt of sin is entirely forgiven at the time of salvation (Rom. 8:1), the consequences of that sin in this present life are not necessarily removed. . . . While divorce (and remarriage) are forgivable sins, they may have lifelong consequences."[39] One of those consequences, obviously, is disqualification from functioning as a leader in the church.

What is so incredible about this argument is that forgiveness entails "not taking into account." But that is exactly what Laney insists upon doing. Christ has forgiven and forgotten, but he enjoins us to hold it against this person till "death do us part." And what multiplies one's perplexity on reading Laney is that the Epistle was written by a person who was complicitous (by his own admission) in the sin of murder. Thus, though Paul can be a leader of the Church, even though guilty of breaking one of the Ten Commandments, he enjoins Timothy to exclude persons who have been treacherously divorced by adulterous spouses! And Laney tells us that divorce and remarriage are not unpardonable sins! On this line of logic, divorced persons should probably be disqualified for a lack of Pharisaical "horse sense." If they had only murdered their spouses, they could have become bishops. But, because they did not have that presence of mind or knowledge of how Christian ethics work, they allowed themselves to be divorced, perhaps even fought the divorce, and ended up disqualified for office. If this is not an instance of Christians shooting their wounded, I'm not sure what would be!

Laney has confused his categories. Becoming a Christian does not remove the need to seek the forgiveness of those previously offended. It does not change "the state you are in." But if repentance at the foot of the Cross and subsequent "fruits" (e.g., going back to a spouse unjustly divorced and seeking restoration—even if rejected by that person) are not enough to render us fit to serve and lead in the Church, then forgiveness means nothing at all in this world—a sub-Christian perspective.

Laney's other argument against the divorced (and not remarried) serving as church leaders is misplaced; it is really an argument against a man serving if he has married a divorced woman. Accepting the interpretation that the women of 1 Timothy 3:11 are the wives of deacons, Laney notes that these women are to be "exemplary in their conduct and faithful in all things."[40] He concludes that a wife's marital condition disqualifies her husband from leadership. The implied premise is that the divorce is a sign of unfaithfulness and of bad conduct. But, of course, this is all begging the question, if Laney has not previously shown us that all divorces are instances of misbehavior or that repentance does not make a difference.[41]

SUMMARY AND CONCLUSIONS

Let us summarize our conclusion drawn from "husband of one wife" alone. If the verse demands marriage, then the divorced are in the same position as the virgins and widowers. Divorce per se is not identified as an offense. Second, if the phrase demands no more than one marriage in a lifetime, the divorced are in the same boat as the widower; again, divorce is not any more morally offensive than the death of the spouse. If the verse proscribes plurality of wives at the same time, the divorced man is qualified to be a leader if he has not remarried, and the remarried man is qualified if his divorce has truly dissolved his first marriage. Only in the case of a man who has divorced and remarried *and* the first marriage was not dissolved does this verse disqualify. And, if it does, he would be disqualified for the same reason as the polygamist, that is, for having two wives at the same time. However, I am convinced that the polygamist is not excluded, and that the first marriage is dissolved. Therefore, I do not believe that this passage of Scripture deals with the divorced/remarried person at all with regard to the divorce/remarriage per se.

But what then *is* the proper interpretation of these texts? The grammar helps a little. In the Greek, two elements are significant. First, the phrase reads, "of one wife husband." Lenski translates it "one wife's husband."[42] Robert Saucy prefers the less marital translation of the terms: a "one woman man."[43] This is entirely permissible, since the Greek words for "woman/wife" and "man/husband" are the same. Both these authors seem to suggest that Paul's primary concern is the prohibition of known fornicators (sexually immoral men) from leadership in the church. And neither would exclude the repentant.[44] In this Greek phrase, the word *one* is put forward, showing emphasis, but it is also anarthrous (without the definite article *the*). The net result of this structure is to stress the singleness of devotion rather than the number of wives. This is a one-woman type of man, a man who is not looking at every toga that passes. Standing out against the background of sexual promiscuity in the Greek and Roman world, he is a man who does not have "eyes of adultery" (2 Pet. 2:14), who does not go to the prostitutes (1 Cor. 6:13–7:2).

Not only does this interpretation fit the cultural background, but it also explains how Paul, who is usually explicit about sexual immorality in lists of sins (e.g., 1 Cor. 6:9 ff.; Rom. 1:21 ff.; Gal. 5:19 ff.), misses sexual permissiveness completely when mentioning qualifications for church office.[45] However, if "one-woman man" is simply idiomatic for "not sexually promiscuous," the gap is filled. In fact, Laney touches upon the key idea when, in combating polygamy, he cites 1 Corinthians 7:2 as prohibiting sexual immorality.[46] Paul is not concerned with the sex one has with a *legitimate* wife (or wives, though the Greeks in Ephesus and Crete had only one), but with *illicit* sex. And even a single person, like himself, could fall to such temptations. Thus, whether we translate the clause "one-woman man" or "one wife's husband," we are to understand that it is directed against *fornication,* not previous legal marriages.

Herein we find another strange phenomenon in the thinking exhibited by such writers as Laney. They would allow a man who has committed simple adultery to be an overseer, but a legally married, then divorced, then legally remarried person would be excluded. Though both are guilty of adultery in their minds, only the divorce and remarriage disqualifies.[47]

If the text wishes to prohibit known immoral persons from becoming church leaders, is it fair to conclude, as Laney does, that "virtually anyone could meet the standard" if it permits the qualification of "one wife at a time"?[48] Of course not. On our reading, a monogamist, a virgin, a widower, a divorced and/or remarried person, or a polygamist might be excluded if they are known to be immoral. But is it fair to conclude that *any* person is immoral simply by falling into one of those categories? None of the categories in themselves are offense-terms. Immorality is an offense. Paul wishes to block the immoral from office—

not the innocent, or even the guilty but repentant. Thus, the qualification sections of these pastoral Epistles may exclude the divorced and remarried from office, but not simply because they have been divorced and remarried. In that sense, these passages are irrelevant to the development of a biblical theology of divorce and remarriage.[49]

CHAPTER 11

Summaries and Conclusions

It now falls to us to summarize our work, draw conclusions, and anticipate objections. We will not attempt to apply our theory to practical situations. That task must be left to another book.

SUMMARY OF THE CHAPTERS

The first chapter centered upon the question of the nature of marriage. We found that marriage is not a mystical, permanent union. I did not deny that the union in marriage is typified in the Bible as an "organic union"; on the contrary, I affirmed that the Scripture does indeed teach this. But, in our analysis of the terms used in the Scripture to express this union ("cleave," "one flesh," and "join"), we found that when they were considered in their biblical context, the conclusion could not be avoided that none of them entails ontological permanency. By this I mean that the Bible does not teach that marriage *is* a permanent union. Just as people break off cleaving, just as some one-flesh unions *should* be ended, just as some joinings are sundered, so too the union in marriage *can* be ended before the death of one of the spouses.

In the second chapter I argued that marriage is, rather, a covenant: an agreement between two people that involves certain stated or implied obligations of each party to the other. Not all promises, even in marriage agreements, are equal. Certain essentials must be pledged. For the man, these are primarily necessary physical provisions. He must not physically abuse his wife. She, on the other hand, has to pledge sexual loyalty to her husband. Permanency in the covenant was implied by the concept of "cleaving," but it is a permanency of intention, not necessarily of fact. By this I mean that the two pledged to fulfill these responsibilities of covenant until death separated them. Or, put differently, they agree to join themselves together *intending* never to end the relationship. This is not to say that they agree to fulfill their covenant responsibilities to each other even if the other sunders the relationship, but that each pledges not to end the covenant by breaking the vows. If both keep their vows, the marriage will in fact be permanent, that is, endure until death separates the couple.

The third chapter considered the sad facts of a fallen and finite world: marriage relationships *are* ended before the death of one of the partners. We found that this sundering occurs when one of the partners intentionally breaks the essential vows. And we observed that God gave instructions regarding the treatment of covenant-breakers. Breach of the *wife's vow* of faithfulness was treated with capital punishment for the offending woman and her lover. Breach of the *husband's vow* of providing led to forced divorce in the case of active or passive physical abuse. The third chapter also considered the sad fact of treacherous divorce. Such divorce, we found, was permitted by God's law for the sake of the woman, who, doubtless, would otherwise be mistreated by her hard-hearted husband. We did not find that such divorce carried with it any approbation of the husband's action as such, though the Law was understood to do so by later generations of Israelite interpreters, specifically the Pharisees.

The fourth chapter considered the apparent plan of God for dealing with a time when the biblical admonitions to execute adulterers ceased to be practiced. We found that in the divine economy divorce took on a larger disciplinary role. This expansion of role did not alter the function of divorce in the Law; divorce was always seen as defensive and disciplinary. But we did find that this disciplinary function was executed with an aim of restoring legitimate marriages. Additionally, we noted that the act of unjust divorce was identified as treachery. This reveals that legal repudiation of the covenant is itself adulterous. Presence in the covenant is required.

In the fifth chapter, which considered the early official teachings of Jesus, we found that he taught nothing new, that he sought to clarify the old, and that, like the prophets, he emphasized the nature of the sin of treacherous divorce as *adultery*. Though the idea of "sexless" adultery struck contemporary ears as foreign, this idea was actually well established in the writings of the prophets. Jesus was simply trying to bring out the ignored and misunderstood implications of the previously revealed standard concerning marriage relations.

The sixth chapter continued this theme, emphasizing the wickedness of a third party alienating marriage partners in order to take one of them into a new covenant. Such meddling was pictured as a form of adultery. We did not find that all remarriage was considered adulterous, but only the kind that involved treachery, and in that case, the moral onus was construed as primarily relating to the divorce of the legitimate partner, not the remarriage as such, at least for the male Israelite.

Chapter 7 concluded the study of the teachings of Jesus by considering passages that essentially restated his previously spoken points. His agreement with the Law and the Prophets was underscored as well. And his insistence that those who marry must follow the moral rules was noted.

Paul's writings were analyzed beginning in chapter 8. His agreement with Jesus' teaching was observed, but we also noted that in application Paul went "beyond" Jesus to speak to issues facing the Church that Jesus did not specifically encounter: what should be the relation of a convert to an unsaved spouse? Yet, the advice given did not differ from the principles of the oracles previously given. Marriage is broken by a breach of vows (separation) not by ontological (i.e., spiritual) iniquities (the sheer fact that the marriage was religiously mixed). We also heard advice that extended other Old Testament principles: the obligation of the wife to give herself sexually to her husband was prescribed to meet the new context of socially required monogamy. This extension was made to avoid the old threat of fornication. As in the Old Testament, remarriage for the innocent party was permitted (assuming that attempts at reconciliation were fruitless), and I even suggested that remarriage for the guilty party was only prohibited when it was in the face of treachery, that it would likely be moral if efforts at reconciliation had been fruitless. Continuing our study of Paul in the ninth chapter, we evaluated his words to the "unmarried." We concluded that Paul advised singleness for the times, but allowed all single people (assuming they were now legitimately single—with all necessary attempts at reconciliation fully tried to whatever degree of success) to marry. This included the remarriage of those validly single as a result of divorce. We also considered Paul's advice to wavering guardians, reminding them that marriage is intended to be permanent—that no one could subsequently end it (without the sin of adultery taking place). We did not find Paul, after morally condoning some divorce and some remarriage, changing his mind either in straightforward teaching sections or by implication in theological analogies.

The tenth chapter weighed allegations that certain Pauline and Petrine texts *indirectly* stand against all divorce and remarriage. Harmonizations were offered to show how our theory, developed to that point, is entirely compatible with these passages, which were expressive of Christian attitudes and actions in marriage. That chapter also analyzed the biblical texts dealing with qualifications for church leadership. Against the interpretation that all divorced and/or remarried persons are excluded from office by such texts, we found no impediment to them per se, but only where unrepentant immorality existed.

THE UNIFIED THEORY STATED

This study leads to the following conclusions: First, marriage is a covenant that should not be broken. A breach of covenant occurs when any of certain biblically minimal (also called "canonical" or "essential") vows are not kept. When the covenant is broken, divorce is available as a defensive action (in the case of active or passive physical abuse and intentional neglect on the part of the husband) and as a disciplinary action (in the case of sexual unfaithfulness on the part of the wife), though the goal of discipline is, first and foremost, restoration of the marriage relationship. In the case of abuse, when a significant instance of abuse has occurred without signs of repentance, divorce may be necessary to protect the person of the spouse. Remarriage to a more desirable (Christian) partner is morally permissible. In the case of un-faithfulness, when a sufficient (but not set) amount of time has passed after the first knowledge of breach, disciplinary divorce is the only morally proper way of dealing with the offender. If such discipline *is not* heeded, remarriage to another is fully permissible and would be subject to no negative admonition from God. If the discipline *is* heeded, then the righteous divorcer is morally obligated to restore the offender to fellowship (even remarriage, if possible). Where the divorce was treacherous rather than disciplinary, the divorcing party is under moral obligation to try to restore the relationship. The offended party is, in turn, under obligation to reestablish the former marriage (if possible). Impediments to restoration (even remarriages) should be removed by the guilty in order to produce the full fruits of repentance. Marriages that themselves were prohibited, for example, the knowing and inten-tional marrying of an unbeliever, must be terminated. However, when a partner who is innocent (e.g., the one who was treacherously divorced or who has sought restoration only to be rebuffed) has remarried, such marriages are not the sorts of "impediments" here referred to and should not be ended; neither should marriages to unbelievers con-tracted in ignorance of the partner's faith or of the divine obligations applying. Where such justifiable impediments exist, the repentant one and the reconciler should at least come to terms of personal (though not marital) reconciliation. Unjust divorcers who have come to see the error of their ways and sought reconciliation with their former spouse, but find restoration of the marriage impossible (either because of a legitimate intervening marriage, or because of the obstinance of the former spouse), are no longer seen as such, and remarriage "in the Lord" is permissible.

On the Nature of the Marriage Union

MARRIAGE IS NOT ESSENTIALLY A SEXUAL UNION

The act of sexual intercourse never, in itself, constituted marriage.[1] In the Bible, premarital sex, if discovered, led to a forced marriage unless the father of the woman insisted otherwise (Exod. 22:16 f.; Deut. 22:28 f.). The legal bond gave the only proper moral context for sexual union (Gen. 2:24). The woman in such cases of premarital sex was considered to have been "defiled." At least one word (*halal*) used in the Old Testament to describe sexual defilement implies a controversion of God's planned order.[2] And the more common term (*tame*) implies "uncleanness," an interruption of the wholeness or wholesomeness of life.[3] Marriage is never typified simply by the sexual act, or even by the idea of "one flesh."[4]

It might be argued that a marriage is not *final* until sexual relations have taken place. Deuteronomy 20:7 speaks of a man who has become engaged to a woman but has not "taken" her yet. The woman is an "unclaimed blessing." The text reveals that the covenant with her has not been consummated. But the term used (*laqah*) is not the most common Hebrew word for marriage, and in the Deuteronomic text it may simply be referring to *consummation* rather than to *marriage* per se. Beyond this, there are a number of other passages that understand the engaged couple to enjoy the same status before law as those persons in a fully consummated union.

In the New Testament, we note that, in spite of the strong marital connotations of "one flesh," Paul is willing to apply the term to the nonmarital sexual relationship between a man and a prostitute. So it seems more correct to say that marriage is the *proper context* of becoming "one flesh" than to say that marriage is becoming "one flesh." Marriage grants the right to have a "one-flesh" union. Insofar as unity is the goal of marriage people should avoid focusing upon separation themes when discussing marriage, and, when possible, problem marriages should be directed back toward that primary goal. The teaching of Jesus, that the two have become "one flesh," would seem logically to require nothing more than this.

Sexual union entails a strong bonding between two persons. But the actual and moral degree of that bonding or influence is at least partly to be determined by the covenantal factors present or absent surrounding the particular sexual union. The absence of such factors directs the persons either to get married (as with premarital sex) or to cease and desist from further relations (extramarital or promiscuous sex, i.e., with a prostitute).

With regard to this question, it is interesting to compare three different sorts of relationships in which a "one-flesh" union occurs, and observe the differences:

PHYSICAL UNION:	PROSTITUTE	CONCUBINE	WIFE
Text:	1 Cor. 6:16	Exod. 21:10	Gen. 2:24
Relation:	"one body" only	slave contract	companion/ covenant
God's Law:	illegal	legal	legal
Treatment:	flee from	treat justly or free	do not sunder relationship

It would seem by consideration of this that the existence of a "one-flesh" relation does not determine the existence of marriage. It may call for it in the case of "premarital sex," but it is not the marriage itself. It is a "right of marriage."

MARRIAGE IS NOT A MYSTERIOUS RELATIONSHIP

There seems to be no scriptural evidence for saying that marriage is a mysterious union. On occasion some will cite Ephesians 5:32, but this "support" really rests upon a mistaken idea that the Greek word translated "mystery" means "beyond human knowledge." That may be the most common element of an English definition of the word, but the Greek definition entails "information knowable only by revelation from God." Understood in its proper light, the antecedent of "this mystery is great" is *not* the husband/wife relationship, which union has been revealed from the days of the Garden of Eden, but the relation of Christ to the Church. The text itself makes this clear when it immediately adds, "but I am speaking with reference to Christ and the Church" (v. 32), and adds further discontinuity by returning to the husband-wife discussion (v. 33) with "Nevertheless, let each individual among you also love his own wife . . ." Another verse that is suggested to express a mystical element in marriage is Malachi 2:14. Steele mentions that the wife (then divorced) is called a "companion." About this word he quotes Brown, Driver, and Briggs as suggesting the meaning of the root is "to unite, tie a magic knot."[5] But I know of no scholar who would argue for magic knots as the meaning of the inspired text. God does not use magic. The knots he ties have already been shown to be like a yoke. It is safer to define the term without mentioning such heathen uses. The resulting definition simply speaks of a companion as one who is closely woven together with the partner in a common enterprise, joined by contract and mutual commitment. It functions in the literature in a similar manner to the word *cleave* that we have dealt with. There really is no textual support for the idea that marriage is either mystical or magical per se.

It might be argued that sexual union entails some mystical element. Since the sexual act is not itself a melding of the two persons back into one person, what is the meaning of "one flesh"? Perhaps there is some element of mystery in what appears to be a simple conjunction of bodies. But even were this true, it misses the point. For we have seen already that marriage is not essentially a sexual or "one-flesh" union anyway. Therefore, it is a non sequitur to show that the "one-flesh" relationship has mysterious elements.

MARRIAGE IS NOT A UNION OF SOULS OR SPIRITS

The initial problem with discussion of spiritual union is definitional. What exactly does it mean? Are we talking about association, to whatever degree of intimacy, or about some more ontological union (union of being)? Often people who refer to marriage as a spiritual union or a union of souls begin talking this way when they attempt to describe the completeness of the marriage union. Steele and Ryrie (quoting Ross) conclude their discussion of marriage "intimacy" by saying: "To become one flesh means becoming a spiritual, moral, intellectual, and physical unity."[6] Obviously this does not mean mixing brain cells or sharing a common nervous system, so what does it mean? Perhaps it means nothing more than that the intimacy of marriage involves the couple "seeing things the same way." They share a common moral standard, think alike, have sexual union. But, still, please, what does common "spirit" mean? Could that be a way of referring to a similar *disposition?* I believe this puts the best face on the matter. But note that all such elements of intimacy only occur if the couple makes the effort to integrate their individual concerns. An estranged couple clearly does not share any of these things. Thus, it would be more proper to say that marriage *may* involve such intimacy, but not that this is what it means to become "one flesh."

If, on the other hand, it be argued that some more ontological union of spirits or souls is intended, then several other problems present themselves for our consideration. The first of these concerns the point of origin of this sort of union and, indeed, the way in which the union is achieved. If union is said to begin when the vows are said, then I rejoin, How does the speaking of vows achieve an ontic bonding of spirits? If it is said to take place in the sex act, one may ask how physical union achieves spiritual bonding. When and how does this bonding occur?

A second reason for doubting that marriage involves a unity of spirits is that such a unity would seem to go beyond the grave. Thus, someone who had more than one marriage partner would have confusing spiritual relationships eternally. This is the very matter dealt with in the confrontation between Jesus and the Sadducees in Mark 12:18–27 (Matt. 22:23–33/Luke 20:27–40). The Sadducees' argument turns on two points: the marriage union remains after death (therefore being a union of the souls of the resurrected) and there is a resurrection of the married persons. The Sadducees slyly knew that if both these propositions were affirmed at the same time, there would be ideological confusion.

Jesus affirms the second proposition but denies the first. Marriages, he says, do not go beyond the grave. "They are neither marrying [i.e., in a marriage state] nor are being given in marriage, but are like angels in heaven." Note that these words do not mean simply that no new marriages will be contracted, but that the marriage state as such does not exist in heaven. In other words, marriage is designed for this world. It is temporal. But how can this be so if marriage entails a union of being of spirits?

The third problem with an ontic union of spirits involves intermarriage. In our study of the use of *cleave* and *one flesh* in 1 Corinthians we noted that marriage unions have spiritual ramifications. Choosing a partner of another faith, against the wishes of God, reveals much about one's spiritual state and will undoubtedly effect further negative changes in one's spiritual life. But to say that marriage has these spiritual ramifications is not to say that marriage effects a union of spirits or souls. Insofar as at least one kind of interfaith marriage (i.e., that caused by the conversion of one of the previously bonded partners) was permitted by the Apostle Paul, we may safely conclude that marriage does not entail spiritual union.

Finally, we note again that Scripture stresses the intimacy of the union in marriage, especially the physical union. The text says that in sexual union the man "knows" his wife. This implies a deeply intimate awareness of how it is with her. Without lessening the biblical understanding of that intimacy, I wish clearly to state that that intimacy is *in* the marriage and not that that intimacy is *essential* to the marriage. It is those who leave and cleave who have the right to become "one flesh."

On the Morality of Biblical Polygamy

INTRODUCTION

When Henry VIII sought the counsel of Luther on the morality of divorcing Catherine, he was told that it would be a lesser evil to simply marry Anne Boleyn as well! This is not considered the best advice given by the German reformer. In fact, it is not advisable for any theologian to write favorably of bigamy or polygamy. Against that advice, and with a certain feeling of personal uneasiness, I offer the following to those interested in what the Bible says on the subject of biblical polygamy. I realize that any attempt to harmonize the polygamy mentioned in the Bible with other biblical passages on the morality of marriage relations will be difficult to accept, because it runs against the grain of much tradition, as well as modern thought. Nonetheless, my research leads me to the conclusion that the Bible fully accepted the polygamous practices of that day and, in fact, encouraged them in certain circumstances. About this conclusion I speak with no apology, because I am convinced at this point that it is fully in harmony with other biblical teaching on the morality of marriage. I consider it my task to present the biblical view of marriage and divorce, not my own wishes or those of my tradition.

THE DIFFERENCE THE FALL MAKES

When Eve was first given, there was no sin—and, with no sin, no need to make provision for situations that might result from sin. It was enough for the two to have each other, and no one else. But sin forever changed that. With the sin of unbelief and the coveting of the fruit, other sins were quick to follow. Among these sins was the coveting of people as if they were items of property to satisfy the desires of others. And along with sin came the punishment God had promised: death and all the ills of the body and mind. All these evils were disruptive to monogamous marriage. Death ended the marriage state, seldom with the partners dying at the same time. Today, the phrase "till death do us part" is the result. Such a phrase is entirely out of place in the Garden of Eden, at least before the Fall. Had Adam and Eve not sinned, they would be alive today and happily married. Those who quote Genesis 2:24 to support the "ideal" of marriage *until death* should recall that the issue is more complex than that.

To say that one may not glibly resort to Genesis 1 and 2 to find norms of behavior for today is not to deny that they may be found in those passages; it is only to warn that the presence of certain behavior in those passages does not settle the question of what normative behavior is. The issue here is hermeneutical. The reader of the Scriptures must carefully consider whether or not conditions have changed since the Garden of Eden. If the conditions *have* changed, then the behavior presented in those passages may no longer be "the only way to act morally."[1] By saying this it is evident that I reject the uncritical acceptance of certain "creation ordinances." The idea behind these words is that the situation in the Garden reflects a sort of covenant, with terms that are still more or less binding today.

To argue that the number of spouses provided in the Garden does not determine the moral norm *since* Eden opens the question of whether or not bigamy is morally permissible. To note that a woman may not, according to the Law, have more than one man at a time eliminates one form of bigamy: polyandry, in which the woman has two husbands. For if she is not permitted to have a man other than *her initial and living husband,* then this logically excludes both marital as well as extramarital relations for her. But the rejection of polyandry does not *ipso facto* prohibit the other sort of bigamy, namely, polygyny, in which the husband has more than one wife.

However, as we have noted, any attempt to argue the moral propriety of polygamy is destined to meet with the wrath of traditional Christian scholarship. In a recent work on Old Testament ethics, Walter Kaiser leans on "creation ordinance" logic borrowed from John Murray's *Principles of Conduct* to begin his arguments against the moral propriety of polygamy. Says he, "The first [procreation] and the seventh [marriage] ordinances in the usual list of creation mandates extending from Genesis 1:28 to Genesis 2:23 are closely related and bear directly on the subject of the family. . . . The monogamous relationship was . . . set forth as the normal intention for marriage—the foundation and cornerstone of the family (Gen. 2:23–24)."[2]

All this is stated with much certainty, but little biblical support. The "first" ordinance is, as John Walton has argued, more like a blessing than a command,[3] and the "seventh" is only to be construed as a command for those who wish to become physically intimate. Beyond these points, it is not at all transparent that monogamy is implicit in the biblical statement in Genesis 2:24. Though it is proper to understand monogamy as the norm for the sort of conditions that existed in the pre-Fall Garden, the alteration of those conditions subsequent to the Fall makes it risky to absolutize monogamy *on the basis of Genesis 2:24*. Arguments from Genesis 2:24 bear the burden of proof that monogamy is required throughout time.

Of course, since Jesus quoted the same passages when he discussed marriage, one expects a quick appeal to him to fulfill this requirement. But such an appeal is in vain. Jesus' quote of this passage is not attempting to affirm monogamy in Matthew 19:5 f. He is insisting that no covenanted person is free to walk away from the partner. The context makes this clear. It only compounds the confusion to appeal to the fact that the Essenes interpreted the "the two shall become one flesh" clause as teaching monogamy. I grant the Essene position, but I question its relevance, for there is no reason aside from the quote of a common source to affirm that Jesus interpreted Genesis 2:24 as they did.

LAWS THAT IMPLY THE MORAL PROPRIETY OF POLYGAMY

The Law of the Levirate

When the effect of the Fall on the conditions of the Edenic world are taken into account, it should be easier to see why it is wrongheaded to absolutize the "ordinance of monogamy." Sin created new conditions for which modifications were necessary, modifications evident in the Scripture itself. For example, covetousness, the desire for another's property, when tied to the death of a married man, presents a situation that God, the protector of the widow and orphan, knew he must legally anticipate. The Lord knew that when a man died without leaving children to care for his property in the best interests of his wife, other, greedy persons would strive to take advantage of the estate. This would be especially true of the siblings of the deceased. They, rather than helping the widow, would be likely to attempt to make the "family" property their own. And especially in cultures hesitant to allow a woman (who was probably from another family) to inherit the property, this "family" interest could easily lead to abuse of her. Further, in a culture with a land-based economy, for a wife to gain rights to property and transfer it to another tribe or family could indeed create chaotic conditions.

God, in his infinite love and wisdom, foresaw the possibilities and devised a profound plan that with one piece of legislation inhibited both greed and economic chaos. It is known as the "kinsman redeemer" or the "law of the levirate." The basic idea is that, when a man died childless, his brother or another "near" kinsman was to take the widow to be his wife. This ensured that someone would be there to take care of her minimal needs, one of which, we have seen, was a chance to have children who would take care of her even beyond the lifetime of this second husband. This arrangement also protected the family of the husband from losing ownership of their property to another, perhaps distant, tribe. The property was, significantly, the possession of the husband's tribe. Still further, the custom protected the widow from being robbed by her new provider. The deceased's brother was prohibited from considering the property his. It was to be passed to the firstborn male child, who was technically considered the offspring of the widow and her first husband. The child had the rights to the property, not the uncle. Thus, the in-laws were able to keep the property in the family as a whole but not for themselves specifically. Any attempt to "short-circuit" the system by failing to marry the widow or by failing to attempt honestly to give her the chance for children was considered a grave social injustice. One only has to read the sad story of Tamar and Onan and Judah in Genesis 38 to see how seriously both human beings and God took this whole matter.

It is interesting indeed to note that, on the one hand, this arrangement far antedated the Mosaic Constitutions and, on the other, that it is the picture of Christ, our kinsman Redeemer (like Boaz). And as far as the Law of Moses is concerned, the arrangement was sanctioned in a severe and straightforward manner. In Deuteronomy 25:5–10 we read that any brother not wanting to do his duty was publicly humiliated, and a lasting stigma was placed upon him. Onan's abuse of the system, because it turned Tamar into a mere sexual object, was treated more severely yet.

So death and sin conspire to inflict loss upon the widow, and God moves in conscience and by Law to protect her. But what would happen if the brother was already married? Could he not plead exemption from responsibility to the widow? For the sake of primal monogamy, would he not be an exception to the levirate rule? Seemingly, the answer is no. Indeed, to the contrary, the stigma of an unwilling kinsman is said to also reflect against "his house." It seems hard to see how this reference to his "house" could fail to imply an existing family with at least one wife and child. There is no provision in Deuteronomy 25:5–10 for married near kin to plead exemption. Had God been concerned about the possibility of (immoral) polygamy, he surely would have included such an exception in the text itself. Such exceptions are not lacking in the Law.[4] Propriety in a fallen world called for polygamy of the potential husband rather than neglect of the widow. Polygamy was not immoral per se; neglect was.

It may well be that other, similar reasons might have given rise to instances of polygamy. The desire for offspring on the part of the husband or the inability or unwillingness of a wife to cooperate with her husband may have contributed to the matter. Perhaps the latter situation was the cause for some of David's marriages subsequent to Michal. It is hard to say. In this regard, we should note that it was not the obligation of the Old Testament woman to have a physical relationship with her husband, as it is in the New (1 Cor. 7:2 ff.). But one should remember that the reason the New Testament requires the wife not to withhold herself from her husband is precisely because the Greek marriage partners had made monogamous vows, and since Paul prohibits recourse to prostitutes (an act never morally proper in either Testament!), he must require wives *not* to defraud their husbands by withholding sex. In Old Testament times, the husband would simply have taken a new wife—if he was able to afford it. In the Old Testament the woman was *well advised* to have relations with her husband or he would take another wife who would. In the New, the apostle simply *requires* the wife to do so. Both Old and New Testaments, however, mandate the husband to have relations with his wife, but then she was not permitted to go to anyone else for sex.

The Fornication Laws

The "fornication" laws are another instance of God's care for social relations in a fallen world. When a man seduced a virgin, the man was to marry her *except* when her father refused (Exod. 22:17). The law does not add, "and the father must refuse if the seducer is already married," nor does it say that the man should marry her unless he is already married. It does say (Deut. 22) that if *she* is already married, both should be executed (Lev. 20). When it makes such a point of the woman's marital condition and makes none about the man's, the silence speaks loudly.[5] We may presume that polygamy was preferable to continued singleness on the part of the woman, who, though the man and/ or she had done wrong, had not done a capital offense. Premarital sex required the cutting of a covenant.

Laws That Regulate Polygamy

Another type of law suggests the moral properness of polygamy. We refer here to those laws that regulated the practice of polygamy itself. For example, in the Exodus 21 passage referred to above, it is clear that the taking of a second wife is not prohibited. But the Law does protect the rights of the first woman. It might be expected that the Bible might elsewhere speak of such laws as "permissions" for the "hardness of hearts," though the text never so speaks. Further, where it does use this phrase (Jesus' comment on Deut. 24:1–4), it is altogether improper to imply that God stoops to permit sin for its own sake or for the sake of the sinner. If the Law regulates polygamy, and nowhere suggests that polygamy is itself a sin, it is dangerous indeed to play the Pharisee and hedge God's Law.

Kaiser, depending heavily upon S. E. Dwight's *Hebrew Wife*,[6] seeks to subvert this line of reasoning by suggesting that, if generalized, it would authorize forms of behavior clearly prohibited in Scripture. Their example is of the rules governing the hire of a harlot (Deut. 23:18). By way of response, one might say that the reader might well assume on the basis of such a verse that harlotry would be permissible, were it not for the fact that the Scripture *does* specifically condemn harlotry; it is by no means clear that the same is the case with polygamy. Given clear scriptural condemnation of harlotry, one may assume that verses prohibiting the harlot's hire from becoming a gift to God should not be used to argue for the propriety of harlotry. The lack of such condemnations of polygamy gives reason to presume the propriety of that practice.

Additionally, it is clear that the verses proscribing the harlot's hire proscribe it because the wages are what they are, i.e., proceeds of fornication. Passages regulating polygamy are present in the text to keep that institution from becoming evil in its possible consequences. We shall look at such argument in a moment, but first, let us consider how Kaiser treats one of these passages: Exodus 21:10–11.[7]

Kaiser believes that this passage does not refer to plural marriage at all. He thinks that by correcting three mistakes in the traditional translation and interpretation of the text, it may be shown to be dealing with the treatment of a woman who has been *rejected* for marriage.

The first correction actually comes in the prior context. In verse 8, he argues, instead of the translation being "If she does not please the master who has selected her for himself" it should read "If she does not please her master so that he does not choose her." His support for this comes from following the preferred and majority reading of the Hebrew, as well as from the various versions, and we may assume that this correction is proper, though I think most interpreters assume this point anyway.

His second correction involves the clause "if he marries another wife" (v. 10). Kaiser thinks that insofar as the previous correction shows that the man rejected this woman as a partner, it should be amended to read, "if he marry another woman *instead* of her," this removing the idea of polygamy and simply preparing the way for a statement of how he is to treat the rejected woman.

This "correction," however, is unacceptable. Kaiser has failed to read carefully the contextual material. Verse 8 deals with the instance of a man rejecting a woman as his wife. The Law required him to let her be redeemed. This, of course, involves her leaving his house and going to that of another. Verse 9 deals with the instance of the rejecting husband providing for her by giving her to his son. This is a sort of redemption, but involved no paying of a bride price. Verses 10 and 11 then deal with the only other instance possible: in which the man *does* take her as his concubine. We may assume this, for were this not the case, she would already be redeemed (therefore not in need of his care) or in the house of his son (being treated like his daughter). The evident purpose of verses 10 and 11 is the protection of a concubine by a man who subsequently decides to take another woman to be his wife or concubine.

The third "correction" suggested by Kaiser involves the nature of the provision ensured for this first woman. The question arises, Was she assured "marital rights," that is, sex, or only, as Kaiser suggests, "ointments"? We have previously discussed this matter, concluding that Kaiser's option is not the preferred one.[8] Here we only need say that if Kaiser is wrong on this suggestion, then his previous "correction" (i.e., that this woman is not a concubine but a rejected woman) would create moral impropriety. Granted the traditional interpretation of "marital rights," the traditional interpretation of verses 10 and 11 referring to polygamy is supported. I side with the tradition in both cases.

PASSAGES THAT APPEAR TO PROHIBIT POLYGAMY

The Association of Polygamy with Other Evils

THE POLYGAMY OF MORALLY CORRUPT MEN

Let us return now to consider the passages that are raised to suggest that Scripture does, in fact, prohibit polygamy or that present polygamy in a poor light, at least. Among "poor light" arguments, we may first note instances where polygamy is associated with men who were morally corrupt. Lamech is the first (Gen. 4:19); Esau is another (Gen. 26:34). Lamech was in Cain's line, and he probably was evil for his treatment of the fellow who wounded him (Gen. 4:23), but none of this is essentially related to his polygamy. In fact, to suggest such association is too much. One could similarly argue that monogamy is evil, because others in Cain's line obviously were married only to one wife. As for Esau, it is not the number of his wives, but their character, that concerned Isaac. In the end, these guilt-by-association arguments are unhelpful. For each instance of the bad sort of polygamist, one could cite a righteous man who had more than one wife—Jacob, Abraham, David, to name but a few. The rejoinder then comes that these "righteous" men were not righteous when they married their second wives. Abraham should not have taken Hagar, because that was against God's plan, which was to bless him through Sarah only. Jacob was a trickster trying to outsmart another trickster (Laban). David sinned greatly in taking Bathsheba to himself.

The reasonable rejoinder replies that Abraham was never wrong in taking Hagar as a concubine or even for having a child by her. What the Scripture condemns in him was his seeking to have *the child of promise* by her. Jacob may have been tricked by Laban, but nowhere in Scripture does it suggest that Jacob was wrong in having two wives. Rachel and Leah certainly thought that God himself was blessing them by giving them babies (Gen. 29 f.). They could, of course, have been wrong in their analysis, but who are we to say? David, on the other hand, married a number of women besides Bathsheba, and when he had taken her to wife, Nathan remarked, "[God] gave your master's wives into your care . . . and if that had been too little, [he] would have added to you many more things like these!" (2 Sam. 12:8). It was not that David had plural wives, but the prior marital status of Bathsheba, that constituted his sin.

Kaiser's argument responding to the citation of 2 Samuel 12:7–8 is a clear indication of how far the myopia of traditionalists extends on this question. He goes to great lengths to show that "Saul's wives" should be translated "Saul's women," and that "lap" should be translated "care." So far, so good. But then Kaiser leaves us with the distinct impression that all that God is telling David is that there were lots of women around to dust the palace furniture. Never once does Kaiser let on that it is the *Bathsheba incident* that is the context of the divine remark. I cannot understand how the reminder of the presence of women *in his care* is meant to speak to David's problem of wayward sexual desire. It is as if God says, "David, why did you have an affair with a married woman, when you had all Saul's women to help you keep the palace tidy?" Rather, I see God saying, "David, why did you commit adultery to slake your desire for sex, when you had all Saul's women to choose from?" Obviously, the women that God has given David are potential mates. And since mating without covenant is the sin of fornication, and since David was already married to several women, we must assume that God is suggesting that polygamy was the proper way to handle David's sexual desire.

POLYGAMY AND FAMILIAL PROBLEMS

This sort of reasoning is unlikely to convince traditionalists. They will simply open new lines of defense. For instance, they will point out that, in Scripture, polygamists are recorded as having problems with their children or that the text says their children fought among themselves. Though it is not to be denied that polygamy contributes to such problems, it must be added that peace with and among the children of monogamy is never ensured either, as the children of Rebekah and Isaac well reveal.

POLYGAMY AS A MINORITY PRACTICE

Kaiser offers us another argument in a quite different direction. He tries to show that there are only a small number (19) of polygamists mentioned specifically in Scripture.[9] He then attempts to give reasons why even this small number were not punished by the government. The reason he finds in the fact that at least nine of the polygamists were absolute monarchs, and three were judges. Who then, he asks, could have called them to account? And as to divine evaluation, he contends that God sent the Flood to punish just such (marital) transgressions.

But is it credible to argue that the number of polygamists specifically mentioned in the text represents anywhere near the actual number that existed through the centuries? Certainly not. As for the matter of punishment, it certainly seems that if God were so concerned with polygamy as to see it as one of the causes for the Flood, he would have seen fit to include, in no uncertain language, a specific condemnation of polygamy—for the common man as well as for kings—in the Mosaic legislation. Violence is prohibited in this way, and it, one should recall, was specifically mentioned as a reason for the Flood. Such cannot be said for polygamy.

Alleged Prohibitions of Polygamy

LEVITICUS 18:18

With regard to more specific condemnations of polygamy we first mention Leviticus 18:18. It is interpreted by some as saying that a man should not take "a woman and another" to be his wife at the same time. Such interpretation is supported neither by the majority of scholars nor by the context. The passage is in a section prohibiting sexual relations involving "near kin," that is, "incest." The proper translation is "a woman in addition to her sister as a rival when she is alive."[10]

Kaiser's comments on this text are confusing and self-contradictory. He argues in one place that the crucial phrase should be literally translated as "one woman to her sister," even though it is a fact that everywhere else it is translated idiomatically as "one woman to another." He points out that the context of the phrase in Leviticus 18:18 is what gives a "definite 'no' " to the idiomatic translation, since the section is referring to "a relationship by blood." All this is in agreement with previous comments made nearly seventy pages earlier in the same book, where he said: "What the text [of Lev. 18:18] forbids then is not polygamy . . . , but it forbids marriage simultaneously to two sisters."[11] But the apparent clarity on this point disappears when he finally concludes that "Leviticus 18:18, then, is a single prohibition against polygamy and abides by the law of incest stated in the same context."[12] It is anybody's guess how a passage that is not teaching a prohibition of polygamy becomes a "single prohibition against polygamy." We agree with Kaiser's earlier statement that the verse is irrelevant.

DEUTERONOMY 17:17

A second verse sometimes quoted in regard to the prohibition of polygamy is Deuteronomy 17:17: "neither shall he multiply wives for himself, lest his heart be turned away."[13] But this verse relates to kings multiplying (foreign) wives as a means of insuring treaties with foreign nations. Such wives would doubtless be idolaters and bring in the kinds of false religion seen in the life and times of Solomon. It is improper to apply this prohibition to even such a king as David, whose wives did not fit the prohibited categories. One should also remember that the context of this verse also prohibits a king from multiplying horses and money. If we were to apply the antipolygamy argument consistently, we would have to imagine that kings were also restricted to one horse and one shekel. On the other hand, if kings could have been true to their inspired limitations by having more than a horse or shekel, then they could have been just as moral by having more than one wife.

PROVERBS 5:15–21

A final Old Testament passage we should examine, one that Kaiser calls "the best statement on the monogamous marriage," is Proverbs 5:15–21. It admonishes the reader to "drink water from his own cistern," to "rejoice in the wife of [his] youth," to be "captivated" and "satisfied" "always" by her love. Kaiser asks with rhetorical force, "Could these instructions possibly be obeyed by a man who had many additional wives?"[14]

Our feelings tell us no. But two things caution us to avoid interpreting the passage in line with Kaiser. First, it is my own belief that the text was penned by Solomon, one of the most celebrated polygamists in all history. I presume that Kaiser himself agrees with this identification. If Solomon did write it, it would certainly seem that he, at least, thought that the answer was yes. Second, a study of the context reveals that the words are not at all aimed at discussing the issue of one wife versus plural wives, but rather covenanted sexual relations as opposed to uncovenanted relations. Kaiser is resorting to eisegesis (reading the meaning into the text rather than out of it). His reading of the text has only rhetorical weight when one brings to the text the romantic definition of "love," not a biblical idea of responsible "love."

MATTHEW 19:5/MARK 10:8

Turning to the New Testament, we might hear reference to Matthew 19:5 and its Marcan parallel. Jesus quotes the LXX of Genesis 2:24, which adds (to the Masoretic text) the word "two" to the phrase: "they shall become one flesh." It is pointed out that the Essene community interpreted this addition as an attack upon the fading practice of polygamy. There is no doubt that the Essene community with their Temple Scroll so interpreted the LXX, but it is not at all clear that the LXX, which was written long before the founding of the Essenes, should be interpreted as the Essenes did. Jesus simply quoted the predominate translation known to his hearers, and that translation included the extra word "two." It is certainly acceptable to use the extra word, especially in the historical context of the Gospel verse. For there Jesus is underscoring that though the two partners in marriage once were independent, by their vows, they have become one team, without the privilege of breaking or walking away from the covenant. For the woman, to be sure, that did mean not contracting another marriage. But for the man, it did not mean anything of the kind. For the man it simply meant that he could not do as the School of Hillel suggested, i.e., end the union simply because he wanted to, for any reason at all. To jump on the Essene interpretation because it is available is poor reasoning. It is a hasty conclusion, not supported by internal evidence.

1 TIMOTHY 3:2, 13; TITUS 1:6

"The Husband of One Wife"

Then there is the verse in the "Pastorals," where Paul admonishes Timothy to make sure that "overseers" and "deacons" are "the husband of one wife" (1 Tim. 3:2, 13 and parallel wording in Titus 1:6). This would seem to be a prohibition so stark that only the intellectually maimed and blind could miss the point! But that is only because several important contextual elements have been forgotten. First, we must remember that the phrase comes in a qualifications list. Such a list, like a vice list, is not the place to find new moral teaching or any teaching per se. Lists are summaries of previous teaching. Thus if we cannot find a prohibition of polygamy up to this point in the teachings of the inspired text, we are in trouble (hermeneutically speaking) finding it there. Second, we should remember that polygamy was considered barbaric by the Greeks and had not been practiced in Ephesus or Crete for several hundred years. This raises the question of why the number one qualification mentioned would be the elimination of a nonexistent practice.[15]

Perhaps the best reason for denying an interpretation of the phrase as a direct condemnation of polygamy is the confusion that would cause in understanding 1 Timothy 5:9. Kent notes that if the earlier passages condemn more than one husband at a time, the latter passage must condemn having more than one husband at a time. But polyandry was probably nonexistent in the Empire at the time. Thus polygyny (and polyandry) would be condemned only if "husband of one wife" proscribes the plurality of wives in divorce and remarriage, and, if the underlying reason for that is the plurality of wives in remarriage. And that in turn depends on the idea that the divorce did not really end the first marriage. I deny that there is sufficient biblical support for either of the last two ideas.

The text, written to a nonpolygamous society, would doubtless have been translated as "a one-woman man," or a man who is not a womanizer—a man with a "woman in every port," or a man who had "eyes of adultery," or a man who frequented the temple prostitutes. In other words, it would be read as a prohibition of fornication and promiscuity—known and prevalent problems in the locations reached by the letters. This interpretation of the passage makes far greater sense of the qualifications list than if general promiscuity and fornication are *not* the point of the passage. For, if these problems were as rampant in Greek society as we know they were, it only stands to reason that this would be a number one concern for the churches in those areas. If the qualifications section is only condemning one kind of marriage (i.e., polygamy), a problem that did not exist in their times, then Paul missed the real issues facing Timothy and Titus. The failure of the list adequately to emphasize purity would be a great omission indeed.[16]

If Paul is indeed intending to prohibit fornicators from holding office in the Church, we can easily find passages in his previous moral teachings which become the basis for the qualifications list. This will come as no news to the reader. But I would like the reader to consider one of those passages: 1 Corinthians 7:1–2. Note carefully that in that passage, directed as it was to a monogamous society, Paul places the admonition to "have your own spouse" in the context of *fornication.* To have your own is contrasted to the many prostitutes on the Acro-Corinth. The recipient of the letter should be a "one-woman kind of man." I take this as virtually synonymous with the qualifications requirement.[17]

The importance of *prior* teaching is not to be underrated in matters of qualifications lists. But I should add that the prior context of moral teaching in this important area should go far back beyond the teachings of Paul. We would expect that Jesus and the Old Testament would confirm this same teaching. We are not simply seeking some vague condemnation of fornication, but some teaching akin to the points we have been making above, i.e., some reference to a covenant partner as an alternative to common women or prostitutes. And along this line, I offer Proverbs 5, mentioned above. The point of the passage is that one's own wife is the proper recipient of one's sexual energy vis-à-vis a common woman—a prostitute. The common woman is everybody's woman. She and her kin are to be avoided in favor of the woman who is covenanted to you. Again, as we have noted above, the man is encouraged to avoid fornication by turning to the woman of one's devotion. Sex is for covenant, not for indiscriminate pleasure. It would seem that biblical writers seek to inhibit fornication by an appeal to the wife, or woman of one's covenant. It is not the number of covenanted ones that is the contrast, but the difference between the many harlots and the covenant partner that is in view.

It is most probable that the qualifications list sees the "husband of one wife" as a condemnation principly of *porneia*—sex with an unmarried woman, though doubtless the clause also prohibited adultery—sex with someone else's wife. Polygamy was out of sight and mind. The issue is not the number of covenant relations the man had—he would only have had one at a time—but his womanizing. This of course does not eliminate the grievous sin of marrying and divorcing in order to have sexual relations with a number of women. But that too is not the issue in polygamy. Such divorcing and remarrying are after the order of legal womanizing. It is unsubstantiated that all polygamy falls into such a category.[18]

"Above Reproach"

Somewhere about this point in the discussion of the qualifications lists, one anticipates that the summary term "above reproach" will be invoked to show that polygamy is prohibited. These words are defined by the terms that follow. But that would answer nothing. Of course, it could be argued that "reproach" is a term that can be defined in other ways, for instance by readers from their own subcultures. But then one might read into the definition things that were only subcultural. And it is the inspired text that is using the term. Therefore I would insist that some other scripture must be brought into the discussion. What then is that scripture? We have considered the major proof-texts and found them wanting. What then?

In defining the term "reproach," one other matter must be brought to bear. It should be remembered that God speaks of himself in relation to his people Judah as having been married at the same time to their sister the Northern Kingdom (Jer. 3:8). Perhaps it should be suggested to God that he choose his metaphors a bit more carefully! These folk are saying that God has spoken of himself like a man who would call himself a murderer or a rapist. One sin is like another in being a sin. If it is a sin to be a polygamist, then God has referred to himself as a Being with a character flaw. We are speaking as fools. Better simply to say that the admonition to Timothy simply requires him to avoid people who are not "one-woman men" or "devoted husbands" or men who do not have "eyes full of adultery."[19] Such a man might have been single. He was to have been a "one-woman type of man." Further, does one really think that God would make such a radical clarification so late in his Word and in a personal letter? The great issues of marriage are dealt with early in Scripture, not in its last written pages. Or, again, does it stand to reason that Abraham or Moses would be prohibited from serving in the Church that shares in their blessings because they had more than one wife? How about David? Will he reign in the Millennial Kingdom, but be unworthy to be a deacon in the Church of Christ? We speak as men.[20]

THE IMPLICATIONS OF "ADULTERY" IN THE "VICE LISTS"

Recently a friend suggested that polygamy should be understood as condemned in the New Testament in the vice lists where adultery is mentioned. His point was that since the readers of such passages as 1 Corinthians 6:9 would have understood *moichos* as including the infidelity of both the woman and the man, it is only proper for the exegete to do the same.

Two responses are in order. First, I again note that such lists are not the place for new teaching. Of course, my friend might respond that this is exactly the point, that such a list presupposes that the Apostle understands the term in exactly the same sense. But to say so does not resolve the problem. For it is certainly possible that Paul might have instructed these persons already in the more Hebraic concept of *moichos*. Also, it is worth adding that Paul had no short way of condemning polyandry and adultery without writing a paragraph. This is especially true since in a monogamous society the reciprocal vow of fidelity itself makes the extramarital relationship of a married man to another woman a sort of adultery insofar as it would be a breach of covenant. And since the same list already condemned fornication, which is what extramarital sex would be for him in their society, there would be no need to make the clarification except to protect the reputation of a true polygamist—of which there were none in that society that needed to be protected! Thus were he to know that his meaning did differ from them on this point, he would also know that it would not be worth the effort to clear up the issue at that time.

An even more telling response to my friend is that the term *moichos* did not as he suggests imply reciprocal fidelity to the Greek or even the Roman mind. In both cultures, the term *adultery* spoke only to the marital status of the woman.[21] In fact, the only evidence Kittel offers is that *moichos* entails a reciprocal element in the Gospel passages, in which it is said that a man who divorces his wife and marries another commits adultery.[22] Yet we contend that neither Jesus nor his hearers understood those words as implying the moral impropriety of polygamy. We offer instead that Jesus means only to reaffirm the older Testament's condemnation of a man who would divorce his wife *in order to* marry another woman (Mal. 2). Without the Gospel passages to support prior moral instruction on the point, the contention that the vice lists would have been understood to teach reciprocal monogamy fails.

The ancients understood the act of sex between any man and a non-married woman to be *porneia,* not *moichos.* Thus it is vital that the vice lists include *porneia* as well as *moichos.*

QUESTIONS CONCERNING THE POSSIBILITY OF MORAL POLYGAMY

Covenantal Issues

Questions yet remain. For example, how is it possible for a man to have more than a single one-flesh relationship at the same time? The answer to this is very complex. Before I answer, I must remind the reader that marriage is not essentially a one-flesh relationship.[23] Marriage is essentially a covenant, involving conditions or agreements that are stated in the contractual side of the covenant. Thus the most proper question would be, "How is it morally possible for the husband to have more than one wife?" To this the answer is far more easy: his agreement with a given wife did not include a monogamous vow. Having made no monogamous promise, he has broken no covenant by taking a subsequent wife.

Social-Order Issues

It is rather easy to understand how it is socially and economically possible for a husband to have more than one wife, while the reverse is unworkable. Remember that Jesus said that no one can serve two masters. The term for "master" is *kurios* (Matt. 6:24; Luke 16:13). In 1 Peter 3:6, Sarah is cited as an example for all wives in their relation to their husbands. Her submissiveness is exemplified by her identification of Abraham as "*kurios.*" In other words, the wife's relation to her husband is one of follower to leader. Putting both ideas together, we should say that no wife can have more than two husbands. But the text does not say, remembering that Abraham had both a wife and a concubine, that a *kurios* cannot have more than one who serves (*doulos*).[24] That is why a husband (*kurios*) may have more than one wife (*doulos*), but the wife may not have more than one husband. The issue is social and economic—relating to the authority structure as represented in marriage. Because of who the husband is there may not be two of him, but because of who the wife is, there might be more than one of her. However unhappily this may strike the modern ear, it is, I believe, scriptural.

Ontological Issues

Given the above answer, another question arises; namely, How is it possible for the husband to have more than a single one-flesh relationship at the same time, while the same is not proper for the wife? If we consider this relation to be organic, an analogy may help. The husband functions as the head, while the woman functions as, let us say, the arm. The head may control more than one arm at a time. But to have two heads attempting to control the same arm would be monstrous. What we are suggesting is that there is nothing logically improper about multiplicity of subordinate elements in an organic union. Nor is there anything improper in the thought that a covenant partner may have more than one covenant at the same time.

CONCLUSIONS

As a result of these studies, I consider biblical polygamy to be a moral practice. I do not find sufficient biblical argument to deny it and find several passages that seem undeniably to affirm it. I am certainly willing to consider any biblical argument my readers might offer, but I am unwilling to accept a poor argument simply because it fits my or their fancy. To date, I find the arguments "pro" quite superior to those "con."

Finally, let me state unequivocally that this subject is only of academic interest to me. I seek to discern the moral propriety of the practice as it impinges upon the divorce passages in the biblical text. Insofar as that practice informs the divorce verses, it is important to this work. I have no interest in seeing polygamy established as a present social policy, nor do I have any personal interest in the practice.

On the Order of the Gospels

It is my belief that a chronological approach is best for understanding the meaning of a text. God is a God of order, and he is fully aware that present understanding is based upon prior understanding. That is why I spent so much time explicating the Old Testament first. But though it is clear that the teaching of Jesus is prior to that of his followers, it is not clear to many exactly what Jesus said to his followers (as opposed to what they said he said) or what sayings Jesus said first.

I am committed, after all, to the fact that the Scripture is harmonious, and, therefore, it should not matter where one starts in order to find consistent teaching on a given subject.[1]

I hold to the view that the Gospel accounts do present to us the teachings of Jesus, that no Gospel writer presumed to put ideas into the mouth of Christ that he did not verbalize in his lifetime on earth. I do not deny that Gospel writers redacted material in order to produce a condensed and logical presentation; nor do I wish to insist upon words, phrases, or verses found in the translations for which there is insufficient textual support.[2] But I presume that Jesus did speak (though in Aramaic) the equivalent of the words as presented unless there is an overriding textual reason for believing otherwise.

I have several other commitments that I think less significant in the discussion at hand, but rather than let readers guess where I stand, I will set them forth with only a brief word of defense:

1. I accept the traditional view of the authorship of the Gospels. I do not think that the higher criticism has presented any compelling reason for believing that other writers are responsible for them.[3]

2. I hold to the priority of Matthew rather than Mark. I agree with R. Thomas that most arguments in favor of Markan priority can be used with equal or better result to affirm Matthean priority.[4] I further suspect that Matthew wrote first a "journal" of the sayings of Jesus (the elusive Q), which he used to construct his not-

strictly-chronological Gospel, a work designed as a *discipleship training manual* (cf. Matt. 28:19 f.).[5]

Luke, the historian, wrote next, restoring the chronological order, using Matthew's Q and other elements from his own research, namely, testimony from the others in the apostolic band.

Mark wrote third, condensing their work. I am not saying that Mark is always shorter in the parallel passages, but that he leaves out whole subjects (like the disciplinary section Matthew includes prior to the divorce dialogue in chap. 18) included in one or both of the other synoptics. Mark's focus seems to be upon the powerful mission of Christ, who appears in Mark's document as a triumphant general—destroying the forces of the Devil. This adds to the doctrinal thrust of the book, which, I think, emphasizes the person and power of Jesus. I believe that this emphasis is intended to encourage converts as to the ability of the Master to help them conquer the problems of their world. Mark, as well, may have used Matthew's Q in the construction of his Gospel.

John wrote last, seeking to preserve omitted acts and teaching of which he was a witness—ordering his material around an apologetical theme. Q was discarded, as both its order and contents were fully preserved in the existing Gospels.[6]

The real issue, I suppose, is not which recorder wrote first, but whether or not the sayings of Jesus recorded by them are all relevant to our discussion. I am not seeking here to open the question of whether or not the writer of Matthew interposed the "exception clause" on top of Jesus' teaching in order to accommodate the more liberal practice of the early Church. Those who argue for this point often hypostatize (create) Matthean and Markan traditions that are seen to be at variance with each other, the Markan being more strict and the Matthean being more liberal. I find absolutely no historical evidence for belief in such a liberal trend in the Church, especially in the area to which we presume the Gospel of Matthew was directed (i.e., Antioch in Syria), nor for the view that a Markan tradition utilized and conformed to Essene influences in the Jerusalem area.

It might be argued that the Matthean "liberalization" of Mark is based upon the fact that *Matthew* was written at a late date to a stage at which the Church was no longer able to sustain the purist teachings of Jesus.[7] But this view has little to commend it. In the first place, it presupposes that Matthew wrote after Mark, the very point at issue. Second, it is not clear from what historical evidence, except the very verses in question, the "Matthean Church" period was unable to bear the absolute prohibition supposed to exist in Mark. After all, the more liberal dating of Matthew and Mark does not encompass the great hiatus one suspects would be needed for such liberalization.

As for the Essene connection with Mark, the best one can say for such an argument is that the Markan material looks similar to the previously written Essene material, but in the face of zero evidence that the Markan writer was dependent on, or even familiar with, the Essene material, I am forced to conclude that this often repeated theory is simply a *"post hoc, ergo propter hoc"* fallacy. I do not count as significant the possibility that Jesus' relation with the isolated Essene communities was mediated by John the Baptist. It is conjecture whether John had significant contact with those communities, and it is compounded conjecture that Jesus ever communicated with John about divorce teachings. The biblical text, which is, after all, about the only historical data we have to go on, gives no incontrovertible evidence of Jesus' familiarity with Essene teachings or presence.

The upshot of these convictions and conclusions is the order of treatment found in the book. Even if my views of chronology could be shown to be in error, I believe that the argument of the book would still ring true. But the presented order seems to fit best with the views mentioned.

On the Possibility of Nonsexual Adultery

In his commentary on Matthew 19:9, D. A. Carson says that

if the remarriage clause is excluded, the thought becomes nonsensical: "Anyone who divorces his wife, except for *porneia*, commits adultery"—surely untrue unless he remarries.[1]

Is this the case? Is it nonsense to speak of "nonsexual adultery"? I believe not.

Consider first the difference between adultery, fornication, and marital sex. All may involve sexual acts, but what makes them different is their relationship to the matter of covenant. The sex of marital sex is moral since covered by covenant. The sex of fornication is a sin because it is not. And the sex of adultery is sin because it breaks the covenantal bonds. The essence of adultery is unfaithfulness. Adultery never takes place unless someone's marriage vow has been broken.

But does an act of sex have to take place in order for the breaking of a vow to be considered adulterous? In one sense, no. According to Jesus in Matthew 5:27–28, an unfaithful thought or, more precisely, a thought of unfaithful sex merits the offense-term *adultery*. Although it is true that the thought is about sexual relations, Jesus' revolutionary saying contradicts the Pharisaical teaching exactly at the point at issue: must sexual acts be committed in order for the term *adultery* to be merited? Thinking of sexual acts is not in itself a sexual act; it is a mental act. I find Carson's treatment of this verse confusing in two respects. First, with Klaus Haacker,[2] he concludes that the second *her* is "unnecessary" if the sin is entirely the man's. The presence of the second feminine pronoun compels us to translate the phrase "so as to get her to lust."[3] The overall idea is that the man looks at the woman with a view to entice her to lust. Carson seems to imply the man's effort must have been successful insofar as the adultery the man commits is committed "with her." Carson goes on to say that this does not lessen the basic thought of Jesus that "the heart of the matter is still lust and intent."

I do not feel so compelled. If the complicitousness of the woman is needed for Jesus' point to carry, it *does* seem that the force of Jesus' teaching is blunted. Would it not be correct to say that if the man's effort to get her to lust fails nothing in this saying identifies him as guilty of adultery? If so, successful effort would be functioning as a sort of condition of the condemnation. But that certainly does not seem to be the point Jesus is trying to make. Rather, Jesus is at pains to say that the man does not have to actually commit an act of sex to be guilty of sin. Every one of Jesus' listeners already knew that an act of sex with a woman not one's wife was either fornication or adultery. What would be the need to tell this to the people? The teaching that Jesus was trying to correct must have been the idea that simple lust was not a sin if the act remained mental. Carson's interpretation definitely seems to return us to that Pharisaical teaching. It seems far easier to see the second *auten* (her) as emphatic. His lustful look has the effect of making him adulterous. Though he has not actually had sex with her in a bed, he has done it "with her" in his mind. The second "her" emphasizes the fact that the woman is actually involved, though only mentally.

Second, I cannot agree with Carson when he says that "*gune* here more likely means 'woman' than 'wife.' "[4] His case would be stronger were he to have cited some biblical instances of *adultery* used in the context of a single woman. Carson is correct in noting that *gune* can mean "woman" or "wife"; the only way we can know which the text intends is by considering the context. But the relevant contextual element in this case is *moicheuo,* "commits adultery." The only instance of *adultery* being used with respect to a single woman is where Israelites— who are the "betrothed" of Yahweh—desired (single) women of the land (heathen)—who are alternative lovers to Yahweh. But in this instance, *adultery* is appropriate insofar as the sexes have been reversed in the figure. It is still a married woman (Israel) who is involved with someone other than her Spouse. Unless Carson can show us instances of *adultery* used of women irrespective of their marital status, the stronger alternative is to translate *gune* as "wife." I follow this latter option.

This does not mean that the Sermon is only relevant at this point to men desiring married women. That would be to miss Jesus' point nearly altogether. The point of principle in his teaching is that one does not have to commit a sin in the external world in order to be guilty of it. Adultery is committed in the mind as well as in the neighbor's wife's bed. So too, a man who lusts after a single woman is guilty of fornication whether he actually consummates the thought or not. The thought is the sin just as the external act is. The principle applies to either sort of sin. However, since here the mental act involves thoughts of the sex act with a (married) woman, I anticipate that some will remain unconvinced.

A further argument arises from the so-called metaphorical use of *adultery*. On a number of occasions, the term *adultery* is used of God's people when they have turned away from his way to follow another.[5] In some instances this sort of "adultery" involved actual sex acts with women of the land.[6] But this is not always the case. Consider, for instance, where Jesus speaks of his generation as "evil and adulterous" because they seek after a sign (Matt. 12:39). I suppose that if one tries hard enough one could see the "seeking after" as implying that the sign is like seeking after another husband (the *generation* being understood as being in the position of the bride of Yahweh), but this seems strained. It is easier simply to see the generation as being unfaithful to Yahweh—no sexual fiction being implied.

The metaphorical use only works if there is a univocal analogue in common between the literal and metaphorical usage. The sexual element is common, but on the metaphorical side it is only a fiction. What we are looking for is an actual, not merely a fictional, analogue. That analogue is *unfaithfulness to the marriage vows*, and that the specific nature of the unfaithfulness need not involve sexuality even in thought. To break God's covenant (Law) in any respect—to turn away from it— is an act of adultery. So too, we argue, to break one's marriage vows in any respect is an act of adultery, and *adultery* is not used "nonsensically" when applied to the breach of nonsexual aspects of the marriage covenant.

Jeremiah 3:20 serves to illustrate this point rather clearly.

"Surely, as a woman treacherously departs from her lover,
So you have dealt treacherously with Me,
O house of Israel," declares the Lord.

Note here that the synonym for *adultery, treachery,* refers to the sin of "turning away" from Yahweh, the "lover." Compare this with Proverbs 2:17, where the woman (wife) is said to "leave the companion of her youth, and forget the covenant of her God." Of course, it could still be subjoined that "turning away" is euphemistic for sexual relations with another, since they turned away from God to others. In that case one needs to compare these ideas with Malachi 2:14, where Yahweh condemns the men of Israel for "dealing treacherously" with their companions, their wives by covenant. In the latter context, it is not clear that every covenant-breaker has gone on to marry another woman. It is enough to have divorced his covenant partner. Malachi goes on to condemn divorce, not divorce *and* remarriage. Is it not manifestly clear that Yahweh is concerned with unjust divorce and labels it "treachery," a synonym in this case for adultery—a breach of the marriage covenant?

Of course, our position is that Matthew 5:32 affirms this Old Testament teaching. When the spurious textual material concerning remarriage has been eliminated, Matthew 5:32 speaks of a man adulterizing his wife by unjustly divorcing her. The adulterization takes place whether or not *that* woman remarries.[7] The next clause is, as argued in chapter 7, independent of the first. If so, the New Testament is consistent with Malachi in identifying a nonsexual form of adultery, that is, the covenant breaking of unjust divorce. It is treachery, clear and simple. And it remains the sin of adultery whether or not either or both of the former partners remarry.

A final reason for concluding that "nonsexual adultery" is not nonsensical is that the man in biblical times could have married another woman in addition to a first wife and not have been guilty of the sin of adultery. There is never a clear instance of the Scriptures stigmatizing a polygamist per se as an adulterer. Adultery involves taking another man's wife.

Carson seeks to minimize this definition by associating it with the Jewish identification of adultery as a matter of theft.[8] It would seem to me that this very identification presses us toward a nonsexual understanding of adultery. We would certainly not want to limit adultery to a breach of the seventh word and not see it as also a breach of the eighth. Deuteronomy 24:1–4 is identified by its placement in the Sermon as involving a breach of the eighth word as well as the seventh. But I do reject any definition of *adultery* that does not see it as a breach of an existing covenant, and I believe that any breach of the marriage covenant merits the offense-term *adultery*.

By seeing marital breach as "adultery" regardless of whether it involves sex, we have an "in-principle" reason for harmonizing the Matthean exception clause, with its sexual connotations, with the Pauline "privilege," which lacks any explicit sexual connotations. Paul's teaching is at one and the same time the same and different from that of Jesus. It is different in that Jesus did not address the question of whether a convert ought to divorce an unbelieving spouse. His words presuppose a marriage of two professing disciples. Thus Paul notes that his admonition goes beyond the explicit teaching of the Lord (1 Cor. 7:12). But the apostolic admonition does not go beyond the moral principle that sundering a marriage ends it, morally speaking, thereby freeing the rejected convert. Unjust divorce (or desertion) is a form of adultery; adultery is a form of *porneia*; and *porneia* is justifiable grounds for divorce and remarriage.

Rather than concur that nonsexual adultery is linguistic nonsense, I argue that the idea is eminently sensible and biblically sound. On the contrary, what is nonsense is arguing that remarriage must take place for adultery to occur.

On the Biblical Terms for "Divorce"

OLD TESTAMENT WORDS

k'rîtût: to dismiss. The technical term for divorce or divorcement is *k'rîtût*. The root of this word is *b'tît*, the word for "covenant," which means to "cut off." The idea of the root is that a covenant was an agreement solemnized by the cutting up of an animal, just as God had cut up the animals and passed between them in the covenant with Abraham (Gen. 15:18). *Theological Wordbook of the Old Testament*[1] notes that the idea of covenant is not magical or mystical but intentional. Subjects of a covenant (i.e., the ones making the covenant) walk between the cut animals, saying by the action that they intend the same destruction of themselves, if they break the covenant, that they have done to the animals. In marriage, the reciprocity of the vows implies that the partners each will the same self-destruction if they break the terms.

Thus, the word for divorcement speaks of the "cutting off" of the offending party. It is as if they have received the self-appointed penalty for breaking their vows. The divorced person is "as if dead" to the former spouse. These ideas reveal how appropriate it was for divorce to become a righteous (though second-best) substitute for the death penalty.

This makes it clear that divorcement was meant to apply only to times when the partner had broken the covenant terms. In those cases, the divorce would function like an execution. The concept behind the term also shows how wrong it would be to cut off the partner who had not broken those terms. In that case, the divorce would be like murdering the innocent. The term *k'rîtût*, then, was meant to convey moral stigma against the divorced person. But that stigma was to be in the context of moral offense. Insofar as divorce could occur to an innocent party, it would be necessary to qualify this stigma.

shillûhîm: "to send away." This is the term used of expelling someone in Genesis 3:23; 12:20. It is used of divorce in Deuteronomy 22:19, 29; and Isaiah 50:1. It seems to convey the idea of an official act, often an act of punishment for breaking (at least implied) covenant. A form of it is used twice in Deuteronomy 24:1–4. There the term may show some contrast between the breaking of covenant and the real reason the man is putting his wife away: uncleanness. Uncleanness is *not* proper grounds for sending away, but the woman has been sent away nonetheless. Certainly this term means to identify the party sent away as having moral guilt. How tragic if there is none.[2]

yāsa': "to go out," used in a technical sense of "emancipation." The Bible uses this term when speaking of Israel's freedom from Egypt and the freedom of the indentured servant from slavery (cf. Exod. 21:2). This freedom ensured the right of emancipated persons to be free to make their own decisions by contrast with the limits of their freedom set by their previous condition of slavery. When freed, they were allowed to make new contracts at will. The significance of this term to our study is that the one-flesh partner of Exodus 21:11 is said to be emancipated from her master (husband) if he mistreats her. The text notes that the contract is off, and the slave's part of the bargain (the return of the "slave/bride price" in the case of default) is not an encumbrance upon her. Her father is, then, free to contract her with another master/husband if he wishes. She is no more tied to her former master than Israel was to Egypt after the Exodus. (And, though in one sense Israel was previously tied to God, the events following the Exodus reveal that emancipated Israel—feminine—is called to make a choice between God and her old master, Egypt.)[3]

NEW TESTAMENT WORDS

The New Testament uses several terms for "divorce." Their primary meanings and distinctions are listed:

apoluo: "to let loose from, let go free" (*apo*, "from," *luo*, "to loose").[4] Bauer, Arndt, Gingrich, and Danker (BAGD) distinguish the meaning of "set free, release, pardon" from that of "let go, send away, dismiss" (including "divorce").[5] I believe that this distinction is too sharp. The "send away" of *apoluo* would seem to involve the "set free, release" of the partner from all vows of the covenant. Implicit in this action is the idea that remarriage is permitted for either party. This is the primary word used in the Gospels for the action of divorce.

chorizo: "to put asunder, separate."[6] BAGD notes that this term speaks of dividing. It is used in the papyri marriage contracts.[7] It is my contention that this word is used connotatively in the biblical divorce legislation as an offense-term, whereas *apoluo* is denotatively (and sometimes connotatively) morally neutral.

aphistemi: "to cause to withdraw."[8] BAGD notes that this word is used of a legal sense of divorce by Paul in 1 Corinthians 7:11 ff.[9] It often appears in the biblical text to speak of canceling a debt (forgiving it) or of simple leaving. In the divorce instruction of Paul it is used three times (1 Cor. 7:1, 12, 13), always with a connotation of moral offense, that is, of withdrawing without moral right. The difference between the use of *aphistemi* and *chorizo* (in 1 Cor. 7:10–15) amounts to the difference between legal (and perhaps physical) departure, for which Paul uses the former term, and moral severance, for which he uses the latter. Both, however, convey the idea of moral infraction. Schlier, in Kittel,[10] notes that *aphistemi* is related to the concept of apostasy and emphasizes the alienation of persons from the fellowship of each other. This relationship obviously shows the offense-term connotation of the word.

apostasion: "a standing off" (*apo*, "from," *stasis*, "standing").[11] BAGD notes that the word is used of a certificate of divorce, conveying the sense of relinquishment of property rights or claims.[12] It is related to the term *apostasy*, which speaks of abandonment. Of course, we have noted on several occasions in the book that the certificate of divorce or even divorce as an act implies a refusal to continue to provide for the former partner. This is the technical term for a writ of divorcement (from the verb *aphistemi* above). The noun form does not retain the offense-term connotation of the verb in the divorce legislation.

On the Divorce Teachings of the Early Church

It is not our primary purpose in this book to analyze the history of interpretations of the biblical text, especially with a view to discover the traditional "Christian" view. In one sense, Christians of all times have the same homework to do. The inspired text determines the limits of position; extrabiblical interpretations serve only as suggestions. Although the positions of the early Church are generally given deference, being closer to the actual teachings themselves, they must neither be given undue weight nor be accepted uncritically.

For our purposes, I wish simply to make several observations. First, none of the writings of the early Church Fathers, in spite of their strong belief in their own correctness, is directly associated with the teaching of either Jesus or one of his disciples. By this, I mean that none of the principal sources cited by such writers as Heth and Wenham[1] personally knew either Jesus or one of the disciples. This means that the writings of these Fathers could not be checked by those authorized by Jesus to "know all the truth" (John 16:13).[2]

My second observation is that a number of writers have mis- or overread the teachings of certain early Church Fathers and have drawn certain unwarranted conclusions from such reading. Because of this, I find it necessary to summarize the key teachings of several of the more important Fathers from Hermas to Augustine. I make no claim to have done an exhaustive study, but only to have been fair and informative in my consideration of them. I also believe my analysis of teachings in this early stage of the development of interpretation to be correct.

HERMAS (ca. A.D. 125)

The earliest statements on the subject of divorce/remarriage among Christians were uttered by Hermas, a well-meaning, but simple, seer of the second century. "Hermas" was probably the pseudonym of a

Jewish Christian who lived in Rome. We know very little about him except what is found in his *Shepherd,* a work wrongly granted canonical status by some in the early Church. In fact, some scholars believe that this work is really the product of three hands over a period of some sixty years spanning A.D. 90–150.[3] In all likelihood, the material with which we have to do is separated from Jesus and his disciples by over a century. The connections between Jesus and Hermas are anybody's guess, but they cannot have been direct.

In the "Mandate" section of his *Shepherd,*[4] a work that bears striking similarity in language to Gospel material but is claimed by its author to have been given by direct revelation to him by his "heavenly guardian," Hermas makes the following points:

1. Failure to divorce a recognized, adulterous wife is complicitous adultery (v. 5).
2. Failure of a disciplining husband to remain unmarried is adultery (v. 6).
3. Failure of a disciplining husband to forgive a repentant wife is a sin worse than adultery (v. 8).
4. The reason that remarriage is prohibited of the disciplining spouse is that remarriage blocks repentance (v. 10).

The most natural explanation of this material is that Hermas sees the problem of remarriage as *ethical,* not *ontological.* The stated reason for the prohibition of remarriage is that it inhibits full repentance. Judging from the reciprocity of the point, it is clear that Hermas is a man of his culture, a monogamous one, for remarriage would not hinder the restoration of an erring wife in a polygamous culture.

Heth and Wenham, however, reject as "an argument from silence" the denial that Hermas knew other (more ontological) reasons for abstinence subsequent to divorce.[5] Instead, they attempt to draw from Hermas' use of the term *adultery* in verse 6 the idea of permanent bond. By relegating the repentance theme to a distinct section more or less unrelated to verse 6, they eliminate it from crucial consideration.

Their analysis is unconvincing. It is they who are guilty of arguing from silence. Insofar as Hermas offers no other reason for remarriage being prohibited, it is they who bear the burden of proof if they think he had another. Their reference to verse 6 simply cannot bear that burden. The reasons are twofold: first, Hermas does not clearly state that the adultery of remarriage offends an indissoluble bond (as Heth and Wenham imply), and second, Hermas speaks of the nondisciplining husband (v. 5) as also guilty of the sin of adultery.[6] In the latter case, there is no sexual offense against the initial bond that Heth and Wenham believe to be the case whenever remarriage occurs.

It is clear that the teaching of this influential Father constitutes a "mixed bag" when considered from a biblical perspective. Heth and

Wenham gladly accept his prohibition of remarriage, but they reject his insistence on disciplining divorce and single forgiveness as "beyond" the teachings of the New Testament.[7] It would seem that their counsel that "a modified form of the early church view . . . has the best chance of answering" available evidence[8] must be taken with caution. They seem set on impressing us with the proximity of the Father's views to the biblical teachings, but feel free to reject those views when they do not seem to live up to the text. They would be better advised simply to consider the text and play down the Fathers, whose views are obviously not completely dependable.

But they do not, and Hermas' views have not only come to their attention, but also to the attention of certain later Fathers in the early Church. Though Hermas' idea of prohibiting all remarriage later dominated the Roman Catholic church, we shall see that that idea was not explicitly accepted by the Fathers for quite a number of years. I consider Hermas unique in his view, at the turn of the first century.

JUSTIN MARTYR (ca. A.D. 150)

The teachings of Justin Martyr come next. His burden regarding our subject seems to be to inhibit the marrying of divorced women. In *First Apology* he quotes Matthew 5:28, 29; 32b or Luke 16:18b; and Matthew 19:11–12.[9] It is to be noted that all the pertinent verses refer to married women. The Martyr's explanatory statement of this biblical material is to the effect that "double" marriages are sins against Christ, and that sinful thoughts as well as sinful actions are condemned. In his *Second Apology* Justin teaches the concept of necessary, disciplining divorce by an offended Christian woman.[10] He ignores the subject of her remarriage.

Heth and Wenham (who would reject the Martyr's teaching on disciplining divorce) consider several possible meanings of Justin's *First Apology*. It could forbid (1) bigamy, (2) successive bigamy or the remarriage of widow(er)s, (3) remarriage after divorce, or (4) all remarriage. Heth and Wenham opt for number 3. However, their reason for doing so is weak. They merely cite the fact that the middle passage condemns a kind of remarriage and infer from an aside criticism of "human law" that Justin must be opposed to the Roman practice of permitting remarriage of the divorced.

But the reference to "human law" is in the context of the verses quoted, none of which unequivocally prohibits the remarriage of an innocent woman after her divorce, much less that of a disciplining husband. It would seem that Justin is simply reflecting upon Matthew's presentation of the divorce legislation.[11] The connection of the three passages is clearly made by Justin, who refers back to the "lust saying" after the citation of the three.

It is, then, far more reasonable to see Justin as condemning (1) lusting after a married woman and (2) marrying her subsequent to her being freed by divorce. Such a man should rather remain single than fulfill his lustful desires, and such a man should understand that whether he accomplishes his goal or only thinks about it, he is guilty of the same sin of adultery before God. Roman law might not hold a man guilty of offense for lusting after his neighbor's wife or for marrying her were she to manage to free herself from her husband, but the Bible does. But Justin does not condemn the remarriage of a disciplining spouse (nor does he in the *Second Apology*), nor does he condemn the remarriage of an innocently divorced spouse. His condemnations are always in the context of a woman's legitimate marriage; that marriage should not be broken up in thought or by action by the man to whom Justin refers (and condemns). This understanding of Justin does not go beyond his statements (as Heth and Wenham do), and it is entirely in harmony with the position set forth in this book.

ATHENAGORAS (ca. A.D. 177)

Athenagoras is the next significant Father. His teachings on the subject are found in his *Plea for the Christians:*

A person should either remain as he was born, or be content with one marriage; for a second marriage is only a specious adultery. "For whosoever puts away his wife," says He, "and marries another, commits adultery"; not permitting a man to send her away whose virginity he has brought to an end, nor to marry again. For he who deprives himself of his first wife, even though she be dead, is a cloaked adulterer, resisting the hand of God, because in the beginning God made one man and one woman, and dissolving the strictest union of flesh with flesh, formed for the intercourse of the race.[12]

Athenagoras places this in a section with obviously ascetic strains. Eunuchs are elevated, and marriage is strictly for procreation. The context also contrasts Christian marriage and behavior with the incestuous licentiousness of the pagans and their gods. The only Christian options are the single life or a single marriage. Remarriage is out of the question. God designed for a man to have no more than one wife in his lifetime.

But what exactly does Athenagoras mean by all this? Crouzel, in his classic work on divorce teachings of the Fathers, suggests three possible interpretations: (1) he condemns remarriage after divorce; (2) he discourages any remarriage (even of widowers); and (3) he condemns any remarriage.[13] To this Heth and Wenham add a fourth: he condemns remarriage of a divorcing man whose former wife dies.[14] Crouzel opts for number 1. Heth and Wenham opt for number 2.

It seems to me that Crouzel is essentially correct, though the fourth option seems a better way to put the point. It is only the man who has deprived himself of his wife who is not free to remarry even if she (subsequently) dies. I would qualify Crouzel by noting that it is a man who "deprives himself" who is condemned. Could it be that Athenagoras only has in mind a man who has unjustly divorced his wife? Would it be proper, given the evidence of the previously considered Fathers, to speak of a disciplining divorcer as a "robber" or a "depriving one"? Probably not.

Seemingly against this conclusion stands the reference to the creation of one man for one woman. Yet that may just be Athenagoras' way of speaking out against the desire for more than one wife, the desire that motivates the unjust divorcer. That is, after all, one way to see Christ's use of the same text from Genesis. The whole teaching is in the context of showing how Christians abhor treachery to the wife of one's youth.[15] The "for" structure of his work does seem to keep the whole teaching in the context of inhibiting remarriage after divorce. But what kind of divorce? I suggest that it is the unjustified kind. In the end, however, we do not have enough evidence from Athenagoras to decide the case. As in the case of Justin (who influenced Athenagoras), the Fathers are not clear about whether or not they condemn all remarriage or just that of the guilty.

THEOPHILUS OF ANTIOCH (ca. A.D. 180)

Defending Christian teachings to his friend Autolycus, Theophilus of Antioch presents marriage material in the same order that Justin did before him: Matthew 5:28, then Matthew 5:32.[16] He reverses the order of the sayings in Matthew 5:32 and adds the "except clause." About this, Heth and Wenham quickly conclude that Theophilus rejects "remarriage of anyone divorced for whatever reason," which would amount to affirming that "marriage is truly indissoluble."[17]

But again I must demur. The relevant chapter in Theophilus' work is entirely in the context of coveting another man's wife. It begins with a reference to lustful looks at another's wife, moves through a quote of Proverbs 4:25 (condemning lustful looks), through a quote of Matthew 5:28, to the inverted quote of Matthew 5:32, and ends with a quote from Proverbs (6:27–29) that once more condemns taking another man's wife. What seems obvious is that Theophilus is condemning remarriage when it is to a woman who has been wrongfully taken from another man. The lustful look takes heart in the fact that the object of desire has been freed by divorce (probably instigated by the woman and the coveting man). Theophilus condemns such "legal adultery." And he condemns the man who unjustly divorces his wife as well! This is all a fitting application of the point with which Theophilus ends chapter 12: "let none of you imagine evil against his brother in your heart."[18] Again, Heth and Wenham have overread the material that prohibits remarriage of the guilty party to be a prohibition of all remarriage after divorce.

IRENAEUS (ca. 185)

In *Against Heresies,* Irenaeus, a crucial Eastern Father (also influenced by Justin) depreciates divorce since it was given because of the hard hearts of men. He seems to say that it is incompatible with the original intent of God in Genesis 2:24. Again, Heth and Wenham jump to the conclusion that such a statement affirms the permanence of marriage, which would be compatible with their thesis that divorce is wrong and remarriage is the sin of adultery.

But again, I must suggest the same caveat I voiced regarding Athenagoras: would Irenaeus speak against the solid tradition of disciplinary divorce mentioned by these earlier Fathers? Unlikely. But then what shall we make of Irenaeus' depreciation of divorce? I suggest that he too is referring to those improperly divorcing. It is that sort of divorce that is incompatible with God's original plan. Disciplinary divorce is out of sight and mind—as is the question of a remarriage after a disciplinary divorce. Such a caveat is not an argument from silence, but from the traditional context.

CLEMENT OF ALEXANDRIA (ca. 153–217)

In the writings of Clement of Alexandria, we have the first extant comprehensive treatment of marriage/divorce/remarriage. Clement clearly teaches that Matthew 5:32a and b are aligned as the tradition now holds them. In his *Stromata* (II.23), he discusses the matter of divorce. The progression of topics is as follows:

1. Affirmation of pure marriage, as a necessity for some.
2. Statement that the Scriptures "allow no release from the union."
3. A quote giving the gist of the Matthew 19:9 prohibition of divorce, ending with the "except clause."
4. Statement that Scripture regards the remarriage of those separated during the lifetime of their spouse as "fornication."
5. Statement of the need for the wife to avoid activities that suggest fornication.
6. A quote giving the gist of Matthew 5:32 (reversing the sayings).
7. The interpretation that the putting away sets the woman up for adultery in remarriage—the second marriage inhibiting a restoration.

8. A comparison of these Gospel ideas to the execution of adulteresses in the Law—harmonizing the two by calling the (divorced?)
adulteress "dead to the commandments," while the repentant one
is born again.

Heth and Wenham insist that in this is a prohibition of remarriage
for the disciplining divorcer. They follow this interpretation with a citation of Clement's association of the "eunuch saying" to the matter of
the remarriage of the disciplining divorcer.[19] Their interpretation of
the latter leans toward implying that Clement denied remarriage to all
such divorcers.[20]

But these conclusions may be questioned. Another reading of Clement is that in the earlier passage he is silent about the remarriage of
the disciplining divorcer, and in the second passage he holds forth
celibacy to some disciples, but not to all. The basis of these more liberal
conclusions is as follows: In the earlier passage Clement clearly permits
the divorce of an adulterous wife, because by her fornication she is
already dead. The crucial point number 4 follows hard on the quote
of the "except clause," not to suggest that the man who disciplines is
guilty of setting up his wife for adultery, or that his remarriage is fornication, but to associate the remarriage of a treacherously divorced
spouse with fornication, a point repeated in number 7—where the
"putting away" is obviously not disciplinary. The disciplining divorcer
could not be judged as occasioning his former wife's adultery by a remarriage, since she is already guilty of that sin and is, in fact, like a
dead woman. Nothing is said about *his* remarriage, only hers. Number
7 only rejects—as inhibiting a restoration—the remarriage of the
treacherously divorced woman.[21] The remarriage of the divorced is beyond the control of the divorcer, and if Clement means to tar all divorcers with the adulterous remarriage of the divorced, then he should
have proscribed disciplinary divorce to save the morals of the offended
spouse. But Clement definitely believes in disciplinary divorce—it is
the parallel to Old Testament execution.

As for the second passage, even Heth and Wenham have to admit
that it does not teach the moral necessity of celibacy for the disciplinary
divorcer. Such is held up as an ideal—as it is for the widower and the
never-married. Those to whom the gracious gift of celibacy has not
been granted may apparently marry without moral condemnation.

It seems best, therefore, to interpret Clement as believing that adultery in the marriage severs it and "kills" the adulterer. The "dead" may
be put away without the fear that their remarriage would bring the
charge of complicity in adultery against the disciplining divorcer, and
such a divorcer who does not have the gift of celibacy may remarry.
Such a position is very near that set forth by the traditional Erasmians,

except that the remarriage of disciplining *male* divorcers is always in view in Clement.

TERTULLIAN (ca. 155–220)

The first great theologian of the West, Tertullian, was an outstanding spokesman for the permanence of marriage. In his famous *On Monogamy*, written during his Montanist period, he makes soundings, like Athenagoras, that marriage lasts past the grave.[22] In that vein, and in the same book, the marriage of widows is prohibited on grounds just slightly more fantastic than the Leviticus 18 arguments of Isaksson,[23] that such remarriage is incestuous.[24] In all, Tertullian's *Monogamy* employs not very precise hermeneutics and is of questionable value to one trying to discover a general view of the early Church.[25]

ORIGEN (ca. 185–254)

Origen, the second of the great Alexandrian Fathers, and the successor of Clement in its catechetical school, followed Clement in prohibiting a woman's remarriage during the lifetime of her first spouse.[26] Heth and Wenham admit that he does require "separation" of a man from his adulterous wife, and that he does not speak of the right of a disciplining male divorcer to remarry, but that owing to his dependence upon Hermas and Clement he must have made the prohibition reciprocal.[27] They therefore place him on their side in denying remarriage to the innocent party in a disciplinary divorce.[28]

Though it is true that Origen speaks of the man who divorces his wife as causing her to commit adultery, it is stated that this man is not divorcing for the ground of "fornication."[29] Beyond this, these authors appear not to take Origen seriously when he speaks of Christ as divorcing Israel and (re)marrying the Church, a clear case of disciplinary divorce followed by remarriage.[30] And, in those passages, Origen insists that Christ, in doing so, did not break the commandment not to sunder the "one-flesh" union, *because he had the grounds of "fornication,"*[31] grounds that Origen identifies as "reasonable" for the "dissolution of marriage."

We have in Origen, then, a Father who did not believe in the indissolubility of marriage, who did believe that one could and should divorce (not merely "separate") if one had the grounds of fornication, and who believed that one who divorced as a discipline could morally remarry. This sounds strikingly dissimilar to Heth and Wenham's position.

There is also an interesting reference in his Matthew commentary, where Origen says that "certain Church leaders have permitted the remarriage of a divorced woman while her husband was alive."[32] This raises the question as to whether or not the crucial Alexandrian Fathers are truly representative of the Church in their rejection of remarriage for women. And, given the ambiguity of the earlier Fathers, as noted earlier, this caveat is significant. Of course, we do not know the names of those to whom Origen referred, so we are not privy to their arguments; nor do we know their significance in the Church tradition. But we do know one Father who stands against the trend in Alexandria:

CHRYSOSTOM, JOHN OF ANTIOCH (ca. 344/45–407)

This influential Eastern Father, John Chrysostom, in his homilies on Matthew's Gospel clearly and unmistakably denies the disciplining divorcer the right to remarry during the lifetime of his former spouse.[33] Though he bases this conclusion upon the Genesis 2:24 text, he does not present a refined position of *ontological* union. We have, therefore, with John, one of the first clear proponents of celibacy following all divorce.

AMBROSIASTER (ca. 366–383)

The name Ambrosiaster has, since the time of Erasmus, been applied to a fourth-century writer of commentaries on Pauline epistles. We do not know his real identity, but he may have been one Hilary, the prefect of Rome about 375.[34] In any case, commenting on 1 Corinthians 7, he goes beyond the disciplinary divorce theme to affirm the right of the innocent husband to remarry. He does not permit this for the innocent wife, however. His rationale centers upon the headship role of the male in marriage. He also allows for a deserted Christian spouse (male or female) to remarry. This is the first clear instance of a Father teaching the so-called Pauline privilege.

Heth and Wenham identify three instances in which they see Ambrosiaster as out of step with the Scriptures and with the early Church: (1) he allows remarriage to deserted Christians; (2) he allows remarriage to disciplining male divorcers; and (3) he discriminates against women in the same situation.

I find their criticism not entirely correct or fair. On the first count, it is true that Ambrosiaster is the first Father whom we know to explicitly teach the Pauline privilege. But that seems no more offensive than to be like Clement of Alexandria, who was the first to clearly teach no remarriage after divorce. The real issue is whether or not Ambrosiaster is correct. I believe he is. Second, though he is the first to clearly and explicitly teach that a disciplining male divorcer may remarry, I have previously argued that, with the exception of the enigmatic Hermas, no previous Father can be said to teach explicitly the reverse. Then, too, we must recall those other "church leaders" who, according to Origen, were permitting divorced women to remarry. Most likely such women were the "innocent parties." This is not far from Ambrosiaster, though it disagrees with count 3. As for count 3, Heth and Wenham are technically correct in noting that Ambrosiaster discriminates against innocent women, but most of these early Fathers do the same thing, that is, speak against the remarriage of divorced women and remain silent concerning innocent men. Perhaps Ambrosiaster should be faulted only for being honest and forthright! Further, we are reminded that the Scriptures themselves are often "faulted" for discriminating against women.[35] Perhaps Ambrosiaster is closer to the tradition than his critics!

THE APOSTOLIC CANONS

By the days of the Council of Nicaea (325), or at least the days of the Council of Antioch (341), a series of deliverances, purportedly from the apostles, were being gathered and presented as such. These canons are the very early (prior to 300) canon law of the Church. Pertinent laws include:

Canon V (VI)
Let not a bishop, or deacon, put away his wife under pretense of religion; but if he put her away, let him be excommunicated; and if he persists, let him be deposed.

Canon XVII
He who has been twice married after baptism, or who has had a concubine, cannot become a bishop, presbyter, or deacon, or any other of the sacerdotal list.

Canon XVIII
He who married a widow, or a divorced woman, or an harlot, or a servant-maid, or an actress cannot be a bishop, presbyter, or deacon, or any other of the sacerdotal list.

Canon XIX
He who has married two sisters, or a niece, cannot become a clergyman.[36]

The main burden of these rules is to preserve the ceremonial purity of the clergy. What obligations laypersons had to follow these rules is not entirely clear. It may be presumed that it is morally wrong for anyone to put away his wife for merely "religious" reasons. But the rest of the rules are more difficult to apply to laypersons. In essence the last three rules (all grouped together in the list) function as disqualifications for church office. They all read alike. But would we be correct in saying that a moral Christian could not marry a servant-maid? It would seem better to treat these rules as the sort of ceremonial defilements we noted in the Old Testament Levitical law. But if this is the case, can it be said that the Church is clearly against the marriage of divorced laypersons by the time of these canons? Apparently not.

THE COUNCIL OF ARLES (314)

The tenth canon of the Council of Arles states:

As regards those who find their wives to be guilty of adultery, and who being Christian are, though young men, forbidden to marry, we decree that, so far as may be, counsel be given them not to take other wives, while their own, though guilty of adultery, are yet living.[37]

What is said is clear. Why it is said is not. It may well be that this synodal meeting reflects the view of the early Tertullian and Justin that such remarriages inhibit the repentance of the guilty wife—thus not implying ontic status to the former marriage, though taking into account moral issues.

THE CANONS OF BASIL (after 370)

The Canons of Basil, found in several epistles of the great Cappadocian father to one Amphilochius, bishop of Iconium, include among them:[38]

Epistle I, Canon IX

Our Lord is equal, to the man and woman forbidding divorce, save in the case of fornication; but custom requires women to retain their husbands, though they be guilty of fornication. The man deserted by his wife may take another, and though he were deserted for adultery, yet St. Basil will be positive, that the other woman who afterward takes him is guilty of adultery; but the wife is not allowed this liberty. And the man who deserts an innocent wife is not allowed to marry.

This intriguing law shows that (Church?) custom was discriminatory against women in cases of fornication and that the bishop discriminated against women in the case of desertion. It is not entirely clear that Basil did not agree with Ambrosiaster that deserted men were morally free to remarry. Note that the emphasis is, again, on inhibiting guilty parties from remarrying but not inhibiting innocent male parties.

Epistle II, Canon XXI

A married man committing lewdness with a single woman, is severely punished as guilty of fornication, but we have no canon to treat such a man as an adulterer; but the wife must co-habit with such a one: But if the wife be lewd, she is divorced, and he that retains her is [thought] impious; such is the custom, but the reason of it does not appear.

This is another interesting statement, and one that is entirely in harmony with the conclusions of this book.

Epistle II, Canon XXXVII
That he, who having another man's wife or spouse taken away from him, marries another, is guilty of adultery with the first, not with the second.

This canon shows that the Church, at this point, does not recognize a one-flesh bond to establish a marriage that is indissoluble. Heth and Wenham would perhaps say that this is not a legitimate marriage, but that evades the point. Why is a legal and consummated marriage (since all marriages are witnessed by God) not able to establish a permanent bond?

Epistle II, Canon XLVI
She that marries a man who was deserted for a while by his wife, but is afterward dismissed upon the return of the man's former wife, commits fornication, but ignorantly: she shall not be prohibited marriage, but it is better that she do not marry.

Note that she does not commit adultery, only ignorant fornication, since she is single—a conclusion drawn in this book.

Epistle II, Canon XLVIII
A woman dismissed from her husband, ought to remain unmarried, in my judgment.

Note that there is less dogmatism in this canon than we might expect if the tradition against (apparently innocent) divorced women remarrying is as "traditional" as Heth and Wenham suggest.

Epistle III, Canon LXXXVII
He that divorces his wife, and marries another, is an adulterer; and according to the canons of the Fathers, he shall be a mourner one year, a hearer two years, a prostrator three years, a co-stander one year, if they repent with tears.

Several things are noteworthy about this canon. First, it does not demand that the remarried couple separate. It speaks of "they" as repenting, and there is no mention of a reconciliation with the first wife. Second, though the first part of the canon is obviously a near quote of scriptural material, the canon attributes the rule only to the canons of the Fathers. It is hard to know what to make of this except to say that the canons often are more concerned with tradition than Scripture. Third, it is confusing why, if the man is an adulterer, he should receive such light treatment, when Canon LVIII states that adulterers shall be mourners four years, hearers five years, prostrators four years, and co-standers for two years. Apparently the canons retained different traditions. Perhaps the reference to the Fathers is half in justification for the laxity of Canon LXXXVII. Lastly, does this canon mean to imply the divorcer had no grounds? If Basil is as soft on a divorced woman as he appears in Epistle II, Canon XLVIII, could he be so harsh on a disciplining divorcer who remarries? Such a conclusion would reverse the standard discrimination against women in favor of men. In all likelihood, Epistle III, Canon LXXXVII, means to judge guilty divorcers who remarry.

Epistle III, Canon LXXX
The Fathers say nothing of polygamy as being beastly, and a thing unagreeable to human nature. To us it appears a greater sin than fornication: Let therefore such [as are guilty of it] be liable to the canons, viz. after they have been mourners one year—let them be prostrators three years—and then be received.

This canon is also interesting in several respects. First, though his language is somewhat colorful ("beastly, and a thing unagreeable to human nature"), it is possible to interpret this canon as reporting no dominical condemnation of polygamy "on the books." Could this immensely important Father have missed the tradition against polygamy that Kaiser, Heth and Wenham, and others insist was there?

If the Fathers did not proscribe polygamy, then it is certainly possible that they did not consider divorced and remarried men (and women?) guilty of moral offense (even if such marriages were thought to entail multiple "one-flesh" relationships).

Of course, it might be argued that Basil is simply reporting that the Fathers did not find polygamy an abomination, while knowing they did consider it some other sort of sin. But to this it must be noted that Basil does not say that the Fathers considered it fornication, much less, as he did, "a sin greater than fornication." Having appealed to the Fathers in the first place, Basil would most likely have cited support of his own milder position *had that support been available*. We know churchmen saw themselves as custodians of the traditions. Where then was the tradition condemning polygamy?

Second, it is to be pointed out that the penalty prescribed is less than that Basil usually commands for fornication. Fornication received: mourner two years, hearer two years, prostrator two years, co-stander one year—a total of seven years' penalty. Polygamy, however, receives only four years! Again, Basil seems to mitigate a growing aversion to multiple marriages with the greater laxity of the past Fathers.

The point is moot, but my view is that Basil probably knew of the strong Greek social condemnation of polygamy but was unable to cite ecclesiastical condemnation, because none existed. He therefore took it upon himself as a leader of the Church to set the tradition.[39]

AUGUSTINE (354–430)

Of final importance to our study is the great theologian of North Africa, Augustine. It is probably from this Father that we find the first clear teaching of marriage as a sacramental bond of indissoluble strength and permanent duration. Making his points in discussions of the three "goods" of marriage, he says (only) of Christian marriages that, based upon the analogy of Christ and the Church (Eph. 5:32), we should see marriage as a living union, in which there is "no divorce, no separation for ever."[40] Augustine thought that marriage was a sacrament because the Vulgate translated "mystery" as *sacramentum*, and it is Augustine himself who is credited with giving this term its present Church meaning, "an outward and temporal sign of an inward and enduring grace."[41] Marriage was a moral obligation and a sacred sign of the union between Christ and the Church. Because of this bonding, the marriage partners were placed under moral obligation to keep their marriage inviolate.

Nonetheless, it is not entirely clear that Augustine means to teach an ontic bond, that is, one that cannot be broken, rather than a moral bond, that is, one that *should not* be broken.[42] Though Augustine gives some voice to "indissolubility," it could be that his is simply an early, unclear statement of the position that marriage (only) *ought* to be permanent. His language seems amenable to the position presented in this book, that whatever oath-bond exists, it has only moral force, and whatever ontic-bond exists, it may be dissolved. On the last point, however, Augustine allows his language to soar (in the service of inhibiting marriage violation) beyond the text of Scripture and set a bad precedent regarding later Church teaching on the duration of *violated* marriages.[43]

It is also clear, however, that Augustine is opposed to the remarriage of the innocent spouse in the case of disciplinary divorce. In *Adulterous Marriages*, he insists that the synoptic writers must agree that all who divorce and remarry are guilty of adultery.[44] And, in the same work, we read of his negative response to the more liberal Pollentius, who advocated the remarriage of disciplinary divorcers.[45] It is tidy to suppose that such statements may only be harmonized with permanence discussions by supposing an indissoluble, ontic union, but I am, as yet, unconvinced that Augustine's theology was as refined in such matters as some would suggest. But if I am wrong in this, it is to be remembered that even the great Augustine may be wrong on a point of exegesis, and that the biblical text must remain the standard of moral teaching.

CONCLUSIONS

It would seem to me that the history of the early Church, up to Augustine, at least, is far more open to the remarriage of disciplining (male) divorcers than Heth and Wenham would suggest. Hermas seems to fire the first shots of a conservative trend away from the permissiveness of the Scriptures, and, though he was an influence on Athenagoras and Irenaeus, it was not until Chrysostom (in the East) and Augustine (in the West) that his position gained much acceptance.

There is also evidence of an alternative tradition that was even more lenient, and that tradition may well have been dominant in the Church, as evidenced by the *Apostolic Canons* and the *Canons of Basil.* It is likely that the reason for the overturning of the lenient tradition was the growing ascetic practice in the Eastern church.

It may also be the case that the ascetic tendencies of most of the conservative Fathers produced biased exegesis of the Gospel texts. But if so, what of the point that Heth and Wenham make in their treatment of Athenagoras? There they seek to deny that conservative early Church Fathers were too ascetically minded. These scholars argue that asceticism was primarily Eastern till the sixth century, at which time it was monasticism that caused conservative trends. In other words, when asceticism came West, that branch of the Church took a more liberal outlook. The Western church, they point out, was less stringent from the beginning. The church ecclesiastical, they suggest, seems to have "bucked" the monastic liberalization by standing nearly unanimous in condemnation of remarriage after divorce (where adultery was the issue).[46]

To this I reply that, aside from Hermas—a source of questionable value—the early, stringent position on remarriage of the innocent begins in the East and spreads West with Tertullian's Montanism. Their point that the Eastern church was more lenient by the sixth century is true, but true in spite of the fact that monasticism was a dominant factor in the East. In fact, there was increasing moral laxity in the sixth century anyway, even in the monastic movements.

Finally, it is to be remembered that aside from puritan monastic movements, the East was never as interested in canon law and systematic ethics as the West. This was increasingly so as the centuries progressed. In any case, it cannot be doubted that asceticism was the personal context of the most stringent of the Fathers cited above (i.e., Hermas, Clement, Tertullian, and Origen—even Basil). It *is* quite reasonable to suggest that their ascetic interests moved them to strict positions on the crucial matter of questionable sexual relations. Their interpretations should therefore be viewed with a critical eye. Morever, I believe that their proclivities more than offset their proximity to the biblical teachings.

What, then, do we conclude from this abbreviated study of the early Fathers? First, we do not conclude that the early traditions of the Church are "nearly unanimous" against *all* remarriage after divorce. It is more correct to present the evidence as a nearly unanimous prohibition of the remarriage of wives and guilty male spouses. Most of the early Fathers mustered to support the idea of no remarriage are really making a point against the remarriage of treacherously divorced women and treacherous divorcers, not disciplining ones. Second, with the exception of Hermas, no major Church Father explicitly prohibits the remarriage of disciplining (male) divorcers until Chrysostom during the fifth century. Third, there is evidence of a more lenient tradition that may have dominated the scene but left no extant or notable spokesman until Ambrosiaster in the latter part of the fourth century. Finally, there is only a shadowy teaching on the absolute indissolubility of the marriage bond until Augustine, and even he may have been referring to the *intended* moral duration of the marriage bond.

Notes

CHAPTER 1: COHESIVENESS IN THE MARRIAGE UNION

1. I accept the traditional authorship of Genesis, believing that Moses edited prior writings in the production of this part of the "historical prologue" to the Law.
2. I distinguish between the human writer and the Divine Author.
3. Karl Barth, *Church Dogmatics*, vol. 3/I (Grand Rapids: Eerdmans, ET 1976), pp. 207–20.
4. Mind that we are not saying that God is physical or has sexual distinctions. We are simply trying to point out that the general personality traits that we associate with the different sexes are both equally derived from the divine personality. God exhibits himself sometimes as the "head" (a male characteristic, 1 Cor. 11:3), sometimes as the "mother hen" (Matt. 23:37). God is neither male nor female. The traits can only be distinguished by and in revelation; but no separation, within him, is possible.
5. Some qualifications will be added to this general truth in subsequent chapters.
6. R. Laird Harris, et. al., ed., *Theological Workbook of the Old Testament* (Hereafter *TWOT*) (Chicago: Moody Press, 1980), Vol. 1, p. 38.
7. Cf. Gen. 24:5, where the servant of Abraham inquires of his master what to do if "the woman will not be willing to follow . . ."
8. One reason there is so much confusion on this matter today may be that parents themselves have never learned this and are therefore unable to teach it to their children. The reader is encouraged to read David Atkinson, *To Have & to Hold* (Grand Rapids: Eerdmans, 1979), pp. 77–82.
9. Ebenezer Henderson, *The Twelve Minor Prophets* (Grand Rapids: Baker, reprint, 1980), p. 13.
10. Some popular seminar speakers teach this distortion.
11. Some parents simply do not know when it is time to "let go." They would make their children their veritable slaves until they died, if given half a chance. They might also attempt to bear responsibilities for the offspring that the offspring themselves ought to bear. Or, someone else might attempt wrongfully to hold the parent accountable. The Scripture would seek to hold each person responsible for his or her own doings.
12. Paul E. Steele and Charles C. Ryrie, *Meant to Last* (Wheaton, Ill.: Victor, 1983), p. 25.
13. J. Carl Laney, *The Divorce Myth* (Minneapolis: Bethany House, 1981), p. 20.
14. Ibid.
15. Steele and Ryrie, *Meant*, p. 25.
16. We will consider the special case of the covenant with the Gibeonites later.
17. I agree with Kant's dictum that "ought" statements imply "can." If Jesus told his listeners they "ought" not to separate, that separation was a real possibility. It seems futile to prohibit the impossible! There are theological arguments for disagreeing

with Kant, but I find them wrongheaded, and too remote for further discussion in such a book as this.

18. A Isaksson, *Marriage and Ministry in the New Temple: A Study with Special Reference to Matt. 19.13[sic]–12 and I Cor. 11.3–16,* trans. N. Tomkinson with J. Gray (Acta Seminarii Neotestamentici Upsalienis 24; Lund: Gleerup; Copenhagen: Munsgaard, 1965).

19. See our discussion of this matter in chap. 7.

20. William A. Heth and Gordon J. Wenham, *Jesus and Divorce: The Problem with the Evangelical Consensus* (Nashville: Nelson, 1985), p. 101.

21. The use of "For . . ." usually implies relation to the prior context, but, since the word is in the quote, this may not be the case.

22. See further treatment of Eph. 5 in chap. 10.

23. K. L. Schmidt, *"Kallao," Theological Dictionary of the New Testament,* ed. G. Kittel, trans. G. Bromiley (Grand Rapids: Eerdmans, 1965), vol. III, p. 822. Hereafter: TDNT.

24. Ibid.

25. The difference between *sunzeugnumi* and *proskallao* appears to be that the latter term emphasizes the intention of the marrying parties, whereas the former emphasizes the fact of their union.

26. A form of the word is found in a similar context and with a similar thrust in Rom. 7:2.

27. Steele and Ryrie, *Meant,* p. 64.

28. Laney, *Myth,* pp. 21, 22.

29. Paul touches on this truth in 1 Cor. 15:39. However, it goes too far to argue, as Isaksson does, that "the original relationship between man and woman forms the explanation of man's strong desire to cleave to his wife. Since man and woman were originally of the same bone and flesh, a man leaves his father and mother and cleaves to his wife, in order that they may become one flesh, i.e., together form a family" (Isaksson, *Marriage,* p. 21). This would appear to imply that Adam, at the first moment of seeing the woman, realized that she was indeed part of his own body. A "hunk of [his] side" is the literal translation. But this is improbable. We know the facts, but Adam was simply observing that her skin was the same kind as his and her bone structure was the same, contrasted with that of the animals.

30. Heth and Wenham summarizing Isaksson (*Jesus,* p. 101).

31. Isaksson, *Marriage,* p. 21.

32. See, for example, Heth and Wenham, *Jesus,* p. 101.

33. Isaksson, *Marriage,* p. 19.

34. Heth and Wenham, *Jesus,* pp. 104, 106.

35. I do not deny that between God and humans (Eph. 5:31) organic union entails a nonphysical mystery.

36. Though it is a point that may be overturned by subsequent argument—see chap. 2.

37. Isaksson, *Marriage,* pp. 20–24.

38. Gordon Wenham, "The Biblical View of Marriage and Divorce 2—Old Testament Teaching," *Third Way* (London, November 3, 1977), p. 9.

39. Perhaps a fictional analogy may help. The fact that I was once a student of a particular school and had a falling out with the administration on some issue will affect my future relations with them and possibly with other schools affiliated with them. It would not inhibit me from matriculating at some other institution not affiliated with them. So too, the fact that a man might not be able to marry the close kin of a former spouse does not imply that he may not legitimately marry someone not so closely related to them.

40. I repeat that we shall treat the defilement of the divorced woman (Deut. 24:4) in chap. 3.

41. I believe that Jesus uses "one flesh" as a near synonym of marriage, insofar as he wishes to speak of marriage as a profound union rather than a mere association—the way the Pharisees seem to have understood it.

42. It is difficult to know what nuanced difference, if any, is intended by Paul. It could

be suggested that Paul prefers such a phrase to keep the "one-flesh" idea for licit marriages, but then why would he not have simply used that phrase and left the "one-flesh" idea completely alone? Then, too, Paul speaks of our relation to Christ in terms of "body" (1 Cor. 12:12). In 1 Cor. 6:15 Paul says that our bodies are the members of Christ—an apparently synonymous way of speaking.

43. A colleague, Thomas Cornman, recently pointed out to me that if marriage is a spiritual union, i.e., a union of spirits or souls, marriage would extend beyond the grave—an extension contrary to the teaching of Jesus in Mark 12:25. The soul, after all, is immortal. The upshot of this dynamic is that marriage must initially have been designed to be a temporal not a spiritual union.

44. See chap. 10.

45. These include marriage as a sexual union, marriage as a spiritual union, and marriage as a mystery.

46. D. A. Carson, in his comments on Matt. 19:4–6 in his Matthew commentary in *Expositors Bible Commentary,* ed. Frank E. Gaebelein (Grand Rapids: Zondervan, 1984), p. 412, argues, "If marriage is grounded in *creation,* in the way God has made us, then it cannot be reduced to a merely covenantal relationship that breaks down when the covenantal promises are broken." Without getting ahead of myself by attempting to exegete that passage, I feel it necessary to comment that the exact nature of the "grounding" remains undefined in that statement. I too would admit that Jesus directs those who ponder the ending of marriage to the Genesis language of organic union. But I do not agree that Jesus necessarily means more than to remind the Pharisees of the fact that marriage is intended to unite till death parts, rather than be the sort of institution they imagine, which may be ended by the man's decision. The most that we can say on this matter is that Jesus uses the fact of organic union in marriage to dissuade the sundering of the covenantal union that is marriage. On the other hand, it cannot summarily be argued as Carson has done that the breaking of (the most basic) covenantal vows will not end the moral obligations of marriage. I believe, in fact, that the breach of such promises supersedes any ramifications of organic union that exist, such that it may be said that the organic union itself has been sundered. The point I make is not that marriage may be reduced *merely* to a covenantal relationship, for I do not deny that under the protection of the covenant an organic union exists, but I believe that it is in error to suggest that marriage is essentially that organic union. It is essentially a covenantal relationship. To stress that the nature of marriage is covenantal rather than ontological does not lessen the impact of divine sanction for marriage. It is, after all, a covenant made before God, who initiated the institution of marriage in the first place. It is a "God-ordained unity" as a covenantal relationship.

CHAPTER 2: A COVENANT OF COMPANIONSHIP

1. A similar text is Prov. 2:17. However, closer inspection of that verse reveals that the companion of her youth, which the adulterous woman is leaving, is probably God himself, and the covenant that she has forgotten is most likely the Mosaic Law. By committing adultery, she has not only deserted her husband, but also her God. By being unfaithful, she has broken the Law, which proscribed adultery.

2. Heth and Wenham, following E. Neufeld's study of marriage in the Old Testament (*Ancient Hebrew Marriage Laws* [London: Longman's, Green, 1944], p. 89), distinguish four "essentials" of marriage: (1) intention of the parties to unite, (2) ratification by the parents, (3) ratification before public witnesses, and (4) physical consummation. Although I do not disagree about the particulars in this list, I do feel that these authors have missed significant "essentials." By ignoring the specifics of what the marriage partners pledge to each other, these authors leave their readers with the impression that marriage is some amorphous union, a covenant without terms. The net result of such explication is either of two undesirable conclusions. First, it could be argued that since the only "essentials" are matters of intention and social agreement, one or both of the partners might simply "opt out" of the covenant—a veritable "no-fault." Or, on the other hand, with Heth and Wenham, one might choose to believe that such a union cannot be broken because there is nothing tangible to break.

Heth and Wenham further this confusion by attacking the idea that marriage is essentially sexual. By analyzing several Mosaic laws, they show that marriage is not essentially sexual. I agree, but find the conclusions, and perhaps the placement, of this analysis to be confusing. It is confusing because, first, Neufeld did argue that consummation is an essential of marriage, and they agreed with him. They do not show how consummation is both an essential of marriage (# 4), yet nonessential when it comes to breach. How is their reader to know that this consummation does not establish a sexual bond that is broken by infidelity? On another level, their presentation is confusing because they do not reveal to their readers that though sexual relations do not make a marriage, sexual infidelity may well be a matter of essential covenantal promise that when breached does, in fact, dissolve moral responsibility of the innocent party to continue according to the agreements of covenant. (Cf. *Jesus*, p. 104.) It seems far less confusing to focus upon essential vows. This is what I attempt to do in this chapter.

3. Although others think that it is derived from the Akkadian *birtu*, "a fetter," which, in turn, is derivative of the word meaning "between." For further information on these matters, consult *TWOT*, vol. 1, pp. 128–30.

4. R. Killen and J. Rea, "Covenant," *Wycliffe Bible Encyclopedia*, eds. Charles Pfeiffer, H. Voss, and J. Rea (Chicago: Moody, 1975), p. 306.

5. We shall return to this discussion in a later chapter, but the reader is encouraged to read the books by James Hurley, *Man and Woman in Biblical Perspective: A Study in Role Relationships and Authority* (Leicester: Inter-Varsity Press, 1981) and Susan Foh, *Women and the Word of God: A Response to Biblical Feminism* (Grand Rapids: Baker, 1979).

6. It is really better to translate the word "bride price" rather than "dowry," as a dowry was given by the father of the bride to the bride as a present when she left the nuclear family, whereas a bride price was paid by the groom to the father of the bride. The dowry is an idea quite later than the times of which we speak.

7. It is estimated that the price came to about ten months' wages for the average Israelite. A man would have to be serious to give such a sum.

8. The text considers such relations between "consenting adults" *seduction.*

9. This conclusion may be supported by an obscure passage in Deut. 21. In vv. 10–14, we read of the case of a prisoner-of-war bride. The girl has no parents to speak for her, and the turn of subsequent events makes it clear that she wants out of the "forced" marriage. The text (which we will discuss again later) seems to be saying that this marriage may (perhaps "should") be *annulled* on that basis—the woman has the right to determine to whom she will be united. I believe in view of these passages it is safe to affirm that the woman functioned as an equal partner in the *making* of the covenant.

10. *WBE*, s.v. "Covenants," p. 387.

11. The reader is encouraged to read the highly instructive article in *MAARAV* 1/2 (1978–79):105–58 by Steven Kaufman: "The Structure of the Deuteronomic Law." I differ a bit with Kaufman on exactly where the division breaks occur but am convinced that, in general, his approach to the material is correct and crucial to the understanding of both Deuteronomy and the Ten Commandments.

12. My colleague at Moody John Walton has made much of the distinction between vows (Heb.: *nadar*) and oaths (Heb.: *shaba*). Vows were promises to God whereby a person pledged to give God something, either an object, a course of action, or a service. To make an oath was to bind oneself by *unbreakable* intention to do a certain action. *Theological Wordbook of the Old Testament* (s.v. "Shaba," vol. II, p. 900) further distinguishes an oath from a covenant. "An oath in the OT is a solemn verbal statement

or pledge that is affirmed, while the covenant is the substance of an agreement itself." Walton argues that in a marriage covenant, the person made a vow, an oath, and a covenant. The oath, he further argues, could not be broken, whereas the vow might be set aside. The implication, I suppose, is that, since an oath is involved, the man could not cease to fulfill his own oath-bound promise simply because his spouse had failed in keeping her oath.

This conclusion, however, could be reasonably and exegetically disputed. First, it is not clear that the marriage covenant involved an oath. I do not note a single biblical instance of such. The closest it comes would be the use of a couple of "oath" terms in Num. 5, where a suspected adulteress was expected to make an oath that she had not been unfaithful to her husband. But this is not the same thing as saying that she had originally made an *oath* to her husband that she would not be unfaithful. Secondly, *TWOT* notes that others could "clear" (Heb.: *naqa*) or free a person from an oath. Abraham made such provision in his instructions to his servant when that servant sought a wife for Isaac (Gen. 24:8). According to Num. 30, fathers and husbands could negate the oaths of their daughters and wives. Even more significant is the fact that the spies made a conditional oath to Rahab at Jericho. They would ensure her safety; she must make sure she stayed inside the doors of a house marked with a red rope.

We therefore contend that it is moot whether or not the basic idea of unalterable attestation in an oath affects the subject of marriage promises. It may be that no such absoluteness was involved in the marriage covenant, or (more likely) that circumstances such as the breach of oath by the spouse could have released the innocent party. In either case, it is going beyond the evidence to argue that the verbal bond in marriage is unalterable, and, therefore, I do not think we need concern ourselves unduly with these distinctions.

13. It may be more proper to speak of the exclusion of all other sexual relations, rather than just with other men. The only other possibilities are with animals (proscribed in Lev. 18:23) or other women (proscribed by implication in Lev. 18:22 as clarified in Rom. 1:26 f.). Thus all *porneia* would be *excluded*.

14. Even though a distinction was to be made between a concubine and a full wife—see our earlier discussion—the man's responsibilities to the concubine still existed.

15. The alternatives to this conclusion are repugnant: (1) God does not *know* about the needs of a full wife, (2) he does not *care* about the needs of a full wife, (3) he does not consider the full wife as of equal worth to the concubine (cf. Lev. 19:20 for a clear statement of the opposite valuing).

16. Indeed, it is most reasonable to presume that the free woman will have *more* rights than the slave. We have already noted above the presence of a law that enjoined greater *responsibility* upon the full wife. Why then presume that she has fewer *rights*?

17. Note that this provision is placed first in the Hebrew text.

18. Walter Kaiser, *Toward Old Testament Ethics* (Grand Rapids: Zondervan, 1983), p. 185.

19. It is interesting to note that elsewhere in his book Kaiser suggests that we follow the Septuagint, and even the reading of the Latin Vulgate, rather than the implications of the Hebrew (cf. p. 187). It seems hard to escape concluding that Kaiser is willing, at times, to grasp at straws to deny the possible morality of polygamy.

20. We should remember that the loss of an eye, or even a tooth, was much more serious in antiquity than it would be today. But it should not be our aim to culturally reduce the seriousness of such a malicious physical attack. Such abuse is inexcusable.

21. "Wife" is the proper translation here, even though, as noted earlier, the Hebrew word in question could be translated "woman." In this instance, to be a man's woman was to be *his*, i.e., his wife.

22. This is supported by the verses mentioned in the earlier discussion of how premarital sex *led* to a required public covenant, without which no marriage was considered to exist.

23. This did not mean that women slaves could not be married and carry on private lives in addition to their continued service.

24. See chap. 10.

25. Cf. chap. 6.

26. This presumes the apostle saw them as being transculturally relevant. If not, then we should be cautious even here!

27. This is not to say that some acts of sexuality in marriage may not be evil. It is possible to defile the marriage bed in thought or act with practices identified in Scripture to be evil. Cf. Heb. 13:4.

28. Geoffrey Bromiley, *God and Marriage* (Grand Rapids: Eerdmans/T & T Clark, 1980), p. 4.

29. For a deeper understanding of the differences between men and women, and how they complement each other, the reader is encouraged to read Arianna Stophenopolis's *The Female Woman* (New York: Dell, 1974).

30. Some will say that my view of marriage is humanistic, since it seems at first to so emphasize the social aspects of the marriage agreement. Such criticism is unfounded. Not only do I recognize such Old Testament statements, but I find them parallel to the saying of Jesus that God "joins" the valid partners together. I take this statement to be simply another way of making the same point about God being the witness and security of the marriage covenant.

31. To these "canons" of covenant one should add the fact, mentioned in the first chapter, that the couple commit themselves to each other on a permanent basis. This does not mean that this commitment to permanence *cannot* be broken, but that it *should not*. If one of the parties does break the vows (e.g., her sexual faithfulness), it would not be a breach of the vow-to-permanence for the offended party to divorce, for in that case, the adultery has already broken the moral bond of marriage and sundered the union.

32. Later I will argue that the breach of the covenant (level 2) by one of the parties who have a legal relationship (level 1) releases the innocent party from moral obligation to continue to fulfill his or her obligations on level 2.

CHAPTER 3: TERMINATION OF MARRIAGE ACCORDING TO THE LAW

1. There is at least a formal difference between breaking a vow and failing to keep one. "Breach" implies moral offense, whereas failing to keep may simply involve the fact that the other partner has nullified the covenant by prior breach. Thus, one ought never to break the oath/vow/covenant of marriage, but one does not break such a vow by not keeping promises to a spouse who has already abrogated the covenant.

2. She *was* his half-sister (Gen. 20:12).

3. "Abimelech" was apparently a title rather than a proper name. I do not follow the unfounded and hasty conclusion that the stories are really just three versions of the same story. Cf. Speiser's treatment in his *Genesis* in the Anchor Bible (Garden City, N.Y.: Doubleday, 1964), pp. 150–52.

4. The statement that what she did was "right" refers, not to the deception, but to her compliance in making the truthful but risky identification of herself as Abraham's sister. Making the identification on her part was not a sin, but obedience. His was the sin insofar as the risk was contrary to his covenant obligation to care for her.

5. Thankfully, my position does not rest solely upon these stories.

6. In point of fact, we might suppose that *death* should be considered the proper punishment for failure to provide, were there not other biblical reasons to suggest that a less stringent punishment is permissible—cf. Exod. 21:10 f.

7. Interestingly, paganizing influences seem to inhibit the death penalty for adultery. Compare also the practice of pagan Rome regarding the punishment for adultery.

According to the Julian Laws, the adulterer and daughter might only be killed with impunity by her father in his or his son-in-law's home if she was caught in the act. A husband could kill with impunity only if the adulterer of his wife was caught in the act in his home. He must divorce his wife. Perhaps the depreciation of women in pagan cultures accounts for this. Since the woman is often understood as a piece of property, she is not worth killing over. Naphtali Lewis and Meyer Reinhold, eds., *Roman Civilization; Sourcebook, vol. II: The Empire* (New York: Harper Torchbooks, the Academy Library, 1966).

8. It is interesting here to note the importance to the text of the woman having children, who will be able to care for her in her old age. Because of this concern, I conclude that any attack upon the well-being of the children is counted as an attack upon the well-being of the mother. This holds true whether the attack is passive or active. Compare this text with Deut. 21:15–17, which insisted upon the husband granting full inheritance rights to the children of unloved wives.

9. In line with the previous note, I also count it justified to end the legalities if the attack (active or passive) is upon the children of the woman. Although it is true that the father, in biblical times, had the right to end his children's lives, it must not be assumed that he exercised this right arbitrarily. If we were to assume this, then the easiest way to circumvent the strictures of Deut. 21:15 ff. would be by simply killing the children of the unloved woman. There is no need to ensure the inheritance of children so easily disposed of. We must rather assume that social pressures inhibited a father's ending of children's lives to the sorts of problems explicit in Deut. 21:18–21.

10. We should also remember that in ancient Israel only the man could initiate divorce. In this case it is presumed that he would not *of himself* initiate divorce and would, therefore, have to be forced to do so by the court.

11. I shall give one qualification to this at a later point. Here, I state the "general rule."

12. Other laws (Lev. 21:14, 22:13) pair the divorced woman with the widow. According to such legislation, the High Priest was not to marry any woman who was a widow, a divorced woman, or a (former) prostitute (e.g., Rahab). The implication of these passages is that there abides with the divorced woman a certain stigma. She has been used by another man. She is not pure. Therefore, she is not good enough for the priest or the High Priest. Her stigma appears to be somewhat less staining than that of the (former) prostitute, because she is lumped with the widow in Lev. 21:14. But we may presume that it is more staining than that of the widow, because she is categorized with the (former) prostitute in 21:7, where the widow is not mentioned as "off-limits" for priests other than the High Priest. It is not clear why these "purity" laws prohibited the priests from marrying these types of women. Clearly the (former) prostitute has (at one time) been guilty of moral offense, but, it must be assumed, she is cleansed of moral guilt by the time of possible marriage. It is also clear that the widow is not morally guilty of immorality simply by being a survivor. The divorced woman seems to stand in the middle. It is best simply to say that the Law viewed her as a woman who was less pure than a virgin, and that a pure virgin is the sort of woman that God wanted mated to the mediators. In other words, her stigma is *ceremonial* in these passages. For other comments regarding God's leaders and divorced mates, see chap. 10.

13. Kaufman, "Structure," pp. 136–37.

14. Since the Israelites were not to take to themselves "women of the land" (Deut. 7:3), we may assume that this woman was taken as a concubine, or that she became a convert to Hebrew religion and thereby qualified for the status of a full wife.

15. Recall that in Exod. 21 the text deals with two sorts of cases: first, cases in which the concubine is released without consummation (v. 8), and then cases in which the consummation is completed (by the son, v. 9, or by the man himself, vv. 10 f.).

16. Again, the reader is asked to wait for discussion of the assumed "right to divorce," implied by such texts, till a later point in the chapter.

17. Note that willful sexual relations practiced by an engaged woman as well as a married woman were punished by execution. Adultery was breach of a vow of monogamy subsequent to its being made. The Israelite women made that vow at the time of the betrothal, not at the point of consummation.

18. And it should also be clear that these penalties could end the marriage of a woman to a man who himself, and not she, is the offender.

19. There is no basis at all in the text for Kaiser's twice-made implication that the former *husband* has, in the meantime, remarried (Kaiser, *Toward,* pp. 200, 203). It is irrelevant to the text if the man has remarried, since polygamy is morally permissible. The law concerns itself only with the remarriage of the woman.

20. I do not take this to be the meaning of that passage. There is no real reason for believing that it is the husband-to-be that is in view. In fact, it is most incredible to suggest that it be such when Exod. 22:16–17, a law clearly dealing with premarital sex, prescribed only forced marriage for the couple. When no offense at all is assigned premarital sex in the Exodus passage, is it likely that a betrothed couple who engaged in sex would be executed? Certainly not!

21. See James B. Hurley, *Man, Woman in Biblical Perspective* (Leicester: Inter-Varsity Press, 1981), p. 100.

22. So David Atkinson in *To Have & to Hold* (Grand Rapids: Eerdmans, 1979), p. 103; C. M. Carmichael, in *The Laws of Deuteronomy* (1974), pp. 203 f.; Kaiser, *Toward,* p. 202; John Murray, *Divorce* (Philadelphia: Presbyterian and Reformed, 1961), p. 12; and others.

23. We needn't suspect that the referent here is exclusively emissions that are the result of masturbation.

24. In fact, the person who has the problem with his toilet practices might as well be someone who simply got "caught short," so to speak, and therefore is not guilty of *exhibitionism.*

25. One noted radio preacher has turned the divine intention upside down by insisting that God is permitting husbands to divorce their hard-hearted wives! But Jesus says, speaking to the husbands, "Because of *your* hardness of heart, Moses permitted *you* to divorce *your* wives," not "Because of the hardness of your wives' hearts, he permitted you to put them away."

26. Murray, *Divorce,* p. 13.

27. Ibid.

28. Ibid., pp. 14 f.

29. I presume that, as in the case of the seduced girl, the father may deny the marriage.

30. Of course, it is possible that, just as God permits the first husband to divorce her and allow her to remarry without specific condemnation, Scripture nonetheless means to imply offense in the case of all the woman's successive marriages. I reject this possibility in view of the contextual implications of both Deut. 24 and Matt. 5 of the woman's innocence. We will discuss fully the implications of the Matt. 5:31 f. passage, which also speaks of stigmatizing/remarriage, in a later chapter.

In interpreting this passage, it is tempting to make the following associations: (1) 24:1–4 parallels 23:17 in treating dependents in such a way that, like chattel property, they are passed back and forth from one sexual partner to another, being defiled in the process; (2) 24:1–4 parallels 24:5 in prohibiting actions that inhibit a person from fulfilling (marital) covenantal obligations; and (3) 24:1–4 is paralleled by Matt. 5:32 in containing an adulterization of the wife by means of a divorce and subsequent marriage to another—the second marriage being seen as "defiling" or "adulterous." Combining these elements, we have an implied condemnation of the divorce (with 24:5) and of the remarriage for which the first husband is responsible (23:17, and Matt. 5:32). The return is not mentioned in Matt. 5:32, because that was unnecessary. Jesus is only trying to clarify those issues in Deuteronomy that had *not* been understood.

Although I am impressed with the above relations, and consider conclusions drawn from them defensible in view of them, I ultimately rejected them for the following reasons: First, Deut. 23:17 does not explicitly discuss the passing back and forth. It was a point important enough to make overtly. Along with this, 23:17 does not closely relate to the major point of a return to the sending agent, the father. And, the more obvious link-terms that could have been used are absent, e.g., "defiled" and "abomination." Second, in 24:5 there is nothing intrinsically wrong with "war." It is not a "defilement." And, again, the emphasis of the latter verse is quite different from 1–4. It is opposed to the "going out," whereas they are concerned with the "coming back." The parallel may have some antithetical, formal relation.

More impressive is the reference to the Matthew "correction" by Jesus. Both passages speak of a divorce. Both speak of remarriage that is defiling. Jesus could be seen as correcting the interpretation that the divorcer and the remarrier of Deut. 24:1–4 are guiltless of adultery—the interpretation of the Pharisees.

But the textual connections between Matt. 5:32a and b are not as strong as a first reading suggests (see chap. 5), and the historical context of the Matthew passage, tied to Jesus' criticism of the Pharisees (especially as seen in Luke 16:18—see chap. 6), suggests another, perhaps better, alternative. Beyond this, nothing in the text of Deut. 24:1–4 proscribes the remarriage of the woman. That is very unusual in view of the context, near and far, of the Law. The return is clearly prohibited. But the going out and the remarrying are not. The Law usually moves quickly to inhibit acts of adultery. If the divorce and remarriage are adulterous as such, why does the Law not say so? A simple proscription of the divorce in the first place would have rendered unnecessary any commandment concerning an abominable return.

I believe that Jesus does identify the act of divorce as adultery on the part of the divorcing husband (see Matt. 5:32a, 19:9, and see chap. 5). But he seems to me to be saying that the divorce was allowed for the sake of the woman, that is, as a provision for her subsequent care. (See chap. 7.) Would it then make sense to understand Matt. 5:32b as a condemnation of the second husband? He would only be providing succor for the unjustly divorced woman—succor for which divorce was permitted in the first place. Highly doubtful. And the rejoinder that the permission was intended, not as provision for her, but as a concession for the hard-hearted husbands, runs amok on Christ's own condemnation of the Pharisees for not demanding the full rate of God's debtors (Luke 16:18). God is no Pharisee who tells the sinners that "boys will be boys!" Moreover, although the remarriage of Matt. 5:32b is clearly involved with adultery, in Deut. 24:1–4 the "defilement," whatever it is, seems only to relate to the matter of the return, which is clearly not in view in Matt. 5:32a or b. When the Law is so clear on executing for adultery that it even supplies a test for the wife of a suspicious husband—with the result that the woman is executed, why would it care so little about the defilement of Deut. 24:4 that it would not even prohibit its occurrence?—especially when the return is prohibited.

For these reasons, I have preferred the harmonizing interpretations of these passages set forth in this book.

31. I far prefer this interpretation to that offered by Yaron—trying to block a potential love triangle. C. Carmichael, in *The Laws of Deuteronomy* (Ithica: Cornell University Press, 1974), p. 205, correctly notes that this does not explain why the rule still applies when the second husband dies (R. Yaron, "The Restoration of Marriage," *Journal of Jewish Studies* 17 [1966]:8–9). I also prefer it to that offered by Gordon Wenham in his "The Restoration of Marriage Reconsidered," *Journal of Jewish Studies* 30 (1979):36–40. In that article Wenham argues that the first marriage made the woman the blood relative of her first husband, and therefore, paradoxically, for her to return would be for her to commit incest with him. Says he: "If a divorced couple wants to come together again, it would be as bad as a man marrying his sister" (p. 40). This interpretation is patently absurd, as I noted in chap. 1. If the marriage act has made them blood relatives, then the second intercourse (if not the first) of their *initial* marriage would be incest—forget the divorce. Any intercourse between near relatives, no matter what their marital status, would be incest. Wenham's "explanation" explains nothing.

32. Murray, *Divorce*, pp. 3–16. His conclusions are reflected in the work of David Atkinson, *To Have & to Hold*, pp. 102–5.

33. P. C. Cragie, *The Book of Deuteronomy: The New International Commentary on the Old Testament* (Grand Rapids: Eerdmans, 1976), pp. 304–5.

34. Yaron, "Restoration," p. 8.

35. Wenham, "Restoration," p. 40.

36. Heth and Wenham, *Jesus*, p. 110.

37. We need not assume that such an inhibition to divorce meant that if such a wife later became an adulteress the husband would not have a right to charge her and have her executed.

38. And, in fact, we do not read of a single instance of such abuse in the Old Testament.

CHAPTER 4: DIVORCE IN THE PROPHETS: DISCIPLINE OR ADULTERY?

1. Lewis and Reinhold, *Roman Civilization*, pp. 48 f.

2. It is probably not proper to see in God's response to David's adultery with Bathsheba a relaxation of the adultery penalties per se, for that event was an unusual case. David could only be executed by a government official beneath himself in the hierarchy. This would probably lead to anarchy or some form of temporary chaos in the kingdom; therefore, God punished him by taking the life of his son by Bathsheba.

3. This, of course, ignores the interpretation of the Song of Solomon as an allegory of such a relation. At this point I do not wish to deny that but only to set forth the case without dependence upon such a questioned interpretation.

4. For a similar analogy with a different starting point, read Ezek. 16:1 ff., where Yahweh is said to have married Israel, whom he had raised from an abandoned child of immoral parents. The betrothal theme in Ezekiel seems to speak of God's relation to Israel dating from the entry into the land, rather than from the Exodus, but in the end, the main strands of the analogy are the same.

5. I hold that Deut. 6–11 is a comment in the stipulations section of the general obligation to be loyal to God. Cf. Kaufman, "Structure," pp. 120 ff.

6. Supportive here are a number of verses that speak of God as a "jealous" God: Exod. 20:5; 34:14; Deut. 4:24; 5:9; 6:15; Josh. 24:19, etc. The discussion of marital jealousy was, of course, a matter of law itself in Num. 5.

7. I shall have more to say about this interesting story and the principles it holds for the divorce discussion, momentarily.

8. We know not the exact time of the writing of the 106th Psalm, but it reflects the same sentiment in its thirty-ninth verse. It could have been penned at anytime from the days of David to the deportation of Judah—though the latter is preferred in view of the clearer touch-points with captivity mentioned in the last two verses.

9. It is not clear from the Hebrew exactly what went on in the restoration. I prefer the interpretation that Gomer, no longer under the protection of Hosea's financial responsibility (cf. Num. 30), had fallen on economically hard times and had had to sell herself into slavery to continue to support herself (cf. Exod. 21). Hosea, in turn, purchased her for himself off the slave block. This seems to make the most sense of 2:16, which has the husband telling the woman that, in the day when she is restored, she will call me "Ishi" rather than "Baali." Since *baali* means "master," as of a slave being purchased, we can see how his immediate freeing of her to become his covenant companion (again) would result in his referring to himself, the same day, as her "Ishi," or *husband-companion*.

10. Francis I. Anderson, *Hosea*, vol. 24, The Anchor Bible (Garden City, N.Y.: Doubleday, 1980), p. 220.

11. Ibid., p. 221.

12. Ibid., p. 222.

13. E.g., H. C. Leupold, *Exposition of Isaiah,* vol. 2 (Grand Rapids: Baker, 1971), p. 190.
14. As in Deuteronomic Law on the eighth commandment: Deut. 23:1–4—which is probably the allusion here as it is explicit in Jer. 3:1 f.
15. The separation theme is, of course, real elsewhere in Isaiah: 54:5 ff. speak of Israel being forsaken only "for a brief moment." Note that the situation in Isa. 54:5 reverses the clear facts presented in all the prophets and seemingly speaks of Israel as an innocent bride forsaken by a hard-hearted husband. Such is not, of course, the case; God is only trying to create sympathy on our part for the restored one, and to emphasize the happiness of the restoration. But that is not to deny that the forsaking was real and that it merited the metaphor of a full divorce. Remember that that "moment" was the seventy years of captivity! The moment was in God's time, in which a "thousand years are but as a day."
16. Anderson, *Hosea,* p. 222.
17. Anderson here appeals to Deut. 24:1–4, which, I have suggested and argued earlier, refers to an *innocent woman* being put away.
18. Note here that the text simply says that *she* attributes those fields to her lovers, whereas 2:8 has already served us notice that these things came from her husband, without her knowing it!
19. Thus if a man murders another, he is known as a murderer subsequent to the crime, though he may not murder someone every day (or ever again). In a similar manner it is proper to speak of a divorced woman as an adulteress (if that was the grounds), though she actually bears no legal relationship to her former husband subsequent to the divorce.
20. The reader should remember that Hebrew verbs do not, strictly speaking, express time/tense, but rather complete or incomplete action. The Hebrew "perfect" is close to our *past* tense, but could express action continuing into the present. See the comment on Mal. 2:14 later in this chapter.
21. When, I argue, the parallel story of Gomer speaks of her as being bought back as a slave by Hosea (cf. 3:2). It was subsequent to the buying back that Hosea restored her to her position as wife.
22. Against this view, apparently Joel 1:8, where Judah is identified as a young woman who weeps for her husband—*ba'-al*—though it is possible to see that book as being written subsequent to the onset of exile but before the ratification of the "new covenant" referred to by Jer. 31. If the later date of writing is presumed, then, again, the term might be taken to refer to the master of a slave girl who has been left desolate by the death of her master, i.e., Israel left by God, the offended Master, to her own devices. The Yahweh/Israel husband/wife analogy is made more difficult yet by the fact that Yahweh had with the sons of Abraham a higher covenant (the Abrahamic) that also bound him unilaterally to union with the children of the "child of promise"—Isaac. Such a dual covenant has no exact parallel in the human marriage-divorce discussion, even though the Eph. 5 passage ties the husband to his wife by analogy to Christ's relationship to the Church, which latter relation arises out of the Abrahamic covenant. In this latter case, there is no *second covenant,* and the stated analogy is entirely silent with regard to the matter of divorce, whereas in the Mosaic covenant with Israel—as we have noted amply earlier—the correspondence with divorce is explicit.
23. *TWOT,* "lō." Vol. 2, p. 463.
24. There is some doubt as to the exact relation in time of the "separation" in Ezra 9 and 10 to that spoken of in Neh. 8, but I see no reason to deviate from the view that the Ezra passages predate Neh. 8 by some twenty years. Cf., for example, John Walton's *Chronological Charts of the Old Testament* (Grand Rapids: Zondervan, 1978), p. 71; or Keil and Delitzsch on *Ezra* (Grand Rapids: Eerdmans, reprint, 1973), p. 135. If this is correct, then we may presume that the Israelites who had preceded Ezra to Palestine already knew the Law requiring separation from the women of the land (Deut. 7:3 ff.). This is quite significant in that it shows that those who had intermarried had done so as an act of unfaithfulness, not simply out of ignorance.

Indeed "unfaithfulness" was precisely the charge brought by the peers of those who intermarried (Ezra 9:2). It will be crucial to understand this in order to properly analyze Paul's admonition in 1 Cor. 7, which is often pictured as countermanding the position set forth by Ezra.

25. Although it is true that this passage is most specifically referring to "fore-telling," I feel that "forth-telling" would also be included under the heading of speaking "presumptuously" a word in God's name.

26. I do not say this with glee. The sadness was real, and the trauma of losing a loved but illicit spouse and the incumbent problems involving the children of that illicit union are tragic, to say the least. But God means business with regard to sin, and the sadness is hardly his fault. The problems were caused by the apostates' sin, not by God's righteous correction.

27. Some have raised the question of whether or not the "marriages" spoken of in these chapters are real marriages. Heth and Wenham (1) suggest that Ezra's language implies that he did not see real marriage as having occurred by 9:14; they agree with George Rawlinson that these relations were mere "illicit connections" ("Jesus and Divorce," in manuscript, p. 163); (2) ask how "could these Israelites have made a covenant with God (Ezra 10:3) to put away their legal 'wives' if it is true that Scripture portrays marriage as a covenant made between husband and wife in the presence of God?" and finally, (3) suggest that Ezra's prayer (9:5–15) indicates that the marriages had not yet taken place.

  To this I respond (1) though the terms used by Ezra are not the normal ones for marriage and divorce, the terms do convey those ideas; and (2) there is no contradiction between the covenant to put away and the covenant to be faithful to their foreign wives, precisely because the marriages were not recognized by God. However, Heth and Wenham miss the mark completely by suggesting that because the "marriages" would be considered "invalid" in the religious sense, they were not marriages in a significant, legal sense. Ezra must have considered them "real" marriages because he speaks of the sin of the people as breaking covenant with God and of *intermarriage* with the people of the land (9:14). It is true that the main body of the Jews had not yet done as the apostates had, but what is the sin of the apostates that is identified? "Intermarriage." He is asking if the people as a whole are going to make a practice of apostasy. Finally, (3) I see nothing in the prayer (9:6–15) that indicates that intermarriage had not yet taken place. Indeed, Ezra says that "we have forsaken thy covenant" (v. 10). These words are in the context of returned exiles (v. 9). In v. 14 Ezra is not saying that no one yet has intermarried, but asking if the rest of the body of the returned exiles are going to follow in the steps of the intermarrying apostates. I do not see that Heth and Wenham have made their case.

  Let us simply say that there were in the time of Ezra legally authorized marriages, that is, legal according to the prevailing legal codes, that were illicit according to the Mosaic Law. The extent to which they were recognized by the people of the land was the very extent to which they should be ended according to the same law, because these "legal" unions were "illicit" in the eyes of God's Law.

28. Cf. the conclusion by J. C. Laney, *Myth*, p. 42.

29. Laney, *Myth*, pp. 40–41.

30. Laney makes note of this fact, but makes no significant use of it in drawing his conclusions (*Myth*, p. 41).

31. This tendency on their part is one of the more aberrant implications of the "Old Dispensational School" of C. I. Scofield and L. S. Chafer. There are newer and better forms of Dispensationalism. Cf. C. C. Ryrie's *Dispensationalism Today* (Chicago: Moody, 1959).

32. Steele and Ryrie, *Meant*, p. 67.

33. Laney, *Myth*, p. 48. I believe that God's attitude toward *improper* divorce is summed up here, but, of course, Laney is referring to *all* divorce.

34. The text is somewhat open to interpretation on the question, Does "has married the

daughter of a foreign god" necessarily refer to real marriages? It is usually granted that this was the case, and I agree with this interpretation.

35. I prefer this translation to one that makes Adam the object of the allusion—so Laney (*Myth*, pp. 47, 48), since the appeal to Adam would have been far less convincing than an allusion to Abraham, the Father of Israel. Herbert Wolf, in his commentary *Haggai and Malachi* (Chicago: Moody, 1976), pp. 93, 94, agrees with me. Joyce Baldwin, in her *Haggai, Zechariah, Malachi*, disagrees, but notes that mine is the preferred interpretation of the Jewish interpreters ([Downers Grove, Ill.: Inter-Varsity, 1972], p. 240). John Walton, of Moody Bible Institute, has pointed out to me that the Hebrew that stands for "that one" is used of Abraham in Isa. 51:2 and Ezek. 33:24. I cannot understand Baldwin's comment that to think of Abraham as the referent weakens the prophet's "main case" (Baldwin, p. 240), except to suggest that she has herself missed the prophet's main argument at this point. She has the prophet arguing for the sanctity of the initial *family*, whereas I see the prophet as arguing for the purity of the *nation* respecting *covenantal* faithfulness, i.e., husband-wife loyalty.

36. It is also likely that these men were taking the women as full wives, not as slave-wives as Abraham did. I have already suggested this as a way to harmonize several apparently divergent Mosaic laws—cf. chap. 2.

37. Laney, *Myth*, p. 48.

38. We shall see that the principle involved here is properly expanded by the Apostle Paul to cover *desertion* (1 Cor. 7:15).

39. I do not wish to quibble over semantics. *Adultery* is most properly a term that implies the unfaithfulness and treachery to a wife's vows. But I feel that I have adequately shown that men who break their covenantal vows to their "husband," Yahweh, deserve the term *adulterer*. A man who vows before God that he will provide for his wife, and then breaks that vow, is justly considered an adulterer toward God, and it is but a small jump to calling him an adulterer toward his wife. But I admit that the text of the Old Testament does not *explicitly* so identify the sin of a man who unjustly divorces his wife. I believe that our Lord does that in his great Sermon on the Mount. But we are getting ahead of ourselves.

40. See the comments on that passage in this chapter.

41. It has been suggested that the Hosea and Malachi cases differ in that the former speaks of a well-grounded divorce, whereas the latter speaks of a groundless divorce. The inference drawn from this is that groundless divorces do not really end the marriage, and well-grounded ones do. But I find that unconvincing. Remember that the Law did allow a treacherously divorced woman to remarry (Deut. 24:1–4). It surely would not have done so if she were an already bound woman. Sexual relations between bound women and men other than their husbands were always clearly identified as adultery, and the punishment was always clearly execution. (See chap. 3.)

42. I do not mean by this that the divorce ends moral obligation to repent and reconcile. But the moral obligation that requires the guilty to repent rests, not in the covenant of marriage itself, but in the deeper obligations of morality at large—for the Israelite, stated in the Mosaic Law. Hence it is proper for the guilty party to be identified as an adulterer or adulteress after the divorce and to say that they have in their continuing adultery broken the covenant with their God (e.g., Prov. 2:17). See my comments on the three levels of obligation in marriage at the end of chap. 2.

43. Marriages between illegitimate partners, e.g., close kin or interfaith marriages, were also "witnessed by God," but with no sense of divine insurance. This distinction helps one untie the semantic knot tied by such as Heth and Wenham when they say that "*all* marriages are witnessed by God" (emphasis added, *Jesus*, p. 112, et passim). Biblically speaking, they are equivocating on the term *witnessed*. And this equivocation leads them to draw confusing conclusions elsewhere (cf. *Jesus*, p. 163).

44. This might be qualified by the presumption that such people would be free to remarry if rejected by their former spouse.

45. Heth and Wenham draw the conclusion from Lev. 18 and Deut. 24 that "legal divorce

does not dissolve the marital union and the relationships established through that marriage." They believe that behind such legislation is the presumption that "some kind of relationship still exists between the original couple" (*Jesus*, p. 112). I agree with their latter statement, but not their first. Just because some relation still exists does not mean that the first marriage has not been sufficiently dissolved for a moral second marriage to be contracted. The very fact that valid second marriages are not forbidden by the text is testimony to this fact. God does not ethically stutter. The only proscriptions on remarriage in the Old Testament relate to the inhibition of further or continued evil. First, the woman is prohibited from returning to her degrading first mate (Deut. 24:1–4), and, second, an unrepentant adulteress is forbidden from continuing her adultery by practicing a second marriage (implied by the prophetic materials such as Jer. 3:1 ff.). But none of these moral and social elements of relationship to the former spouse imply a continuing marital bond of the sort inferred by Heth and Wenham. In fact, Deut. 24, far from evincing such a bond (so Heth and Wenham), absolutely denies one exists. For if such a continuing bond existed, the legislation could not possibly have morally denied a bonded husband the right to recover his own wife. Heth and Wenham must clearly seek a different definition of the "relationship" than they suppose.

CHAPTER 5: THE TEACHINGS OF JESUS ON DIVORCE

1. In this book, we will presume that the material in the Sermon preceded the Matt. 19/Mark 10 discussion with the Pharisees, with the Lucan (16:18) statements intervening. We will treat the statements in the text as genuine statements by our Lord. For those interested in the ordering and other methodological considerations, appendix C provides further information.
2. Note that 5:16 is conceptually different from 5:13–15. The initial verses paint a picture; 16 begins the admonition. After a brief digression concerning entrance into the kingdom (balanced by a similar digression, 7:13–23, that ends the "salt" section, 7:1–23), Jesus tells his listeners how to shine as a light before their neighbor in their behavior toward the neighbor (5:21–48), in their behavior toward God (6:1–18), and in their behavior toward themselves (6:19–34). Note the phrase "before men" that occurs in 5:16 and a similar phrase that occurs in 6:1, 5, 16. Note also the structural concept of light that reoccurs in 6:22, 23.
3. This somewhat peculiar order is the same as Jesus employs in the combined parallel accounts of his conversation with the "rich young ruler" (Matt. 19:16–29/Mark 10:17–30). I intend to deal with the structuring of the Sermon in more detail in a later work on biblical ethics.
4. See the excellent programmatic essay by Steven Kaufman: "Structure."
5. This against John J. Kilgallen, "To What Are the Matthean Exception-Texts (5,32 and 19,9) an Exception?" *Biblica* 61 (1980):102–5.
6. Cf. chap. 3.
7. I confess that I used to believe that he did, and once lectured at a gathering of theologians and Bible scholars on the subject. I suspect that I sounded rather convincing; I heard few objections. But I am now unconvinced by the kind of argument I used. There is a far better way to handle the text.
8. The phrase "you have heard that the ancients were told" identified the collection into two groups of threes.
9. The oft-alleged statement that Shammai permitted divorce only on the grounds of adultery seems to be better directed to Shammai's school. See Hurley's *Man, and Woman*, p. 100 (see chap. 3, n. 21), where he shows that Shammai's own position probably did not include adultery insofar as Shammai never quotes in his discussion of the Deut. 24:1–4 passage any of the adultery passages in the Law. Moreover, the presumption by Talmudic scholars is that Shammai meant by "unchastity" behavior characteristic of an adulteress, such as immodest dress, going without the veil, and

"spinning in the streets" (not as in turning around, but as in working on a spindle while waiting for a "john")—jSot 1.1.

10. Murray, *Divorce*, p. 20.

11. Ibid., p. 21.

12. Murray correctly notes that Deut. 24:1–4 has within it the implicit command for a divorcing husband to give his wife a writ. This is to say that, aside from questions regarding the right of the husband to divorce her, it is proper for him to clarify the resulting relationship by means of a writ (*Divorce*, p. 20). That this is implicit is clear once one realizes that Deut. 24:1–4 is designed to protect the wife from the husband's hard-hearted actions. It would be folly to permit her to be free from the man while at the same time legally clouding her freedom.

13. Laney, *Myth*, p. 66.

14. Bruce Metzger, *A Textual Commentary on the Greek New Testament* (London: United Bible Societies, 1971), pp. 13–14, 47–48.

15. One of the sadder and more frustrating experiences for me personally has been dealing with a friend who, though exceedingly conservative in his view of the Bible, is unwilling to admit that the Bible could voice such an exception. Knowing the grave lack of textual support for his view that the clauses are not genuine, he persists in the belief that "someday his prince will come," so to speak, and a flood of manuscripts will appear with the offending clauses omitted. Until that time he is willing to act as if the mythical manuscripts were reality and the better textual option. If such an approach to textual criticism were to become popular, the heretic Marcion should appeal for better treatment by the early Church.

16. Heth and Wenham, *Jesus*, p. 179.

17. Ibid., p. 247.

18. Carson, "Matthew," p. 415. Similar arguments are found in Dupont (*"Mariage et divorce dans l'evangile." Matthieu 19, 3–12 et parallèles* (Desclée de Brouwer, 1959), pp. 102–6).

19. B. Vawter, "The Divorce Clauses in Mt. 5,32 and 19,9," *CBQ* 16 (April 1954):160–62.

20. Heth and Wenham, *Jesus*, pp. 188–89.

21. Q. Quesnell, " 'Made Themselves Eunuchs for the Kingdom of Heaven' (Matthew 19:12)," *CBQ* 30 (1968):340 ff.; G. J. Wenham, "May Divorced Christians Remarry?" *Churchman* 95 (1981):150–61; Dupont, *"Mariage,"* pp. 93–157.

22. Carson, "Matthew," p. 416.

23. Cf. Kilgallen, "Exception," pp. 102–5.

24. Carson, "Matthew," p. 417.

25. Heth and Wenham, *Jesus*, p. 14.

26. Ibid., p. 15. They call this position the "nullity" view of the exception clause and draw from it the conclusion that fornication nullifies the marriage—"a legitimate marriage has never occurred." Fornication does not justify a real divorce, but only an annulment, and remarriage for the innocent husband would not be justified either. I rejoin that the exception clause is subjoined to a term that means "divorce," not merely annulment—for annulment to be at issue, the verse would have to relate to *porneia* occurring during the betrothal period, and that cannot be the main identification of the relationship that exists between the woman put away and the divorcer.

27. Steele and Ryrie, *Meant*, pp. 96–98.

28. Isaksson, *Marriage*.

29. So Heth and Wenham, *Jesus*, p. 176.

30. Ibid., p. 172.

31. This against Murray and others who insist that the disciplinary measure was *purely* optional.

32. Heth and Wenham, *Jesus*, pp. 173–74.

33. The reader can easily understand why I am not impressed with Laney's objection that Jesus and the Pharisees are not discussing betrothal but rather marriage in Matt. 19. Although this is true, it too misses the point that the Jewish mind would have

seen betrothal unfaithfulness as a foregone conclusion had the discussion become more specific. Cf. *Myth*, p. 70.

34. W. K. Lowther Clarke, "The Exceptive Clause in St. Matthew," *Theology* 15 (1927), pp. 161–62, and *New Testament Problems* (New York: Macmillan, 1929), pp. 59–60; Charles C. Ryrie, *The Role of Women in the Church* (Chicago: Moody, 1970), pp. 40–50, and *You Mean the Bible Teaches That?* (Chicago: Moody, 1974), pp. 45–46; C. Laney, *Myth*, pp. 71–77; and F. F. Bruce, *Paul: The Apostle of the Heart Set Free* (Grand Rapids: Eerdmans, 1977), p. 185.

35. Heth and Wenham further break this option down into those who make the interfaith marriages Jew-Gentile: J. Bonsirven, *Le divorce dans le Nouveau Testament* (Paris: Desclée, 1948); H. Baltensweiler, "Die Ehebruchsklauseln bei Matthäus zu Matth. 5:32; 19:9," *Theologisches Zeitschrift* 15 (1959):340–56, and *Die Ehe im Neuen Testament* (Zurich: Zwingli, 1967). The reference in Heth and Wenham is chap. 7.

36. Heth and Wenham, *Jesus*, p. 163.

37. Putting all this in the context of the day in which Jesus addressed the disciples, it would not have sufficed for Herod simply to have sent Herodias away. She had to be "put away." The public marriage required a public declaration that the relationship was completely severed (legalities and all). This brings us to probably the most telling response to Heth and Wenham. In Luke 16:18, Jesus does refer to an illegitimate marriage (i.e., Herod's) with the normal word for "marriage." But this illustration is of a different sort of "illegal marriage," so I put this discussion in a footnote.

38. I do recognize that some forms of dispensational theology relegate the Sermon to ages past or future, but do not wish here to take the time to refute them.

39. Laney, *Myth*, pp. 71–78.

40. Joseph A. Fitzmyer, "The Matthean Divorce Texts and Some New Palestinian Evidence," *Theological Studies* 37 (1976), pp. 213–21.

41. Laney, *Myth*, p. 78.

42. Heth and Wenham, *Jesus*, pp. 165–66.

43. Ibid., p. 161.

44. Murray, *Divorce*, p. 21.

45. Cf. Guy Duty's *Divorce & Remarriage* (Minneapolis: Bethany, 1967).

46. So W. Baur, W. Arndt, F. W. Gingrich, F. Danker, *A Greek-English Lexicon of the New Testament Greek and Other Early Christian Literature*, 2d ed., revised (Chicago: University of Chicago Press, 1979), s.v. "porneia"; J. H. Thayer, *A Greek-English Lexicon of the New Testament*, corrected ed. (New York: American Book Co., 1886), s.v. "porneia"; Thayer; etc. Kittel, Hauck/Schulz, *TWNT*, s.v. "pornā," vol. VI, pp. 579–95, is vague, choosing to spread the smorgasbord of scholarly opinion, with a slight leaning toward a restrictive definition, but only because of the views of scholars already sufficiently criticized in this book and in Heth and Wenham.

47. Laney's objections are actually brought to bear against the idea that you can be divorced/remarried on the grounds of "adultery." I have tried to cull out his objections to the definitional issue alone. Both Laney's arguments are found in *Myth* on pp. 68–69.

48. See Laney, *Myth*, p. 52, and also Steele and Ryrie, *Meant*, pp. 105, 112.

49. Laney, *Myth*, p. 77. Actually the word in the Matthew 15:19 and Mark 7:21 texts is *moicheia*, a variant of *moichos*.

50. But it is probable in this latter case that God picks out the more likely instance of fornication to highlight it against the backdrop of the marriage discussion.

51. Note that even the discussion of a woman's groundless divorce of her husband (5:32b)—see chap. 6—has the complicitous male as the focus of attention in the Sermon.

52. This perhaps goes some way toward explaining why Paul speaks of his "instruction" (1 Cor. 7:11 ff.) as his own, not the Lord's. The issue in the instruction is not *porneia*, at least in the usual sense of that word, but, rather, failure to provide and to stay in the covenant, especially the (unsaved) husband's failure to remain with the (be-

lieving) wife—a matter of failure to provide. Thus Paul is legitimately applying the principles of the Law (Exod. 21:10 f.), though not directly using the instruction of Jesus.

53. Cf. Heth and Wenham, *Jesus*, pp. 198–99.
54. His mercy and forgiveness must be seen in the context of forgiveness and the fruits of righteousness.
55. I will restate this important criticism in chap. 7, when we deal with the commonly misunderstood idea that Moses' concession was a compromise on behalf of hard-hearted husbands.
56. Murray, *Divorce*, pp. 21–22.
57. Ibid., p. 22 n.
58. Ibid., pp. 23 f.
59. R. C. H. Lenski, *The Interpretation of St. Matthew's Gospel* (Minneapolis: Augsburg, 1943), pp. 232–33.
60. Murray, *Divorce*, p. 22.
61. This "natural" appears to me to be grammatically "unnatural."
62. Murray, *Divorce*, p. 23.
63. It would seem to me that the upshot of this in the Sirach passage would be to see the aorist passive form tied to the context as producing the effect of an aorist middle: by her action she has made herself to suffer adultery.
64. Murray, *Divorce*, p. 23.
65. Ibid., p. 24.
66. We know it to be "unjust" because the angry person is told to "be reconciled"—a word that implies guilt on the part of that person.
67. Carson ("Matthew," p. 153) rejects Lenski's theory—which is assigned solely to B. Ward Powers, "Divorce and the Bible," *Interchange* 23 (1938):159—"because it has no counterpart in [Matt. 19:3–12]." He further contests that "stigmatizes her as an adulteress (even though it is not so)" is not proper, because the Greek uses the verb, not the noun. Carson says that "the verbal construction disallows Powers's paraphrase."

  However, neither of Carson's points is convincing to me. In the first place, why is it necessary that all the points in Matt. 5 appear also in Matt. 19? Carson does not tell us. Secondly, Carson seems favorable to the NIV's translation of the verb as "causes her to become an adulteress." Does this translation not turn the verb into a noun as well? Why not simply translate it "causes her to become stigmatized as an adulteress"?

  Confusion enters this discussion, however, when later in his commentary Carson rejects "makes her an adulteress" in favor of the traditional makes her "to commit adultery" ("Matthew," p. 417). Of course, I prefer to translate the clause "causes her to be adulterized," which, I think, more properly translates the verb as a verb, but I think that Lenski's and Powers's idea is not wholly wrongheaded. As I noted earlier, *stigmatization* could be involved in the "adulterization" as a secondary concept, which determined the choice of the passive voice by Matthew.
68. Carson, "Matthew," p. 152.
69. BAGD, s.v. *"poieo."*
70. I have already argued that the saying about divorcing an innocent woman is essentially *independent* of the second saying concerning someone marrying a divorced woman (5:32b).

CHAPTER 6: THE TEACHINGS OF JESUS ON DIVORCE, CONTINUED

1. Further support for the idea that this woman is also guilty of adultery will be presented a bit later on, when we look at the possible relations of this logion to the preceding one.

2. It is hard to find a proponent of this position, but I suspect that certain of the early Fathers come very close to it. Justin Martyr, for instance, probably quotes this verse along with ones relating to male lust and male celibacy. He passes in silence over the matter of women marrying divorced men (*First Apology*, chap. 15). But it may simply be that we do not have enough of this Father's teaching to comprehend its true breadth. (See appendix F.)

3. Lenski, *Interpretation*, p. 230.

4. Ibid., pp. 234 f.

5. The problem of knowing which voice Jesus intended would not have occurred to his listeners, since Aramaic—which we presume Jesus spoke—has no middle voice to confuse with the passive. He would have conveyed his point with a pronoun like *himself*.

6. Although the middle is used less often in Greek, the deponent passive or middle *moikatai* ("commits adultery"), in the same verse, conveys the sense of an active or middle. Further, the deponent *apolusasa* tied to the pronoun ("her") in the potentially parallel clause in Mark 10:12 yields something very much like a middle: "her, the one having dismissed." The more obvious parallel in Luke 16:18b is not helpful, because it uses exactly the same term as in our question.

7. I would choose her over the guilty woman, who is alluded to in the except clause.

8. Nor does it help to look for "a" person in the first saying, since both the divorcer and the divorcée have the definite article.

9. I shall return to this matter later to argue more forcefully from context that the middle is the correct alternative.

10. *Moikeuthanai*, on the other hand, comes from the verb *moikeuo*, which is not deponent, thus permitting Lenski's and my previous consideration of *moikeuthanai* to be *passive*.

11. Thus, all Lenski's attempts to substantiate the form as passive (or middle) are useless. Murray, who replied to Lenski, argued for the middle voice. His arguments support the concept of the verb as deponent, though he does not speak to that point directly. Murray, in voicing his opposition to Lenski, strongly objects to interpreting the verb form as a *passive*, choosing instead to identify it as a *middle*. To support his position, he cites similar verses, some of which employ exactly the same verb form, which clearly show that there is adultery in remarriage (Matt. 19:9; Mark 10:11; and in the LXX: Jer. 3:8; 5:7; 7:9; 9:1; 23:14); he insists that the verb intends "active participation in the sin of adultery" (*Divorce*, p. 23). Although some of the verses chosen by Murray would seem to imply that active participation comes only when the woman is guilty already (cf. the passages in Jeremiah), his contention seems well grounded when it comes to the Gospel usages of this particular verb form. A fair consideration of all the instances seems to reveal without a shadow of a doubt that Jesus is employing the more rare form for the purpose for which it was created: *emphasis*. This man who marries this woman is himself committing adultery.

12. I presume that this position would be held by Heth and Wenham, e.g., *Jesus*, p. 135. They do not spend much time on this part of Matt. 5:32. They make two incidental comments about clause *b*, and call it an "unqualified conditional" statement (*Jesus*, pp. 135, 223, n. 71). Elsewhere (p. 50), they seem to agree to call it an "unconditional statement." But I suspect that this is just a slip. The former is correct. They criticize the NEB and the NIV for translating 32b in a manner that identifies the woman of clause *b* as the guilty woman of clause *a*, thereby limiting the condemnation of remarriage to that class of divorced women.

13. Though it is in a section of criticism of the Erasmian view, the following seems to be a statement of Heth and Wenham's own position: "For, if the woman cannot remarry she is not technically divorced, but separated. The marriage bond with her husband still exists: that is why remarrying a divorced woman is adultery (5:32b). Thus her former husband is really becoming a bigamist if he takes a second wife since the marital bond with his former spouse has not been dissolved" (*Jesus*, p. 50).

14. They comment of the Erasmian view: "[To suppose] that the divorced adulteress is

refused the right of remarriage, but the innocent husband may remarry (= Erasmian view) . . . is effectively to allow polygamy!" (Heth and Wenham, *Jesus,* p. 50).

15. Believing biblical polygamy to be moral, we can see why, as Robert Gundry correctly notes, "Matthew writes nothing about the question of the remarriage by the husband who has divorced his wife for unchastity" (*Matthew: A Commentary on His Literary and Theological Art* [Grand Rapids: Eerdmans, 1982], p. 90). Of course not; polygamy presumed the right of a husband to take another wife. But I do not agree with him when he immediately and boldly states that "Luke gives an unambiguous negative answer" to the question of the man's right to remarry. See chap. 7 on this point.

16. Chap. 2 and appendix B.

17. Murray, *Divorce,* p. 26.

18. Ibid., p. 42.

19. Ibid., pp. 70–72.

20. Though in the illustration chosen here there is no exact parallel, because there is a sense in which the body of the guilty remarrier is no longer the property of the former spouse. Divorce is somewhere between theft and death, for which there cannot be restitution.

   Elements of this position are the most likely interpretation of some practices in the early Church. (See appendix F.) Those Fathers consistently insisted upon disciplinary divorce—they did not see it as disrupting an ontological and especially a moral bond. They saw the refusal to so divorce as a moral lapse. Thus, they must have felt that that sort of bond was broken by the offense. Second, in the clearest cases, Justin Martyr, for instance, it is evident that the reason for inhibiting the remarriage of the divorced parties is to facilitate the repentance of the guilty. This expansion goes beyond the text before us, but they used others to support it.

21. See the point made by Gundry, *Matthew,* p. 91.

22. Even if the divorce was not in a Jewish court, that fact is unimportant.

23. And I do not see adequate reason for denying the genuineness of the latter dominical saying.

24. The Old Testament, of course, condemns all three. Lust: As a man thinks in his heart, so is he (Prov. 23:7). Divorce: Let no one deal treacherously against the wife of your youth (Mal. 2:15). Remarriage: She goes from him and belongs to another— harlotry (Jer. 3:1–11).

   David lusted and wrested from Uriah his rightful wife. There was no reason to force Uriah to divorce her, because David got rid of Uriah by a different kind of treachery—death (2 Sam. 11). About all that can be said in David's behalf is that he committed no treachery against any other of his wives in the process!

25. Though it is doubtful the Pharisees would have verbally supported such an impression, we must remember that the teaching Jesus wished to correct may in this case have been a matter of Pharisaical *omission* rather than public teaching. Note that the "you have heard" is missing from this combined saying.

26. Josephus, *Antiquities of the Jews,* 18.5.4.

27. Laney, *Myth,* pp. 51–60.

28. Murray, *Divorce,* pp. 43–54.

29. *Luke,* vol. 16, *The Pulpit Commentary,* ed. H. D. M. Spence and Joseph S. Exell (Grand Rapids: Eerdmans, 1950), p. 65.

30. Laney, *Myth,* pp. 58–60.

31. This in disagreement with Hoehner's comment to that effect in *Herod Antipas: A Contemporary of Jesus Christ* (Grand Rapids: Zondervan, 1972), p. 138 n.

32. Incidentally, such analysis reveals that this parable is a "prophetic parable," for John's Gospel relates that God, in his ever-wooing grace, did in fact send them a departed one named Lazarus to serve as a warning of their pending fate. But according to John 11 f. they only wished to send Lazarus back to his grave, in order to preserve their "place" in the nation. How desperately sad!

33. Heard in classes at Trinity Evangelical Divinity School of Deerfield, Ill., 1970–72.

34. To be more specific, I would add that the condemnation is of the guilty party who has not attempted to reconcile. I do not believe that the text means that a guilty party may not remarry if the "innocent" party refuses to reconcile. The passage clearly deals with a process of divorce to marry another. There is no thought here at all of a guilty party who has tried to reconcile, has been unable (for one reason or another) to have the marriage restored, and has subsequently found a new partner. I see no prohibition here of that sort of remarriage. Remember that the paradigm case of restitution is God and Israel. Israel, the guilty party, should have come to their senses and sought reconciliation to God. But God would never have turned them away if they had! Human spouses, alas, show how unlike God they are in this respect. Those "innocent" parties who are so inclined should take the parable of the unforgiving steward to heart.

CHAPTER 7: THE TEACHINGS OF JESUS ON DIVORCE, CONTINUED

1. Since the Scripture does not place any moral onus upon one divorcing for such a ground.
2. Cf. tape series on divorce by J. MacArthur, Jr.
3. Nor would it have been in the best interest of any Pharisaical school to have Jesus *agree* with them. At this juncture in his ministry, the questioning Pharisees were indeed trying to discredit, not credit, the Nazarene!
4. Joachim Jeremias, *Jerusalem in the Time of Jesus* (Philadelphia: Fortress, 1969), p. 371. This is only the figure for one city near Jerusalem, but in view of the lack of data, this must stand as typical unless amended by subsequent studies. I cannot see that the geographical area in which the question arose ("beyond the Jordan") would differ markedly from the sociology of the town cited.
5. It is true that divorce was far more prevalent among the Pharisees themselves (cf. Hill's *Matthew*, as cited in Carson's "Matthew," p. 411), but this is not the point. The argument is that the Pharisees were trying to discredit Jesus among the common people, not among themselves.
6. Luke 3; Matt. 11; and probably Matt. 5:32 f. and Luke 16:18.
7. See my discussion of the Old Testament teachings, especially chaps. 3 and 4.
8. So John MacArthur in his tape series on divorce.
9. In this light, we cannot but be astonished by the remarks of John MacArthur when he asserts that God, by the concession, is permitting righteous men to put away incorrigibly treacherous wives! (Hear his tapes on the subject of divorce/remarriage.)
10. Dana and Manty, *A Manual Grammar of the Greek New Testament* (New York: Macmillan, 1927), p. 202.
11. I actually have heard conservative evangelicals affirm this option. Some have spent days searching the context of Deut. 24:1–4 to find the places where the inspiration breaks! Marcion could have been an inerrantist! But even Murray adopts this view of Moses. Says he: "The Mosaic permission was, therefore, a departure from the creation ordinance and from the practice to which it obligated men." I see this as making God a compromiser of moral principle. D. A. Carson suggests the abrogation rests in the fact that "Jesus' judgments on the matter are therefore both lighter (no capital punishment for adultery) and heavier (the sole exception being sexual sin)" ("Matthew," p. 417). I cannot agree to either point. In the first place, as the introductory statements in the Sermon reveal, Jesus is not *making* law, only *interpreting* it. Second, Jesus is only accommodating the prevailing law with regard to execution— as did the prophets Hosea and Jeremiah. Jesus does not want to fight the issue of whether it was proper for foreign overlords to suspend capital punishment. Divorce was clearly an acceptable substitute, *under the circumstances,* for capital punishment, but Jesus does not wish to make the substitute judicial or to give it legal status. Moreover, I believe that Carson's interpretation of Deuteronomy is incorrect and

that that has misled him regarding the second point. That God permitted the protective divorce of innocent wives by husbands set on breaking their vows by divorce does not mean that God gave moral sanction to the men so divorcing their wives on the basis of Deut. 24. God has always morally permitted divorce only on the grounds of infidelity to vows. Any other divorce implicates the divorcer in adultery.

12. This is especially true of the Hillite school.
13. Lev. 20 required her to be executed for that offense.
14. It is sad to note that Heth and Wenham, in their work on the divorce teaching of Jesus, take such a cavalier attitude toward the God/divorce/Israel language of the Old Testament. They say that one should not take such language seriously, because if one does, one will also have to take the God/polygamy language seriously. Exactly! And properly! But the *a priori* reigns in their thinking. (*Jesus,* p. 136.)
15. Cf. appendix D.
16. Heth and Wenham mention word frequencies and stylistic tendencies in Matthew's early chapter that confirm this rule; *Jesus,* pp. 99–100.
17. Ibid., p. 114.
18. Ibid.
19. Ibid., p. 133.
20. Ibid., pp. 115–16.
21. Ibid., p. 117.
22. Ibid.
23. This is not to say that the idea of required divorce in such cases would be improper. See both my chapter on the prophets and Heth and Wenham's own findings regarding the views of the early Church Fathers! (*Jesus,* chap. 2.)
24. I also believe that had it been there, it probably would have supported the "Erasmian" option: "Except where there has been fornication, divorce and remarriage is adultery."
25. D. A. Carson makes almost precisely the same point about this alternative. Cf. "Matthew," p. 416.
26. At no point is the weakness of Heth and Wenham's "syntax argument" more evident than in their attempts to illustrate what they mean. In a footnote (*Jesus,* p. 234, n. 20) they offer the following example, introduced by the comment that cremation by a killer is "suspect," since murderers sometimes do that to destroy evidence:

> 1. To kill someone and cremate them is murder. (Cf. Luke 16:18; Mark 10:11, 12)
> 2. To kill someone, if it was not by accident, is murder. (Cf. Matt. 5:32)
> 3. To kill someone, if it was not by accident, and to cremate them is murder. (Cf. Matt. 19:9)

They forthwith conclude that "killing as such and cremation are always murderous. Only accidental killing not followed by cremation is not murderous. Only divorce for immorality not followed by remarriage is not adulterous."

This is an illustration of questionable value. In the first place, "killing" and "cremation" are, "as such," morally neutral as far as I am concerned. And though this fits my understanding of the parallel term in the Scripture (i.e., "divorce" and "[re]marriage") I am sure that Heth and Wenham do not hold either biblical term to be morally neutral. "Divorce" is said to be absolutely prohibited (p. 198). The only way I can understand this is to say that divorce is always a moral wrong. (See back cover of *Jesus.*) Thus, unless Heth and Wenham believe that "killing" is absolutely prohibited, they have chosen a poor analogy. And as for "remarriage," they say it is always the sin of adultery (ibid.). It is possible that they think cremation always to be wrong, but they do not say that it is "as such" in their illustration. Thus they have chosen a very poor analogy indeed.

Next, notice that the statements themselves are ethically suspect. Who would make such a statement as number 1? The state might well execute a murderer and cremate the body. Would that be murder? Hardly! Number 2 is also only a general way of talking. Execution is not "accidental," but it is not murder. Therefore, number 3 is also not a true statement. The state may execute (not by accident) a murderer and cremate the body, but not be guilty of murder. Here common and careless manners of speaking have been paraded before us as ethical reflection. And make no mistake about it, the application to the divorce discussion is just as careless and misleading.

It is true that the Bible says that divorce and remarriage are adultery in Luke 16:18, but it is open to question exactly what that means. Just as one could say that to kill and cremate is murder, reflection on other ethical truths reveals the statement about killing to be only a general rule. So, too, the statements in Luke and Mark may only be general rules. It is true that just as it is not proper to describe accidental homicide as murder, it is also true that it is not proper to describe divorce grounded in *porneia* as adulterous. However, to argue that divorce is yet some other kind of sin would be as wrong as calling accidental homicide a moral offense. Moreover, to suggest that killing (though accidental) when followed by cremation is the whole of it murder is as clearly nonsense as suggesting that divorce (which is not adultery) when followed by remarriage is the sin of adultery. Just as it is improper to say that killing and cremation *as such* are always murderous, so too it is improper to conclude that divorce and remarriage are always adultery. And although it is true that accidental homicide not followed by cremation is *not* murderous, it is certainly wrong to say that accidental homicide followed by cremation *is* murderous. Can the form of disposal of a body *as such* make either the killing or the combination of killing and disposal murder? So too, it is improper to speak of divorce for *porneia* when not followed by remarriage as only "not adulterous." Actually, the relation of this last pair is so confusing that it is hard to see what Heth and Wenham are driving at.

A better illustration would be:

1. To legally nullify a contract and make another is dishonest. (Luke 16:18)
2. To legally nullify a contract, unless it is because of improper actions on the part of the partner, is dishonest. (Matt. 5:32)
3. To legally nullify a contract, unless it is because of improper actions on the part of the partner, and to make another contract is dishonest. (Matt. 19:9)

In each, the issue is the improper nullification of a contract. Number 1 is the simple statement that it is wrong to break a valid contract for the purpose of making another. The second is an even simpler statement, but the exception to the rule is stated as well. In the third, the two are put together, informing us that it is wrong to break a contract (unless there is justification) simply to make another. The making of the second contract is only mentioned as evidence that the nullifying party is capable of making and keeping contracts. Otherwise, it would not have been wrong for the party of the first part to go ahead and make a contract with the party of the third part. And if the ending of the contract was legitimate, then one should think nothing of the setting of a new contract.

27. For further treatment of the except clause's meaning, see chap. 5.
28. Heth and Wenham, *Jesus,* p. 218, n. 17.
29. See appendix B.
30. It is my belief that Deut. 24:1–4 is the proper location to look for teaching relative to this subject rather than Luke 16:18, since in the latter verse Jesus is simply trying to identify the failure of Pharisees to teach and follow *existing* Old Testament morality.
31. Codex Vaticanus, especially.
32. Sinaiticus includes it.
33. I do not mean to minimize the sin of the women being invalid partners. I only wish to point out that had they been valid and the prior marriages left unbroken, there would have been no condemnation by God through the prophet.
34. Cf. chap. 5 and the comments of Heth and Wenham, *Jesus,* p. 120.
35. BAGD, s.v. "Kai."

36. Cf. chap. 2.
37. Cf. chap. 8.
38. I shall have more to say about "all things being equal" and the point at which guilty parties are released from their obligation to "not remarry" when we look at the emphasis of the individual Gospel records.

   "And he who marries a divorced woman commits adultery." Though some early manuscripts support this clause, it seems to have been assimilated from Matt. 5:32b. In any case, we have previously discussed this clause in chap. 6.
39. Heth and Wenham, *Jesus,* p. 104.
40. They do believe that there is a proper ground for divorce.
41. William Gothard (Supplement to the Supplementary Alumni Book, vol. 5, 1979, p. 2) alleges astonishment; D. A. Carson ("Matthew," p. 419) properly denies it.
42. Laney, *Myth,* p. 65.
43. Cf. chap. 5 for a full discussion of the meaning of this term and a treatment of the different views that are held about its intended meaning.
44. Carson, "Matthew," p. 419.
45. Heth and Wenham, "Jesus and Divorce" (in manuscript), p. 40.
46. Ibid., p. 41.
47. Heth and Wenham, *Jesus,* p. 56.
48. Ibid., p. 54; W. D. Davies, *The Setting of the Sermon on the Mount* (Cambridge: Cambridge University Press, 1964); D. R. Catchpole, "The Synoptic Divorce Material as a Traditio-Historical Problem," *Bulletin of the John Rylands University Library* 57 (Autumn 1974): 95.
49. Heth and Wenham, *Jesus,* p. 63.
50. Carson, "Matthew," p. 419.
51. Of course, Carson, being a strong Calvinist, might well argue that human and natural causation is not at odds with divine sovereignty, but that conclusion is foreign to the statement of the text at this point. All Jesus says is that celibacy can arise from different causes.
52. Quesnell, "Eunuchs," pp. 341–42 (see chap. 5, n. 21); Dupont, *Mariage,* pp. 161–220 (see chap. 5, n. 21); Hermas, *Mandate,* 4.4.1–4; J. D. M. Derrett, *Law in the New Testament,* and *TDNT* 6:592, lines 2–5. Derrett's view, highlighted by Heth and Wenham in an appendix to *Jesus* (pp. 204 f.), arises from his undebatable commitment to the interpretation of Gen. 2:24 as teaching indissoluble monogamy (his = exclusively his). The exclusivity I do not doubt, but I deny the monogamy. The woman was to be exclusive to him but not the reverse. Derrett has overread the text. This false start causes him to make further mistakes in interpretation down the way. Seeing Deut. 24:1–4 as a prohibition of all remarriage since remarriage defiles an existing relation creates a three-in-one monstrosity. Jesus is presented in the Gospels as permitting an offended spouse only to clean his house of the adulteress—but not to remarry, since his one-flesh relation, though defiled, still exists. Remarriage of the innocent is a breach of the seventh commandment, which is interpreted by Derrett as forbidding the marriage of any unmarried people who will not or cannot marry. Believing the Bible teaches that the one-flesh bond can be multiple (for the male) and broken (by willful breach of covenant), I reject Derrett's theory.
53. Heth and Wenham, *Jesus,* p. 59.
54. Cf. ibid., pp. 58–61.
55. I agree with D. A. Carson, who rejects Dupont (*Mariage,* pp. 161–222) and Moloney ("Matthew 19, 3–12 and Celibacy: A Redactional and Form-Critical Study," *Journal of the Study of the New Testament* 2 [1979]:42–60), who argue that the eunuch statement means to exclude *remarriage.* As Carson notes, " 'eunuch' is a strange figure for continence after marriage, especially since if the divorced spouse died, the survivor could remarry (Dupont's view)." Carson, "Matthew," p. 418.
56. And, I might add, this interpretation is quite in accord with the "Erasmian" position. I hasten to note, however, that neither I nor Murray wish to be "modern proponents of Erasmus." That identification, now made popular by Heth and Wenham in *Jesus,*

creates unfortunate guilt by association for many who do not appreciate Erasmus's non-Reformational Catholicism.

57. See chap. 5 for a more detailed consideration of these options.

58. It is my belief, mentioned in an earlier note, that Mark wrote last and abbreviated the material of Matthew/Luke/Q—Q being done by the hand of Matthew, and comprising his discipular journal. I mean no depreciation to Mark's work or that of the Holy Spirit in authoring the Gospel. I mean only that Mark, the writer, was at work selecting according to a purpose.

59. Cf. chap. 8 on Paul's teaching.

60. I add to this my previous comments about Mark's Gospel seeming to be used more in geographical areas where women did divorce their husbands, so that it would be more appropriate for the clause to be found in this Gospel.

61. Interestingly, the effect of the John 8:2 ff. story is the same. Jesus refuses to hear the blemished testimony of men who have set the woman up for the charge of adultery.

62. This is not to say that some mystical bond still exists but that morality is not so blinded by legalities that it cannot see the nexus of covenant violation.

63. From the Old Testament we may well be in doubt as to the propriety of the *guilty* wife remarrying. I conclude that the guilty husband who remarries has not committed adultery in his remarriage per se, though this oversimplifies the situation. He has committed adultery in the treacherous divorce of his wife, and he has done so simply for the sake of marrying some other woman. And, although the Scriptures never state that the second wife is guilty of adultery, we may presume that, if she is a party to the treachery, she is guilty of the same sin. It seems difficult to suppose that only the husband is guilty of it when he *conspires with* the second woman.

64. I am not contradicting what I just said. The principle (i.e., do not break convenantal vows) is found in Exod. 21 as well as in Exod. 20:14 and is behind the explicit teachings of Jesus. It is the specific application of that principle to the failure to provide that passes unmentioned. Yet even here, note that Christ's condemnation of groundless divorce as the sin of adultery comes very close to the point of Exod. 21:11. It falls short, however, of noting the freedom of the woman to divorce and remarry. I suspect that Jesus found this latter point so obvious that it needed no mention.

CHAPTER 8: THE TEACHINGS OF THE APOSTLE PAUL ON DIVORCE

1. To restate the principle: I believe that when writers speak to a topic, it is wise to think their thoughts after them, allowing for development of their thinking and understanding later comments as expansions of earlier teachings. By saying this I do not mean that the Author of the Scriptures himself gets a better grasp of the issues, but that the human instrument often does. The human instrument also finds in the continuing circumstances occasion to pen further, inspired instruction in righteousness.

2. I realize that this sort of statement is open to the criticism that Paul himself did not know that his different writings—directed to churches in different locations—would be collected into the volume we now call the New Testament. Thus, his teaching may well have no intention of specific development. Nonetheless, it would still be proper to consider the first part of 1 Cor. 7 before the second and to look for a logical explanation for the seeming negation of a permission granted in the earlier part of the chapter. And since Romans, written after 1 Corinthians, contains sentiments very similar to the latter part of 1 Cor. 7, it is logical to treat them together. It is also logical to treat the passages that clearly and directly speak to the divorce/remarriage issue before those that may only do so indirectly. Thus, I feel that there are other than chronological reasons for the pattern set forth.

3. I mean here to disparage the rather unfortunate dispensationalism of such as D. H. Small, which has led him offhandedly to dispense with the Gospel teachings as relevant only to the dispensation of the "Kingdom," a kingdom that is not now, but once (Jesus' time) and future (the "millennium"). Cf. D. Small's *The Right to Remarry* (Old Tappan, N.J.: Spire Books, Fleming H. Revell Co., 1977).

4. We must remember that in Greek society the women were seen as lesser persons whose rights to have sex would have been deemphasized. They would have had a better chance of getting the court to permit them to divorce the man than to mandate the man to have sex with them. Moreover, they would have been laughed out of court were they to have been seeking the court to inhibit sexual relations by their husbands. On the man's side, the courts would simply have wondered why a man who could not get sexual relations from his wife would not simply go to the prostitutes. To a husband who wanted to end sexual relations, the courts would have responded with the same confusion.

5. Note the interesting relation here to Paul's ideas in 5:9–13. It is not wrong to associate with the people of the world, but it is wrong to be organically united with them.

6. Vis-à-vis those from the house of Chloe.

7. In what I have just said, I do not mean to imply that Paul's language makes monogamy morally normative. Lenski exemplifies this traditional mistake of seeing reciprocal monogamy in this wording. "His own wife" and "her own husband" "clearly" entail monogamy to him (R. C. H. Lenski, *The Interpretation of I and II Corinthians* [Minneapolis: Augsburg, 1937], p. 274). The grammar and ideas simply state that sex should be under covenant—i.e., the man should have a relationship with a woman who is "his" according to the law, and the woman should not have sexual relations with a man who is not hers by law. It is entirely proper to speak of Sarah as Abraham's wife—she was his. It is certainly proper as well to call the legal spouse of a woman "hers," regardless of the number of his wives. For proof of this, simply note 1 Pet. 3:5 f., where Sarah the polygamous wife of Abraham is cited as an example of a woman who was "submissive to [her] *own* husband." The Greek word is the same in both cases (*idios*) and means "proper." The contrast in 1 Cor. 7:2 is between a woman who is a harlot (chap. 6) and a woman who is properly related by law.

8. Gordon Fee, "1 Corinthians 7:1 in the NIV," *Journal of the Evangelical Theological Society* 23 (1980):307–14.

9. This is not to deny that Paul prefers celibacy, all things being equal. And at whatever point Paul begins to elevate celibacy, he goes beyond the teachings of Jesus, but in an entirely proper way. Jesus had simply said that those who choose celibacy are not under the requirements binding upon married men. Paul promotes celibacy to ensure maximum time of service for the kingdom (7:28 ff.).

10. And I do wish to note that the roles set forth in this summary might be reversed, though that reversal may seem less likely as we observe human nature.

11. Fee, "Corinthians 7:1," p. 312.

12. Heth and Wenham speak of the "Intentional Fallacy"—"the error of supposing that Paul assumes permission to divorce and remarry in the event of Matthew's exception even though he gives no indication of this and hints elsewhere that only the death of a spouse permits remarriage" (*Jesus*, pp. 138–39).

13. First Corinthians is dated at A.D. 56, Matthew in the 60s, and Mark in the 50s—but in all likelihood subsequent to his problems with Paul, thus placing the writing after 1 Corinthians, i.e., the late 50s.

14. Heth and Wenham argue that divorce is always wrong, but that a person forced to divorce his spouse on the ground of *porneia* is not held guilty—the offender is guilty of adultery (*Jesus*, pp. 198–99). This is a strange ethic. A man intentionally divorces his guilty wife, an act that Heth and Wenham believe is absolutely prohibited, but his wife is charged with the guilt of his offensive divorce? How can his intentional, wrong action, i.e., divorce, not yield guilt for him?

15. Ibid., pp. 139 ff.
16. Cf. chap. 6.
17. It is appropriate here to note that *chorizo*—separate—does not denote, but connote, divorce. It is unthinkable in a landed and city-state society that a spouse would desert the partner and pick up somewhere else. This term, found in 1 Cor. 7:10 and 15, has in view a sundering of the covenant by divorce, but the sundering rather than the legal process is the emphasis.
18. See also appendix E, which gives short definitions of the key biblical terms used to speak of divorce.
19. For example, the former spouse might have remarried.
20. Recall too that many of his readers were *diaspora* Jews, persons whose ancestors had been dispersed from Israel because of their adulterous relations with the gods and peoples of the lands.
21. By saying this I do not mean to imply that such reason may not have been inspired by the Holy Spirit.
22. His words to this effect in his second letter doubtless are spoken to head off any misunderstanding of the very teachings at hand. This is to say that the Corinthians might possibly have seen the material in 7:12 ff. as some sort of sanction of the very sins practiced by the Jews of Ezra's time.
23. I must insist upon the hermeneutical rule that both a principle of morality and its application, once stated in the Word of God, are binding on all ages unless explicitly abrogated. I decry the employment of the hermeneutical theory of a kind of dispensationalism that wields the ax of disharmony at the tree of God's transdispensational moral character.
24. Of course I hasten to stress that the marriage in view must have been an act of rebellion, not an act of ignorance, and that the conversion of the spouse sufficiently resolves the problem in a way not requiring legal separation, i.e., divorce. See chap. 3 for more information on this subject.
25. It is interesting to speculate about the marital condition of Paul himself. The only thing we know for sure is that at the writing of these words, he was unmarried (cf. 7:8). But what was his marital status before? Some have suggested that Paul's words about being a "Hebrew of the Hebrews" and a Pharisee (Phil. 3:5) imply that he was once a member of the Sanhedrin. If this speculation is correct, then it is possible that he was once married, as Sanhedrin members almost certainly were. I regard his membership in this august body as unlikely, as he seems too young. Nevertheless, Paul was the Sanhedrin's "special prosecutor," and it would seem that such a responsible position would have demanded the sort of Pharisee that would have been considered socially and emotionally mature.

In any case, it is *probable* that since Paul was a Pharisee he was married. Pharisees were men of age. Men of age in Israel were more likely than not married. Second, since it is *im*probable that his wife predeceased him at this point in his life, it is *probable* that his wife had divorced him as a result of his own dramatic conversion. That he does not mention her is not surprising. We know that Peter was married, but he himself does not mention his wife in any of his writings or speak of her at any point in Acts. If he was silent about her and she was a believer, why should Paul haul out his dirty linen concerning his former wife, who was not? Now mind, I am not saying that Paul *was* a divorced man. We do not know that. I am only saying that it is actuarially *probable*. And, if I am right in this educated speculation, then Paul may have known firsthand what he was talking about.

Interestingly, Clement of Alexandria, in the third book of his *Stromata*, chap. 7, supposes Saint Paul to have been married.
26. To this extent we follow Heth and Wenham, *Jesus,* pp. 138, 139.
27. Ibid., p. 140.
28. Cf. chap. 7.
29. A. Robertson and A. Plummer, *A Critical and Exegetical Commentary on the First Epistle*

of *St. Paul to the Corinthians*, 2d ed., *International Critical Commentary* (Edinburgh: T. & T. Clark, 1911), p. 143.

30. Heth and Wenham, *Jesus*, pp. 140–41.
31. Ibid., p. 141.
32. Lenski, *I & II Corinthians*, p. 297.
33. I believe that any who have counseled such folk will readily attest to the feelings of bondage and anticipated guilt that center precisely in this matter!
34. Heth and Wenham, *Jesus*, pp. 141–43.
35. See also appendix E.
36. Heth and Wenham, *Jesus*, p. 143.
37. Ibid.
38. See chap. 1.
39. Some would suggest that the principle set forth by Heth and Wenham, that conversion does not make a difference, goes too far when it comes to suggesting that an improperly divorced couple remarry where one of them (even the guilty party) has converted. It may be contended that that conversion places the convert under the biblical admonition not to marry an unbeliever, and that remarriage, as a fruit of repentance, is not warranted in such a case. I am sympathetic to this interpretation, but I cannot say that I find compelling biblical reasons for affirming such an application of principle.

In the first place, conversion usually compels the convert to make right the sins of the past. The thief must steal no more but, like Zaccheus, will restitute in multiple kind (Luke 19:1–10). The covenant-breaker will seek to make right by the covenant. It would be totally against moral principle to claim special privilege to abrogate responsibility regarding a valid vow simply because you had turned from sin to the light of God's Way. Since the broken covenant was a morally valid one, it must be presumed that conversion would move the convert to reestablish the former covenant and fulfill its terms. This means remarrying the unbeliever.

A friend has suggested that a middle way may exist: the male believer may fulfill his obligations to his former wife by means of paying the alimony and child support, though not by resuming the marriage in its fullest extent. Again, I am sympathetic to such an approach, but scriptural warrant seems elusive. The Scripture, it seems, recognizes all or nothing. Since the woman has a right to the body of her husband, and since sexual relations should only occur when a socially recognized marriage exists, it would seem that the Christian man who seeks to fulfill his duty by paying alimony is not really fulfilling *all* his duties.

Additionally, it must be remembered that, in such a remarriage, the believer is not rebelliously taking an illicit partner. Rather, he is resuming a relation with a legitimate partner. The remarriage is not, in one sense, by choice. And, it is certainly not an act of spiritual adultery. I can, therefore, find no compelling reason to admonish the believer not to resume the marriage with the unsaved former spouse.

40. I am in agreement with those who argue that a woman who deserts her husband is presumed to have another man waiting. Even if she does not remarry, desertion or divorce legally frees her to marry, and divorce/desertion is clearly a public statement that a couple wish to end the relationship, i.e., break the covenant. It is probable that the social conditions in Israel in the days of Jesus, which definitely limited desertion, made it true, for all practical purposes, that the only reason that a man could divorce his wife was "fornication."

CHAPTER 9: THE TEACHINGS OF THE APOSTLE PAUL ON DIVORCE, CONTINUED

1. J. M. Ford, "Levirate Marriage in St. Paul (I Cor. vii)," *New Testament Studies* 10 (1964): 361–65.

2. G. Delling, *"parthenos"* in *TDNT*, vol. 5 (1967), p. 836.
3. J. K. Elliot, "Paul's Teaching on Marriage in 1 Corinthians: Some Problems Considered," *New Testament Studies* 19 (Jan. 1973):219–25.
4. Robertson and Plummer, *Corinthians*, pp. 158–60.
5. Heth and Wenham, *Jesus*, p. 147.
6. This view was suggested to me by a colleague, Dr. William Baker, at Moody Bible Institute.
7. Lenski, *I & II Corinthians*, p. 326.
8. BAGD, s.v. "παρθένος."
9. Heth and Wenham, *Jesus*, p. 144.
10. Ibid.
11. In point of fact, I deny that 24–35 speaks primarily to the already engaged. That seems to be an interpretation Heth and Wenham draw backwards from their view of the man in 36 ff. as the fiancé—another interpretation I do not accept.
12. In my opinion Heth and Wenham (*Jesus*, p. 144) make too much of their findings in Liddell and Scott (H. Liddell and R. Scott, *A Greek-English Lexicon*, 9th ed., revised and augmented throughout by H. Jones [London: Oxford, 1940], s.v. *"agam-os"*). That lexicon points out that the primary meaning of *agamos* is "unmarried, single." The definition goes on to apply this to men as either "bachelor or widower." It would be interesting to see how frequently *agamos* refers only to widowers in the literature. As it is, Heth and Wenham have little lexically to support their limitation of *agamos* to *widower*. Further, though Liddell and Scott do not mention divorced men in their application, it is surely hasty to conclude that divorced persons could not be called *agamos*. What else could they be called? Were they not considered to be in the unmarried state? Liddell and Scott do not explicitly exclude divorced men from the term.
13. Heth and Wenham, *Jesus*, pp. 146–47.
14. C. Brown, *New International Dictionary of New Testament Theology*, s.v. *"Chorizo:* Divorce, Separation and Remarriage," vol. 3 (1978), p. 537.
15. Heth and Wenham, *Jesus*, p. 147.
16. See my comments on Fee in the previous chapter.
17. Heth and Wenham, *Jesus*, p. 146, emphasis theirs.
18. Cf. BAGD, s.v. *"agamos."*
19. Heth and Wenham, *Jesus*, p. 147.
20. Of course there is also the likelihood that 27b is meant to include widowers as well.
21. Heth and Wenham, *Jesus*, p. 147.
22. It is likely that divorced people would get married, because we presume that they got married in the first place in order to satisfy their needs morally. But I have met a number who decided to stay single subsequent to their divorce in order to better serve the Lord.
23. Heth and Wenham, *Jesus*, p. 84.
24. Cf. chap. 4.
25. I do not wish to make more of this point than necessary. There is, for example, a whole nest of questions surrounding the propriety of substitution of what seems to be a lesser penalty for one more severe. But that is not my task at this moment—I need not decide that issue for my earlier arguments to hold true.
26. Chap. 2.
27. Cf. chap. 1.
28. E.g., Lenski, *I & II Corinthians*, p. 331.
29. It could be argued that to put her in jeopardy regarding temptation is a moral matter. If it really is such, then I think the latter interpretation, i.e., desire for security, sufficient in itself to carry the overall interpretation offered here.

It is most interesting that the word chosen by Paul to express unbecoming behavior (*askamoneo*) is very closely related to the term used by the LXX translators in Deut. 23:14 and 24:1—the "unseemly thing." Insofar as the term in 1 Cor. 7:36 does not imply immoral behavior but only behavior that could result in immoral behavior, I believe that it supports my interpretation of the behavior in Deut. 24:1 as not immoral either. I note further that, in the case of Deut. 24:1, the behavior of the woman might lead to the breach of the husband's marriage vow to properly care for his wife—he might physically abuse her. The resulting concession is intended to protect her from that abuse. Here in 1 Cor. 7, another concession is being made: to inhibit the virgin's potential fornication (resulting from her being seduced as a biologically needy woman), Paul prompts her guardian to let her get married. Both passages have the better interests of the woman in view—an interesting parallel!

30. This parallel may suggest that Paul was in possession of the common source for both Matthew and Mark, thus, in turn, suggesting that Paul meant to harmonize all his teachings with the "exception clause," which from all dependable, historical evaluation was included in that common source.

31. It is the case, as well, that this section is parallel to 7:27, where divorce, as I have argued earlier, is a very likely implication of "released." This in turn implies that the divorced and the widow are in the same category—a point made by the older testament and one I have noted on more than one occasion.

32. Heth and Wenham, *Jesus*, p. 142.

33. See Rom. 7:3.

34. It is also worth pointing out that Heth and Wenham are confusing in their use of "legal" in their argument. If a divorce writ does not free from "legal" obligation, what, pray tell, does? They must mean "moral" bond.

35. Cf. chap. 4 in its treatment of the "Abraham reference" in Mal. 2.

36. See my discussion of this verse in chap. 8.

37. Here, Paul presumes that the death penalty is proper, vis-à-vis the later substitute of divorce. This could indicate that he is speaking literally of the Mosaic Law in v. 1 when he says he speaks to those who know the Law. He could be referring to the Law even as distinct from the "prophets," for whom divorce was the norm.

38. Interestingly, all the early Church Fathers agree with my view that Jewish law in the days of Jesus held a husband morally bound to divorce an adulterous wife. (See appendix F.)

CHAPTER 10: MISCELLANEOUS TEACHINGS OF THE APOSTLES

1. Even Steele and Ryrie draw such an inference. See *Meant*, pp. 77–79.

2. Cf. chap. 4.

3. Of course, under the Law, patience was more severely limited. A single act of adultery was to lead to the execution of the guilty. The government was not to practice patience. We are to presume that governments differ from individuals in such matters.

4. Cf. *International Standard Bible Encyclopedia*, 1st ed., s.v. "forgiveness."

5. BAGD, s.v. "agape."

6. Some critics seek to belittle this idea by saying that it is logically possible that a person could be no longer married and not even know it! Though there is some truth to this, the humor in it arises largely from a misunderstanding of the terms and ideas. In any covenant, it is possible that one of the partners might break the covenant without informing the other. In that case, as of the time of the offense, it is not morally (and perhaps legally) necessary for the offended partner to continue to fulfill his or her side of the covenant. But the offended partner may not know of the breach and may continue to give. So much for the moral issues.

It is highly unlikely, however, that the legal aspect would be ended without notice. And that is usually what we mean by "marriage." Thus, it is possible that a man whose wife has been unfaithful would not know it. Her action has morally reduced her status such that her legal husband has no moral reason to act as a husband toward her. But unfaithful wives seldom inform their husbands of their affairs! Thus, because the legal status exists and because he is ignorant of her affair, he will continue to act as a husband toward her. Were he to be made aware of her affair, he might, with moral sanction, cease to act as a husband toward her. The legal action of divorce merely clarifies their status and states their independence or freedom from obligation. Ethically speaking, the offended party does not cease to act as a spouse because of being treated unkindly—a matter of friendship—but because the offense in view has by its nature changed the status of the (former) partner.

7. Laney, *Myth,* pp. 122–23.

8. Cf. chap. 2.

9. Heth and Wenham, *Jesus,* p. 136.

10. The sort of argument Laney uses here exemplifies very bad hermeneutical habits. It ignores stated analogues in one location in favor of unstated analogues in another.

11. There *are* legitimate theological alternatives to the assumption that Christ would never divorce the Church. Arminian theology would do so, at least with regard to a part (i.e., the individual believer) of the whole. And, consider, as well, that though Christ might not divorce the church, or true believers, Christ does say that he will spew professing but imitation believers out of his mouth (Rev. 3:16). And who are these imitation believers? They are people who spoke the vows of commitment to Christ but who continually sin and are unrepentant about their sanctions (1 John 34 ff., Heb. 6:4 ff.). Are these not very much like a spouse who makes a profession of faithfulness but then continually and unrepentantly breaks those vows? Christ will not cut off the true believers, but a true believer would never continually sin and refuse to repent. He has not promised *not* to abandon the truly unfaithful. So there are certain assumptions here too that are not beyond question.

12. I recognize that these statements will not ring sound in the ears of fellowships that do not hold to a premillennial eschatology as I do. Some see in the Church a continuation of the bride, Israel, and they see the covenant with the Church as the promised "new covenant" of Jer. 31. In all of these opinions, it is important to remember that the final disposition of the matter of remarriage does not rest solely upon this passage in Eph. 5.

13. Cf. the previous chapter, in its discussion of 1 Cor. 7:39 and Rom. 7:2.

14. The citizen is to act with knowledge to the foolishness of government officials (2:15 ff.), and the slave is not to respond to the harshness of a master with more harshness, but rather long-suffering (2:20). Thus, if the woman is told not to dress gaudily, this perhaps identifies wherein the husband is disobedient. Or perhaps the text refers to the husband's sexual looseness. After all, it would be the loose women of the world—prostitutes—who would dress so. Thus, the wife is enjoined to be "chaste" and respectful.

15. Laney, *Myth,* pp. 92–94.

16. Ibid., p. 100.

17. Ibid.

18. Cf. 1 Tim. 5:20. This verse makes it mandatory for elders to publicly rebuke "those who continue in sin."

19. Luke 17:3; and note that this admonition appears in the context of condemning the Pharisees for not rebuking Herod Antipas for his divorce/remarriage sins with Herodias!

20. Laney, *Myth,* pp. 95–99.

21. This view is mentioned without explicit proponents in Homer Kent, Jr.'s, *The Pastoral Epistles* (Chicago: Moody, 1958), p. 126.

22. Again, a view mentioned sans supporters by Kent, *Pastoral Epistles,* pp. 128–29.

23. Some early Church Fathers held this view. See appendix F.

24. Laney, *Myth,* p. 95.

25. Ibid., p. 96.

26. Ibid.

27. But, having said as much, we must consider the possibility that whatever this practice is, it might prohibit polygamy indirectly. I shall have more to say about the principle at issue here at a later point. But let us note at this time that it is highly unlikely

that the *institution* of polygamy would be indirectly prohibited. For though it is Paul's habit to make new applications of principles resident in the teachings of Christ and the Old Testament (1 Cor. 7:10, 25; 9:9 f.), it is not his habit to make major alterations of permissions. Would it be likely that Paul would change the acceptableness of polygamy if it had been allowed all the way up to the time of the writing of this personal letter? Most likely not. Of course this presupposes that neither Jesus (cf. Matt. 19:5) nor he himself (cf. 1 Cor. 7:2) had altered the Old Testament practice of polygamy, which played an implied but integral part in the levirate and fornication laws, and which was expressly condoned in the cases of David (2 Sam. 12:8) and Abraham (Mal. 2:15). (See appendix B for the arguments supporting these points.)

28. It may well be that, as Acts 10 reveals a relaxation of the food laws of the old priestly system, Acts 8:26 ff. reveals a relaxation of the law concerning mutilated persons being in the assembly. I know that it is argued that "eunuch" does not necessarily mean a castrated male, but I suggest that that is still the preferable understanding unless there is proof otherwise.

29. Cf. chap. 4. And this is a logical inference from applying the oracle of Malachi to the priestly group, whom we know from Ezra had been a part of the marrying of the women of the land—though we do not know if they had also been guilty of divorcing their Hebrew wives in the process.

30. Robert L. Saucy, "The Husband of One Wife," *Bibliotheca Sacra* 131 (July-September 1974):230.

31. Kent, *Pastoral Epistles,* p. 128. Some synods of the early Church were opposed to "lawful" digamists, i.e., widowers marrying again. The Synod of Laodicea, in its first canon, tries to correct strictures against the digamists. *The Canons of Basil* speaks of no other penance than that required of "digamists" being required of remarrying widowers (Canon 24).

32. Laney, *Myth,* p. 100.

33. Kent takes the interesting perspective that divorced men are *not* the husband of one wife (*Pastoral Epistles,* p. 130). But this is unimpressive when he has previously denied the interpretation that leaders must be married (pp. 128–29).

34. Laney, *Myth,* p. 96.

35. Ibid.

36. Ibid., p. 98.

37. Ibid., p. 118.

38. This is not to say that breaches of the "canons" of covenant would not do so. Cf. chap. 2.

39. Laney, *Myth,* p. 119.

40. Ibid., p. 99.

41. Not to mention the question of his conclusion regarding the exact nature of these women.

42. R. C. H. Lenski, *The Interpretation of St. Paul's Epistle to the Colossians, to the Thessalonians, to Timothy, to Titus and to Philemon* (Columbus, Ohio: Augsburg, 1937), pp. 580–81.

43. Saucy, "Husband," p. 229.

44. Cf. ibid., p. 240.

45. Peter certainly does not—2 Pet. 2. John (1 John 2:15 ff.), Jude (v. 4), and James (2:11) mention sexual matters as being problems in the Church.

46. Laney, *Myth,* p. 96.

47. Laney argues that "becoming one flesh does not in and of itself make a marriage," but that sexual intercourse always results in a one-flesh relationship, which is a "mystical, spiritual unity" (*Myth,* p. 21). Laney later disqualifies the divorced/remarried, but he never suggests that those who have fornicated or committed adultery *without* divorce/remarriage are disqualified.

48. Ibid., p. 96.

49. This interpretation also makes sense of the 1 Tim. 5:9 phrase "one husband wife." On my interpretation that text simply means to exclude from church aid notoriously

promiscuous women. In earlier life they depended on their lovers, let them turn to them now in their old age! Paul does not, on the other hand, wish to disqualify the holy women, even if they were married more than once—and even if that had come about through divorce.

CHAPTER 11: SUMMARIES AND CONCLUSIONS

No notes.

APPENDIX A: ON THE NATURE OF THE MARRIAGE UNION

1. This is in disagreement with such as the early position of Norman L. Geisler in his *Ethics: Alternatives and Issues* (Grand Rapids: Zondervan, 1971), pp. 199–200.
2. *TWOT*, s.v. *"halal."*
3. *TWOT*, s.v. *"tame."*
4. Geisler suggested that in Heb. 13:4 "marriage" and "marriage bed" are in parallel. It would seem, however, that the text of Hebrews is simply affirming long-standing biblical teaching that the place for bed-relations is marriage. Fornication and adultery are defiled beddings. Such argument goes well beyond the text to argue that "bed" and "marriage" are coterminous. In fact, if they are the same, it would seem that people could not commit fornication, but only marriage! Never adultery, but only bigamy. This is, of course, absurd. I understand that Geisler no longer holds this view. (Cf. Heth and Wenham, *Jesus*, p. 228, n. 35.)
5. F. Brown, S. Driver, and C. Briggs, *Hebrew and English Lexicon of the Old Testament* (London: Clarendon, 1972).
6. Steele and Ryrie, *Meant*, p. 27.

APPENDIX B: ON THE MORALITY OF BIBLICAL POLYGAMY

1. For example, I believe that heterosexuality is presented in Gen. 1 and 2 as the only moral sexual behavior, because the concept of the heterosexual Image is revealed as constituting what it means to be human. Additionally, later Scripture affirms that homosexuality is immoral. The conditions of the Fall do not change the normativeness of heterosexuality as the "way it is meant to be" in marriage and in life in general. On the other hand, monogamy is simply stated as a fact of Adam's heterosexual relationship. Monogamy is not stated as transdispensationally and transculturally normative.
2. Walter Kaiser, *Toward Old Testament Ethics* (Grand Rapids: Academie Books/Zondervan, 1983), p. 153.
3. John Walton, in private conversations at Moody Bible Institute, where he teaches.
4. It is probable that Boaz was married when he fulfilled his responsibility to Ruth. Although we have no explicit evidence, and the text mentions no other wife, several things suggest that this was so. First, Boaz was not a young man, and in that culture, older men were almost always married unless their wives had preceded them in death. Second, it is unlikely that Boaz was a widower, because in all societies, men usually die at a younger age than do their wives, not vice versa. In addition to this, Boaz was a man of property, and this too would have implied a married man since property and maturity went hand-in-hand. Adding these together, we see that it is probable that to become Ruth's redeemer Boaz had to become a polygamist. This conclusion may be wrong as a matter of fact, but until factual evidence is brought forth to show this, the probabilities mentioned make it the best interpretation. By contrast, the interpretation that Boaz was single has only silence to support it; probability is against it. That the text mentions no other wife is weak support (if it is support at all), since the text of Scripture often passes in silence over the wives of the men mentioned.

5. We may presume that the parallel case of a virgin being *raped* by a married man (Deut. 22:29) would suffer the stated exception of Exod. 22, as that law was already on the books and was so similar to the rape legislation. This would be supported by the consideration that if the father of a seduced girl who had given tacit permission to the intercourse was able to negate the marriage requirement, it would stand to reason that the father of a girl who had *not* given such permission would be protected as well. In any case, the text of Deuteronomy agrees with that of Exodus in not making potential polygamy an issue.

6. S. E. Dwight, *Hebrew Wife* (New York: Leavitt, 1836), p. 20.

7. Kaiser, *Toward,* pp. 184–85.

8. Chap. 2.

9. Kaiser, *Toward,* p. 183.

10. Note that this verse would not even have hampered Jacob from marrying Rachel subsequently to Leah, because he did not take Rachel as a "rival," that is, to make Leah jealous and to humiliate her.

11. Kaiser, p. 116.

12. Ibid., p. 168.

13. E.g., Kaiser, *Toward,* p. 188.

14. Ibid., pp. 189–90.

15. Perhaps an analogy can help us understand the peculiarity of the traditional interpretation of this phrase: A Chicago bishop writes a priest in Oklahoma requiring him to make sure that his altar boys do not "eat at each other." Would it be likely that the priest would reflect upon the fact that certain Indian tribes in that area were reputed to have practiced cannibalism hundreds of years ago? Would he think of tribes of people in the contemporary world that still practice cannibalism? Highly unlikely! The priest would understand that the phrase was idiomatic for division and strife. It is my suggestion that the same is implied in the case at hand.

16. See also chap. 10.

17. Homer Kent gives the peculiar argument that a condemnation of polygamy is unlikely because polygamy could not have been a major problem in the Church, since it was prohibited in the Roman Empire. But then he goes on to say that 1 Cor. 7:2 is a proscription of polygamy. Why would not his same arguments stand against such an interpretation of 7:2? (*Pastoral Epistles,* p. 127).

18. It is also interesting to note some of the statements of the early Church Fathers on this matter, though I hasten to remind the reader that our concern is almost exclusively with the biblical teaching. In the *Canons of Basil,* Canon 21, we read: "A married man committing lewdness with a single woman is severely punished as guilty of fornication, but we have no canon to treat such a man as an adulterer; but the wife must co-habit with such a one: But if the wife be lewd, she is divorced, and he that retains her is [thought] impious; such is the custom, but the reason of it does not appear." Canon 80 is even more to the point: "The Fathers say nothing of polygamy as being beastly, and a thing unagreeable to human nature. To us it appears a greater sin than fornication." Does it not appear, then, that it was simply the Greek prejudice against polygamy wherein arose the moral stigma against the institution? With those who hedge the biblical laws—Tertullian and Clement of Alexandria for instance—and with Basil, the married man's nondivorcable *fornication* with another, nonmarried woman becomes *adultery,* and convenantal polygamy becomes a sin greater than fornication.

19. See the helpful article on these texts by Robert Saucy, "Husband" (see chap. 10, n. 30). He does not go as far as he should, but he does much in overturning the traditional misinterpretations.

20. I speak to those who accept such eschatology. Others must still consider the language from which "premillennialists" derive such conclusions.

21. Cf. Bernard I. Murstein, *Love, Sex, and Marriage through the Ages* (New York: Springer, 1974), pp. 54–56, 59 f., 76 f., 78–82.

22. "*Hauck,*" "*moikeuo,*" etc., in *Kittel,* vol. 4, pp. 729–35, esp. 733 f.

23. If this is not understood, the reader needs to return to chap. 1.

24. Though it is true that *doulos* is used indirectly of both the husband and the wife (e.g., 1 Cor. 7:15), in those contexts the spouse is not identified as a *kurios*. Additionally, in 1 Cor. 7:15, the "sister" is the primary referent. In all likelihood, the implied *kurios* is the very law that binds them. It is their husband, and they cannot have more than one law to govern them. This seems to be precisely the point of Rom. 7:1 ff.

APPENDIX C: ON THE ORDER OF THE GOSPELS

1. Presuming of course that there is not a Dispensational change that has occurred between different biblical pronouncements.

2. I hold to the results of textual criticism.

3. Cf. Donald Guthrie's *New Testament Introduction* (Downers Grove, Ill.: Inter-Varsity Press, 1965).

4. Cf. Robert Thomas, "Source Criticism," in *A Harmony of the Gospels* (Chicago: Moody, 1978), pp. 274–79.

5. If I am correct in this conclusion, then focusing one's attention upon Matthew—rather than Mark or Luke—to learn about how disciples should act in the trying situation of a troubled marriage is the correct procedure.

6. It seems to me that the foregoing schema is the most reasonable presuming the correctness of note 1 above.

7. D. R. Catchpole, "Synoptic Divorce Material," pp. 92–127; R. H. Stein, " 'Is It Harmful for a Man to Divorce His Wife?' " *Journal of the Evangelical Theological Society* 22 (1979):115–21; H. Reisser, *Dictionary of New Testament Theology*, 1:500.

APPENDIX D: ON THE POSSIBILITY OF NONSEXUAL ADULTERY

1. Carson, "Matthew," p. 416.

2. Klaus Haacker, "Der Rechtsatz Jesu zum Thema Ehebruch," *Biblische Zeitschrift* 21 (1977):113–16.

3. Carson, "Matthew," p. 151.

4. Ibid.

5. See chap. 4 for a more detailed treatment of some of these verses.

6. Ezra 9 and 10 documents one of the most famous instances of this sort of thing.

7. Heth and Wenham make the very reasonable point against Murray and other Erasmians that not all divorced people do get remarried, so that it should not be thought that clause *b* must be tied to *a* in order for *a* to make sense (*Jesus*, p. 119).

8. Carson, "Matthew," p. 151.

APPENDIX E: ON THE BIBLICAL TERMS FOR "DIVORCE"

1. *TWOT*, s.v. "*Kārat.*"

2. *TWOT*, s.v. "*Shillûhîm.*"

3. *TWOT*, s.v. "*Yāsa'.*"

4. W. E. Vine, *Expository Dictionary of New Testament Words* (Westwood, N.J.: Fleming H. Revell, 1940), s.v. "divorce" (hereafter "Vine").

5. BAGD, s.v. "*apoluo.*"

6. Vine, s.v. "*apoluo.*"

7. BAGD, s.v. "*chorizo.*"

8. Vine, s.v. "*chorizo.*"

9. BAGD, s.v. "*aphistemi.*"

10. Kittel, vol. I, p. 512, "*Aphilagthos.*"

11. Vine, s.v. *"Aphilagthos."*
12. BAGD, s.v. *"apostasion."*

APPENDIX F: ON THE DIVORCE TEACHINGS OF THE EARLY CHURCH

1. Heth and Wenham, *Jesus,* chap. 1.
2. It is to be noted that those to whom the Spirit of Truth is promised are not Christians in general (as many Protestants suppose) or the ongoing magisterial Church (as Catholics suppose) but rather those disciples who had been specifically chosen by Christ (15:16), those who had been with him from the beginning (15:27), those whom he would shortly leave and to whom he would shortly return (16:16).
3. Cf. *NIDCC,* s.v., "Hermas."
4. Hermas, *Shepherd,* 4.1.4–10.
5. Heth and Wenham, *Jesus,* p. 26.
6. Though he does not explicitly use that word of the man, what else could "becomes guilty of her sin and a partner in her adultery" mean?
7. Heth and Wenham, *Jesus,* p. 52.
8. Ibid., p. 216.
9. Justin Martyr, *First Apology,* chap. 15.
10. Justin Martyr, *Second Apology,* 2.1–7.
11. That seems safer than interposing Luke between the clearly Matthean passages, when a Matthean option is available.
12. Athenagoras, *Plea for the Christians,* chap. 23, trans. B. P. Pratten, in *Ante-Nicene Fathers,* vol. II (Grand Rapids: Eerdmans, n.d.), pp. 146–47.
13. *L'église primitive face au divorce du premier au cinquieme siècle* (Paris: Bauchesne), p. 60.
14. Heth and Wenham, *Jesus,* p. 29.
15. I do not deny that Athenagoras would have disparaged polygamy, but I do not think that is the point of the prohibition to "marry again."
16. Theophilus of Antioch, *To Autolycus,* 3.13.
17. Heth and Wenham, *Jesus,* p. 31.
18. A quote of Zech. 7:10.
19. Clement of Alexandria, *Stromata,* III.6.50.
20. Heth and Wenham, *Jesus,* pp. 32 f. See also Quesnell, "Eunuchs," pp. 347–49 (see chap. 5, n. 21).
21. Clement immediately mentions the Law, and probably has Deut. 24:4 in mind when he refers to the inhibition.
22. Tertullian, *Monogamy,* chap. 9.
23. See chap. 1 of this book.
24. Tertullian, *Monogamy,* chap. 7.
25. It is interesting, however, that in Tertullian's "orthodox period" he employs an argument against the remarriage of disciplining divorcers akin to that of Hermas, who was also from the West: remarriage inhibits repentance (*On Patience,* chap. 12). I do not agree that remarriage inhibits repentance, only marital restoration, and such restoration is not necessary, according to the dictates of the Scriptures. Tertullian seems to have gone from the wrong to the bizarre in his rationalizing of his ascetic position. By the end of his life (in *Monogamy,* bk. II), he came to view marriage as but tolerated adultery! (So S. Thelwall, in his "Elucidation" of that section of Tertullian in *Ante-Nicene Fathers,* vol. IV [Grand Rapids: Eerdmans, n.d.], p. 73.)
26. Origen, *Commentary on Matthew,* 14.22, 23, 24.
27. Heth and Wenham, *Jesus,* p. 35.
28. Ibid., pp. 37 f.
29. Origen, *Matthew,* 14.24.
30. Ibid., 14.17, 19.

31. Ibid., 14.17.
32. Ibid., 14.23.
33. Chrysostom, *Homily* on Matt. 19:1 ff.
34. So Augustine, according to the article "Ambrosiaster" by G. T. D. Angel in *NIDCC*, pp. 32 f.
35. Heth and Wenham's citation of 1 Cor. 7:3–4 notwithstanding (*Jesus*, p. 38).
36. The translations here are those found in *The Nicene and Post-Nicene Fathers*, 2d ser. vol. 14, ed. Henry Percival (Grand Rapids: Eerdmans, n.d.), pp. 594–95.
37. Quoted in Heth and Wenham, *Jesus*, p. 43.
38. *Nicene and Post-Nicene Fathers*, vol. 14, pp. 604–11.
39. Basil was famous for his monastic rule. He, as much as any Eastern prelate, was responsible for spreading monasticism in the Eastern church. This is to be kept in mind regarding comments to be made shortly concerning the influence of asceticism on the teachings of divorce and remarriage in the early Church.
40. Augustine, *On Marriage and Concupiscence*, 1.2.
41. *NIDCC*, s.v., "Sacrament."
42. This important distinction has been mentioned often in this book, and is not often clearly made in the earlier literature, especially by those who speak of the "indissolubility" of marriage. Some who do recognize it believe that the two are complementary and *mutually implicit* (e.g., E. Schillebeeckx, *Marriage: Human Reality and Saving Mystery*, trans. N. D. Smith, 2 vols. in 1 [New York: Sheed & Ward, 1965], p. 283). I hold that the ideas may be complementary, but that there is no sufficient evidence of an indissoluble, ontic bond in the realm of marriage.
43. For another treatment along the same lines, see Atkinson, *To Have & to Hold*, pp. 40–43 (see chap. 3, n. 22).
44. Augustine, *Adulterous Marriages*, 1.11.12.
45. Ibid., 2.1–4.
46. Heth and Wenham, *Jesus*, p. 30.

Index